D1344503

OIL AND GOD

OIL AND GOD

Sustainable Energy Will Defeat
Wahhabi Terror

Elie Elhadj

Universal Publishers
Irvine • Boca Raton

Oil and God: Sustainable Energy Will Defeat Wahhabi Terror

Universal Publishers, Inc.
Irvine • Boca Raton
USA • 2018
www.universal-publishers.com

978-1-58112-607-5 (pbk.)
978-1-62734-263-6 (ebk.)

Typeset by Medlar Publishing Solutions Pvt Ltd, India

Publisher's Cataloging-in-Publication Data

Names: Elhadj, Elie.
Title: Oil and God: Sustainable Energy Will Defeat Wahhabi Terror/Elie Elhadj.
Description: Irvine, CA: Universal Publishers, 2018. | Includes bibliographical
  references and index.
Identifiers: LCCN 2018932500 | ISBN 978-1-58112-607-5 (pbk.)
  | ISBN 978-1-62734-263-6 (ebook)
Subjects: LCSH: Wahhābīyah--Saudi Arabia--Influence. | Terrorist
  organizations--Middle East. | Arab Spring, 2010--Influence. | Renewable
  energy sources--Political aspects. | Petroleum industry and trade--Political
  aspects. | BISAC: POLITICAL SCIENCE/Terrorism. | BUSINESS &
  ECONOMICS/Industries/Energy.
Classification: LCC BP195.W2 E44 2018 (print)
  | LCC BP195.W2 (ebook) | DDC 297.8/14--dc23.

To

My Daughter Sarah

For Her Big Heart in Helping Syria's Refugees

SYNOPSIS

Religious extremism in the Middle East surfaced after the dismemberment of the Ottoman Empire in 1918. What caused the transformation from a tolerant Sunni Hanafi empire to the ferocious religious wars which now plague the Middle East?

Oil and God is an unabashed realpolitik study of the culprits. It analyses the complex relationships between and among the different players in Middle Eastern affairs and the stake each has in the region's sectarian wars. The book explores the roots of the current jihadist movements, Wahhabi culture, the Arab Israeli conflict, the Khomeini revolution, and the sectarian wars in Iraq and in Syria.

Oil and God examines the tensions that fuel events such as the Arab Spring and the different histories, cultural values, and religious priorities that underlie the level of success each country has had on its trajectory to democracy with the credibility of an insider.

Oil and God relates US oil geopolitics to Saudi Arabia's symbiotic union with Wahhabism. The terrorists of 9/11 were Wahhabis. The book investigates why the US occupied Iraq, not Saudi Arabia.

Oil and God contends that hegemony over oil exports is world hegemony and that US control over Saudi oil is a non-lethal weapon of mass destruction. The book holds that national security concerns of the big oil importers, China, continental Europe, India, and Japan, will drive renewable energy development to end oil imports. When that happens, US protection of Riyadh will wane, Saudi cash will dwindle, Wahhabi terror will diminish, and democracy will have a chance to take root in Arab lands.

Oil and God is a must read for students, academics, business people, journalists, and politicians.

TABLE OF CONTENTS

ACKNOWLEDGMENTS

After a thirty-year career in finance and banking in New York, London and Riyadh, I became a student again in order to seek answers to questions on the cultures, politics and reform prospects of Arab countries. I was fortunate to join London University's School of Oriental and African Studies (SOAS) in 1998, where it was possible to access focused and relevant regional scholarship.

My research examined the contrasting political economies of water in Saudi Arabia and Syria, published in 2006 under the title: *Experiments in Achieving Water and Food Self-Sufficiency in the Middle East, the Consequences of Contrasting Endowments, Ideologies, and Investment Policies in Saudi Arabia and Syria*.

Concurrently, I wrote *The Islamic Shield, Arab Resistance to Democratic and Religious Reforms*, published in 2006, updated in 2008. *The Islamic Shield* argued that Arab resistance to religious reforms would make it almost impossible for a Muslim Martin Luther to emerge.

Oil and God follows *The Islamic Shield*. It incorporates two events that shook the Middle East since the September 11, 2001 attacks by 19 Wahhabi terrorists on New York and Washington D.C. The first is the Arab Spring of 2011. The second is the empowerment of Iran since 9/11/2001.

SOAS is a community of gifted researchers, a uniquely eminent center for scholarship. During and since my SOAS years of study, Professor Tony Allan has been inspirational. A giant thinker and the consummate gentleman, I shall forever remember the many hours of engaging discussion we have had over the past two decades. I have benefited from discussions with members of Professor Allen's SOAS/King's College Research Group.

I am grateful to Peggy, my wife, who expertly edited the manuscript and energized the journey of my writing. Last, but certainly not least, is the contribution made by my daughter Sarah. Her enthusiasm for knowledge on the Middle East and her many questions helped clarify what might have otherwise been vague.

CHAPTER SUMMARIES

Chapter One: *Oil and God* in Brief

The first chapter summarizes *Oil and God*. It explains the factors that shape the book. Given the strong attachment of Middle Eastern Muslims to Islam, two policy implications are concluded. First: religious minorities must never rule over the majority—witness the calamitous destruction of Syria at the hands of the Assad family's 10% Alawite minority. Secondly, if governments in the Arab world are to become representatives of the people, and respectful of the rule of law and human rights, democracy is a must. As examples of the undemocratic Middle East, Saudi Arabia's exploitation of Wahhabi Islam and the ayatollahs' exploitation of Shi'ism in Iran are described.

The book argues that oil hegemony means world hegemony. For Washington, it is important to influence/control the oil politics of Saudi Arabia, the world's biggest oil exporter and swing producer, not because America needs Saudi oil, but to assert Washington's superpower status. Control over a big proportion of world's oil exports is like a non-lethal weapon of mass destruction (WMD). The nexus of US politics, Saudi oil and God is discussed, and the delicate and complicated US/Saudi relationship is considered from both American and Saudi viewpoints.

Oil has protected the al-Saud regime before and after 9/11. The Bush administration ignored Wahhabi culpability. Instead, it occupied Iraq, which led to Iran's control over Iraq and the empowerment of the ayatollahs in the Middle East.

The combination of oil and God allows Saudi Arabia's kings to act like hostage takers, forcing oil-importing countries to tolerate their regime to avoid the risk of oil interruption. It is only when demand for imported oil by US rivals, like China; the world's largest oil importer, continental Europe, India, and Japan is replaced by sustainable sources of energy such as solar, wind, hydropower, and nuclear fusion, that Wahhabi terror will be defeated.

Oil and God is shaped by the interaction between the effects of two epic events since 9/11/2001. The first is the Arab Spring. Beginning in 2011, it planted a resilient seed in the heads of Arabs that parliamentary democracy is compatible with Islam, a serious blow to the Wahhabi doctrine, which teaches that democracy is a Western conspiracy to destroy Islam. The second event is the empowerment of Iran since 9/11 by US presidents G.W. Bush and Barack Obama.

Today, Saudi Arabia is caught between the democratic values of the Arab Spring and the Wahhabi ideology of al-Qaeda and the so-called Islamic State. To claim the high religious ground, the al-Saud regime is expected to maintain the fundamentals of the Wahhabi culture it introduced in 1932. To maintain its grip on power, the regime will not adopt an iota of genuine democratic reform.

Chapter Two: Islam, the Arab Masses, and Arab Rulers' Exploitation of Islam to Stay in Power

Chapters Two and Three are intended to enhance understanding and appreciation of the pivotal role Islam plays in the private lives of Muslims, and the politics of the Middle East.

Chapter Two addresses the strong attachment the Arab peoples has to Islam. It explains how moderate Muslims, Islamists, and jihadists relate to the Islamic text. The chapter explains how Arab rulers use the palace ulama (Muslim scholars thought to have serious knowledge of theology and sacred law) to exploit the Qur'anic Verse 4:59 in order to turn blind obedience to their benefactors into a form of piety. The belief in predestination helps the ulama to remind the faithful that, even an unjust ruler is ordained by God. Chapter Two looks at how jihadist leaders justify rebellion against the Muslim ruler, in a challenge to Verse 4:59.

Chapter Three: Islamic Beliefs and Sects

The third chapter outlines the basic beliefs a good Muslim must adhere to. The belief in predestination and the fear of innovation are addressed.

Chapter Three compares the process of Sunni law-making with Shi'ite law-making. It describes the four sources of Sunni law: The Qur'an, Prophetic Sunna, Analogical Deduction, and Consensus of the ulama. This contrasts with only three sources of Shi'ite law: The Qur'an, Prophetic Sunna (according to Shi'ite sources), and Shi'ite ulama's intellectual reasoning.

This chapter discusses the concept of the infallible Shi'ite Imams, the doctrine of the return of the Hidden Twelfth Imam to the Earth, the effect the doctrine has had on the reporting of the Shi'ite Prophetic Sunna, the delegation of the Hidden Imam's boundless authority and infallible judgment to Shi'ite ulama. All of these constructions are anathema to Sunni ulama.

Also discussed in Chapter Three is Grand Ayatollah Khomeini's revolutionary assertion that the senior-most Shi'ite cleric, as the deputy of the Hidden Imam, has the right to oversee all religious, social, and political affairs of Iran. This doctrine handed Khomeini and his successors absolute theocratic authority/dictatorship.

The Appendix to Chapter Three considers how the Sunni ulama elevated the Prophetic Sunna into a source of law equal to the Holy Qur'an.

Chapter Four: Combating Jihadism

Notwithstanding the imperative of obedience to Muslim authority in Verse 4:59, jihadists invoke Hadith injunctions that sanction rebellion against an Islamic ruler if he becomes impious or unjust.

This chapter attributes the breeding of suicide bombers to charismatic political leaders mixing an explosive cocktail made up of three ingredients: Jihad injunctions, predestination dogma, and the promise of houris (beautiful damsels) in paradise. The cocktail alone is safe. To explode, it needs a spark. The spark can be any number of despairing domestic and/or foreign triggers.

To combat jihadi terror, Chapter Four advocates deactivating these combustible ingredients and defusing the sparks. The chapter concludes that as long as oil is the main source of global energy, the combustible cocktail is unlikely to be deactivated and the sparks are unlikely to be defused.

Chapter Four concludes that representative democracy can be an effective medicine to combat the appeal of jihadism. It also considers how the Muslim Brotherhood's embrace of representative democracy might defeat Wahhabi terror.

Chapter Five: The Effect of Saudi Oil on Derailing the Arab Spring's Political and Islamic Reforms

The fifth chapter asserts that the Arab Spring is not expected to sweep through the Arab world smoothly. Oil will stand in the way of reforms in Saudi Arabia and Egypt until it is driven out of world markets by renewable energy. Meanwhile, however, non-oil exporters like Tunisia and Morocco will be able to develop democratic governance without outside hindrance.

The US has been protecting the al-Saud regime for the past 70 years. Why? To control Saudi oil production and price politics and make global oil supply a part of its arsenal of non-lethal weapons of mass destruction. Not even Wahhabi culpability for 9/11 was sufficient to challenge US protection of the al-Saud regime. Instead, President George W. Bush devastated Iraq, an adventure that empowered Iran. President Obama further empowered Iran with his policies in Iran, Iraq, and Syria.

Chapter Five argues that Washington will protect the al-Saud regime despite its dictatorial rule, hatred-of-the-other culture, human rights abuses, and gender inequality. Ease of dealing/controlling one absolute king who owes his throne and life to US protection is far simpler and more effective than managing scores of parliamentarians and political leaders in a democratic setting. Washington will not pressure the Saudi King to reform for fear that pressure might weaken his control over Saudi Arabia and disrupt oil exports.

Given the strong cultural and societal connections between Egypt and Saudi Arabia, Egypt will not be allowed to evolve democratic rule either. Riyadh, with help from Washington, will keep democracy away from Egypt in the future, just as they did since 1952, except for the year between June 30, 2012 and July 3, 2013, under the democratically elected president, Muhammad Morsi.

Chapter Five presents the view that the Muslim Brotherhood's embrace of parliamentary democracy in Egypt could have ushered in an era of modernizing Shari'a (Islamic law). How? In a poor country like Egypt, modern laws to reduce poverty and raise employment must be enacted. The new laws would, of course, be labeled as un-Islamic by Islamists. The debates would open taboo subjects, suppressed under blasphemy laws and cultural norms for centuries. The debates would go a long way to modernizing Shari'a laws.

Chapter Six: The Al-Saud Wahhabi Governance

Chapter Six describes the five constituencies that form the Saudi power pyramid: The al-Saud royals, Wahhabi ulama, tribal sheikhs, the defense and national security establishment, and merchant families. It considers how Wahhabism evolved during the twentieth century, boomeranged on 9/11, then metastasized into increasingly violent terror groups: Boko Haram (Nigeria), the so-called Islamic State (Iraq and Syria), al-Qaeda (regional), Shabab (Somalia), and the Taliban (Afghanistan).

A hopeful sign is the recent emergence of certain Saudi ulama as agents of political change, calling for elections and separation of government powers. The chapter ends with an argument invoking Verse 42:38 and Prophetic Ahadiths (plural of Hadith; or, words of the Prophet) to counter the Wahhabi palace ulama's contention that democracy is incompatible with Islam.

Chapter Seven: The US Invasion of Iraq, the Empowerment of Iran, and Opening Sunni/Shi'ite Gates of Hell

Chapter Seven explores the reasons that could have driven the G.W. Bush administration (2000–2008) to wreak its revenge for the 9/11 attacks on an innocent country, Iraq, instead of Saudi Arabia.

The chapter argues that wittingly or unwittingly, Mr. Bush handed Iraq to Iran on a silver platter without Iran having to fire a shot. President Obama (2008–2016) added to Bush's performance. He embraced Iran's sectarian proxy prime minister in Baghdad, Nouri al-Maliki (2006–2014); midwifed the P5+1 nuclear agreement (signed in July 2015); prematurely removed all US troops from Iraq (December 2011), and handed Syria to Iran. The cost to the US was huge. The cost to Iraq and Syria was far greater.

The march of Shi'ism opened the gates of hell in the Muslim Middle East. These wars have already destroyed, not only most of Iraq, but also most of Syria and Yemen, killed and injured more than five million, and created more than fifteen million refugees. Now that Pandora's Box has been opened, the Shi'ite/ Sunni wars will rage for decades.

Chapter Seven examines Iran's strategic influence in Iraq and what lurks behind Iran's desperate drive to control the Shi'ite dominated southern Iraq and the Baghdad government.

It ends with addressing Iraq's superior religious credentials in the world of Shi'ism to that of Iran and the stronger attachment of Arab Shi'tes to Iraq than Iran.

Chapter Eight: The Bible Faces the Qur'an in Palestine

Chapter Eight focuses on the root cause of the Palestinian/Arab-Israeli conflict and on contemplating a solution based on a single state for Arabs and Jews. The chapter starts by describing Islam's veneration of Judaism. The Qur'an praises Abraham as the first Muslim, and describes Islam as the "religion of Abraham."

Two events embittered the Arab peoples. The first was the Sykes-Picot Agreement (May 19, 1916). It was secretly negotiated by London and Paris to carve up the Levant between them. The second was the Balfour Declaration (November 2, 1917). The British Foreign Secretary, Lord Balfour, offered lands Britain never owned in Palestine to the Zionist Federation.

To justify offering Palestine as a Jewish home, Zionist leaders promoted the slogan: "A land without people to a people without land." However, as far back as 1893, the lowest estimate of the number of Palestinians was 410,000.[1] According to the 1922 census, Mandatory Palestine had a population of 673,000 Palestinians (589,000 Muslims plus 84,000 Christians) and 71,000 Jews.[2]

---

[1]MidEastWeb.org, "The Population of Palestine Prior to 1948." http://www.mideastweb.org/palpop.htm

[2]Ibid.

The founding of modern-day Israel was based on a biblical covenant, which politicized the Bible. In reaction, the Qur'an was politicized. Unless the Bible is depoliticized, wars between Arabs and Jews could go on for a thousand years.

Chapter Eight argues that a purely Jewish Israel is impossible to attain, unless the Palestinian Israeli citizens simply vanish. It also argues that a two-state solution is not viable, due to a myriad of thorny issues: Jerusalem, borders, security for Israel and Palestine, water rights, Jewish settlers, the status of the Palestinian Israelis, and the right of return for the refugees.

Instead, a single, democratic, and secular state for Palestinians and Jews based on equal citizenship and constitutional protection of religious, ethnic, and national identities promises to be a better long-term prospect. President Trump's decision on December 6, 2017, to recognize Jerusalem as Israel's capital has effectively put an end to the two-state solution, leaving the single-state as the only alternative.[3]

The Palestinians did not take anything from Israel. For a durable long-term peace, Israel should not stonewall the Oslo Accords and the Arab Peace Initiative.

As the Palestinian problem festers, downtrodden Palestinians and Arabs, exploited by charismatic politicians, will turn to God for deliverance. Israeli policies have been driving increasing numbers of otherwise moderate Muslims toward Islamism and jihadism.

The chapter ends by quoting an essay written by Avraham Burg, former speaker of Israel's Knesset (1999–2003) and a former chairman of the Jewish Agency titled "The end of Zionism".

Chapter Nine: Sectarianism, Dictatorship, and the Destruction of Most of Syria

Chapter Nine addresses the Syrian revolution; what led to it, weaponizing it, Islamicizing it, the myriad parties involved in it, the horrendous toll of it, and finally a likely solution.

The chapter argues that in religion-gripped Syria, it is unsustainable for a non-representative totalitarian, Assad-ruled 10% Alawite minority to

---

[3]The White House, "Statement by President Trump on Jerusalem", (December 6, 2017). https://www.whitehouse.gov/briefings-statements/statement-president-trump-jerusalem/

rule over and abuse the 75% Sunni majority forever. It has already brought disaster.

The Assad regime stands on three pillars. The first is multiple brutal security forces. Amnesty International documented 38 types of terrifying torture methods used by the regime. The second is exploitation of Sunni Islam. The palace clerics threaten the faithful with God's wrath if they fail to obey Assad blindly, exploiting Verse 4:59. The third is a bombastic war of words against Israel to justify the alliance with Iran and the imposition of emergency laws since 1963 that terrorize the populace.

Fifty years of police state cruelty were challenged on March 18, 2011 with small protests in the city of Dar'a. Within a few days, Assad had weaponized the protests. He ordered the army to shoot to kill. To avoid the ire of Western public opinion for killing unarmed civilians, he Islamicized the revolution. In a Machiavellian strategy of blackmail legitimacy, he released hardened jihadists from prisons, to make the East and the West choose between tyranny or the jihadists.

The Assad regime has decapitated organized opposition for the past 50 years. There were no political parties or community leaders to lead the uprising. Some 1,500 different groups appeared on the battlefield.[4] The revolution suffered from relying on Saudi Arabia and Qatar. The two states hate each other. They are US protectorates. President Obama ignored both.

Obama's intentions against the revolution became clear quickly. He prevented the supply of anti-warplane guns and repudiated his own red line on Assad's use of chemical weapons on August 21, 2013. Without US support, the revolution was doomed. Most of Syria was destroyed, with two thirds of Syria's 20-million population dead, injured and displaced. By aiding in the destruction of Syria, Obama empowered Iran beyond the Bush years.

Only Moscow and Washington can resolve the Syrian calamity, most likely through a barter exchange, a cease fire arrangement to be monitored by a U.N./Arab force, removal of Assad, democratic elections, and a truth and reconciliation commission. It would be sensible to create a democratic system of governance with self-ruled regions within a federal Syria, based on sectarian and ethnic lines: Alawites, Christians, Druzes,

---

[4]Royal United Services Institute for Defence and Security Studies (RUSI), *Understanding Iran's Role in the Syrian Conflict*, Edited by Aniseh Bassiri Tabrizi and Rafaello Pantucci, (August 2016), P. 33. https://rusi.org/sites/default/files/201608_op_understanding_irans_role_in_the_syrian_conflict_0.pdf

Isma'ilis, Sunnis, Arabs, Armenian, Assyrians, Circassian, Kurds, Syriacs, and Turkman.

The US can take advantage of Syrians' hatred of Assad and Russia to arm a new Syrian army from amongst the 12 million Syrians displaced inside and outside the country, and who lost homes and relatives. Washington could turn Syria into an Afghanistan for Russia without the involvement of American troops, save for advisors and weapons. Whether the Trump White House would choose to invoke this option is uncertain, given Mr. Trump's mysterious fascination with Mr. Putin.

CHAPTER ONE

OIL AND GOD IN BRIEF

What's in a Book's Title?

The title to this book is inspired by certain facts:

- In a world addicted to oil, hegemony over oil means world hegemony. In the hands of the US, influence/control over Saudi oil export volumes and pricing politics is a non-lethal weapon-of-mass-destruction.[1] The oil weapon adds to the two other non-lethal weapons of mass destruction in the US arsenal: Dominance in global food exports and trade, and the US dollar as the main reserve currency for world central banks.[2]
- The 1945 security-for-oil understanding between Saudi Arabia's King Abdulaziz al-Saud and US President Franklin D. Roosevelt. Thus far, the understanding has survived six kings (all children of Abdulaziz) and 13 US presidents.[3]

---

[1]A lethal weapon of mass destruction destroys life and property within the affected area. An oil embargo brings the entire economy of an enemy to a standstill, while preserving life and property.

[2]65% of world reserve currencies is denominated in US dollar. As the world's main currency used to measure value and settle trade transactions, all Eurodollar interbank dealings, including the dollar payments resulting from forex transactions must clear in New York's *Clearing House Interbank Payment System (CHIPS)*. On an average day, 270,000 transactions totaling around $1.5 trillion are cleared. CHIPS helps US authorities enforce US sanctions against foreign countries.

[3]Adam Taylor, "The First Time a US President Met a Saudi King," *The Washington Post* (January 27, 2015). https://www.washingtonpost.com/news/worldviews/wp/2015/01/27/the-first-time-a-u-s-president-met-a-saudi-king/?utm_term=.72453beb4c18

- To claim legitimacy, the al-Saud kings have been exploiting an extreme reading of the Qur'an and Prophetic Sunna (acts and words of the Prophet Muhammad) by Wahhabi ulama (clerics/scholars) for the past century. They preach hatred of the other, jihad injunctions, predestination dogma, and the promise of houris (beautiful damsels) in paradise for the martyrs. On 9/11/2001, this combination turned nineteen Wahhabi jihadists into flying bombs.

It should be emphasized that the belief in God's tenets alone can be a force for good in the private life of an individual. Also, oil alone is innocuous. It is the combination of oil politics and manipulation of God's dictums by palace clerics that is toxic.

Unless noted otherwise, reference to Saudi Arabia throughout the book implies the rest of the Gulf Cooperation Council (GCC) member states as well. Formed on May 25, 1981, the GCC includes Bahrain, Kuwait, Oman, Qatar, Saudi Arabia, and United Arab Emirates.

Conclusions

Oil and God argues that the Arab Spring planted a resilient seed in the heads of the Arab masses: Parliamentary democracy is compatible with Islam. This idea is a serious blow to the Wahhabi indoctrination that democracy is a Western conspiracy to destroy Islam. The Arab Spring holds the promise of democratizing and modernizing Shari'a laws in non-oil exporting Arab countries that are far away from Saudi Arabia, like Tunisia and Morocco (see Chapter Five: *The Arab Spring—The First Wave: Non-Oil Exporting Countries* and Chapter Nine: *The Arab Spring*).

As for Saudi Arabia, matters are different. *Oil and God* argues that as long as oil imports by America's rivals, like China, continental Europe, India, and Japan is strong, Washington will want to influence/control Saudi oil production volume and price politics, not because the US needs Saudi oil, but because oil can be a strategic non-lethal weapon of mass destruction in Washington's hand (see Chapter Five: *Washington's Middle East Politics is the Politics of Oil*). To this end, the US has for the past seventy years, protected the al-Saud regime, despite its non-representative, archaic, totalitarian reign, its deep institutional corruption, its hatred-of-the-other indoctrination, its gender inequality and human rights abuses, its cruel penal code, and worldwide Wahhabi proselytization. To protect the oilfields and the king, some 35,000 American soldiers are stationed in air force and naval bases in Bahrain, Kuwait, Qatar, and the United Arab Emirates.

Oil protected the al-Saud regime before 9/11 and after 9/11. Even after Wahhabism boomeranged on 9/11, killing over 3,000 in the United States and costing an estimated $2 trillion,[4] and after 15 of the 19 Wahhabi terrorists turned out to be Saudis, the Bush administration looked the other way.[5] Instead, Bush bombed Iraq back to the stone-age in a misadventure that ended in Iran's control over Iraq and the empowerment of the ayatollahs of the city of Qom (see Chapter Seven). Mr. Obama empowered Iran further. He pursued policies in Iraq beneficial to Tehran (see Chapter Five) and handed Syria to Iran (see Chapter Nine).

Since 9/11, the handing of Iraq and Syria to Iran emboldened Iran's Supreme Ayatollah. Proxy Shi'ite/Sunni and Arab/Persian wars between Iran and Saudi Arabia followed, killing, injuring, and displacing millions, and devastating most of Iraq, Syria, and Yemen. Whether this horrific destruction is deliberately connected to 9/11 or not, the fact remains that since 9/11, the Muslim Middle East has been burning with no end in sight.

Aside from influencing/controlling Saudi oil politics, why does Washington protect the al-Saud kings? Two reasons: first, it is easier to manage one man, the king, who owes his life and throne to US protection than it is to manage the dozens of politicians in a democratic setting; secondly, the fear that pressuring the king to reform might weaken his hold on power and disrupt oil exports (see Chapter Five: *The Delicate and Complicated US/Saudi Relationship*).

Benefits from renewable energy are cumulative. The first phase, the subject of this book, argues that once America's rivals and big oil importers like China, continental Europe, India, and Japan generate sufficient energy from renewable sources to stop the importation of oil, Saudi Arabia will cease to be of much interest to Washington, Wahhabi cash will diminish, and jihadist terror will decline.

In the second phase, as renewable energy drives oil out of global demand, the environmental benefits will become enormous.

---

[4]Institute for the Analysis of Global Security, "How much did the September 11 terrorist attack cost America?" (2003–2004). http://www.iags.org/costof911.html

[5]It is hard to think that the Saudi government was involved in the recruitment or execution of the attacks. Rather, they were criminal acts by individual terrorists, bred by the Saudi Wahhabi way of life.

As long as Saudi Arabia is the world's biggest oil exporter and swing producer, the al-Sauds will be caught between two extremes. The first being the democratic values of the Arab Spring. The second is the Wahhabi ideology of the likes of al-Qaeda and the so-called Islamic State. Facing the two challenges, the al-Saud regime can be expected to at least maintain its own Wahhabi credentials if it wants to keep its claim to the high Wahhabi ground. The al-Sauds and Wahhabism are symbiotically attached—Wahhabism is their claim to legitimacy. Also, Wahhabism is a sharp psychological weapon to fight the "heretical" Shi'ite Iran. Lifting the ban on women driving motor vehicles or relaxing the harshness of the religious police, are merely cosmetics.

Global Dependence on Oil and Gas

Despite environmentalists' campaigns against the use of fossil fuel and the successes in developing efficient sustainable electricity generation from solar and wind technologies, global consumption of oil between 1980 and 2015 increased by 56%, from 61 million barrels per day to 95 million barrels per day (see Chapter Five: *Washington's Middle East Politics is Politics of Oil*).[6] Multiple decades will elapse before sustainable energy sources are allowed by the oil, auto, oil-using power generation plants, and banking industries to grow sufficiently to meet global energy demand. Also, Russia, with its huge oil and gas production and exports, will do all it can to prolong the life of fossil fuel. Resistance by millions of workers and by investors and lenders to write-off trillions of dollars in equities, bonds, and loans are formidable. Additionally, world oil reserves are plentiful.[7]

Oil income in GCC states represents the lion's share of government revenues. In 2014, oil contributed 86% of Bahrain's government revenues, Kuwait 80%, Oman 88%, Qatar 80%, Saudi Arabia 77%, and United Arab Emirates 64% (in the UAE, non-oil re-exports are significant, especially from Dubai).[8]

---

[6]YCHARTS, "World Oil Consumption Historical Data". https://ycharts.com/indicators/world_oil_consumption

[7]Ryan McQueeney, "How Much Oil Is Left In The Earth?" *Nasdaq*, (November 18, 2016). http://www.nasdaq.com/article/how-much-oil-is-left-in-the-earth-cm711409

[8]International Monetary Fund, "Economic Diversification in Oil-Exporting Arab Countries," Annual Meeting of Arab Ministers of Finance, Manama, Bahrain, (April 2016), PP. 8 and 13. https://www.imf.org/external/np/pp/eng/2016/042916.pdf

Saudi Arabia's proven oil and gas reserves in 2015 stood at 266 billion barrels (21.9% of world's reserves) and 8.6 trillion cubic meters of natural gas.[9] In 2016, Saudi Arabia produced 10.46 million bbl./day, of which 7.62 million bbl./day were exported, (around 20% of world oil exports), making Saudi Arabia the world's biggest oil exporter.[10] When oil exports from the rest of GCC states are added, total GCC oil exports rises to around 35% of world oil exports.[11]

In the event of war, US forces in GCC bases can dominate Iran and Iraq to control their oil exports; thus, raising US control over Middle Eastern oil to around 45% of world oil exports.

Further, the cost of Saudi oil production is the lowest in the world. While the net of tax average cash cost (capital spending + production costs + administration/transportation costs) of producing a barrel of oil or gas equivalent in 2016 in the UK was $44.33, Nigeria $24.88, Venezuela $17.14, US (shale) $16.93, US (non-shale) $15.96, and Russia $10.77, in Saudi Arabia it was $8.98.[12]

Global Hostage-Taking: No power seems capable of putting the Wahhabi genie back in the bottle. The combination of oil and God has given Saudi Arabia's kings the power to act as if they were hostage takers. In the al-Sauds' symbiotic union with Wahhabism, the oil-importing world is being forced to tolerate Wahhabi extremism in order to avoid the risk of darker regimes that might replace the al-Sauds and interrupt the flow of oil. As such, the cycle of violence will not end and the hostages will not be released until the world's demand for oil importation is replaced by sustainable energy sources like, solar, wind, hydropower, and nuclear fusion.

Middle Eastern Peoples' Strong Attachment to God

The great majority among the followers of the three monotheistic religions in the Middle East are passionate in their belief in God. In this book, the focus will be on Shi'ite and Sunni Muslims (See Chapters Two and Three).

---

[9]Organization of the Petroleum Exporting Countries, "Saudi Arabia Facts and Figures," *2015*. http://www.opec.org/opec_web/en/about_us/169.htm

[10]Wael Mahdi, "Saudi Arabia Breaks Records on Oil Exports and Output for Year," *Bloomberg*, (February 20, 2017). https://www.bloomberg.com/news/articles/2017-02-20/saudi-arabia-breaks-records-on-oil-exports-and-output-for-year

[11]Index Mundi, *Oil—exports > TOP 20*. http://www.indexmundi.com/g/r.aspx?t=20&v=95&l=en

[12]The Wall Street Journal, "Barrel Breakdown," (April 2016). http://graphics.wsj.com/oil-barrel-breakdown/

A Zogby survey of eight Arab countries conducted in 2015 shows the respondents' belief in the importance of religion in their future:

Religion has an important role to play in my country's future.

	Morocco	Egypt	KSA	UAE	Bahrain	Kuwait	Jordan	Palestine
Agree	77	90	88	89	63	93	75	86
Disagree	23	10	12	11	37	7	25	14

Zogby Research Services, LLC, "Muslim Millennial Attitudes on Religion and Religious Leadership," *Tabah Foundation*, (2015). https://d3n8a8pro7vhmx.cloudfront.net/aai/pages/11165/attachments/original/1452881049/Millenials_2015_FINAL.pdf?1452881049

In a 2013 survey by the Pew Research Center in seven countries in the Middle East and North Africa, 91% answered that it is necessary to believe in God to be a moral person.[13] In the same survey, Shari'a (Islamic law) won the approval of the great majority of Arabs as official law: Iraq (91%), Palestinian Territories (89%), Morocco (83%), Egypt (74%), Jordan (71%), Tunisia (56%), and Lebanon (29%).[14]

As Iranians prepared to elect a new president on June 14, 2012, a survey by the Pew Research Center (conducted between February 24 and May 3), found that 83% of Iranians say they favor the use of Sharia law, 40% think religious figures should play a large role in politics and an additional 26% of Iranians say religious figures should have some influence in political matters.[15]

Policy Implications: Islam is deeply ingrained in the hearts and minds of Middle Eastern Muslims. The word Islam means submission to the will of the one and only God. The word Muslim means the person who submits to the will of God. Islam regulates a Muslim's every waking minute, including personal hygiene, diet, healthy living, good manners, and family affairs. Islam rules the theological, ritual, judicial, political, social, ethical, and business realms. Serious theological issues separate Sunni clerics and congregations from Shi'ite clerics and congregations.

It is understandable if Western analysts, academics, and politicians do not focus on the role of religion in shaping the daily lives and politics of the peoples of the Middle East. Centuries of secularism in Europe have made Western men and women oblivious to the role of religion. To avert

---

[13]Pew Research Center, "The World's Muslims: Religion, Politics and Society." (April 30, 2013). http://www.pewforum.org/2013/04/30/the-worlds-muslims-religion-politics-society-overview/

[14]Ibid.

[15]Pew Research Center, "Iranians' Views Mixed on Political Role for Religious Figures," (June 11, 2013). http://www.pewforum.org/2013/06/11/iranians-views-mixed-on-political-role-for-religious-figures/

sectarian wars and evolve liberal democracies in the Middle East, two imperatives should be observed:

First, Minority Sects Should Never Rule Over the Muslim Majority: Religious minority rule converges on dictatorship, sectarianism, and corruption. Lacking majority support, the dictator entices other minorities, along with a small proportion among the majority—typically, the merchant class—to form a narrow ruling group. The dictator rewards the ruling group with impunity to violate the law. Huge disparities in wealth, income, and political power between the ruling group and the downtrodden majority breed an economic and political stratified society akin to a system of apartheid. Corruption is the glue that keeps such ruling groups together. If the glue is dissolved, the whole structure collapses. Ultimately, the pressure cooker explodes. There will be a revolt. Witness the calamitous destruction of Syria at the hands of the 10% Assad Alawite minority rule over the 75% Sunni majority.

Secondly, Democracy is the Antidote to Dictatorship: Except for Morocco, Tunisia and Turkey,[16] Sunni and Shi'ite rulers in the Middle East, whether kings, presidents, or ayatollahs, are non-representative dictators. A common denominator among the palace ulama is the exploitation of the Qur'anic Verse 4:59 to stay in power, which demands obedience to the Muslim ruler:

> *Obey God and obey God's messenger and obey those of authority among you.*

To become transparent, accountable, and respectful of the rule of law and human rights, representative democracy is a prerequisite. Such ideals, however, are alien to Arab rulers. The so-called "secular" military tyrants in Cairo or Damascus, for example, exploit Verse 4:59 just as much as the Kings of Bahrain or Jordan. As for the Saudi King, he goes beyond Verse 4:59. His palace clerics propagate that democracy is a Western conspiracy to destroy Islam, despite the fact that:

1) Non-Arab Muslim-majority countries like Bangladesh, Indonesia, Malaysia, Pakistan, and Turkey (50% of the estimated 1.5 billion world Muslims) enjoy multi-party elections, representative democracy, even women presidents and prime ministers.

---

[16]Lebanon is excluded due to its special religious and ethnic circumstances.

2) The 90 year-old Muslim Brotherhood Organization is democratic.[17] It has been an integral part of the Arab Spring's three democratic governments in Morocco (2011), Tunisia (2011), and Egypt (2012)—until Saudi Arabia in 2013 helped General Abdulfattah al-Sisi to overthrow and imprison Egypt's first and only democratically elected President, Muhammad Morsi.

3) Saudi modernist ulama have been reinterpreting the Islamic text "to create a modern state based on representation, accountability, and freedom" within a civil state that "rejects theocracy."[18] (See Chapter Six: *Certain Saudi Ulama as Agents of Change*).

The political conceptions of the Saudi modernists are akin to the conclusion reached by the al-Azhar University's Egyptian scholar and Shari'a judge, Ali Abd al-Raziq (1888–1966)[19] in his book on Islam and the basis of political authority.[20] Abd al-Raziq can find no clear evidence that there was any kind of organized Islamic governance during the Prophet's lifetime nor that the Prophet had any function except the prophetic function; he was not sent to exercise political authority, and he did not do so. According to Abd al-Raziq, the Prophetic mission is purely spiritual.[21]

Saudi Exploitation of Wahhabism to Claim Divine Rule: The al-Saud family does not belong to the family of the Prophet or his Quraish Tribe. They invoke the opinion of certain scholars such as, al-Ghazali (d. 1111), Ibn Taymiyya (d. 1328), and Ibn Jama'a (d. 1333), who opined that no matter what the origin of the ruler's authority might be, he must be obeyed, provided that he consults the ulama.[22] They ignore the opinion of scholars who stipulate that the caliph should belong to the Quraish tribe (see Chapter Six: *The Ruling Group. Thousands of al-Saud Royals*).[23]

---

[17]Established in Egypt in 1928, the Brotherhood is the Arab world's oldest Sunni political party, with a large following, estimated at around two million.

[18]Madawi al-Rasheed, *Muted Modernists. The Struggle Over Divine Politics in Saudi Arabia*, (Oxford University Press, 2015), PP. 2–6.

[19]Faizal Gazi, "The First Muslim Secularist," *The Guardian*, (April 9, 2009). https://www.the-guardian.com/commentisfree/belief/2009/apr/09/religion-islam-secularism-egypt

[20]Suad T. Ali, *A Religion, Not a State: Ali Abd al-Raziq's Islamic Justification of Political Secularism*, (The University of Utah Press, 2009).

[21]Albert Hourani, *Arabic Thought in the Liberal Age 1789–1939* (Cambridge University Press, 1997), P. 186.

[22]Ibid. PP. 14–18.

[23]Such as Abu al-Hasan al-Mawardi (d. 1031), Ibid, P. 10.

Saudi palace clerics teach that Islam is the perfect religion and Wahhabism is the true Islam. They praise the Saudi King as being the most ardent protector and promoter of the "true" faith. They preach that blind obedience to the king (waliy al-amr) is a form of piety. They teach that only Wahhabis enter paradise.[24] Their teaching engendered a hatred-of-the-other culture. They entrenched their belief in predestination, turned jihad into a virtuous act deserving paradise, and ignored the peaceful and the tolerant Verses in the Qur'an and the Sunna. Instead, they focused on the violent and the intolerant. They preach that Islam and Westernization leads to mixing of the sexes, the opening of nightclubs, the discarding of the veil, the charging of interest on bank loans, and the celebration of non-Islamic holidays, such as Christmas, Mother's Day, and Labor Day.[25] In addition, they deny women many of their human rights, to nullify the potential political opposition of 50% of the Saudi society. (See: Chapter Six, *Manifesting Wahhabism in Saudi daily life*).

Aside from justifying and bolstering the al-Saud king, Wahhabism was a useful strategy in the fight against communism in the Arab world, which pleased Washington. Also, Wahhabism was an important tool used to recruit and energize jihadists in Afghanistan's war against the Soviet Union (1978–1989), which added to Washington's approval of Wahhabi Riyadh.

On the other hand, the Wahhabi cult metastasized into terror groups like al-Qaeda, Boko Haram, the so-called Islamic State, al Shabab, and the Taliban. A former imam of the Grand Mosque in Mecca said of the so-called Islamic State, "We follow the same thought [as ISIS] but apply it in a refined way .... They draw their ideas from what is written in our own books, from our own principles."[26]

The Qom Ayatollah's Exploitation of the Hidden Imam to Claim Divine Rule: Shi'ites accept only the authority of the Prophet and the twelve Imams (see Chapter Three: *Wilayat al-Faqih or Rulership of the Senior-Most Shi'ite Jurist*). The Imams are descendants of Ali bin Abi Talib,

---

[24]The Prophet reportedly said that Islam would split into 73 sects but only one sect would go to heaven. This has spurred Wahhabi ulama to claim that theirs is the righteous sect and to expropriate paradise.

[25]Madawi al-Rasheed, *A History of Saudi Arabia* (Cambridge University Press, Cambridge, UK, 2003), P. 191.

[26]"Leading Saudi Cleric Says IS and Saudi Arabia 'Follow the Same Thought'," *Middle East Eye*, (January 28, 2016). http://www.middleeasteye.net/news/top-saudi-cleric-says-and-saudi-arabia-follow-same-thought-626782255

the fourth caliph, cousin and son-in-law of the Prophet and father of his two grandsons, Hasan and Hussein.

The majority of Shi'ites today believe that the Twelfth Imam, Muhammad al-Muntazar, disappeared as a child around 874, and that he is in a state of occultation (disappearance) until his return to the Earth to usher justice and prosperity. While the Twelfth Imam is hidden, the Shi'ite clerics act as his deputies, uncovering his judgment on all matters for the masses. They interpret the Islamic script according to their personal reasoning, in the name of the Hidden Imam.

In 1979, Grand Ayatollah Ruhollah Khomeini asserted the right of the senior-most Shi'ite cleric, as the deputy of the Imam, to oversee all religious, social, and political affairs of the Shi'ite community.[27] The new governance system is called Wilayat al-faqih. It wields absolute theocratic dictatorship. The faqih is the supreme power over the parliament, the judiciary, and the executive branch. He appoints members of the Council of Guardians, which vets candidates for parliament and the presidency and has veto power to reject parliamentary laws that do not conform to Shi'ite principles.[28]

Who Is Behind Today's Wars Among Shi'ites and Sunnis?

Four culprits loom large behind the growth of jihadism over the past three generations and the deepening of the Shi'ite/Sunni divide today. The first is Wahhabism (see Chapters Five and Six). With the formation of the Saudi state in 1932, hatred-of-the-other has become a part of the Wahhabi way of life, propagated in schools, mosques, and the media. Discrimination against Shi'ites has become particularly venomous. The second factor is the Khomeini revolution of 1979. It exacerbated the Shi'ite/Sunni divide and was the catalyst behind the eight long years of the Iran/Iraq war (September 1980–August 1988). The third factor is the American occupation of Iraq (see Chapter Seven). It opened the gates of sectarian hell in the Muslim Middle East. G.W. Bush's misadventure in Iraq and Obama's inaction in Syria empowered Iran and ignited proxy wars between Saudi Arabia and Iran in Iraq (see Chapter Seven), Syria (see Chapter Nine),

---

[27]Moojan Momen, *An Introduction to Shi'i Islam*, (Yale University Press, New Haven, CT, 1985), P. 196.

[28]US Library of Congress, "Iran Country Report". http://lcweb2.loc.gov/frd/cs/irtoc.html.

and Yemen. The fourth catalyst behind extremism and jihadism today must be blamed on Israel (see Chapter Eight). Israeli and US denial of a connection between its occupation, oppression, and humiliation of Arabs and Palestinians and the growth of jihadism is similar to Saudi Arabia's denial of a connection between the Wahhabi way of life and the atrocities of 9/11.

The harsher life becomes in a religious Middle East, the closer to God the faithful get. The belief in God, predestination, jihad, and the delights of paradise make martyrdom more attractive than living under occupation, oppression, and humiliation.

A New Middle East Map: Wahhabism radicalized Sunni Islam and polarized Muslims. The Khomeini revolution weaponized Shi'ism. Empowered by the Bush and Obama administrations, Iran has become the self-appointed protector of Shi'ites everywhere, especially Arab Shi'ites. Proxy sectarian wars have destroyed most of Iraq, Syria, and Yemen. Shi'ite communities in Bahrain, Kuwait and Saudi Arabia are restive. Harmony among religions, sects, and ethnicities in the Middle East has died.

The Sykes-Picot Agreement of May 19, 1916 between London and Paris divided Greater Syria and Iraq between the two European powers. Sykes-Picot assumed that the rather peaceful relations of most of the previous six centuries under the tolerant Hanafi Sunni rite of the Ottoman Sultans would be maintained. However, with the arrival of the Saudi Wahhabi state (1932), all that has changed. Hatred-of-the-other culture poisoned the well of religious and sectarian good will and harmony. Atrocities were committed against Christians, Yazidis, and Shi'ites, even Sunnis who reject Wahhabi extremism. A new map along Swiss lines of autonomous self-ruled regions within federal states—drawn along sectarian and ethnic lines—has become a viable and necessary alternative.

The Nexus: US Politics, Saudi Oil, and God

In a world addicted to crude oil, energy hegemony means world hegemony. To achieve hegemony over world energy, the US must influence and/or control Saudi Arabia's oil and gas production and pricing politics. Control over world energy supplements US dominance over global food exports and the US dollar as the main reserve currency of central banks worldwide. Oil, food, and the dollar are three formidable non-lethal weapons.

The 1945 security-for-oil understanding between King Abdulaziz and President Franklin D. Roosevelt served the al-Saud kings well. Not even the 9/11 atrocity could make G.W. Bush punish Riyadh for breeding the 9/11 terrorists. Instead, Iraq was destroyed, only to be captured by Iran.

US Protection of Saudi Arabia: For the past seventy years, successive US administrations have protected the al-Saud regime through different means (see Chapter Five: *US Protection of Saudi Arabia*):

1) Some 35,000 US soldiers are in air force and naval bases in Bahrain, Kuwait, Qatar, and United Arab Emirates.
2) Brigades of American engineers and tons of spare parts keep the hundreds of billions of dollars in weapons, energy, chemical, electric, and desalination plants operational in Saudi Arabia.
3) Former senior US officials, captains of industry, media moguls, lobbyists, and think-tank researchers are generously paid by the Riyadh ruling group as lawyers, advisors, consultants, investment managers, and business partners, etc.

While US foreign policy is supposed to spread American values such as representative democracy, free speech, gender equality, and human rights, the Saudi regime has been exempted from such lofty ideals. Washington has protected Riyadh despite its non-representative, non-participatory governance. Saudi Arabia's exploitation of the most extreme interpretation of the Islamic text finally boomeranged on 9/11.

In response to 9/11, Afghanistan was invaded in October, 2001 and Iraq in March 2003. Harvard University's Kennedy School estimated in 2013 that the war in the two countries cost the US between $4 trillion and $6 trillion.[29] Brown University's Watson Institute for International and Public Affairs estimated that the wars in Afghanistan and Iraq cost US taxpayers nearly $5.6 trillion.[30] These estimates do not include the cost of the destruction of infrastructure and cities in Afghanistan and Iraq, nor the millions of lives lost and those injured with life-long disabilities.

---

[29]Linda J. Bilmes, "The Financial Legacy of Iraq and Afghanistan: How Wartime Spending Decisions Will Constrain Future National Security Budgets," Harvard University: Faculty Research Working Paper Series, (March 2013). https://research.hks.harvard.edu/publications/workingpapers/citation.aspx?PubId=8956&type=WPN

[30]Neta Crawford, "US Budgetary Costs of Post-9/11 Wars Through FY2018: $5.6 Trillion," *Watson Institute for International and Public Affairs, Brown University,* (2017). http://watson.brown.edu/costsofwar/papers/2017/USBudgetaryCostsFY2018

The relationship between Washington and Riyadh is delicate and complicated. It forces the two countries to tread carefully in dealing with one another.

The Delicate US/Saudi Relationship—The View from Washington: Washington would not seriously pressure the Saudi King for the following two reasons:

1) Ease of dealing with one absolute king who owes his throne and life to US protection compared with having to manage scores of parliamentarians and religious and political leaders in a democratic setting.
2) Fear that a confrontation might weaken the king's hold on power and cause chaos in oil markets.

The Delicate US/Saudi Relationship—The View from Riyadh: Saudi Kings realize the importance of US protection for the survival of their enterprise. Nonetheless, they have not and never will acquiesce to US (or to any other power's) suggestions or pressure to implement truly genuine religious and political reforms. Wahhabism is the al-Sauds' justification to rule over the disparate, staunchly independent, and higher-pedigreed tribal sheikhs. Not a whiff of representative democracy would be allowed to develop—it would collapse the king's absolute rule.

The Two Recent Events that Shook the Middle East

This book is shaped by the interaction between the effects of two huge events since 9/11. These events shook the Middle East to its core: (1) The 2011 Arab Spring, and (2) The empowerment of Iran by G.W. Bush and Obama.

One—The 2011 Arab Spring

The Arab Spring in Tunisia (2011), Morocco (2011), and Egypt (2012) may be described as the most significant development in the modern history of the Arab world. The Arab Spring planted a resilient seed in the heads of the Arab masses, namely, that parliamentary democracy is compatible with Islam. This development represents a serious blow to

Wahhabi indoctrination that democracy is a Western conspiracy meant to destroy Islam.

The Arab Spring was led by the downtrodden Arab masses, the internet generation, and the Muslim Brotherhood. The Brotherhood embraced representative democracy and participated in multi-party democratic elections in Tunisia, Morocco, and Egypt. It won parliamentary majorities and formed coalition governments with secular parties, defying Wahhabi anti-democracy teaching and preaching.

In 2013, however, one year after Egypt's first ever democratic election for president brought President Mohammad Morsi to power, Saudi Arabia collaborated with army General Abdulfattah al-Sisi in a coup d'état against Morsi. The legitimate President was thrown in jail, where he still is at the time of this writing, five years later. The coup delivered Egypt back into the clutches of yet another dark military dictatorship. It damaged the cause of democracy, justice, and human rights in the Arab world (except in Morocco and Tunisia). It shielded the al-Saud regime from the winds of democracy from Egypt.

The Existential Threat Posed by a Democratic Egypt to Saudi Arabia: A democratic Egypt could be a catalyst for political change in Riyadh. The Saudi King is frightened that a Brotherhood parliamentary democracy in Egypt would spill over to his own realm. He fears that with its Islamic credibility, the Brotherhood's parliamentary democracy would undermine his legitimacy. A Brotherhood parliament could modernize Shari'a laws and evolve a less austere, less extreme, and gentler way of life than Wahhabism, which the Saudi populace would embrace.[31] (See: Chapter Five, *How Might a Brotherhood Parliament Pose an Existential Risk to Saudi Arabia?*)

The Arab peoples, especially the young internet generation, are ready to embrace modernized Shari'a laws. A poll of over 5,300 Muslims between the ages of 15 and 34 conducted by Zogby Research Services during October and November 2015 in eight Arab countries (Bahrain, Egypt, Jordan, Kuwait, Morocco, Palestine, Saudi Arabia, and United Arab Emirates), found respondents to be overwhelmingly of the opinion that there needs to be renewal in the language used to talk about Islam in

---

[31]Elie Elhadj, "The Arab Spring and the Prospects for Genuine Religious and Political Reforms," *Middle East Review of International Affairs (MERIA) Journal* 16, no 03, (Nov. 14, 2012). http://www. rubincenter.org/2012/11/the-arab-spring-and-the-prospects-for-genuine-religious-and-political-reforms/

sermons, talks, and public outlets.[32] The survey was commissioned by the Tabah Foundation to explore attitudes of the Muslim millennial generation, specifically with respect to their attitudes toward religious identity, authority and religious leadership, religion and politics, personal religious devotion, reform, and religious extremism.

Not surprisingly, therefore, Riyadh and Abu Dhabi have been on a crusade to demonize the Brotherhood and lobby governments and the media in Europe and the US to declare the Muslim Brotherhood a terrorist organization.

Two—The Empowerment of Iran Since 9/11

On September 11, 2001, the earth shook. Nineteen Wahhabi terrorists committed the ultimate crime when they flew passenger airplanes into office buildings in Manhattan and Washington DC. In retaliation, the Bush administration ignored Wahhabi culpability. Instead, it pulverized Iraq, only for Iran to dominate Baghdad (see Chapter Seven). Mr. Bush's Iraq project created a Shi'ite Crescent from Iran to Iraq, Syria, and Lebanon. The Obama White House, as if to continue what G.W. Bush had started, allowed Iran to help destroy and occupy Syria (see Chapter Nine).

The Bush and Obama administrations turned the Fertile Crescent into an Iranian domain for the first time since the advent of Islam fourteen centuries ago. They emboldened Iran's supreme leader, Ayatollah Ali Khamenei, to embark upon an aggressive crusade against his Sunni Arab neighbors. Tehran's empowerment triggered proxy wars in the Middle East between Iran and Saudi Arabia. These wars brought the US (and UK) huge weapons contracts. They also bred the so-called Islamic State.

G.W. Bush Hands Iraq to Iran: The Bush administration avoided punishing Saudi Arabia for Wahhabi culpability for 9/11. It feared destabilizing the king's control over the country, especially in the Shi'ite populated oil-rich Eastern Province, where practically all Saudi oil and gas fields and chemical installations are located. A loss of the king's control could have disrupted oil exports by the likes of al-Qaeda's Saudi sympathisers, and/or Saddam Hussein (in 2003), and/or the Qom ayatollahs. Instead, Mr. Bush

---

[32]Zogby Research Services, LLC, "Muslim Millennial Attitudes on Religion and Religious Leadership," *Tabah Foundation*, (2015). https://d3n8a8pro7vhmx.cloudfront.net/aai/pages/11165/attachments/original/1452881049/Millenials_2015_FINAL.pdf?145288104

opted for turning centuries-old Sunni rule in Iraq on its head. The Bush project failed. It handed Iraq to Iran on a silver platter without Iran directly firing a bullet (see Chapter Seven).[33]

To rally the US public behind the war against Iraq, the Bush administration propagated that Baghdad had:

1) A connection to al-Qaeda.
2) Attempted to obtain uranium from the Central African country of Niger.
3) Attempted to acquire more than 100,000 high-strength aluminum tubes for gas centrifuges for use in enriching uranium.
4) Possessed chemical and biological weapons, and continued development of weapons of mass destruction.

Iraq denied all accusations. The first three were discredited before the war had even started. Discrediting the fourth had to wait until after Iraq was occupied.

How might the falsehoods be explained? Senator Angus King said on January 12, 2017, "Intelligence that was tailored to fit the demands of the policymakers."[34] Further, in his memoir, *My Life, Our Times,* published in November 2017, former British Prime Minister Gordon Brown charges that the US defense department knew that Iraq did not have weapons of mass destruction but kept Britain in the dark.[35]

The rush to war might be explained by the Bush administration's ostensible aims to:

1) Control Iraq's vast oil reserves.
2) Hand US companies billions of dollars in re-construction contracts.
3) Bolster Israel's security.
4) Quench Mr. Bush's personal hatred of Saddam Hussein.
5) Spread democracy in the Arab world.
6) Use Iraq as a launching pad to change the regimes of Iran and Syria.
7) Replace the Cold War against the former USSR with a new enemy.

---

[33]By contrast, the eight-year Iraq/Iran war was the 20th century's longest war (September 1980–August 1988), and cost both sides a million dead and many times this number of injured.

[34]CNN Transcripts, "Confirmation Hearing of Mike Pompeo for CIA Director," (January 12, 2017). http://transcripts.cnn.com/TRANSCRIPTS/1701/12/ath.02.html

[35]Michael Savage, "Gordon Brown Says Pentagon Misled UK over Case for Iraq Invasion," *The Guardian,* (November 5, 2017). https://www.theguardian.com/world/2017/nov/05/iraq-weapons-mass-destruction-america-misled-britain-gordon-brown

The Bush administration might have reasoned, also, that even if, in a worst case scenario, the Iraq project fails and Iran dominates Iraq, the new situation would still be beneficial to Washington; an empowered Iran would not only get into Shi'ite/Sunni wars with Saudi Arabia thousands of miles away from the US, it would also bring billions of Saudi Dollars in weapon purchases from US companies to fight Iran.

Barack Obama's Strategies that Empowered Iran: To gain insight into Mr. Obama's attitude toward Middle Eastern affairs, the interview he gave to the *Atlantic* magazine in April 2016 is revealing. (See: Chapter Five, *A Window into Mr. Obama's Middle East Politics—The Atlantic Magazine Interview*). He exhibited a jaded view of Wahhabism and the house of Saud. He expressed "derision" toward the "Washington Playbook," which "compel[led] him to treat Saudi Arabia as an ally," denunciation of Saudi Arabia's "state-sanctioned misogyny," fulmination at the "Arabization" of Indonesia's Islam, and realization that "the large majority of 9/11 hijackers were not Iranian, but Saudi.[36] He told his interviewer, "Saudis need to 'share' the Middle East with their Iranian foes.[37]

Three strategies may be cited behind Obama's empowerment of Iran (see Chapter Five: *Obama's Three Strategies That Empowered Iran*).

The first was the P5+1 nuclear agreement with Iran. After seventeen years of US refusal to meet with Tehran, until UN demands to suspend all nuclear activities were met, the State Department announced on April 8, 2009 a departure from its previous policy: The US would join the P5+1 talks with Iran.[38] On July 14, 2015, the Joint Comprehensive Plan of Action (JCPOA) was reached. In return for a delay of 15 years in its nuclear program, Iran gained access to $100 billion in frozen assets and became able to export oil.[39]

The second strategy was Obama's Iraq policy. He supported the anti-Sunni pro-Iran Iraqi Prime Minister, Nouri al-Maliki (2006–2014). Also, he prematurely removed on December 18, 2011, US troops from Iraq.

---

[36]Jeffery Goldberg, "The Obama Doctrine," *The Atlantic,* (April 2016 Issue). https://www.theatlantic.com/magazine/archive/2016/04/the-obama-doctrine/471525/

[37]Ibid.

[38]"US to Join Nuclear Talks with Iran, State Department Says," *CNN,* (April 8, 2009). http://edition.cnn.com/2009/POLITICS/04/08/us.iran.nuclear/

[39]"Iran Nuclear Deal: Key Details," *BBC,* (January 16, 2016). http://www.bbc.co.uk/news/world-middle-east-33521655

US senators and diplomats warned Obama about the dangers his Iraq policies are creating for US interests in the Middle East (see Chapter Seven).[40]

The third strategy that empowered Iran was Obama's handing of Syria
to Iran. Since the eruption of the Syrian revolution on March 18, 2011
against the Assad family's fifty-year of sectarian tyranny, Obama not only
refused to supply defensive anti-aircraft guns to Syria's anti-regime forces,
but prevented other countries from supplying the weapons as well, with one
excuse or another. He gave Assad and his Iranian protectors the green light
to fly thousands of bombing raids, unopposed on Syrian cities and villages.
He handcuffed the Syrian revolution. He repudiated his own infamous red-
line warning against the use of chemical weapons,[41] which Assad defied on
August 21, 2013, killing 1,400 people near Damascus.[42] He was not about
to risk a breakdown in the P5+1 negotiations, which Iran reportedly threatened.[43] Further, when Russia intervened militarily on September 30, 2015
to protect the Assad regime, Obama looked the other way.

Seven years later, an estimated 500,000 civilians are dead, (possibly a
million), including 55,000 children,[44] millions more injured, and Twelve
million people displaced (see Chapter Nine).

Risks Obama Ignored: A student of history, the son of a father who
"came from a Kenyan family that includes generations of Muslims,"[45]
Obama ignored realities like the deep theological gulf that separates
Shi'ites from Sunnis and the ethnic rivalries and history of wars between
Arabs and Persians. He also disregarded recommendations by American
officials and experts on Syria and Iraq to change course. A plan developed

---

[40]Peter Beinart, "Obama's Disastrous Iraq Policy: An Autopsy," *The Atlantic*, (July 23, 2014).
https://www.theatlantic.com/international/archive/2014/06/obamas-disastrous-iraq-policy-
an-autopsy/373225/

[41]James Ball, "Obama Issues Syria a 'Red Line' Warning on Chemical Weapons," *The Washington
Post*, (August 20, 2012). https://www.washingtonpost.com/world/national-security/obama-issues-
syria-red-line-warning-on-chemical-weapons/2012/08/20/ba5d26ec-eaf7-11e1-b811-09036bcb
182b_story.html?utm_term=.be111a7b6235

[42]"Syria Chemical Attack: What We Know," *BBC*, (September 24, 2013). http://www.bbc.co.uk/
news/world-middle-east-23927399

[43]Pamela Engel, "Obama Reportedly Declined to Enforce Red Line in Syria after Iran Threatened
to Back Out of Nuclear Deal," *Business Insider UK*, (August 23, 2016). http://uk.businessinsider.com/
obama-red-line-syria-iran-2016-8

[44]I Am Syria, "Death Count in Syria: 470,000—Children: 55,000." http://www.iamsyria.org/
death-tolls.html

[45]"Barack Obama's Speech at Cairo University: Full text," *The Telegraph*. (June 4, 2009). http://
www.telegraph.co.uk/news/worldnews/barackobama/5447513/Barack-Obamas-speech-at-Cairo-
University-Full-text.html

in the summer of 2012 by then-Secretary of State Hillary Clinton and then-CIA Director David Petraeus to arm and train vetted Syrian rebels was rebuffed.[46] In June 2016, more than 50 State Department diplomats signed an internal memo sharply critical of US policy in Syria, calling for military strikes against Assad forces, which he brushed aside.[47]

How Might Obama's Empowerment of Iran Policy Be Judged? From a US perspective, Obama's rewriting of the "Washington Playbook" brought America a number of benefits:

1) Opened the door for US companies to trade with Iran, closed since the Khomeini revolution and the taking of US hostages in 1979 for 444 days.
2) Entangled Shi'ites and Sunnis in endless wars thousands of mile away from America.
3) Forced Saudi Arabia and the rest of GCC rulers to seek an even tighter alliance with Washington and to purchase more weapons.
4) Drove Saudi Arabia (and other GCC states) to seek an alliance with Israel.

The Future of the Obama Legacy in the Muslim Middle East: Obama's empowerment of Iran may have three, conflicting future policy implications: First, it may have been short-sighted. It could be reversed because Saudi Arabia benefits America more than Iran. Secondly, perhaps Obama's decisions were a clever strategy that should be maintained since it enhances US business opportunities with Iran's 85 million consumers, while at the same time it does not reduce Saudi (and GCC) purchases of US weapons. Thirdly, the better policy might be to retain aspects of the old "Washington Playbook" combined with Obama's edited version. (See Chapter Five).

Oil has protected the al-Saud regime before and after 9/11. Whether the horrific destruction in Iraq (since 2003), Syria (since 2011), and Yemen (since 2015) is wittingly or unwittingly connected to 9/11, the fact remains that Arab countries which are innocent of the blood of 9/11 have

---

[46]"White House Rebuffed Clinton-Petraeus Plan to Arm Syrian Rebels: Report." *Reuters*, (February 3, 2013). https://www.reuters.com/article/us-usa-syria-clinton/white-house-rebuffed-clinton-petraeus-plan-to-arm-syrian-rebels-report-idUSBRE91201220130203

[47]"US Diplomats Rebuke Obama on Syria and Call for Strikes on Assad." *Huffington Post*, (June 20, 2016). http://www.huffingtonpost.com/entry/diplomats-obama-syria-assad_us_5763668ce4b0fbbc8be9e7ed

been burning since 9/11, while Saudi Arabia (15 terrorists) and the UAE (2 terrorists) escaped unscathed.

The Donald Trump White House: Mr. Trump reduces complex multifaceted, long-term balanced relationships with other countries into a balance of payments issue. Saudi Arabia is no exception. In addition to providing the US with big balance of payment surpluses, Donald Trump expects the King to:

1) Normalize Saudi relations with Israel.
2) Bring the Palestinians to yield on Israeli settlement terms.
3) Help destroy the so-called Islamic State.
4) Moderate Riyadh's Wahhabi teaching and preaching.

Will the King oblige? To protect his throne, the Saudi King shall do his utmost to deliver whatever Donald Trump instructs.

In return, what does the Saudi King expect from Donald Trump? Given his bitter disappointment in Obama's politics, King Salman performed an act of pre-emptive surrender to Trump. During Mr. Trump's visit to Riyadh on May 20, 2017, Saudi Arabia purchased weapons and civilian goods totaling $500 billion, to be delivered over the next ten years.

The King's wish list includes:

1) Reversal of Washington's Empowerment of Iran Since 9/11.
2) Adding the Muslim Brotherhood to the list of terrorist organizations.
3) Punishing Turkey and Qatar for supporting the Muslim Brotherhood.
4) Shutting down Qatar's Al Jazeera media Network.
5) Protection from the Justice Against Sponsors of Terrorism Act (JASTA).

Will Donald Trump oblige? It is unlikely that Mr. Trump will deliver much of what the King wishes. In the master/servant relationship that exists between Washington and Riyadh, what can the King do? Nothing.

Breeding Jihadists and Combating Jihadi Terror

Oil and God argues that ambitious, charismatic politicians dressed up in Wahhabi garb have been turning angry men and women into walking bombs (see Chapter Four).

The Breeding formula: Three ingredients create an explosive cocktail:

Jihad injunctions + predestination dogma
+ promise of houris in paradise = Dynamite.

The dynamite alone is safe. To explode, it needs a spark. The spark can be any number of despairing domestic and/or foreign triggers. The domestic spark might be unemployment, poverty, injustice, oppression, sexual frustration, government tyranny, etc. The foreign sparks can be old and recent humiliations and defeats, such as:

1) Sykes-Picot Agreement (May 19, 1916), which divided the Levant between Britain and France.
2) Balfour Declaration (November 2, 1917), which created Israel in 1948 and the ensuing refugees, defeats, shame, and anger. It politicized the Bible, which in turn politicized the Quran. Seventy years later, ten million Palestinians are in refugee camps and under Israeli occupation.
3) Washington's handing of Iraq and Syria to Iran and the triggering of proxy wars between Shi'ites and Sunnis.

With every new disappointment, some Sunni moderates become Islamists and some Islamists become jihadists. What was al-Qaeda a few years ago has metastasized into a variety of more extremist strands in many countries.

Combating Jihadi Terror: To fight the appeal of jihadist recruitment, the dynamite must be deactivated and the domestic and foreign sparks defused.

To deactivate the dynamite:

- Wahhabi clerics' control over Saudi Arabia should be ended. Similarly, Shi'ite ayatollahs' control over Iran should be ended. Also, the historicity of the Qur'an and the Sunna ought to be examined scientifically by credible Sunni scholars with an open mind to determine the authenticity of the holy text.

To defuse the domestic spark:

- Arab states should embrace democratic rule.

To defuse the foreign spark:

- In Palestine, de-politicize the Bible and the Qur'an.

However, none of the remedies is even remotely likely to materialize under existing sectarian, ethnic, nationalistic, economic, and political conditions; above all, the grip of God over the peoples of the Middle East and a world addicted to crude oil are the largest impediments.

The Samuel P. Huntington Hypothesis

Samuel P. Huntington hypothesized in 1993 that "the principal conflicts of global politics will occur between nations and groups of different civilizations."[48] Religious and sectarian wars in the Middle East today validate Huntington's hypothesis.

Following the defeat and dismemberment of the Ottoman Empire in the aftermath of First World War in 1918, the tolerant rule of the moderate Hanafi Sunni Ottoman Sultans came to an end. Over the next century, five political events, dressed-up in religious garb, spilled rivers of blood in the region and terrorism around the world. These were, the founding of Wahhabi Saudi Arabia (1932), the creation of the Jewish State of Israel (1948), the Shi'ite revolution of Ayatollah Khomeini in Iran (1979), the September 11, 2001 attacks by Wahhabi terrorists against the US, and the birth and empowerment of the Shi'ite Crescent (2003–2016).

---

[48]Samuel Huntington, "The Clash of Civilizations?" *Foreign Affairs,* Summer 1993. https://www.foreignaffairs.com/articles/united-states/1993-06-01/clash-civilizations

CHAPTER TWO

ISLAM, ARAB MASSES, AND ARAB RULERS' EXPLOITATION OF ISLAM TO STAY IN POWER

Introduction

Studies that overlook the influence of religion on Middle Eastern politics can only reach myopic conclusions. Neglecting the Islam factor in the politics of the Middle East is like navigating a ship without a compass. Religion is as important today in the study of events in the Middle East as it was a thousand years ago. Recognizing the stresses cultural differences may create, Samuel P. Huntington wrote, "The great divisions among humankind and the dominating source of conflict will be cultural ... The clash of civilizations will dominate global politics. The fault lines between civilizations will be the battle lines of the future."[1]

Deep collective memories connect age-old historical events with the present. Muslims' First Civil War was in 657. It was over the succession to the Prophet. It was between the fourth caliph (successor to the Prophet) Ali bin Abi Talib (656–661), who was the Prophet's cousin and son-in-law, and Mu'awiyah bin abi Sufyan, Governor of Syria (639–661), who became the fifth caliph (661–680) after the death of the Prophet in 632. Mu'awiyah ushered in the Umayyad caliphate in Damascus (661–750).

The First Civil War took place along the banks of the Euphrates river in Siffin, near Raqqa, Syria. 1361 years later, a new page on sectarian wars

---

[1] Samuel Huntington, "The Clash of Civilizations?" *Foreign Affairs*, Summer 1993.

was written when the Alawite Assad regime lost Raqqa to the Wahhabi so-called Islamic State. About four years later, on October 17, 2017, Raqqa was liberated by Kurdish and Arab fighters of the Syrian Democratic Forces (SDF) backed by the airpower of the US-led coalition.[2]

In this and the next chapter, the religious principles that define Muslims in general, and Arabs in particular, will be outlined.

Tight Attachment

The word Islam means submission to the will of the one and only God. The word Muslim means the person who submits to the will of God. To Muslims, God's word in the Holy Qur'an asserts that Islam is the perfect religion and the ideal way of life for all peoples and all time:

> Qur'an 6:38: *Nothing have we omitted from the Book.*
> Qur'an 16:89: *We have sent down to thee the Book explaining all things.*

Four factors combine to make Muslim Arabs feel like God's supreme race:
The first is the pride Arabs take in the fact that God's words in the Qur'an were revealed in Arabic, the language of paradise. There are many verses to this effect. Here are two examples:

> Qur'an 12:2: *We have sent it down as an Arabic Qur'an so that you may learn wisdom.*
> Qur'an 41:3: *A book, whereof the verses are explained in detail; a Qur'an in Arabic, for people who understand.*

Knowledge of Arabic determines the extent to which a person understands Islam. The Qur'an, the Sunna [Prophetic actions (Sira) plus Prophetic words/sayings (Hadith)], and the writings of the early scholars and jurists are all in Arabic. Non-Arab ulama must speak, read, and write Arabic in order to explain Shari'a rules to their non-Arabic

---

[2]Patrick Cockburn, "Raqqa: Isis 'capital' liberated by US-backed forces—but civilians face months of hardship with city left devastated," *The independent*, (October 17, 2017). http://www.independent. co.uk/news/world/middle-east/raqqa-liberated-isis-defeat-latest-mine-clearance-sdf-camp-residents-medicine-aid-a8005881.html

speaking congregations. Such intermediation introduces local customs, cultures, political leanings, and the personal interests of the translators into the interpretation of the Text. Indeed, capturing the precise meaning of the Qur'an in translation is difficult, often leading to differing conclusions.

The second factor is Arabs' pride in the belief that God described them in Qur'anic verse 3:110 as: *The best of peoples evolved for mankind.*

The third factor is Arabs' feeling of honor that the Prophet was an Arab from the Meccan tribe of Quraish. To Arab pride, every Companion of the Prophet who reported His words and actions, as well as the founders of the four Sunni schools of jurisprudence that survive today (Hanafi, Hanbali, Maliki, Shafi'i) were all Arab, although, Abu Hanifa was the grandson of a Persian slave.[3] All fifty-five caliphs since the death of the Prophet in 632 and up until the Mongols destroyed the Arab Abbasid Empire in 1258 were Arab from the Quraish tribe. The scholar al-Mawardi (d. 1031) stipulated that the caliph should belong to the Quraish tribe.[4]

The fourth factor in Arabs' pride is that Islam's holiest shrines are located in Arab lands: Mecca, Medina, and Jerusalem.

The Arab peoples are gripped by their love of Islam and its way of life, individually and as a community. The ethno-linguistic connection makes Islam an Arabic religion. To the great majority of Arabs, Islam is a medal of distinction. They see themselves as the guardians over the purity of Islam. A Zogby survey shows how important it is for an Arab Muslim to be known as a Muslim:

How important is it to you that those you meet know that you are a Muslim?

	Morocco	Egypt	KSA	UAE	Bahrain	Kuwait	Jordan	Palestine
Important	92	95	83	98	52	91	68	83
Not important	8	5	17	2	48	8	32	17

Source: Zogby Research Services, *Muslim Millennial Attitudes on Religion and Religious Leadership*, Tabah Foundation, 2015.

According to a survey by the Pew Research Center published in April 2013,[5] 74% of Muslims in seven countries in the Middle East and North

---

[3]Albert Hourani, *History of the Arab Peoples*, (Faber and Faber, London, 1991). P. 397.
[4]Hourani, *Arabic Thought in the Liberal Age 1789–1939*, P. 10.
[5]Pew Research Center, "The World's Muslims: Religion, Politics and Society," (April 30, 2013). http://www.pewforum.org/2013/04/30/the-worlds-muslims-religion-politics-society-overview/

Africa region (MENA) want Islamic law (Shari'a) to be the official law of the land. On a country by-country basis, the percentages were as follows: Iraq (91%), Palestinian Territories (89%), Morocco (83%), Egypt (74%), Jordan (71%), Tunisia (56%), and Lebanon (29%).

The relationship between Arab Muslims and non-Arab Muslims has always been strained. Behind the hostility stands the occupied people's natural dislike of occupiers. Since the dawn of Arab conquests, and following the death of the Prophet in 632, non-Arab Muslims rebelled against their new masters for religious, political, and economic equality. Nationalism, ethnicity, old rivalries and wars among Arabs, Persians, and Byzantines added fuel to the fire. As early as 685, ethnic revolts erupted. Al-Mukhtar led a revolt in Kufa, central Iraq, against the Umayyad caliph in Damascus. Mukhtar claimed that he was acting in the interest of the 'weak' and the Mawali (early non-Arab Muslims).[6]

World Muslims are estimated at 1.5 billion; 1.25 billion are Sunnis and 250 million are Shi'ites. Four Sunni schools of jurisprudence survive today and are named after their founders. The vast majority of Sunnis belong to three schools: Abu Hanifa (d. 767), with followers in West and Central Asia and the Indian subcontinent, Malik (d. 795) in North and West Africa, and Shafe'i (d. 820) in East Africa, South Arabia and the Malay Archipelago. These Sunni schools are relatively moderate and followed by 97% of the world's peace-loving Muslims.

Ahmad bin Hanbal (d. 855) established the fourth Sunni school. Due to its extremism, Hanbalism has never had much of a following. Its fortunes improved, however, since the al-Saud/Abdulwahhab partnership formed Saudi Arabia in 1932 and embraced bin Hanbal's teachings. Despite Riyadh's deep pockets since the 1973 quadrupling of oil prices, which financed the construction of thousands of Wahhabi mosques and schools and the dispatching of preachers in an aggressive global program of proselytization, the Wahhabi/Hanbali following is still a tiny percentage among world Sunnis, estimated today at around 3%.

Three Degrees of Attachment: Notwithstanding the inherent difficulties in categorization, it will be useful to recognize three levels of attachment to Islam: moderate, Islamist, and jihadist. Within each category, there are shades in the degree of individual commitment.

---

[6]Hugh Kennedy, *The Prophet and the Age of the Caliphates, the Islamic Near East from the Sixth to the Eleventh Century* (Longman, London and New York: 1996), PP. 95–96.

Moderate Muslims are those who are tolerant of other beliefs and ways of life. They accommodate modern thought and values. Moderates represent the majority of the Arab peoples.

Islamists aspire to live in an Islamist state. In an Islamist state, Shari'a is the source of legislation, ideology, and way of life. Except in Wahhabi Saudi Arabia, where Islamists represent the majority of Saudis, in other Arab countries Islamists are tiny minorities.

Jihadists are a violent minority. They are angry, fanatical, despairing, and vengeful. They see only the violent and the intolerant. They ignore the peaceful and the tolerant. They regard the Muslim who does not follow their ways as kafir—a heretic, an apostate; thus, they call them takfiris. Apostasy is punishable by death.

Jihadists believe they are perfection. Terrorizing the innocent is justified. Prayer absolves all sins and the jihadists do not feel remorse. They welcome martyrdom as a means to inherit paradise. Charismatic Wahhabi leaders exploit jihadists' belief in predestination and readiness for self-annihilation. Jihadists are Wahhabis; including the followers of al-Qaeda, Boko Haram, al Shabab, the Taliban or the so-called Islamic State. Wahhabis, however, are not necessarily jihadists. Jihadists are only a very tiny minority among the estimated 3% of world Sunnis who are Wahhabis.

Verses for the Moderate, the Islamist, and the Jihadist

Men and women of different persuasions find different inspirations in the Qur'an, often on the same subject.

The Moderate: The moderates choose the peaceful and the tolerant Verses. They represent the vast majority. Here are examples of verses that appeal to moderate Muslims:

> Qur'an 2:62: *Those who believe, and those who follow the Jewish [scriptures], and the Christians and the Sabians ... shall have their reward with their Lord; on them shall be no fear, nor shall they grieve.*
>
> Qur'an 2:136: *We believe in God, and the revelation given to us, and to Abraham, Isma'il, Isaac, Jacob and their progeny, and that which was given to Moses and Jesus, and to all the prophets by their Lord. We make no distinction among them and we submit to God in Islam.*
>
> Qur'an 2:256: *Let there be no compulsion in religion.*

Qur'an 18:29: *The truth is from your Lord, so let* anyone *who wishes to, believe, and anyone who wishes to, disbelieve.*

Qur'an 29:46: *Do not argue with the People of the Book[7] unless in a fair way, apart from those who act wrongly, and say to them: we believe in the revelation which has come down to us and in that which came down to you; our God and your God is one; and it is to him we bow.*

Qur'an 109:6: *Unto you, your religion, and unto me, mine.*

The moderates focus on a segment of Verse 5:82 that praises Christians and their priests:

> *You will find ... nearest ... in love to the believers are the people who say: 'we are Christians' because amongst them there are priests and monks and they are not arrogant.*

Indeed, Islam recognizes and reveres all Christian and Jewish prophets and messengers. The Qur'an dedicates an entire chapter, Surah number 14, which contains fifty-two verses to Abraham, and Chapter 12 with 111 verses to Joseph. To Mary, the mother of Jesus, the Qur'an dedicates Chapter 19 with its 98 verses. Muslims believe that God revealed Islam in order to restore the religion of Abraham to its original tenets, after Christian priests and Jewish rabbis corrupted its true message. To Muslims, Islam represents the original, true, and unadulterated religion of Abraham. The Qur'an refers to Islam in 2:135 as being the Religion of Abraham.

The Islamist: Islamists choose to concentrate on the intolerant verses instead of the peaceful and the tolerant ones. An Islamist would focus, for example, on the remaining segment of Verse 5:82, which condemns the Jews:

> *You will find the Jews and the idolaters strongest in enmity to the believers.*

The Islamists concentrate also on those Verses that condemn Christians and Jews, along with their priests and rabbis. For example:

Qur'an 2:65: *You are well aware of those among you who profaned the Sabbath, and to whom We said, 'Be as apes despicable'.*

---

[7] The "People of the Book" are the Christians and the Jews.

> Qur'an 5:51: *Take not the Jews and the Christians for your friends and protectors: they are but friends and protectors to each other. And he amongst you that turns to them is of them.*

The moderate and the Islamist would relate to the intolerant differently. While an Islamist justifies hostility to the Christians and Jews of the present day, a moderate sees the intolerance in the verses as being directed, not against today's Christians and Jews, but against those Christians and Jews who had purportedly conspired against the Prophet and his followers fourteen centuries ago.

The Jihadist: The jihadist, concentrates on the Verses that urge fighting non-believers. For example:

> Qur'an 8:60: *Against them make ready your strength to the utmost, that you may strike terror into the enemies of God and your enemies.*
>
> Qur'an 9:29: *Fight those who believe not in God nor the Last Day, nor hold that forbidden which has been forbidden by God and his Messenger, nor acknowledge the religion of truth, even if they are of the People of the Book, until they pay the protective tax [jizya] with willing submission, and feel themselves subdued.*
>
> Qur'an 9:73 and 66:9: *Oh Prophet engage the non-believers and the hypocrites in a jihad, and deal with them most ruthlessly, for their abode is in hell and to hell with them.*

It should be noted that the Qur'an is not the only holy book that contains violent passages. The Bible, too, shares in this characteristic.[8]

---

[8]"Their children also shall be dashed to pieces before their eyes; their houses shall be spoiled, and their wives ravished" (Isaiah 13:15–16, 704). "Now therefore kill every male among the little ones, and kill every woman that hath known man by lying with him. But all the women children that have not known a man by lying with him, keep alive for yourselves" (Numbers 31:17–18, 188). "And utterly destroyed the men, and the women, and the little ones, of every city, we left none to remain" (Deuteronomy 2:34, 199). "And ye shall overthrow their altars, and break their pillars, and burn their groves with fire; and ye shall hew down the graven images of their gods, and destroy the names of them out of that place" (Deuteronomy 12:3, 211). "And they utterly destroyed all that was in the city, both man and woman, young and old, and ox, and sheep, and ass, with the edge of the sword" (Joshua 6:21, 244). "The righteous shall rejoice when he sees the vengeance. He shall wash his feet in the blood of the wicked" (Psalms 58:10, 608). "I will tear your flesh with the thorns of the wilderness and with briers," (Judges 8:7, 277). "The Lord had smitten many of the people with a great slaughter" (I Samuel 6:19, 307) (Holy Bible, London: Eyre and Spottiswoode Limited, 1979).

Descriptions of the great delights that await the faithful in paradise make a jihadist's career worthwhile. Dozens of verses tantalizingly describe the eternal bliss that awaits the faithful in paradise. For example:

> Qur'an 18:31: *For them will be gardens of Eden; beneath them rivers will flow; they will be adorned with bracelets of gold, and they will wear green garments of fine silk and heavy brocade, they will recline on raised thrones.*
>
> Qur'an 44:52–54: *In the midst of gardens and springs ... dressed in fine silk and in rich brocade ... we shall join them to companions with beautiful, big, and lustrous eyes.*
>
> Qur'an 47:17: *And rivers of wine delightful to those who drink it.*

Arab Rulers' Exploitation of Islam to Stay in Power

In all Arab monarchies and republics, Islam is the religion of the state. (In Syria, it is the religion of the president). Also, Shari'a law is either the *main* source of legislation, *a principal* source of legislation, or the *basis* of legislation. The exceptions are Tunisia and Jordan, where Shari'a is not mentioned. Even the supposedly "secular" Saddam Hussein, added in 1991 the words 'God is Great' (Allahu Akbar) to the Iraqi flag. Arab personal status laws follow Shari'a laws, including those of Syria, despite the 50 years of a so-called "secular" Assad regime. The only modern family law in the Arab world is in Tunisia, where polygamy and Shari'a courts were abolished in 1956.

Blind obedience to authority is a core demand of Sharia law. Arab kings and presidents alike use Islam as a weapon to prolong their dictatorships. The word "Islam" means submission or surrendering to God, to the Prophet, and to Muslim authority.

> Qur'an 4:59: *Obey God and obey God's messenger and obey those of authority among you.*

Such wording occurs many times throughout the Qur'an. Further, traditions attributed to the Prophet amplify Qur'anic instructions. In answering how a Muslim should react to a ruler who does not follow the true guidance, the Prophet is reported to have said, according to *Sahih Muslim*:

He who obeys me, obeys God; he who disobeys me, disobeys God. He who obeys the ruler, obeys me; he who disobeys the ruler, disobeys me.[9]

Similar wording or its equivalent occurs two dozen times in *Sahih Muslim*. And to emphasize the point, the Hadith collections of Abi Dawood and ibn Maja quoted the Prophet as imploring Muslims to hear and obey their ruler, even if he were an Ethiopian slave.[10] Al-Bukhari quotes similar sayings.[11]

The belief in predestination cements the injunction of blind obedience to Islamic authority as being the predestined will of God. As a result of these injunctions, a culture of obedience to hierarchical authority developed in Arab societies: The male ruling over the female, the father over the children and wife (wives), the older over the younger, the teacher over the student, employer over the employee, etc. In the political realm, to sanctify their drive to capture the citizenry's blind obedience, Arab kings and military presidents, having imposed their rule by force, mobilize the palace ulama to inculcate in the masses the belief that obedience to the Muslim ruler is a form of piety.

Saudi Arabia goes further. Security measures aimed at eliminating the potential political opposition of 50% of the population, namely, women, are turned into divine dictates, notwithstanding the Qur'an's even-handedness in promising paradise to Muslim women and men equally:

Qur'an 40:40: *Whoever does right, whether man or woman, and is a believer, will enter Paradise.*

Blind Obedience and the Belief in Monotheism

Like Judaism and Christianity, monotheism reigns supreme in the Islamic faith. The first article in Islam is '*La Ilaha Illa Allah,*' meaning, "there is no God but God." The concept of monotheism helped the development of blind obedience to authority. Monotheism transferred in one swoop all the powers that had been the preserve of the many gods of the pre-Islamic polytheist Arabs into the hands of the one and only omnipotent god,

---

[9]*The Six Books, The Hadith Encyclopaedia, Sahih Muslim*, traditions 4746 to 4763, PP. 1007–1008 and traditions 4782 to 4793, PP. 1009–1010.

[10]Ibid., *Sunan Abi Dawood*, tradition 4607, P. 1561, and *Sunan Ibn Maja*, tradition 42, P. 2479.

[11]Ibid, *Sahih al-Bukhari*, traditions 7137 and 7142, P. 595.

Allah. As the Messenger of Allah, the Prophet's authority became rooted in the unlimited powers of Allah.

After the Prophet's death, the caliphs claimed his authority. The first four caliphs (632–661) were Companions of the Prophet, so they asserted firsthand knowledge of how the Prophet would have reacted to new situations. By controlling the financial and the military might of the state, later rulers—the Umayyad caliphs (661–750), the Abbasid caliphs (750–1258), and the Ottoman Sultans (1280–1918)—controlled not only the political sphere of the state but also the religious sphere. Today, Arab monarchs and presidents are absolute rulers in the tradition of their caliph predecessors. Pandering ulama energetically preach that blind obedience to king or president (waliy al-amr) is a core doctrine of the Islamic faith, a form of piety.

Blind Obedience and the Desert Habitat

Extreme temperature fluctuations, dry and burning summer winds of over 50 degrees Celsius (122 degrees Fahrenheit), freezing winter nights, a topography of seemingly endless open spaces, mirages and moving sand dunes, low-density population, loneliness, personal freedom, scarce resources and often a limited quantity of food and clean water have contributed to shaping the personality, beliefs, and the way of life of the Bedouin. Survival requires the efficient use of the desert's meager provisions. Any waste of clean water, for example, could have dire consequences, including death. There is little margin for error here. To Hitti, "Nomadism is as much a scientific mode of living in the Nufud [a part of the Arabian Desert] as industrialism is in Detroit or Manchester".[12]

Under such conditions, solidarity and harmony among tribesmen are critical for protecting the scant necessities of the tribe from waste in internal disputes. Solidarity and harmony require blind obedience to the authority of the father, the clan's elders, and the tribe's leader. The tribal community needs to be managed by the most able manager. The tribe's leader must be obeyed if the tribe's resources are not to be wasted. Tribal obedience to tribal hierarchy is a natural strategy for the Bedouin's survival. The Prophet, being a product of desert living, enshrined blind obedience to authority in the Islamic creed.

---

[12]Philip Hitti, *History of the Arabs*, 10th edition (MacMillan Press Ltd., London, 1970), P. 23

CHAPTER THREE

BELIEFS, DEVELOPMENT OF SHARI'A LAWS, AND SECTS

Introduction

In answering a question in a 2013 survey by the Pew Research Center in seven countries in the MENA region as to whether it is necessary to believe in God to be a moral person, 91% answered in the affirmative.[1] A Zogby survey, also, shows the respondents' overwhelming belief in the importance of religion in the future of the eight countries surveyed:

Religion has an important role to play in my country's future.

	Morocco	Egypt	KSA	UAE	Bahrain	Kuwait	Jordan	Palestine
Agree	77	90	88	89	63	93	75	86
Disagree	23	10	12	11	37	7	25	14

Zogby Research Services, *Muslim Millennial attitudes on religion and religious leadership*, Tabah Foundation, 2015.

In another expression of the importance of religion to Arabs, the same survey asked an interesting question: Have you seen or heard traces of atheism in your locality, community, and society? The response was overwhelmingly negative, except in the United Arab Emirates. Why is the answer so different in the UAE? Because 88% of the UAE population is

---

[1]Pew Research Center, "The World's Muslims."

comprised of expatriate workers,[2] as well as the fact that Muslim residents consider a good proportion of non-Muslims as atheists. The survey further showed that a third expression of Arab Muslims' love of Islam is the belief that it represents the truth.

Have you seen or heard traces of atheism in your locality, community, and society?

	Morocco	Egypt	KSA	UAE	Bahrain	Kuwait	Jordan	Palestine
Yes	3	5	3	51	6	4	7	8
No	97	95	97	49	94	96	93	92

I believe in Islam because I am convinced of its truth.

	Morocco	Egypt	KSA	UAE	Bahrain	Kuwait	Jordan	Palestine
Agree	77	90	100	90	100	100	100	90
Disagree	23	10	<1	10	0	<1	0	10

In Iran, a Pew Research Center survey conducted between February 24, 2012 and May 3, 2012 found that an 83% of Iranians say they favor the use of Shari'a law, 40% think religious figures should play a large role in politics and an additional 26% of Iranians say religious figures should have some influence in political matters.[3]

Another expression of Muslims' attachment to Islam is the meteoric growth of Islamic banking and finance, from zero in 1980, to an estimated market size in 2016 of between $1.66 Trillion to $2.1 Trillion, with expectations of $3.4 Trillion by end of 2018.[4]

Beliefs

To profess the faith, a Muslim must perform the five daily prayers (at sunrise, noon, afternoon, sunset, and night), fast during the month of Ramadan from sunrise to sunset, give alms (zakat), and make the pilgrimage to Mecca once in a lifetime, if possible. Islam demands the belief in the

---

[2]"UAE's Population—By Nationality," *BQ magazine*, (April 12, 2015). http://www.bq-magazine.com/economy/socioeconomics/2015/04/uae-population-by-nationality

[3]Pew Research Center, "Iranians' Views Mixed".

[4]Islamic Finance, "The Size of the Islamic Finance Market." (June 14, 2016). https://www.islamicfinance.com/category/market-information/market-size-and-growth/

inimitability and the uniqueness of God, in the truthfulness of the Prophet Muhammad's mission, in the divinity of the Qur'an, and in the final Day of Judgment. To Muslims, Islam is the perfect religion. In the Pilgrimage of Farewell, the Prophet declared:

> Qur'an 5:3: *Today, I have perfected your religion for you, and I have completed My blessing upon you, and approved Islam for your religion.*

The faithful are enjoined in many Verses and Prophetic traditions to engage in holy war (jihad) in the service of Islam against the enemy and against personal sinful temptations. Islam prohibits usury, gambling, and to Sunni Muslims, image representations. It also prohibits eating pork and drinking wine.[5]

Islam regulates every waking minute, including personal hygiene, diet, healthy living, good manners, and family affairs. It also rules the theological, ritual, judicial, political, ethical, and business realms of society. Islam distinctively amalgamates the spiritual and the temporal into an inseparable unit. Islamic law regulates personal affairs, including marriage, divorce, and inheritance. Its moral and ethical codes demand chastity, honesty, charity, justice, and societal peace. The ulama have for more than a thousand years preached that God's Law is unchangeable, sent to Arabians through the Prophet as the perfect way of life for all mankind everywhere, as suitable for today as it was in the seventh century.

The extent to which the Prophetic Sunna [sayings (Hadith) and acts (Sira) of the Prophet] regulate the tiniest details of a Muslim's daily life may be appreciated from the extensive coverage of the Sunna in the six Sunni canonical collections. Shi'ites have their own Hadith collection. Al-Bukhari, the most revered among the Sunni Hadith collectors, quoted some 7,500 Prophetic sayings and acts that deal with how the Prophet reportedly reacted to the myriad circumstances that he encountered day and night during his mission. Five other collectors add to the coverage. A close second in importance is Muslim (d. 875) whose collection contains 7,563 traditions. The remaining four collectors are Ibn Majah (d. 886),

---

[5]Wine is promised in Paradise:
  Qur'an 47:15: *The parable of the Paradise which the pious and the devout are promised is that of a garden wherein there are … rivers of wine delectable to those who drink it …*

with 4,341 traditions, Abi Dawood (d. 888) with 5,274 traditions, al-Tirmithi (d. 892) with 3,956 traditions, and al-Nasai (d. 915) with 5,761 traditions.

Muslims who pray regularly and fast Ramadan may feel as if they commit no sin. The Prophet was reported as saying:

> *– Ablution and prayer absolve all previous sins.*[6]
> *– Fasting the month of Ramadan absolves all previous sins.*[7]

To Muslims, the Prophet is a human messenger of God, without divinity. He is the greatest of all prophets, the last, and the final prophet. This view is disputed by Twelver Shi'ites who believe that the Hidden Imam, the twelfth descendent from Ali bin Abi Taleb, the Prophet's cousin and husband of His daughter, Fatima, will return one day to the earth and bring justice and prosperity. The Zaidis, or Fivers, believe in the doctrine of the Hidden fifth Imam, Zaid (d. 740). The Isma'ilis, or Seveners, believe in the doctrine of the Hidden seventh imam, Ismail (d. 760).

To Muslims, the Prophet is the most venerated, loved, and honored human being. The tiniest details of every known moment in the life of the Prophet evolved into an ideal standard to be emulated faithfully. The Sunna even dictated the form of greetings and good wishes. A good Muslim must not make his own unguided determination, or worse, follow a foreign custom.[8] Ahmad Bin Hanbal (d. 855), founder of the orthodox Hanbalite rite, the inspiration behind Wahhabism, is reported to have never eaten watermelon because he had not been able to find any Prophetic precedent on the subject.[9]

The Prophet symbolizes the very essence of the Muslim self. There cannot be a greater injury to a Muslim than disrespecting the Prophet. Sunnis prohibit human imaging for fear of falling into polytheism (Shi'ites do not share this prohibition). Such prohibition explains why Sunni art has, over the centuries, been focused on calligraphy and geometrical shapes.

The Belief in Predestination: To Muslims, God's Will determines success, failure, and destiny. There cannot be the smallest of movement nor the least amount of strength to perform the tiniest of tasks without

---

[6] *The Six Books, Sahih Al-Bukhari*, tradition 164, p. 16 and *Sahih Muslim*, tradition 538, P. 719.

[7] Ibid. *Sunan Abi Dawood*, traditions PP. 1371 and 1372, P. 1325.

[8] Ignaz Goldziher, *Muslim Studies*, ed. S. M. Stern, translated by C. R. Barber and S. M. Stern, Vol. II. (Aldine Atherton, Chicago and New York, 1967, first published 1890), P. 29.

[9] Noel J. Coulson, *A History of Islamic Law*, (At the University Press, Edinburgh, 1999), P. 71.

the Will of God, '*the most magnificent, the all-powerful,*' goes one of the most common Arabic sayings, repeated many times every day by many throughout the Arab and Muslim world. '*There is no escape from what has already been written,*' goes another. Daily conversations are dominated by references to God's will, God's wish, God's permission, God's help, God's compassion, God's name, and dependency on God. If a person dies on the operating table, family and relatives usually attribute the death to the will of God, not to a mistake of the surgeon. Even a corrupt ruler is seen as an act of God, just as an act of terror and self-annihilation is justified as being inspired and ordained by God. God's powers are immense in all spheres. God's supremacy is loud and clear throughout the Qur'an.

In early Islam, the debate over free will had been robust. The Qadarite school of thought, developed in the 700s, was the first Islamic philosophical movement to advocate the belief in free will. Around 748, Mu'tazilism, a spectacular philosophical movement, defended the free will doctrine and the imperative of intellectual reasoning in matters of faith. Mu'tazilism placed reason above revelation. Mu'tazilite thought survived for about three centuries, despite opposition from orthodox scholars. Mu'tazilism became the official doctrine of the Abbasid state during the reign of caliph al-Mamoun (813–833). However, orthodoxy won, and Mu'tazilism was eventually obliterated. Orthodoxy shut the gates of personal philosophical reasoning. The proponents of free will lost out to the advocates of predestination.

Shutting the gates on intellectual reasoning was a tragic retrogression in the development of Islamic thought, locking Muslim societies in stagnation, at a time when the Western world was charging ahead with the Renaissance, Reformation, Enlightenment, and the Industrial Revolution to unprecedented prosperity and military might.

Discouraging Innovation: To those who believe in the ways of the righteous ancestors (Salafists), innovation is a sin. They hark back to the imagined virtuous ways of seventh century Arabia. Desert living brings fear of change. Innovation might upset the delicate balance between nature's limited endowment and man's requirements. The Prophet reportedly said:

– *The most evil of all matters are those that get modernized.*[10]
– *Beware of innovation, for every innovation is heresy, and every heresy leads to the wrong path.*[11]

---

[10] *The Six Books, Sahih al-bukhari*, tradition 7277, P. 606.
[11] Ibid. *Sunan Abi Dawood*, tradition 4607, P. 1561 and *Sunan Ibn Maja*, traditions 43 to 46, P. 2479.

The Prophet's widow, Aisha, said that the Prophet had rejected any deviation from His teachings.[12] Salafists, however, extend the prohibition to, for example, eating with forks and knives, because the Prophet did not eat using forks and knives.

The lack of innovation in the Ottoman Empire (1280–1918) during the European Industrial Revolution of the eighteenth century was among the main factors that led to the defeat and dismemberment of Islam's last empire. During that period, while Europe was charging ahead with industrialization, in Ottoman lands, free thought was stifled, intellectual curiosity smothered, and innovation discouraged. Three centuries after the printing press was introduced in Europe, the Ottoman ulama still considered printing in Arabic and Turkish to be an undesirable innovation. The long delay in introducing the printing press into Ottoman life was symptomatic of the rigidity that slowed Ottoman progress at a time when Europe was opening new frontiers of knowledge. Bernard Lewis wrote, "Seyh-ul-Islam Abdullah Efendi was persuaded to issue a fatwa authorizing the printing of books in Turkish on subjects other than religion. The printing of the Koran, of books on Koranic exegesis, traditions, theology, and holy law was excluded as unthinkable … Finally, on July 5, 1727, an Imperial Ferman [meaning edict, or decree] was issued, giving permission for the establishment of a Turkish press."[13] However, fifteen years later, in 1742, the press was shut down, not to be reopened until forty-two years later in 1784.

The Development of Sunni Law-Making

In addition to the Qur'an and the Sunna, two sources of law evolved for Sunnis around the eighth and ninth centuries. These are known as Analogical Deduction (Qiyas), and Consensus of the Ulama (Ijma'). Formed in liberal Iraq and led by Abu Hanifa (d. 767), the founder of the Hanafite school of jurisprudence, Analogical Deduction (Qiyas) is derived from Jewish law.[14] Propounded by the conservative Medanese school and led by

---

[12]Ibid. tradition 4606, p. 1561 and *Sunan Ibn Maja*, tradition 14, P. 2477.

[13]Bernard Lewis, *The Emergence of Modern Turkey* (Oxford University Press, Oxford, UK, 1961), P. 51.

[14]Joseph Schacht, *An Introduction to Islamic Law* (Oxford University Press, Oxford, UK, 1982), P. 21.

Malik bin Anas (d. 795), the founder of the Malakite school of jurisprudence, the Consensus of the Ulama (Ijma') seems to have been modeled on Roman law.[15] Qiyas and Ijma' enabled what later became Sunni Shari'a law meant to cover human actions not addressed in the Qur'an and the Sunna. Together, the four sources address, for Sunnis, all likely doctrinal and juridical requirements.

In addition to the Hanafite and Malikite rites, Sunnis adopted two further rites. The first is the Shafi'ite rite, named after its founder Muhammad bin Idris al-Shafi'i (d. 820), and the Hanbalite rite, named for its founder Ahmad bin Hanbal (d. 855), who wrote the most orthodox and austere among the four rites, and thus the least popular over the past millennia.

Hitti points out that the establishment of these four schools crystallized traditional dogma in such a way that there could be no further development of doctrine or law, and the possibility of ijtihad (forming new opinions regarding the Qur'an or Sunna) was forever closed to the Sunnis.[16] Through the consensus of the ulama, decisions of great significance were taken. Hitti wrote, "The vulgate text of the Qur'an was canonized, the six canonical books of the Hadiths were approved, the miracles of the Prophet were accepted, lithographic reproductions of the Qur'an were authorized, and the necessity of belonging to the Quraish was dispensed with, in favor of the Ottoman caliphs."[17]

The conquests of Byzantine Syria and Egypt, along with Sassanid Persia, brought the early Arabian Desert people into the comparatively advanced commercial, cultural, and social conditions of the conquered societies. The laws of the Medinese society were inadequate, and because the conquered people were not yet Muslims, the laws of their new Islamic society were not applicable.[18] It is natural, therefore, that the early Muslims would be influenced by the cultures of Syriac Monophysite Christianity and the developed intellectual and cultural life of the Babylonian Jews.[19] For example, Islam's scale of the five religious qualifications—obligatory, recommended, indifferent, reprehensible, and forbidden—derive from

---

[15]Ibid. P. 20.

[16]Philip Hitti, *History of the Arabs*, 10th edition (MacMillan Press Ltd., London, 1970), PP. 399–400.

[17]Ibid. P. 398.

[18]Philip Hitti, *Syria: A Short History* (MacMillan & Co. Ltd., London, 1959), P. 113.

[19]Hugh Kennedy. *The Prophet and the Age of the Caliphates: The Islamic Near East from the Sixth to the Eleventh Century*, (Longman, London and New York: 1996), P. 119.

stoic philosophy.[20] Also, in penal law, it is apparent that stoning to death as a punishment for unlawful sexual intercourse, which does not occur in the Qur'an, was introduced from Mosaic law.[21] The popular and administrative practice of the late Umayyad period was transformed into the religious law of Islam.[22]

Shi'ite Doctrinal Split from Sunnism

The Shi'ite/Sunni divide finds its roots in the controversy over the succession to the Prophet. The Prophet died in 632. He left no male children and devised no criteria to choose a successor, nor did He establish an outline of the successor's authority and duties. The Qur'an does not address these issues, either.

The succession controversy plunged the Muslim community into conflict and bloodshed immediately after the Prophet's death. It split the Muslim polity over various questions. Must the Prophet's successor belong to the family of the Prophet? Must he belong to the Prophet's Meccan tribe of Quraish? Must he be an Arab? Is his rule hereditary? Must he be obeyed regardless of his deeds? Can he be replaced? If yes, under what circumstances, and by whom?

According to Shi'ite ulama, it is incontrovertible that the Prophet had "designated" his cousin, Ali bin Abi Talib as his immediate successor. For them, the successor to the Prophet can only be passed from one successor to the next from among the progeny of Ali and his wife Fatima, (the Prophet's daughter) via their two sons, Hasan and Hussein, through a divinely inspired designation. Sunni ulama disagree.

Shi'ites cite many Prophetic traditions from Shi'ite as well as Sunni sources to prove that the Prophet had publicly and unambiguously designated Ali as his immediate successor. As an example, Ahmad bin Hanbal, the orthodox Sunni collector of some 30,000 Prophetic traditions and founder of the most extreme among the four Sunni schools of jurisprudence that survive today, related that while the Prophet was traveling back to Medina after his last pilgrimage in 632, he stopped at Ghadir Khum

[20]Schacht, An Introduction to Islamic Law.
[21]Ibid. P. 15.
[22]Ibid. P. 27.

(near Mecca) and took Ali's hand and said, "Of whomsoever I am Lord, then Ali is his Lord. O God! Be thou the supporter of whoever supports Ali and the enemy of whoever opposes him."[23] To Shi'ites, this plus other evidence, prove without any doubt that Ali was to be the Prophet's chief assistant and immediate successor. To Sunnis, however, the evidence is insufficient to conclude that the Prophet had designated Ali as his immediate successor.[24]

Ali's son Hasan, first grandson of the Prophet, had renounced his claim in 661 in favor of his father's archenemy, Mu'awiyah, the fifth caliph (661–680) and founder of the Umayyad dynasty (661–750) in Damascus, Syria, in return for a generous subsidy for life. Ali's other son Hussein, the second grandson of the Prophet, was killed in 680 in Karbala, Iraq, while attempting to claim the leadership of the Muslim world from Mu'awiyah's successor, his son Yazid. The tenth of the Muslim month of Muharram (called Ashura) commemorates the martyrdom of Hussein. Annually, Shi'ites exhibit astonishing displays of emotion, passion, self-flagellation, and sorrow, especially in Karbala, where Imam Hussein is buried.

Authority of the Imams

Twelver Shi'ites, the majority of Shi'ite Muslims today, aside from the Prophet's authority, accept only the authority of the twelve infallible imams. These are all descendants of Ali and Fatima. The imams have become legendary. Shi'ite writers of every generation sought to prove their unique qualities. For example, Moojan Momen writes that the birth of the imams, "were miraculous, the baby imam being born already circumcised and with his umbilical cord already severed; that they spoke immediately on birth

---

[23]Moojan Momen, *An Introduction to Shi'i Islam*, (Yale University Press, New Haven and London, 1985), P. 199.

[24]Sunnis and the Shi'ites disagree on many issues, including the number of children the Prophet had. Shi'ites believe that Fatima was the Prophet's only biological daughter. Sunnis believe that the Prophet fathered three other daughters in addition to Fatima—Umm Kulthum, Ruqayah, and Zainab. Sunnis believe that these three girls were the biological daughters of the Prophet and his first wife Khadija. Shi'ite scholars, however, dispute the claim. They argue that Fatima was the Prophet's only biological daughter. They contend that Khadija was too old to have given birth to so many children after her marriage to the Prophet, supposedly at the age of forty. Shi'ite scholars argue that the girls were more likely the daughters of Khadija's second husband, or even the daughters of Khadija's deceased sister, Hala, whom Khadija brought up after Hala's death, possibly before Khadija married the Prophet.

(and sometimes from within their mother's womb) praising God ... that each performed miracles and was possessed of supernatural knowledge."[25]

Twelver Shi'ites, believe that the Twelfth Imam, Muhammad al-Muntazar (the awaited one), the ninth descendent in Imam Hussein's progeny, disappeared as a child around 874, and that he is in a state of occultation (absence, disappearance), a Hidden Imam, until his return to the Earth someday to restore justice and bring prosperity.

Sunni Muslims reject such notions categorically. To them, the Prophet Muhammad is God's last and final Prophet:

> Qur'an 33:40: *Muhammad is ... the Messenger of God, and the seal (last, final) of the Prophets.*

The words *seal, last, final*, are translations of the Arabic word *khatam* in Verse 33:40. The Arabic word, *Khatam* means also *signet ring, band*.

No aspect of the history of Shi'ite Islam is as confused as the stories relating to the Twelfth Imam. Momen cites the following version of the story of the Twelfth Imam, his occultation, and return, as the one that is usually presented in books published for popular reading:

> The mother of the Twelfth Imam was a Byzantine slave-girl named Narjis Khatun (or Saqil or Sawsan or Rayhana). In the more fully elaborated versions of the story, she becomes the Byzantine emperor's daughter who was informed in a vision that she would be the mother of the Mahdi. She was bought by the Tenth Imam, Ali al-Hadi, for his son the Eleventh Imam, Hasan al-Askari. The Twelfth Imam was born in 868 (some sources vary by as much as five years from this date) in Samarra. He was given the same name as the Prophet, Abul-Qasem Muhammad. The usual miraculous accounts of his talking from the womb, etc. may be passed over to the only occasion on which he is said to have made a public appearance. This was in 874 when the Eleventh Imam died. It appears that none of the Shi'ite notables knew of the birth of Muhammad and so they went to the Eleventh Imam's brother, Ja'far, assuming that he was now the Imam. Ja'far seemed prepared to take on this mantle and entered the house of the deceased Imam in order to lead the funeral prayers.

[25]Momen, *An Introduction to Shi'i Islam*, P. 23.

At this juncture, a young boy came forward and said, "Uncle, stand back! For it is more fitting for me to lead the prayers for my father than for you." After the funeral, Ja'far was asked about the boy and said that he did not know who the boy was ... The boy was seen no more, and Shi'ite tradition states that from that year, he went into occultation.[26]

While the Twelfth Imam is hidden, the Shi'ite ulama act as his representatives, or deputies, uncovering for the masses what the Hidden Imam would have ruled on all matters. To perform their duties, the Shi'ite clerics interpret the Qur'an and their version of the Hadith collections according to their personal reasoning, though in the name of the Hidden Imam.

Twelver Shi'ite ulama rely on their Intellectual Reasoning (Aql, meaning "brain" in Arabic) in making those judgments. To the Shi'ite ulama, Intellectual Reasoning is what the consensus of the Sunni ulama (Ijma') plus analogical deduction (Qiyas) are to the Sunni ulama.

The concept of the occultation is strikingly similar to the biblical messianic concept of the return of Christ to Earth. It is curious that in the more elaborate versions of the story, the mother of the Hidden Imam saw a vision informing her that she would be the mother of the Mahdi, a story similar to that of the mother of Jesus, Mary, who was informed by the Angel Gabriel that she would be the mother of Jesus.

The Development of Shi'ite Law-Making

By inventing the concept of the all-encompassing, all-knowing, all-powerful Hidden Imam, and by appointing themselves as the Hidden Imam's representatives on the Earth, the Shi'ite ulama went beyond the demand of blind obedience to Muslim authority in Verse 4:59, which their Sunni co-religionists invoke. By expropriating the infallible Hidden Imam's unlimited powers, the Shi'ite clerics rendered their pronouncements infallible. In so doing, they rendered themselves the lawgivers.

The Shi'ite masses hold the senior Shi'ite clerics as exemplars. They are the reference for imitation, or marja' taqlid. A grand ayatollah (the greatest sign of God) is a marja' taqlid. Worldwide, a small number, perhaps

---

[26]Ibid. PP. 161–162.

around ten at any one time, are grand ayatollahs. The grand ayatollahs do not report to one another. They are equal. Should opposing opinions arise between two ayatollahs on interpreting what the Hidden Imam might have thought, the Hidden Imam must manifest himself and give a decision. If he does not, the truth must lie with both parties.[27] The distinguishing element among the ayatollahs is the size of their following, which determines the level of their income, educational institutions, and charitable work.

Moreover, as the Hidden Imam is thought to be among the body of the Shi'ites incognito, and since the Hidden Imam is considered the most learned and all-truth-knowing, there is always the possibility that one of the Shi'ite ulama might indeed be the Hidden Imam.[28] Such a belief creates a unique aura of respectability and authority around Shi'ite clerics, especially those regarded as the marja' for emulation. This aura is further enhanced by stories in popular culture of the Hidden Imam manifesting himself to prominent Shi'ite ulama.

Shi'ites can follow the teaching of the marja' of their choice. Because a marja' interprets Shi'ite law according to his personal reasoning and, because the teachings of a dead marja' are invalid, then, Shi'ite law, unlike Sunni law, can, theoretically at least, evolve with life's changing circumstances. In reality though, caution as well as self-interest has limited the initiatives that differ from traditional thought and precedents.

A survey by the Pew Research Center conducted between February 24, 2012 and May 3, 2012 as Iranians prepared to elect a new president on June 14, found that 83% of Iranians say they favor the use of sharia law, 40% think religious figures should play a large role in politics, and an additional 26% of Iranians say religious figures should have some influence in political matters.[29]

Summary and implications: While Sunni Shari'a is composed of four sources: Qur'an, Sunna, Analogical Deduction, and Consensus of the Ulama, Shi'ite Shari'a is composed of three sources: Qur'an, Sunna (Shi'ite version), and Intellectual Reasoning. Serious religious and political implications flow this difference.

A Shi'ite individual is free to follow and obey the grand ayatollah of his choice. Shi'ites have a clear, recognized, and assertive central Islamic

---

[27]Ibid. P. 186.
[28]Ibid. P. 199.
[29]Pew Research Center, "Iranians' Views Mixed".

authority, vested in the few grand ayatollahs that exist in the world at any one time. Ayatollahs pull their worldwide congregations together. They provide uniformity in religious opinions (fatwas).

On the other hand, issuance of Sunni fatwas is fragmented. It lacks centrality, coordination, or uniformity, even on the same subject. Today, under the banner of Consensus of the Ulama, Sunni fatwa issuance is vested in government appointed committees or councils of senior scholars in each Sunni country independently of one other. Council members do the political bidding of their benefactors. Aside from the official bodies, a huge number of Sunni fatwas have also been issued outside the councils by self appointed minor and unqualified clerics, leading to confusion, contradictions, and disagreements.

Conflict Between Shi'ites and Sunnis Over the Hadith and Other Differences

On the Prophetic Hadith, Shi'ite scholars reject the Sunni Hadith collections. The Shi'ites emphasize the Prophet's alleged naming of Ali as His immediate successor and stress the Prophet's affection for Ali's children. Twelver Shi'ites assembled four of their own canonical Hadith collections by three authors: Abu Ja'far al-Kulayni (d. 939), Abu Ja'far Muhammad bin Babouya (d. 991), and Abu Ja'far al-Tusi (d. 1067), who wrote two collections. Additionally, three other authors during the 1600s produced highly regarded Shi'ite Hadith collections—bin Murtada (d. 1680), bin Hasan (d. 1692), and Majlisi (d. 1699).

It should be noted that while the first three collectors lived approximately a century after the six Sunni canonical collectors, the three collections of the 1600s were produced five hundred years later, during the life of the anti-Sunni Safavid Dynasty (1501–1736). Shah Ismail (1487–1524) converted Persia's Islam from Sunnism to Twelver Shi'ism. He made Shi'ism the state religion in order to introduce fervor into Persia's long running confrontations with the Sunni Ottoman Sultans. Safavid politics, wars, and rivalries with Istanbul could have colored the anti-Sunni Hadith collections of bin Murtada, bin Hasan, and Majlisi.

There are two major differences between the Hadith collections of the Shi'ites and the Sunnis. The first is that, while Hadith traditions to Sunnis record the sayings and actions of the Prophet, to Twelver Shi'ites, the Hadith records the sayings and actions of the Prophet as well as those of the twelve infallible imams. The second difference is that for a Prophetic tradition to be credible to Shi'ite Muslims, it must be transmitted through one of the imams. Shi'ite Muslims reject the first three caliphs, Abu Bakr (632–634), Omar (634–644), and Uthman (644–656) as usurpers of the caliphate from Ali (656–661). Shi'ites do not consider Abu Bakr, Omar, or Uthman, or the Prophet's Companions who supported these caliphs, as reliable transmitters of traditions. Sunnis, on the other hand, revere the first three caliphs and their supporters, as well as Ali. These four caliphs are collectively described by Sunnis as the four rightly guided caliphs.

In addition, Shi'ites venerate the imams' tombs and other religious figures and family members, while Wahhabi Sunnis bury their dead in unmarked tombs (but not the Hanafites, Malikites, and Shafi'ites). Shi'ites respect historical monuments and works of art, while Wahhabis do not (for fear of falling into polytheism). Indeed, the Wahhabi Taliban dynamited the Buddhas of Bamiyan on March 2001 and the Wahhabi so-called Islamic State destroyed parts of Syria's Palmyra in 2016, as well as the Mosul museum and the Ninevah ruins in Iraq.[30] Like the Taliban and the so-called Islamic State, Wahhabis in Saudi Arabia destroyed 98% of the country's historical and religious sites since 1985, according to estimates by the Islamic Heritage Research Foundation in London.[31] Shi'ites display pictures of the imams and the Prophet, while Sunnis do not. Shi'ites permit Mut'a marriage (the woman gets paid for her companionship for a specified period of time) while Sunnis do not. Wahhabis, permit Misyar marriage (the couple live apart, with the man visiting the woman at her home without obligation) while Shi'ites do not.

Shi'ism may be described as a Persianized version of Arabian Islam. Shi'ism incorporates the ethnic and age-old cultural differences and rivalries between Arabs and Persians, and the memories of their wars over the long sweep of history.

---

[30]Andrew Curry, "Here Are the Ancient Sites ISIS Has Damaged and Destroyed," *National Geographic*, (September 1, 2015). http://news.nationalgeographic.com/2015/09/150901-isis-destruction-looting-ancient-sites-iraq-syria-archaeology/

[31]Carla Power, "Saudi Arabia Bulldozes Over Its Heritage," *Time magazine*, (November 14, 2014). http://time.com/3584585/saudi-arabia-bulldozes-over-its-heritage/

Wilayat Al-Faqih, or Rulership of the Senior-Most Shi'ite Jurist

Grand Ayatollah Ruhollah Khomeini asserted the right of the senior-most Shi'ite cleric, as the deputy of the Hidden Imam, to oversee all religious, social, and political affairs of the Shi'ite community.[32] Khomeini's conception means that the senior-most Shi'ite cleric has the same authority and can perform the same functions as the Hidden Imam, without being equal to the Hidden Imam in status.[33]

The new concept is revolutionary, and an inflection point in the history of Middle Eastern politics. It heightened the Shi'ite/Sunni divide, pitting Shi'ite ayatollahs against Saudi ulama. Fears that Ayatollah Khomeini would embark upon a crusade to destabilize Iraq and Saudi Arabia and the rest of GCC states following the 1979 revolution in Iran fueled the twentieth century's longest war between Iraq and Iran (September 22, 1980–August 20, 1988). Since that time, proxy wars between Iran and Saudi Arabia have destroyed much of Iraq, Syria, and Yemen, and magnified the discontent among the Shi'ite communities in Bahrain, Kuwait, and Saudi Arabia.

Wilayat al-faqih yields absolute theocratic dictatorship. Control by the Shi'ite religious establishment over the political and spiritual lives of Iranians is vested in two religious institutions enshrined in Iran's constitution. The first is the Office of the Supreme Faqih. The second is the Council of Guardians. The Supreme Faqih possesses power over the parliament, the judiciary, and the executive branch. He appoints members of the Council of Guardians, which approves candidates for parliament and the presidency. It has veto power to reject parliamentary laws that do not conform to Shi'ite religious principles.[34]

Controversy Over the Concept of Wilayat Al-Faqih: The issue of a supreme worldwide Iranian faqih is controversial. Not all Shi'ite clerics subscribe to Khomeini's construction. His opponents regard the new theocracy as illegitimate, both ideologically and theologically.

There have been clerics who preferred not to interfere in politics. This group included many high-ranking Shi'ite ulama, particularly Ayatollah Burujirdi and his successors, Ayatollahs Shari'atmadari (stripped of his rank as grand ayatollah after the discovery of his involvement in a 1982 plot

---

[32]Momen, *An Introduction to Shi'i Islam*, P. 196.
[33]Ibid.
[34]US Library of Congress, "Iran Country Report". http://lcweb2.loc.gov/frd/cs/irtoc.html.

against Grand Ayatollah Khomeini), Gulpaygani, and Mar'ashi-Najafi.[35] Ayatollah Mohammed Kazemeini Burujirdi, an advocate of the separation of religion from politics, was arrested in October 2006 in Tehran amid clashes between his supporters and police.[36] He and seventeen of his followers were tried by a special court with jurisdiction over Shi'ite clerics and sentenced to death on charges, including "enmity against God". After an appeal, the death sentence was reduced to eleven years in prison. He was banned from practicing his clerical duties. His home and belongings were confiscated. He has suffered physical and mental abuse while in prison.[37]

The Unsustainability of Wilayat Al-Faqih Concept: Currently, there is only one supreme faqih in the world; namely, Grand Ayatollah Ali Khamenei in Iran, who is the first successor to the founder of wilayat al-faqih construction, the Grand Ayatollah Ruhollah Khomeini. The wilayat al-faqih raises serious questions regarding the scope and long-term viability of the concept. At the heart of the controversy is a dispute over authority. Is the religious and political authority of the supreme faqih in Iran intended to extend beyond Iran? If yes, is the supreme faqih's religious authority over world Shi'ites envisioned to be akin to that of the Pope's authority over world Catholics? Must the ayatollahs outside Iran subordinate their authority to Iran's supreme faqih?

Hezbollah is the only body of Shi'ites outside Iran that pledges allegiance to the Iranian faqih. Hezbollah was established by the Iranian Revolutionary Guard in 1982. It has been funded and armed ever since that time by the Iranian government, ostensibly to confront Israel, but in reality, to enhance Iran's regional reach. Hezbollah's deputy secretary general Sheikh Naim Qassem was quoted as saying in August 2011, "wilayat al-faqih is the reason for Hezbollah's establishment."[38]

Typically, ayatollahs have followings among Shi'ites in different countries. Ayatollah Ali al-Sistani, for example, the senior-most ayatollah at the Najaf Hawza (center of Shi'ite learning and issuance of binding religious opinions) in the holy city of Najaf in Iraq is the spiritual guide to as many as 80% of

---

[35]Momen, *An Introduction to Shi'i Islam*, P. 19.

[36]Sadeq Saba, "Iran Arrests Controversial Cleric," *BBC*, (October 8, 2006). http://news.bbc.co.uk/2/hi/middle_east/6032217.stm

[37]Tom Lantos, "Ayatollah Mohammad Kazemeini Boroujerdi," United States Congress Human Rights Commission. https://humanrightscommission.house.gov/defending-freedom-project/prisoners-by-country/Iran/Ayatollah%20Mohammad%20Kazemeini%20Boroujerdi

[38]"Hezbollah MP credits Wilayat al Fakih for saving Lebanon," *YALIBNAN*, (November 2, 2014). http://yalibnan.com/2014/11/02/hezbollah-mp-credits-wilayat-al-fakih-saving-lebanon/

world Shi'ites.[39] Does the Supreme Faqih in Iran envisage Sistani handing him all or a part of the estimated $700 million he receives annually from his followers in the form of the khums tax (fifth, or 20%) of their saving?

Can the Shi'ite world have more than one supreme faqih? If the answer is no, in what country should the one faqih be located? Should it be in Iran by virtue of Iran's size and power? In such a case, would he consider that he has the religious right to claim political authority over the Shi'ite majority of Bahrain, which is ruled by the Sunni minority of the al-Khalifa clan? What about the Shi'ite minorities in Muslim countries like Saudi Arabia or Pakistan, or in non-Muslim countries like India? Or, should the one and only supreme faqih be located in Iraq by virtue of Iraq's religious signifi- cance as the sanctuary for seven Shi'ite imams—especially, in the holy city of Najaf (the site of Ali's burial shrine), or the holy city of Karbala (the site of Ali's son Hussein's burial shrine)?

Demographics: Many Islamic sects and doctrines came into existence and disappeared. Today, around 85% of the estimated 1.5 billion Muslims in the world are Sunnis. Shi'ite Muslims number around 250 million, liv- ing mainly in Iran (majority of around 70 million), Pakistan (minority of around 25 million), Iraq (majority of around 20 million) and Azerbaijan (majority of around 8 million). There are Shi'ites in Yemen (minority of Zaidis of around 10 million), Saudi Arabia (minority of Shi'ites and Isma'ilis of around 4 million), the rest of the Arabian Peninsula (around 1.5 million), Syria (minority of Alawites and Isma'ilis of around 3 million), and Lebanon (minority of around 2 million). In addition, there are minori- ties of Shi'ites in Afghanistan, India, Russia, and Turkey.

Shi'ite Rebellions: Many rebellions, though certainly not all in early Islam, find their roots in the controversy over the succession to the Prophet. The Shi'ite partisans of Ali and his direct descendants proved to be prolific producers of heterodoxies. Momen lists 51 sects that arose during the first two and a half centuries after the death of the Prophet.[40] The majority of these sects disappeared. Many of the doctrines and concepts behind these groups, however, were incorporated into the development of Twelver Shi'ism in the Tenth Century. What follows is a description of two surviving Shi'ite sects. A third, the Alawites of Syria, will be discussed in Chapter Nine.

---

[39]Alireza Nader, "Iran's Role in Iraq," *Rand Corporation*, (2015), P. 4.
http://www.rand.org/content/dam/rand/pubs/perspectives/PE100/PE151/RAND_PE151.pdf
[40]Momen, *An Introduction to Shi'i Islam*, PP. 45–60.

Zaydis: Zayd died in 740 in a rebellion against the Umayyad caliphate in Damascus. Zaydis are the partisans of Zayd, grandson of the third imam, Hussein bin Ali, which makes Zayd the fifth imam since Ali. Thus, the Zaydis' alternative name is the Fivers. They are found today in Yemen. The Houthi rebels fighting Saudi Arabia today are Zaidis. They represent around 40% of Yemen's 27 million people. Zaydis are concentrated in the rugged Northern Yemeni Mountains bordering Saudi Arabia.

Zaydis advocate that any member of the Prophet's family claiming to be imam must assert the title publicly and back up his claim with force.[41] Unlike other Shi'ites, Zaydis do not accept that the imamate must be "designated," and they reject that the imamate should follow any strict hereditary principle, except that the imam must be a descendant of Hasan or Hussein. Additionally, in variance with other Shi'ites, Zaydis accept Islam's first three caliphs as legitimate, reject the messianic concept behind the belief in occultation and with it the infallibility of the Hidden Imam.[42] As such, Zaidism is the closest Shi'ite doctrine to Sunnism.

Isma'ilis: The Isma'ilis, or Seveners, believe in the doctrine of the Hidden seventh imam, Ismail (d. 760), the third grandson of the third Shi'ite imam, Hussein. Isma'ilis were once the most significant among Shi'ite sects. They dominated the Islamic stage between the 900s and the 1200s. They believe in the allegorical, esoteric meaning of the Qur'an. As in the Pythagorean system, the number seven held sacred importance. The Seveners serialized cosmic and historical happenings by the number seven.[43]

The Isma'ilis succeeded in establishing areas of influence and ruling dynasties that survived many decades, sometimes a few centuries, in defiance of the central Abbasid authority in Baghdad. While Sunnis today represent some 85% of Muslims, with the remaining 15% being Shi'ite, the opposite was true around the twelfth century. Around a thousand years ago, most Muslims were under the control of one Shi'ite sect or another: the Qarmatians, the Fatimids, the Hamdanids, the Assassins, and the Buyids. Today, numbering around 15 million worldwide, Ismai'ilis are found in Syria and Saudi Arabia, as well as in Central and South Asia, Africa, Europe, North America, and Australia.

---

[41]W. Montgomery Watt, *Islamic Political Thought*, (Edinburgh University Press, Edinburgh, 1999), P. 114.

[42]Momen, *An Introduction to Shi'i Islam*, PP. 49–50.

[43]Hitti, *History of the Arabs*, P. 442.

Conflicts that Loom Large Behind the Sunni/Shi'ite Divide

According to the August 2012 Pew Research Center survey, 53% of Egyptians, 50% of Moroccans, and 43% of Jordanians consider the Shi'ites to be non-Muslims.[44] The reason is due in part to historical events that are still remembered today. Two cataclysmic events occurred in the twelfth and thirteenth centuries during which the Shi'ites sided against their Sunni coreligionists.

The first event was the Mongols' obliteration of Baghdad and the Abbasid caliphate in 1258. Sunni historians have accused Shi'ites of being responsible for the fall of Baghdad and the murder of the caliph.[45] As evidence, they argue, that while Baghdad was destroyed, Hilla, the Shi'ite center, was spared.[46]

The second event was Shi'ite complicity with the Christian Crusaders against the Sunnis in the twelfth and thirteenth centuries. During this period, Shi'ites, especially the Isma'ilis and the Nusayris (Alawites) often fought on the side of the Crusaders against the Sunni forces.[47]

Opening the Gates of Hell in Shi'ite/Sunni Wars Today: During their first failed rebellion against Istanbul, the al-Saud/Abdulwahhab hatred of Shi'ites reached the unprecedented level of invading Karbala and destroying the holiest of Shi'ites' holies, the venerated tomb of the Imam Hussein in 1801. With the formation of the Saudi state in 1932, hatred-of-the-other teaching in schools, mosques, and the media became a part of the cultural fabric of Saudi society. Wahhabism radicalized Islam and polarized Muslims. In 1979, the Khomeini revolution exacerbated the Shi'ite/Sunni divide. The long brutal Iran/Iraq war (September 1980–August 1988) intensified the hatred between Shi'ites and Sunnis.

Then, came the American occupation of Iraq. It flung open the gates of sectarian hell in the Muslim Middle East like never before. The G.W. Bush project in Iraq and Obama's inaction in Syria empowered Iran further. They ignited nasty proxy wars between Saudi Arabia and Iran that have already destroyed most of Iraq, Syria, and Yemen, thus far. It also heightened hostility between the Shi'ites and Sunnis in Bahrain, Kuwait, and Saudi Arabia.

An Attempt to Unite Shi'ism and Sunnism: In a Pan-Islamism step, on July 6, 1959, during the presidency of Gamal Abdulnaser,[48] Sheikh

---

[44]Pew Research Center, "The World's Muslims."
[45]Momen, *An Introduction to Shi'i Islam*, P. 92.
[46]Ibid. PP. 91–92.
[47]Ibid. P. 93.
[48]The fatwa might have been requested by Nasser.

Mahmoud Shaltout, the Rector of al-Azhar University in Cairo, issued a religious opinion (fatwa) recognizing Twelver Shi'ism as a "legitimate Islamic school of law." The text of the fatwa reads:

> Islam does not require a Muslim to follow a particular Madh'hab (school of thought). Rather, we say, every Muslim has the right to follow one of the schools of thought which has been correctly narrated and its verdicts have been compiled in its books. And, everyone who is following such Madhahib [schools of thought] can transfer to another school, and there shall be no crime on him for doing so.
>
> The Ja'fari school of thought, which is also known as "al-Shia al-Imamiyyah al-Ithna Ashariyyah" (i.e., The Twelver Imami Shi'ites) is a school of thought that is religiously correct to follow in worship as are other Sunni schools of thought.
>
> Muslims must know this, and ought to refrain from unjust prejudice to any particular school of thought, since the religion of Allah and His Divine Law (Shari'ah) was never restricted to a particular school of thought.
>
> Shaykh al-Azhar, 1959.[49]

Grand Ayatollah Muhammad Sadiq al-Sadr, father of Iraqi leader Muqtada al-Sadr, preached national unity in Iraq to bridge the Shi'ite/Sunni divide.[50] He called on his followers to pray in Sunni mosques, a call that brought throngs of his followers to do so (see Chapter Seven: *Apprehension over Iran—Muqtada Al-Sadr*).[51]

On the level of the Shi'ite/Sunni individual, it should be noted that Shi'ites and Sunnis in the once tolerant Iraq were members of a harmonious community. Marriages among Shi'ites and Sunnis in Iraq were common until the 2003 American occupation, which empowered Iraq's Shi'ites, and turned Shi'ites and Sunnis of the same family against one another.

---

[49]The fatwa was promulgated at the theological center at al-Azhar, Dar Taqreeb al-Madhaahib al-Islamiyyah (center for bringing closer together the various Islamic schools of thought). https://hastoneest.wordpress.com/2011/09/27/dar-al-taqreeb-al-madhahib-al-islamiyyah-and-al-azhar-university-on-shia-and-sunni/

[50]"Iraq's Muqtada Al-Sadr: Spoiler or Stabilizer? Middle East Report N°55," *International Crisis Group*, (July 11, 2006). https://www.files.ethz.ch/isn/20115/55_iraq_s_muqtada_al_sadr_spoiler_or_stabiliser.pdf

[51]Ibid.

CHAPTER THREE—APPENDIX 1

ELEVATION OF THE PROPHETIC SUNNA TO A SOURCE OF LAW EQUAL TO THE QUR'AN

Around two-and-a-half centuries after the death of the Prophet, the ulama laid down the foundation that helped them control Muslims' life. They succeeded in making the Prophet's reported words and actions a source of law equal to the Qur'an. This happened despite the fact that the Qur'an never made the Sunna a source of law, and despite God's attestation that, as the word of God, the Qur'an contains everything mankind needs to know.

After the death of the Prophet in 632, it quickly became clear to Muslim rulers that Qur'anic law did not cover every aspect of life in the Arabian Desert, let alone life in the territories of the Byzantines and the Persians, which the Muslims conquered soon after the Prophet's death. The Qur'an deals primarily with personal status matters, such as marriage, divorce, and inheritance. Of the 6,236 Verses contained in the 114 chapters (Suras) of the Qur'an, the vast majority is concerned with theological matters, religious duties, rituals, and recounting Biblical stories. No more than approximately eighty Verses deal with legal topics in the strict sense of the term, writes Coulson.[52] Hitti put the legislative Verses at around two hundred, mostly in the Medinese portion, and especially in Chapters Two and Four.[53]

Muslim scholars argue that the actions and sayings of the Prophet reflected the general provisions of the Qur'an and gave guidance in matters on which the Qur'an was silent.[54] Incorporating the attributed sayings and actions of the Prophet into Islamic Shari'a made the Prophet more than the deliverer of God's message. He became "the divinely certified exemplar,

---

[52]Coulson, *A History of Islamic Law*, P. 12.
[53]Hitti, *History of the Arabs*, PP. 396–397.
[54]Hourani, *History of the Arab Peoples*, P. 67.

whose practice itself had a revelatory status. It was through His personal words and acts, and only His, that the commands of the Qur'an could be legitimately interpreted."[55]

Adding the Sunna of the Prophet to the Qur'an expanded the narrow coverage of Qur'anic law. It thrust the ulama class into the daily affairs of Muslims.[56] The role of the ulama became more extensive as more and more Prophetic traditions describing the Prophet's words (Hadith) and actions (Sira) were discovered. By the ninth century, hundreds of thousands of often contradictory and partisan traditions in favor or against every imaginable matter affecting the individual, the family, the tribe, the city, the mosque, rituals, personal conduct, personal hygiene, business affairs, and others, were ascribed to the mouth of the Prophet. Each transmitter claimed that he had been told by *x*, that *y* had told him, that *z* had told him, that *f* had told him, and so forth, claiming the Prophet had said this or done that.

The Six Sunni Canonical Collections: Scholars verified the authenticity of every attribution (*matn*) and the integrity of every attributer into every chain of attributions (*isnad*). Eventually, a few thousand traditions were accepted as authentic, with six collections elevated to canonical rank by Sunnis.

The most revered and authoritative collection is that of Muhammad bin Ismail al-Bukhari (d. 870). Al-Bukhari, a Persian, traveled for sixteen years throughout Persia, Iraq, Syria, Hijaz, and Egypt, collecting 600,000 traditions from 1,000 sheikhs. Of these, he selected, according to Hitti, 7,397 traditions, classified them according to about one hundred subject matters,[57] and included them in a book entitled *Sahih al-Bukhari* (Sahih means correct, sound).[58] Al-Bukhari's collection is considered second only to the Qur'an in authenticity, to the extent that, according to Hitti, an oath sworn on it is as valid, as one taken on the Qur'an.[59]

---

[55]Marshall G. S. Hodgson, *The Venture of Islam: Conscience and History in a World Civilization: The Classical Age of Islam*, Vol. 1. (University of Chicago Press, Chicago, 1977), PP. 327–328.

[56]The Lutheran reformation of the sixteenth century separated the Catholic church from the state. Devoid of intermediaries between God and man, Luther's conception of the relationship between Christians and God became similar to the original conception of Islam regarding the relationship between Muslims and God. Christians, followers of a religion based on priesthood, evolved under the Lutheran revolution into a group that was less controlled by clergy, while Muslims, the followers of a non-church-based religion, became controlled by the ulama class.

[57]Hitti, *History of the Arabs*, P, 395.

[58]The number of al-Bukhari's traditions is 7,563, according to the April 2000 edition of *The Six Books*.

[59]Hitti, *History of the Arabs*, P. 395.

A close second in importance is the collection of Muslim bin al-Hajjaj (d. 875) of Naysabur, Iran, with 7,563 traditions. The other four collections are those of ibn Majah (d. 886), with 4,341 traditions, Abu Dawood (d. 888), with 5,274 traditions, al-Tirmithi (d. 892), with 3,956 traditions, and al-Nasai (d. 915), with 5,761 traditions.[60] The collections are repetitive in some cases, individually and among each other. Shi'ite Muslims have their own Hadith collections (see above: *The Conflict between Shi'ites and Sunnis over the Hadith and Other Differences*).

Notwithstanding the reported integrity of the collectors and the care that they must have taken to ensure the credibility of the thousands of attributers and the authenticity of the hundreds of thousands of Prophetic traditions that grew over 250 years, it remains impossible to know with absolute certainty whether every word and comma in every attribution by every memorizer is authentic and reliable.

Possible Influences of Early Political History on the Collectors: During the first two-and-a-half centuries after the Prophet's death, the generations of Hadith attributers and collectors were witnesses to many doctrinal, legal, and political conflicts.

Aside from the Arab conquests that established one of the world's largest empires, major intra-Muslim conflicts erupted. There were four major civil wars, seven state capital cities, and numerous violent political and religious rebellions. These events spilled rivers of blood and divided the nascent nation of Islam (umma) into many factions and sects. Under such circumstances, it is fair to say that some attributors, not to mention the collectors, had financial, political, career, and other personal interests in the outcome, or they might have simply forgotten what was said or heard over ten generations.

The first Muslim civil war was between the fourth caliph, Ali (656–661), and Mu'awiyah (the fifth caliph and founder of the Umayyad dynasty in Damascus). The second civil war (680–692) was during the reigns of Muawiyha's successors against another claimant of the caliphate, Abdullah ibn al-Zubair. In 683, ibn al-Zubair was recognized as a rival caliph to the Umayyads in parts of Arabia, Egypt, Iraq, and Syria, until he was killed at Mecca in 692. The third civil war culminated in 750 with the destruction of the Umayyad dynasty in Damascus and the arrival of the Abbasid

---

[60]The numbers of the traditions of the five compilers are from the April 2000 edition of *The Six Books. The Hadith Encyclopaedia*, Darussalam Publishing and distribution, Riyadh, Saudi Arabia, 2000.

dynasty in Baghdad. The fourth civil war (811–813) was between al-Amin and al-Mamoun, the two sons of the caliph, Haroun al-Rashid (786–809). Eventually, the former was killed and al-Mamoun reigned from 813 to 833.

Additionally, there was the cataclysmic event in 680 that eventually shook the foundations of the world of Islam and caused a permanent split between Shi'ites and Sunnis to this day—the rebellion and the resultant killing of Imam Hussein bin Ali at Karbala, Iraq.

The first capital city was Medina, the Prophet's adopted city, where he took refuge in 622 to escape Meccan persecution. Medina remained the capital during the rule of the first three caliphs (632–656). In 656, Ali, the fourth caliph, made Kufa, Iraq his base. Mu'awiyah (the fifth caliph) made Damascus the capital of the new Umayyad caliphate in 661. Damascus remained the capital of fourteen caliphs until the Abbasids destroyed the Umayyad Caliphate in 750. The Abbasids moved the seat of the caliphate to Iraq, although transitionally to al-Hashimiyyah before Baghdad was built, starting in 762. In 836, the eighth Abbasid caliph, al-Mu'tasim (833–842), moved the capital to Samarra (a short distance north of Baghdad on the Tigris River). The sixteenth Abbasid caliph, al-Mu'tadid (892–902), moved the seat of government back to Baghdad in 892. Meanwhile, in 756, Cordova became the capital of the Umayyad caliphate in Spain, rivaling and outlasting the Abbasids in Baghdad.

To uncover the truthfulness of hundreds of thousands of Prophetic sayings and actions that supposedly had occurred some ten generations earlier must have been a daunting task. The monumental size, the old age, and the significance of the issues involved raise questions regarding the genuineness of some of the traditions.

Logistical Challenges: That al-Bukhari (810–870) examined 600,000 traditions means that, even if he had spent forty years of his sixty-year life exclusively on the one and only task of compiling the *Sahih*, working fourteen-hours a day without taking a vacation, a sick day, or working on anything else—be it to earn a living or compose other books, he would have had to study an average of more than forty traditions every day,[61] or one tradition every twenty minutes. However, we know that al-Bukhari wrote

---

[61] 40 years × 365 days per year × 14 hours of work per day = 204,400 hours
600,000 traditions over 204,400 hours = 2.93 traditions per hour
2.93 traditions per hour × 14 hours per day = 41 traditions per day
60 minutes per day over 2.93 traditions per hour = 20.5 minutes per tradition.

twenty-one books in addition to the *Sahih*.[62] If we take Hitti's statement that al-Bukhari spent sixteen years of travel and labor in order to produce his *Sahih*, then he would have had to investigate the provenance of an average of 103 traditions every day, or, one tradition every eight minutes.[63]

Al-Bukhari had to ensure the personal integrity of the thousands of attributers over ten generations. The volume of traditions attributed to some memorizers is bewildering. "Abu-Huraira, a Companion of the Prophet ... and a most zealous propagator of his words and deeds, reputedly transmitted some 5,374 Hadiths; Aisha transmitted 2,210, Anas Bin Malik, 2,286, and Abdullah, the son the second caliph, Omar Bin al-Khattab, 1,630."[64] Other transmitters with large volumes of attributed traditions include Jabir Bin Abdullah, with 1,540, Abu Said Al-Khudari; 1170, Ibn Masud; 748, the second caliph Omar; 537, and the fourth caliph Ali; 536.[65] Some of these figures are in dispute.[66]

With the Abbasids' victory over of the Umayyads in 750, the invention of pro-Abbasid, anti-Umayyad Prophetic traditions was a tool used to legitimize the Abbasids.[67] The six canonical collectors lived under Abbasid rule during the turbulent decades of the 800s. The Abbasid Hadith transmitters, upon whom the six collectors relied, were in turn reliant on transmitters who had lived for almost one hundred years under the rule the Abbasids' great nemesis, the Umayyads (661–750). Abbasid politics and fervent hatred of the Umayyads may have played a role in choosing or ignoring attributers, as well as altering certain attributions considered pro-Umayyad.

Scholarly Observations: As observed by the Indian Islamic thinker Muhammad Ashraf: "Had the Qur'an and Hadith been of equal importance, Muhammad's Companions would have written down his sayings."[68] It is curious that, not only the Companions, but not one among the first

---

[62]Muhammad Mustafa Azami, *Studies in Hadith Methodology and Literature* (American Trust Publications, Indianapolis, Indiana, 1977), PP. 88–89.

[63]16 years x 365 days per year x 14 hours of work per day = 81,760 hours
600,000 traditions over 81,760 hours = 7.34 traditions per hour
7.34 traditions per hour × 14 hours per day = 102.77 traditions per day
60 minutes per day over 7.34 traditions per hour = 8.17 minutes per tradition.

[64]Hitti, *History of the Arabs*, P. 394.

[65]Azami, *Studies in Hadith*, PP. 26–27.

[66]G. H. A. Juynboll, *Muslim Tradition: Studies in Chronology, Provenance and Authorship of Early Hadith.* (Cambridge University Press, Cambridge, UK, 1983), P. 29.

[67]Hitti, *Syria: A Short History*, PP. 150–151.

[68]Alfred Guillaume, *Islam.* (Penguin Books, London, 1954, Reprinted 1990). P. 165.

four caliphs regarded by Sunnis as "rightly guided," nor the fourteen Umayyad caliphs, or the first six Abbasid caliphs, found the need to collect and write down the Hadith traditions. According to historical sources, Omar, the second caliph (634–644) was not in favor of *Ahadith* [plural of Hadith] being disseminated, much less being set in writing.[69]

It is, therefore, reasonable to conclude that the Sunna represents a man-made corpus of rules organized by the ulama to suit the political agendas of the caliphs and the ruling elites. It follows that in order to determine its authenticity, the historicity of the Islamic text ought to be subjected to scientific examination by credible open-minded scholars. Nonetheless, the Prophetic traditions draw a useful portrait of society during the lifetime of the Prophet.

---

[69]Juynboll, *Muslim Tradition: Studies in Chronology*, P. 26.

CHAPTER FOUR

COMBATING JIHADISM

B
lind obedience to authority in Verse 4:59 does not extend to the authority of non-Muslims over Muslims. Led from the mosque in the twentieth century, Islamic liberation movements freed Arab countries from British rule (Egypt, Iraq, Sudan), French rule (Algeria, Tunisia, Syria, Lebanon), and Italian rule (Libya). Even within Islamic sects, Shi'ite Muslims have been active politically for centuries against what they regard as the injustices of their Sunni coreligionists.

Jihadist Justification for Rebellion

Notwithstanding the imperative of obedience to Muslim authority, Jihadists who have a different agenda from moderate Muslims, invoke Hadith injunctions that sanction rebellion against an Islamic ruler if he becomes impious or unjust. Muslim, Abi Dawood, and al-Nasai all attribute to the Prophet the saying:

> *Whoever of you sees an evil action, let him change it with his hand, and if he is not able to do so, then with his tongue, and if he is not able to do so, then with his heart.*[1]

---

[1] *The Six Books, Sahih Muslim*, tradition 177, P.688; and *Sunan Abi Dawood*, tradition 4340, P. 1539; and *Sunan Al-Nasai*, tradition 5011 and 5012, P. 2411.

Jihadists rely also on millennium-old opinions of jurists like Abulmaali al-Juwayni (1028–1085), Abulwafa bin Aqil (1040–1119), and Ibn al-Qayyim al-Jawziyya (1292–1350), who supported rebellion against unjust Muslim rulers. Charismatic leaders rallied the disaffected masses to remove the Egyptian, Libyan, and Tunisian presidents from office and have sustained the popular uprising against Syria's Assad regime since March 2011. Al-Qaeda and the so-called Islamic State are in rebellion against the al-Sauds' alleged corruption of "true" Wahhabism.

During the uprisings, it was normal to hear from one mosque in Cairo, Damascus, or Tripoli (Libya) passionate calls for obedience to the sitting ruler (*waliy al-amr*), while equally passionate urgings for rebellion against the same ruler were made from another nearby mosque.

The Breeding of Jihadists

Politicians dressed-up in garbs of piety, from Muhammad bin Abdulwahhab to Osama bin Laden, and Abu Bakr al-Baghdadi have been invoking jihad injunctions, predestination dogma, and promises of paradise to produce walking bombs.

Jihad injunctions + predestination dogma + paradise's delights = Dynamite.

To explode, the dynamite needs a spark.

It should be emphasized that the dynamite alone is harmless. Similarly, the sparks alone are harmless. It is the combination of the dynamite and the sparks that triggers an explosion.

The spark can come from any number of frustrating, despairing domestic and/or foreign fires. The domestic spark can be poverty, unemployment, injustice, oppression, sexual frustration, human rights abuses, hopelessness, etc. The foreign sparks can be anger over Western, Russian, Shi'ite, and Alawite wars against Sunnis in Iraq, Syria, and Yemen, and Israel's humiliation of Palestinians and Arabs.[2]

The collapse of the Ottoman Empire a century ago led to the release in the Middle East of the dark forces of religious extremism and hatred of other religions and sects. The new development contrasts with the religious tolerance that characterized the previous six centuries under the

---

[2]The relative weightings of the factors behind the sparks differ from one jihadist to another.

rule of the Sunni Hanafi Ottoman Sultans (1280–1922). For example, Sultan Bayezid-II (1481–1512), opened the Empire's door to Jews to settle in Ottoman cities, as they were forced out by Catholic Spain and Portugal (see Chapter Eight: *Islam's Veneration of Judaism*). The Sultans did not compel their Christian and other non-Muslims subjects in the Balkans in the Sixteenth Century to convert to Islam. Had they made Islam the only religion in the Balkans, the sectarian atrocities of the 1990s would most probably not have happened.

The sparks not only ignite the dynamite, but also contribute to breeding more jihadists. Domestic and foreign frustrations have been driving moderate Muslims into Islamism and Islamists into jihadism and terrorism. This provokes a more severe governmental response, which, in turn, drives more moderates into orthodoxy and the more orthodox into jihadism and terrorism, and so on.

9/11 might be seen as a deliberate plan by bin Laden to provoke a severe and long-term American retaliation, which would deepen the enmity between the Muslim peoples and the West and ignite what Samuel Huntington calls the clash of civilizations.[3] Seventeen years after 9/11, what was only al-Qaeda has metastasized into Wahhabi strands competing to become the most savage.

Although, Wahhabism is the common denominator among these groups, the leaders are rivals. Al-Qaeda's chief Ayman al-Zawahiri is at war with the so-called Islamic State's caliph, Abu Bakr al-Baghdadi. Both Zawahiri and Baghdadi are after the crown of Salman, the Saudi King. Riyadh is at war with al-Qaeda and the so-called Islamic State in a fight for the al-Sauds' self-preservation, not to protect the world from the scourge of terror, which the Saudi regime bred in the first place.

After the removal of the Taliban regime of Afghanistan in December 2001, the killing of Osama bin Laden on May 2, 2011 by US Navy Seals, the degradation of the physical capabilities of al-Qaeda, and liberation of Mosul (July 10, 2017) and Raqqa (October 17, 2017) with most of the territories captured by the so-called Islamic State, a new breed of jihadists emerged—the lone-wolf terrorist. These men belong to many nationalities and ethnicities. Using a knife or a motor vehicle, they have terrorized Berlin, London, New York, Nice, and Stockholm.

---

[3]Huntington, *The Clash of Civilizations*.

The Globalization of Terrorism: The process of globalizing terrorism involved three strategies:

The first is to pull the universal nation of Islam (umma) together:

> Qur'an 3:103: *And hold fast, all together, unto the bond with God, and do not draw apart from one another ...*

The Prophet had reportedly said:

> - *The relation of a believer to another believer is like a building whose parts support one another.*[4]
> - *The solidarity of Muslims in their mutual love, mercy, and sympathy, is that of a body; if an organ aches, the whole body sympathizes with it with sleeplessness and fever.*[5]

The second strategy is to rally the faithful to defend the nation of Islam (umma) under attack from "infidel Crusaders." Injustices suffered by Muslims in the twentieth century made it possible for bin Laden's message to find listeners. His *Letter to America* in November 2002 listed grievances in Chechnya, Iraq, Kashmir, Lebanon, Somalia, Palestine, and Jerusalem, in addition to citing US protection of corrupt rulers who act as "agents" exploiting the umma's wealth, and stationing military forces on Muslim lands.[6]

The third strategy is to preach intolerant Verses. Combined, these strategies extended the recruitment of jihadists to many ethnicities and nationalities around the world, widened the geographical spread of the confrontation, lengthened the list of jihadist complaints beyond Arab grievances, and awakened the consciousness of political jihad.

To Combat Jihadi Terror, Deactivate the Dynamite and Defuse the Sparks

A war against ideas is far more difficult to win than bombing terrorist hideouts. To fight jihadi terror, or at a minimum, to blunt the jihadists'

---

[4] *The Six Books, Sahih al-Bukhari*, traditions 481, P. 40 and tradition 6026, P. 510; and *Sahih Muslim*, tradition 6585, P. 1130.

[5] Ibid. *Sahih Muslim*, traditions 6582 and 6585 to 6589, P. 1130.

[6] The letter is available on the *Observer Worldview* published in translation from Arabic on November 24, 2002 at: http://observer.guardian.co.uk/worldview/story/0,11581,845725,00.html

recruitment appeal, it is necessary to deactivate the dynamite and defuse the sparks.

How to Deactivate the Dynamite? The way to deactivate the dynamite is to stop manufacturing it. Saudi palace ulama turned Wahhabism into a religious cult. A hundred years of Wahhabi textbooks and mosque sermons have shaped a societal discourse dominated by hatred-of-the other culture, jihad glorification, belief in predestination and the delights of Paradise. The Wahhabi ulama created the recipe for manufacturing walking bombs. Thus, to stop the dynamite, the educational curriculum must be freed from ulama control. Teaching of the sciences, the arts, philosophy and European languages instead of religious dogma would free the mind from the demagoguery of predestination, fate, and superstition, such as the psychotic explanations of the evil eye and the machinations of angels and djinn (genies). Graduating employable workers in business and industry renders young men and women too busy and prosperous to be interested in acts of terror. Additionally, fiery sermons in mosques must be detoxified, and the regurgitation in the media of classroom and mosque rhetoric must stop.

How Likely Is It That the Dynamite Will Be Deactivated? Serious Wahhabi reforms will not happen, at least while oil is in big demand. The US is the only power that could apply pressure on Riyadh, but it will not do so for fear that the king's hand might be weakened and the oil markets disrupted. The *International Religious Freedom Report for 2015* of the US Bureau of Democracy Human Rights and Labor reveals that since 2004, despite Saudi violation of religious freedoms and human rights, the US Secretary of State has waived the sanctions that come with designating Saudi Arabia as a "Country of Particular Concern" due to the important national interest of the US.[7] Not even 9/11, in which 19 Wahhabis, 15 of whom were Saudis, was a big enough catastrophe for the G.W. Bush administration to punish Saudi Arabia. Instead, Iraq, an innocent party, was demolished and became dominated by Iran.

The al-Saud regime will reject calls for genuine political reforms. Political reform dilutes the king's totalitarian absolute authority. Reform would force a governance system mired in corruption, non-accountability,

---

[7]US Department of State, Bureau of Democracy, Human Rights and Labor, "International Religious Freedom Report for 2015, Saudi Arabia." http://www.state.gov/j/drl/rls/irf/religiousfreedom/index.htm?year=2015&dlid=256287

and absence of transparency to become participatory, transparent, and accountable. The al-Saud will never allow such development to happen.

Genuine religious reform would erode the king's claim of being the "servant of the two holy mosques" and the most ardent protector of the purest form of Islam. Without Wahhabism, the regime becomes illegitimate. The king would not grant Saudi women meaningful human rights, such as a modern personal status law like that of Turkey, or a modern court system like that of Tunisia. Why? Because in treating women like chattel, the regime nullifies the political opposition of half of Saudi society. As for the recent changes such as lifting the ban on women's driving cars and limiting the powers of the religious police, these are cosmetic changes that exist in every non-Wahhabi Muslim society.

Sustainable solar, wind, hydropower, and fusion sources of energy are sharp weapons in the fight against jihadism. It is only when US rivals like China, continental Europe, India, and Japan become independent of the importation of oil that the US will lose its oil leverage. Only then, will Washington abandon its protection of the al-Saud regime. Only then will serious religious and political reforms have a chance to evolve in Riyadh (and Egypt) unhindered. It is only then that the world will begin to break free from the Wahhabi cult.

Now that the Wahhabi genie is out of the bottle, no power seems capable of putting the genie back in. Wahhabi groups sprang up in several parts of the world. Support for these groups comes from enormously wealthy individuals in Saudi Arabia and the rest of the GCC states. Most dangerous of all, however, is the recent birth of the lone-wolf jihadist. All the lone wolf needs, is Wahhabi inspiration plus a knife, or a stolen car.

The Sparks

Intensifying the sparks include the collective memories of the occupation of the Arab world by Britain, Italy, and France in the nineteenth and twentieth centuries; support by Western powers of non-representative; tyrannical Arab regimes since independence; Israeli humiliation of Palestinians and Arabs since the creation of Israel in 1948; and the recent Sunni/Shi'ite wars in Iraq, Syria, and Yemen.

The Sykes-Picot Agreement (May 19, 1916): Arabs are embittered over the duplicity and ingratitude of Britain and France during the

First World War (1914–1918) toward their Arab allies. The Great Arab Revolt, launched by the Sharif of Mecca, Hussein bin Ali, on June 5, 1916, declared support for Britain and France in the middle of the war. In fighting on the side of Christian Britain and France, Sharif Hussein stabbed his Turkish co-religionist rulers in the back. Arab leaders trusted that their European allies would grant them independence from Ottoman rule if Istanbul was defeated. Instead, London and Paris carved up and divided Greater Syria and Iraq between them, using the excuse that these countries were not ready for independence. The fact that the Agreement was concluded behind the back of Sharif Hussein only two weeks before he declared the Arab Revolt is all the more painful (For details, see Chapter Nine).

The Balfour Declaration (November 2, 1917): Arabs are deeply aggrieved over the Balfour Declaration. The British Foreign Secretary, Lord Balfour, volunteered Palestinian lands to the Zionist Federation, lands, which, Britain neither owned, nor had authority over. Balfour declared to Lord Rothschild that the British Government viewed "with favor the establishment in Palestine of a national home for the Jewish people."[8] The part of the Declaration, which specified that, "Nothing shall be done which may prejudice the civil and religious rights of existing non-Jewish communities in Palestine," did nothing to prevent the painful result of this Declaration (see Chapter Eight). According to Palestinian sources, in 1948, "over 800,000 Palestinians ... [were] expelled from 531 towns and villages, in addition to 130,000 from 662 secondary small villages and hamlets."[9] This turned Arab frustration to fury. Jewish sources put the number of the refugees at around 650,000.[10]

Article 11 of the United Nations General Assembly Resolution 194, dated December 11, 1948 was resolved but never implemented: "The refugees wishing to return to their homes and live at peace with their neighbors should be permitted to do so at the earliest practicable date and that

[8]"Balfour Declaration: Text of the Declaration," *Jewish Virtual Library*, (November 2, 1917). http://www.jewishvirtuallibrary.org/text-of-the-balfour-declaration

[9]Palestine Land Society, http://www.plands.org/en/books-reports/books/right-of-return-sacred-legal-and-possilble/from-refugees-to-citizens-at-home

[10]Mitchell Bard, "The Palestinian Refugees," *Jewish Virtual Library*. http://www.jewishvirtualli-brary.org/jsource/History/refugees.html

compensation should be paid for the property of those choosing not to return and for loss of or damage to property.[11]

Moshe Dayan, former Israeli defense minister, stated in a 1969 speech before students at the Israeli Institute of Technology in Haifa that:

> Jewish villages were built in the place of Arab villages. You do not even know the names of these Arab villages, and I do not blame you because geography books no longer exist. Not only do the books not exist, the Arab villages are not there either. Nahial arose in the place of Mahlul; Kibbutz Gvat in the place of Jibta; Kibbutz Sarid in the place of Huneifis; and Kefar Yehushua in the place of Tal al-Shuman. There is not a single place built in this country that did not have a former Arab population.[12]

Arabs resent the labeling of their struggle against the occupation as terrorism while the occupier's actions are considered to be self-defense. The victim has become the villain—a thoroughly exasperating situation to the Arab masses (for details, see Chapter Eight).

Other Grievances: The occupation of Iraq by the US in 2003 opened the gates of hell to Shi'ite/Sunni wars in Iraq and beyond. In Syria, the revolution against Assad's fifty years of tyranny, (plus that of his Iranian and Hezbollah and Russian protectors) along with the destruction of much of Syria, has deepened the sectarian enmity among Sunnis on the one hand, and Alawites and Shi'ites on the other.

The events that have shamed and angered the Arab masses for the past 100 years cannot be compartmentalized. The US occupation of Iraq cannot be isolated from the occupation of Greater Syria by Britain, and France before them, nor from the occupation of Iraq, Egypt, and the Sudan by Britain, nor of Libya by Italy, Algeria and Tunisia by France, nor Palestine by Israel. Today, Iraq, Syria, and Palestine are inextricably entwined in the minds of Arabs as examples of injustice and humiliation. Nor can these examples be separated from the misrule of Western-supported tyrannical, non-representative, corrupt Arab kings and presidents under which these

---

[11]United Nations General Assembly, 194 (III), *Palestine—Progress Report of the United Nations Mediator*, (December 11, 1948). https://unispal.un.org/DPA/DPR/unispal.nsf/0/C758572B78D1CD0085256BCF0077E51A

[12]Noel Ignatiev, "Zionism, Anti-Semitism and the People of Palestine," *Counterpunch*, (June 17, 2004). http://www.counterpunch.org/2004/06/17/zionism-anti-semitism-and-the-people-of-palestine/

masses have suffered. For the masses, all such grievances translate into a common denominator—humiliation. The longer the grievances persist, the more despair will grow, and the more dangerous the radicalization will become.

Each one of the victors' triumphs has scarred the collective memory of the Arab generations. The effects of the events that demeaned Arab pride and sensibilities have been accumulating in the Arab mind and psyche long after the victors thought they had gotten away with their victory. It is as if every man, woman, and child who was killed, every young man whose bones were crushed, every home, which was bulldozed and every olive tree, which was uprooted has accumulated in the Arab collective memory. The comment section in Arabic newspapers and social media provide a window into the despair sweeping the oppressed Arab masses.

How to Defuse the Sparks? In Iraq, the Shi'ite dominated government's discrimination against Sunnis must end. Iraqi Sunnis will increasingly embrace Wahhabi extremism. The birth of the so-called Islamic State's ideology must serve as a warning.

In Syria, genuine democratic elections supervised by the United Nations should be held to determine the political future of the country. Elections must include the Muslim Brotherhood. Syria's Brotherhood had a tradition of participating in democratic elections and partnering with secular political parties of coalition governments until the military coup on March 8, 1963, which ended democracy in Syria, dissolved the parliament, dismissed the cabinet, and removed the last legitimate president, Nazim al-Qudsi.

The Israeli/Palestinian conflict has been an extremely serious source of Arab frustration and dishonor for the past seventy years. For Israel and the United States to deny responsibility for having helped create the environment that allowed jihadism to grow among Arabs is as deluded and dangerous as the al-Saud rejection of a connection between the Wahhabi way of life and the terrorists of 9/11. A single democratic state for Palestinians and Jews is the durable sustainable solution, not the two-state solution.

In Sunni ruled Arab countries, Shi'ites must become equal citizens to Sunni citizens. Otherwise, Arab Shi'ites will become easy targets for exploitation by the ayatollahs.

Parliamentary democracy should be encouraged by Washington, especially in Egypt. A Doha Institute for Graduate Studies survey in 2015 of 18,311 face to face interviews conducted in 12 separate Arab countries shows that the most important factors in combatting the so-called Islamic State and ending the threat of terrorism include supporting democratic transition in the region (28%), resolving the Palestinian cause (18%), ending foreign intervention (14%), intensifying the military campaign against ISIL (14%), and solving the Syrian crisis in line with the aspirations of the Syrian people (12%).[13]

How likely Is It That the Sparks Will Be Defused? The sparks will not be defused for two reasons: First, from a Western point of view, the Sunni/Shi'ite proxy wars between Saudi Arabia and Iran in Iraq, Syria, and Yemen have kept Muslims busy killing each other thousands of miles away from American and European cities. Secondly, as Saudi Arabia (and its GCC brethren) face the far more powerful enemy in Tehran, they must cling to US protection more tightly than ever. They will also cling to Israel. They will pay whatever invoice Washington and Israel demand. They will flood US and European weapon manufacturers with expensive orders for the most sophisticated war machines, whether they have the skills to keep the equipment operational or not. Coinciding with President Trump's visit to Saudi Arabia on May 20, 2017, weapon contracts totaling $110 billion were agreed, with the package surpassing more than $300 billion over a decade.[14] Beyond weapons, $200 billion in contracts were also exchanged, ranging from power and healthcare sectors, to the oil and gas industry and mining.[15] With such purchases, Mr. Trump did not utter a word to his Saudi hosts about their non-representative autocratic rule, or human and women's rights abuses, or proselytizing Wahhabi extremism around the globe.

As for the Arab-Israeli conflict, there is no realistic hope for a sustainable solution. Israel is the hegemonic power in the Middle East. It enjoys Washington's unlimited support. Palestinians and Arab states are underdeveloped, weak, and divided. Arab regimes are dependent for survival on support from the same world powers that created Israel in 1948 and that have been protecting it ever since that time [US, UK, France,

---

[13]Doha Institute for Graduate Studies, Arab Center for Research & Policy Studies, "The 2015 Arab Opinion Index: Results in Brief," (December 21, 2015). http://arabcenterdc.org/wp-content/uploads/2016/01/2015-Arab-Opinion-Index-Results-in-Brief.pdf

[14]Steve Holland, "US nears $100 billion arms deal for Saudi Arabia: White House official," *Reuters*, (May 12, 2017). http://www.reuters.com/article/us-usa-trump-saudi-idUSKBN18832N

[15]Javier E. David, "US, Saudi Firms Sign Tens of Billions of Dollars of Deals as Trump Visits," *CNBC*, (May 22, 2017). https://www.cnbc.com/2017/05/20/us-saudi-arabia-seal-weapons-deal-worth-nearly-110-billion-as-trump-begins-visit.html

and U.S.S.R (and its successor Russia)]. Under such conditions, negotiations between the all-powerful Israel and the defenseless Palestinians are futile (see Chapter Eight). President Trump's decision on December 6, 2017, to recognize Jerusalem as Israel's capital adds salt to the wounds of Palestinians, Arabs, and Muslims.[16]

What about the risk of growing radicalization and jihadi violence in Western cities if the dynamite and/or the sparks are not defused? The benefits to Western economies from war and mayhem in the Muslim Middle East outweigh the potential loss of life in Western cities. The risk of terrorism can be mitigated through better policing and intelligence work. While it is true that the risk cannot be eliminated completely, the residual risk may be regarded as acceptable collateral damage. In the US, during the ten years between 2002 and 2011, the annual average number of those killed as a result of jihadist terror was 31, while in 2015 the number of people killed by firearms alone was 13,286 and injured was 26,819.[17]

How Might the Muslim Brotherhood's Representative Democracy Defeat Wahhabi Terror?

Representative democracy is an effective medicine to combat the appeal of jihadism and the recruitment of jihadist. Democratic governance goes a long way to placate the anger that constantly charges the domestic spark. Separation of government powers, competition among political parties, free speech, free elections, accountability, and transparency in government affairs are all important factors to restore the missing respect for human dignity and rights in Arab countries. Already, a sizable body of Arabs believe in democracy. According to an April 2013 Pew Research Center survey, the median of those who support democracy is 55% in the seven MENA region countries (Iraq, Palestinian Territories, Morocco, Egypt, Jordan, Tunisia, Lebanon).[18]

The recent democratic election gains by the Muslim Brotherhood in Egypt, Jordan, Kuwait, Morocco, and Tunisia discredit Saudi clerics' teaching that Islam and democracy are incompatible and that democracy is a

---

[16]The White House, "Statement by President Trump on Jerusalem."

[17]"Guns in the US: The statistics behind the violence," *BBC*, (January 5, 2015). http://www.bbc.co.uk/news/world-us-canada-34996604

[18]Pew Research Center, *The World's Muslims*.

Western conspiracy to destroy Islam. The Arab Spring planted a resilient seed in the heads of the Arab peoples, men and women, young and old, that free elections and representative democracy are compatible with Islam.

Democracy is one thing, but modernizing Shari'a Laws is another, and far bigger challenge. For a democratically elected parliament and government to be able to modernize Shari'a Laws, they must above all possess religious credibility. The Brotherhood possesses the Islamic credibility required. How might the Brotherhood effect such a transformation?

Arab Spring governments realize that unless they reduce poverty and unemployment quickly and convincingly, they stand no chance for re-election. They realize that dogmatic and rhetorical religious and nationalistic posturing will produce neither jobs, housing, health services, nor prosperity. They have little choice but to enact modern laws that would reorder national budgetary priorities away from military spending and toward human development and economic growth. To raise employment and per capita income, the new governments will have to welcome foreign capital and encourage the flow of dollars and euros from tourism. They will have to introduce policies to reverse high population growth rates. To make graduates employable, emphasis must be placed on teaching the sciences and philosophy rather than religious dogma such as predestination.

There will be confrontations between the new governments and the anti-modernization Islamists, salafists, and jihadists with Wahhabi inspiration and Saudi cash. These groups will assail the new laws as un-Islamic. The Muslim Brotherhood leadership and ulama, with their credibility and serious knowledge of Islamic law and theology, must counter the attacks with impressive arguments from the Muslim Text in favor of the Islamic nature of the new laws.

The confrontation between the two sides could isolate the anti-modernization voices, cement democratic governance, modernize Shari'a laws, and evolve a more tolerant, less austere, less extreme, and less coercive existence than the Wahhabi way of life. The confrontation could break new grounds in debating sensitive religious questions, buried for centuries under blasphemy laws and age-old cultural norms.[19]

The previously mentioned 2015, Zogby survey on "Muslim Millennial Attitudes on Religion and Religious Leadership" shows that the respondents

---

[19]Elhadj, "The Arab Spring and the Prospects for Genuine Religious and Political Reforms."

in eight Arab countries would welcome "a renewal in the language to talk about Islam in sermons, talks and public outlets."

There needs to be a renewal in the language used to talk about Islam in sermons, talks and public outlets.

	Morocco	Egypt	KSA	UAE	Bahrain	Kuwait	Jordan	Palestine
Agree	90	90	72	64	78	66	76	78
Disagree	10	10	28	36	22	34	24	22

Zogby Research Services, *Muslim Millennial attitudes on religion and religious leadership*, Tabah Foundation, 2015.

The survey also found that the topics addressed by scholars, preachers and speakers "need to be updated to be relevant to people today."

The topics and issues which scholars, preachers and speakers address need to be updated to be relevant to people today.

	Morocco	Egypt	KSA	UAE	Bahrain	Kuwait	Jordan	Palestine
Agree	79	93	85	69	76	81	63	75
Disagree	21	7	15	31	24	19	37	25

Are Western Fears of the Muslim Brotherhood Exaggerated? Yes, Western fears of the Muslim Brotherhood are exaggerated. A Brotherhood regime does not necessarily mean its policies will be anti-Western or anti-American any more than a secular regime would be. Three examples will illustrate the point. Saudi Arabia is the world's most extreme Islamist regime; yet, Riyadh has been obsequious to and protected by (initially London and later by Washington) Western powers. Secondly, in the case of Tunisia's Annahda party, while Islamic, refused to add Shari'a law as a source of legislation in the country's constitution, despite demands by Islamists.[20] Thirdly, Syria, a so-called "secular" regime, has been anti-democracy, anti-Western and anti-American for decades.

Indeed, Syria is more Islamic today than it was in 1963 when Hafiz Assad and his compatriots seized power. Like the 1973 constitution, the 2012 constitution makes Islam the religion of the president [Article 3 (1)] and enshrines the Islamic Shari'a as a main source of legislation [Article 3 (2)].[21]

---

[20]George Sadek, "The Role of Islamic Law in Tunisia's Constitution and Legislation Post-Arab Spring," *Library of Congress*, (May 2013). https://www.loc.gov/law/help/tunisia.php

[21]Carnegie Middle East Center, *The Syrian Constitution—1973–2012*. http://carnegie-mec.org/diwan/50255?lang=en

Shari'a laws and courts continue to regulate Muslims' personal status affairs in Syria. Further, religious dogma has taken center stage. During periods of drought, Bashar Assad, supposedly an eye doctor, orders Syria's mosques to perform special rain prayers.[22] It is difficult to imagine how a future Muslim Brotherhood participation in parliament and in a coalition government in Syria could be more religious or more belligerent toward Europe and America than the Assad regime. That the Assad regime warns Western countries against the Muslim Brotherhood is typical of its well-practiced cry-wolf ritual of blackmail legitimacy.

The Brotherhood is not a unified body. It does not have a central authority formulating strategies and dictating policies. Each Arab country has its own Brotherhood organization. The local chapters do not report to each other. The Brotherhood organizations in Egypt, Morocco, Jordan, Kuwait, Syria, and Tunisia have chosen elections and representative democracy as a way of political life. This is a monumental development that should be applauded and encouraged by the United States and its allies, who preach the virtues of representative democracy on every turn and often use it as a tool to pressure non-democratic countries. It is a choice between the Wahhabi war on democracy and the Brotherhood's defense of democracy.

There is the risk that a government dominated by the Brotherhood might betray the democratic process and decide to build a dictatorship instead. In such a case, there is the hope that the masses, who brought the Brotherhood to power, would ensure that the new governments would not trample over democratic rule. Also, if a Brotherhood chapter reneges on democratic governance in a specific country, the remaining chapters would pressure the reneging chapter to tow the line.

In an Arab world gripped by religious fervor, the Muslim Brotherhood provides the best hope to isolate the Wahhabi assault on democracy and democratic institutions. The Brotherhood can be the catalyst that ushers parliamentary democracy and modernizes Shari'a laws and courts. Achieving Islamic and political reforms outweighs the risk involved in supporting Brotherhood governments in the Arab world.[23]

---

[22]Scott Lucas, "Syria: Assad Sees Imminent Victory, as God Answers Prayers for Rain and Snow," *EA Worldview*, (February 4, 2014). http://eaworldview.com/2014/02/syria-assad-sees-imminent-victory-god-answers-prayers-rain-snow/

[23]Elhadj, "The Arab Spring and the Prospects for Genuine Religious and Political Reforms."

CHAPTER FIVE

THE EFFECT OF SAUDI OIL ON DERAILING THE ARAB SPRING'S REFORMS

The Shape of Arab Governance

Until the Arab Spring's democratic elections produced legitimate rulers in Tunisia (October 23, 2011), Morocco (November 25, 2011), and Egypt (June 30, 2012), not a single Arab country had a semblance of democratic governance.[1] Since the end of the Second World War, independent Arab countries have all been in the grip of non-representative absolute monarchs or non-representative absolute royal presidents. Typically, Arab rulers hold on to power for life until forced to leave upon:

- Natural death: President Gamal Abdul Nasser of Egypt (1970), King Hussein of Jordan (1999), President Hafiz Assad of Syria (2000), and Saudi Arabia's kings, Abdulaziz (1953), Fahd (2005), Khalid (1982), and Abdullah (2015).
- Being killed: King Faisal of Iraq (1958), President Abdul Kareem Kassem of Iraq (1963), President Saddam Hussein of Iraq (2006), King Faisal of Saudi Arabia (1975), President Anwar el-Sadat of

---

[1] Lebanon is excluded due to its religious and ethnic special circumstances

Egypt (1981), President Ibrahim al-Hamdi of Yemen (1977), President Ahmad al-Ghashmi of Yemen (1978), Libyan leader Colonel Muammar Qaddafi (2011).

- Dethroned in palace intrigue: King Saud of Saudi Arabia (1964), Sultan Sa'id bin Taimur of Oman (1970), Sheikh Shakhbut bin Sultan al-Nahyan of Abu Dhabi (1966), Emir Khalifa Bin Hamad al-Thani of Qatar (1995).
- Overthrown by a military coup: King Muhammad al-Badr of Yemen (1962), President Abdulrahman al-Iryani of Yemen (1998), President Nazim al-Qudsi of Syria (1963), Prime Minister Sadiq al-Mahdi of Sudan (1989), President Mohammad Morsi of Egypt (2013).
- Removed in a popular uprising: President Hosni Mubarak of Egypt (2011), President Zein al-Abdeen bin Ali of Tunisia (2011), President Ali Abdallah Saleh of Yemen (removed 2012, killed 2017).

It is noteworthy that non-Arab Muslim countries like Bangladesh, Indonesia, Malaysia, Pakistan, and Turkey, which contain around one half of the estimated 1.5 billion world Muslims, have multi-party elections, representative democracy, and women presidents and prime ministers. Similarly, millions of Muslims living in non-Muslim democracies participate in the political life of their countries.

Aside from the two Arab Spring countries; the Kingdom of Morocco and the Republic of Tunisia, Arab rulers are of two types:

1) Military presidents—Having seized power by force, they pretend to be modernizers. They contrive farcical, un-contested referendums. Approvals between 90% and 100% are the norm from Egypt (Nasser, Sadat, Mubarak, Sisi), to Iraq (Saddam Hussein), Libya (Qaddafi), Sudan (Bashir), Syria (Assad father and son), and Tunisia (bin Ali).

2) Kings, emirs, and sultans—These men are tribal sheikhs crowned for life. They leave government palaces upon death or removal, often by a son or a brother. In place of the theatrics of rigged referendums, mile-long lines of happy looking men, (women not allowed) are drafted to display allegiance to the monarch during religious and national festivals. The celebrants typically wish to ingratiate themselves with the ruler or his entourage to get jobs they do not merit, contracts they don't deserve, or just to be seen at the right place and time in order to enhance their image among neighbors and friends.

The Arab Spring—The First Wave: Non-Oil Exporting Countries

On December 17, 2010, the Arab world shook. Muhammad Bouazizi, a 26-year-old vegetable street vendor from the poor town of Sidi Bouzid, Tunisia (200 miles south of Tunis, the capital), set himself on fire in front of the governor's office. He had been humiliated by the confiscation of his vendor cart, and ignored by the municipality, which refused to see him about the matter. It was the last straw that broke Bouaziz's back. He self-immolated. He died on January 4, 2010. Bouazizi's tragedy sparked widespread protests against President Zine al-Abidine bin Ali's 23-years (November 7, 1987–January 14, 2011) of non-representative, corrupt police state regime. On January 14, 2011, bin Ali fled to Jeddah, Saudi Arabia.

The Tunisian uprising was swift, effective, and inspirational to the Arab masses everywhere. Within days, at least five downtrodden men in Egypt followed Bouazizi's example, with one dead in Alexandria.[2] On January 25, 2011, thousands of anti-government protesters demanded the end of Mubarak's almost 30-year dictatorship (October 14, 1981–February 11, 2011). They clashed in Cairo's Tahrir Square with Mubarak's brutal police. The protests spread to other cities. On February 11, 2011, Mubarak resigned. He handed power to the defense minister.

The Arab Spring may evolve Arab democratic and religious reforms in two waves. The first wave involves non-oil-exporting countries that are far away from the oilfields of the Eastern shores of the Arabian Peninsula. Tunisia, a republic, and Morocco, a kingdom, are examples. In Tunisia, the Islamic Annahda Party was the leading winner in the democratic parliamentary elections in October 2011. Annahda won 90 seats in the 217-member parliament and led a coalition government.[3] In the October 2014 elections, Annahda won 69 in the 217-member parliament[4] and joined a coalition government under the leadership of the secular party, Nidaa Tunis.[5]

---

[2]"Egyptian Workers Burn Themselves to Protest Transfers," *Signalfire*, (January 21, 2011). http://www.signalfire.org/2011/01/21/egyptian-workers-burn-themselves-to-protest-transfers/

[3]"Tunisia's Islamist Ennahda party wins historic poll," *BBC*, (October 27, 2011). http://www.bbc.co.uk/news/world-africa-15487647

[4]"Secularist Nidaa Tounes party wins Tunisia election," *BBC*, (October 30, 2014). http://www.bbc.co.uk/news/world-africa-29828706

[5]"Tunisia's Ennahda to Join Coalition Government," *Al Jazeera*, (February 1, 2015). https://www.aljazeera.com/news/2015/02/tunisia-ennahda-join-coalition-goverment-150201172336735.html

In Morocco, in the November 2011 elections, the Islamic Justice and Development Party won 107 seats in the 395-member parliament and led a coalition government.[6] In the October 2016 parliamentary elections, the Islamic Justice and Development Party won 125 seats in the 395-member parliament.[7] On April 5, 2017, it formed a coalition government with five other Moroccan political parties.[8]

The Arab Spring—The Second Wave: Saudi Arabia

The second wave of democratic and religious reforms could reach Saudi Arabia only after green sustainable energy replaces crude oil imports by America's rivals, China; the world's biggest oil importer (8.4 million bbl./day in 2017),[9] India (3.789 million bbl./day in 2016), Japan (3.181 million bbl./day in 2016), and continental European countries.[10] It is only then that the door to representative democracy could open to the people of Saudi Arabia and without American intervention to stop it. Until then, absolute monarchies, seventh century laws, and religious dogma will govern in the name of divine rule.

Washington's Middle East Politics is the Politics of Oil: In a world addicted to crude oil, energy hegemony means world hegemony. As long as global demand for oil by America's rivals (China, continental Europe, India, and Japan) is strong, the US will protect the al-Saud regime despite its corrupt non-representative dictatorship, dark record of human rights abuses, proselytizing hate-of-the-other culture, radicalizing Islam, and polarizing Muslims. In return for US protection, the six Saudi kings and their father, King Abdulaziz, maintained an obsequious relationship with the thirteen US presidents since Franklin D. Roosevelt. The kings

---

[6]"Islamist PJD Party Wins Morocco Poll," *BBC*, (November 27, 2011). http://www.bbc.co.uk/news/world-africa-15902703

[7]"Moderate Moroccan Islamists Win Election, Coalition Talks Seen Tough," *BBC*, (October 8, 2016). http://www.reuters.com/article/us-morocco-election-tally-idUSKCN1280EP

[8]"Morocco's King Names New Coalition Government," *Al Jazeera*, (April 6, 2017). https://www.aljazeera.com/news/2017/04/morocco-king-names-coalition-government-170405185201695.html

[9]US Energy Information Administration, "China Surpassed the United States as the World's Largest Oil Importer in 2017," (February 5, 2018). https://www.eia.gov/todayinenergy/detail.php?id=34812

[10]CIA World Factbook. https://www.cia.gov/library/publications/the-world-factbook/rankorder/2243rank.html

followed Washington's advice/instructions on oil export volumes and pricing politics.[11]

US influence/control over Saudi oil is important, not because the US needs the oil, but because Saudi Arabia, as the world's biggest oil exporter[12] and swing producer, is capable of decreasing or increasing the volume of its oil exports at anytime in order to drive oil prices up or down.

Additionally, in case of a confrontation with America's oil importing rivals, US influence/control over Saudi oil can be a non-lethal weapon of mass destruction. The oil weapon supplements two other non-lethal weapons of mass destruction in the US arsenal: food production and the dollar as the main reserve currency for world central banks.

Saudi insistence on using the US dollar in the oil trade helps maintain the dollar as the main reserve currency for world's central banks.

Washington has protected the al-Saud regime faithfully for the past seventy years. Not even when 15 of the 19 Wahhabi terrorists who flew passenger planes into buildings in New York City and Washington D.C. turned out to be Saudi nationals, killing over 3,000 people and costing an estimated $2 trillion,[13] would the Bush administration retaliate against Riyadh. Instead, Iraq was sacrificed on the altar of Saudi oil. It was invaded in March 2003, occupied, and much of it demolished. Nine years later, on December 18, 2011, the US withdrew from Iraq,[14] leaving the field empty for Iran to fill and the ravaged country to suffer further destruction until this day. The occupation of Iraq led to Iran's control over Iraq, to the birth of the Shi'ite Crescent proxy wars between Saudi Arabia and Iran in Iraq, Syria, and Yemen. The Shi'ite Crescent heightened tension in the Shi'ite communities of Bahrain, Kuwait, and Saudi Arabia against their Sunni rulers.

The wars in Afghanistan and Iraq cost trillions of dollars. In a working paper in 2013, Harvard University's Kennedy School estimated that the Afghanistan and Iraq wars cost the US between $4 trillion and $6 trillion.[15]

---

[11]"Saudi Minister Yamani: 'Kissinger Was Behind 1974 Oil Shock,'" *Executive Intelligence Review* 28, no. 4, (January 26, 2001). http://www.larouchepub.com/eiw/public/2001/eirv28n04-20010126/eirv28n04-20010126_008-saudi_minister_yamani_kissinger.pdf

[12]7.62 million bbl./day, around 20% of world oil exports, Index Mundi, *Oil—exports > TOP 20.*

[13]Institute for the Analysis of Global Security, "How much did the September 11 terrorist attack cost America?" 2003–2004. http://www.iags.org/costof911.html

[14]"Last US troops leave Iraq, ending war," *Reuters*, (December 18, 2011). http://www.reuters.com/article/us-iraq-withdrawal-idUSTRE7BH03320111218

[15]Linda J. Bilmes, "How Wartime Spending."

Brown University's Watson Institute for International and Public Affairs estimated that the wars in Afghanistan and Iraq cost US taxpayers nearly $5.6 trillion.[16] This latter calculation does not include the cost of the destruction of the infrastructure in Afghani or Iraqi cities, nor the millions of lives lost or those who now live with life-long disabilities.

Washington's protection of Saudi Arabia will change if China, India, Japan and other big oil importing rivals of the US free themselves from the shackles of dependence on oil imports, energy from oil as a weapon in the US arsenal would vanish, and with it, US protection of the Saudi regime. When that happens, Wahhabi cash will dwindle and, with it, terror will decline.

JASTA vs. Saudi Arabia: On September 9, 2016, two days before the 15th anniversary of the al-Qaeda attacks,[17] the US House of Representatives approved a bipartisan bill that would allow the Saudi government to be held responsible for any role in the 2001 assault.[18] The US Senate had passed the Justice Against Sponsors of Terrorism Act (JASTA) unanimously on May 17, 2016. On September 23, 2016, Mr. Obama vetoed the JASTA. On September 28, 2016, the US Congress overturned the veto. [see below: *Protection from the Justice against Sponsors of Terrorism Act (JASTA)*].[19]

While US foreign policy is supposed to promote democracy and human rights, the Saudi regime is the exception. Why the inconsistency? The answer is that the relationship between Washington and Riyadh is delicate and complicated.

---

[16]Neta Crawford, "US Budgetary Costs of Post-9/11 Wars Through FY2018: $5.6 Trillion.

[17]It is difficult to imagine the Saudi government having a hand in the planning or execution of 9/11. Rather, the atrocity was engineered by a Saudi and committed by nineteen Wahhabi terrorists, brought up with the teachings and preaching of clerics in Saudi Arabia for the past one hundred years.

[18]"Bill Passed by US Congress Allowing 9/11 Victims' Families to Sue Saudi Arabia Could Be Defeated by Presidential Veto," *The Independent*, (September 9, 2016). http://www.independent.co.uk/news/world/americas/bill-passed-by-us-congress-allowing-911-victims-families-to-sue-saudi-arabia-could-be-defeated-by-a7234716.html)

[19]"Congress overrides Obama's veto of 9/11 bill letting families sue Saudi Arabia," *The Guardian*, (September 29, 2016). https://www.theguardian.com/us-news/2016/sep/28/senate-obama-veto-september-11-bill-saudi-arabia

The Delicate and Complicated US/Saudi Relationship

The View from Washington: Saudi Arabia is effectively an American protectorate (see the next section: *Manifesting US Protection of Saudi Arabia*). Washington must have been conscious of the damage Wahhabi indoctrination in Saudi Arabia is capable of inflicting upon the world, yet it would not pressure Saudi Arabia's kings to democratize and secularize for two reasons:

1) US capacity to impose its will on the Saudi King is limited by the fear that excessive pressure might weaken the king's hold on power, causing chaos in world's oil markets. Should the king lose control, the door might open to disruptions in oil exports by the followers of al-Qaeda or the Shi'ites of the oil-rich Eastern Province, or external enemies, like Iran, or Saddam Hussein (before his removal from power in 2003). If that were to happen, the US would need to intervene to ensure the smooth flow of oil to world markets; making the wars in Iraq and Afghanistan look like child's play.
2) Ease of dealing with one absolute king who owes his throne and life to US protection, compared with having to manage the scores of parliamentarians and political leaders in democratic settings.

The View from Riyadh: Saudi monarchs are aware of the need for US protection to deal with the many vulnerabilities they face—internal conflicts with the Shi'ite and Isma'ili citizens (see below: *The Threat from Saudi Arabia's Internal Sectarian Divisions*), external threats from powerful hostile neighbors on the East, North, and the West. Also, there are growing challenges from the Muslim Brotherhood's democratic Islam, on one hand, and from the likes of al-Qaeda and the so-called Islamic State over the "true" Wahhabi creed, on the other. Despite these dangers, Saudi monarchs would never yield to pressure from Washington, or any other power, to democratize, or seriously loosen their embrace of Wahhabism, let alone secularize (see below: *Obstacles in the Way of Moderating Wahhabism*). Ever since the patriarch of the family, Abdulaziz, launched the al-Saud clan's second rebellion against the Ottoman rulers of Arabia 115 years ago, successive Saudi Kings have used the Wahhabi creed to legitimize their claim to authority.[20] Without Wahhabism the regime becomes illegitimate. Wahhabism is the glue that keeps the tribes and the al-Sauds together. Dissolve the glue and the whole structure will collapse. Wahhabism and the al-Sauds are symbiotically attached, notwithstanding the cosmetic changes King Salman effected recently to appease President Trump, like lifting the ban on women driving cars and attending sporting events. As for democratization, the possibility is zero.

Furthermore, the al-Sauds realize that Washington will protect them as long as Saudi Arabia remains the world's biggest oil exporter and swing producer and that the imports of Saudi oil by US rivals continue to be strong.

Manifesting US Protection of Saudi Arabia: The US has been protecting the al-Saud kings since oil was discovered in big quantities 70 years ago. US protection of the al-Sauds regime is manifested in a number of ways:

1. American technicians, engineers, and spare parts sent to keep operational the hundreds of billions of dollars in sophisticated US weapons sold to the Saudi Ministry of Defense and Aviation and the National Guard over the past forty years. Weapon purchases are a form of protection money Saudi Kings pay.

    Under President Trump's White House, the price of American protection skyrocketed. On a campaign rally in Wisconsin in 2016, Candidate Trump said, "Nobody's going to mess with Saudi Arabia because we're watching them. They're not paying us a fair price. We're losing our shirt."[21] The Saudi King reacted quickly to the new language. President Trump's visit to Saudi Arabia on May 20, 2017 yielded $500 billion in business contracts. Almost a year later, Mr. Trump, clearly addressing Saudi Arabia and the rest of GCC member states during a White House press conference with French President Emmanuel Macron on April 24, 2018, said: "Countries that are in the area … would not be there except for the United States … They wouldn't last a week. We are protecting them."[22]

[20]The first rebellion was in 1805, when Mohammad Bin Saud allied himself with Mohammad Bin Abdulwahhab, the pioneer of Wahhabi doctrine. The two men charged the Istanbul sultans with corrupting the true tenets of Islam. The first rebellion was unsuccessful. Mohammad Ali, Egypt's ruler, acting on behalf of the Ottoman Sultan, Mahmoud II (July 1785–July 1839) crushed the Saud/Abdulwahhab rebellion in 1817.

[21]Stephen Adler, Jeff Mason and Steve Holland, "Exclusive: Trump complains Saudis not paying fair share for US defense," *Reuters*, (April 28, 2017). http://www.reuters.com/article/us-usa-trump-mideast-exclusive-idUSKBN17U08A?il=0

[22]Steven Nelson, "Trump: 'Immensely wealthy' Arab countries 'wouldn't last a week' without US support," *Washington Examiner*, (April 24, 2018). https://www.washingtonexaminer.com/news/white-house/trump-immensely-wealthy-arab-countries-wouldnt-last-a-week-without-us-support

2. Until 2003, the US maintained a large air force presence at the Prince Sultan air base outside Riyadh. In a cosmetic move, it relocated to the nearby al-Udeid Air Base in Qatar. The move was intended to "purify" the land of the two holy mosques from the military presence of "infidels" to calm bin Laden's followers. Al-Udeid is a few minutes flying time away from Saudi Arabia's Eastern Province where the world's richest oil fields are located. With around 10,000 US troops, al-Udeid Air Base is the largest US base in the Middle East.[23]

   Additionally, Bahrain is home to the US Fifth Fleet, hosting approximately 7,000 Navy personnel.[24] Its Khalifa bin Salman deep-water port can accommodate aircraft carriers.[25] Out of Sheikh Isa Air Base, the US Air Force operates F-16s, F-18s, and P-3 surveillance aircraft.[26]

   In Kuwait, the US has 15,000 troops in two air force bases[27] and seven camps scattered around this small country.[28]

   In the UAE, there are about 3,500 US military personnel stationed at Dhafra, and it is the only overseas base with F-22s.[29]

   US forces in Bahrain, Kuwait, Qatar, and UAE protect not only the oil installations and the regimes of the four tiny states, but, of course, the world's richest oil fields in Saudi Arabia's Eastern Province and the al-Saud regime. Further, these forces ensure the uninterrupted shipping of around 17 million barrels of oil per day through the narrow Strait of Hormuz. And, in case of war, the US armada will be able to control oil exports from Iran and Iraq as well.

3. While all other countries maintain a single diplomatic presence in Riyadh, the US has always maintained large diplomatic presence in Riyadh, Jeddah, and Dhahran. With eyes and ears to the ground, American diplomats must have heard for years, anti-democracy

---

[23]GlobalSecurity.Org, "Al Udeid Air Base, Qatar". http://www.globalsecurity.org/military/facility/udeid.htm

[24]Ibid.

[25]Ibid.

[26]Ibid.

[27]The Heritage Foundation, "2015 Index of US Military Strength, Assessing the Global Operating Environment, Middle East." http://index.heritage.org/military/2015/chapter/op-environment/middle-east/

[28]Military Bases.com. "Kuwait." https://militarybases.com/kuwait/

[29]Rajiv Chandrasekaran, "In the UAE, the United States Has a Quiet, Potent Ally Nicknamed 'Little Sparta,'" *The Washington Post*, (November 9, 2014). https://www.washingtonpost.com/world/national-security/in-the-uae-the-united-states-has-a-quiet-potent-ally-nicknamed-little-sparta/2014/11/08/3fc6a50c-643a-11e4-836e-83bc4f26eb67_story.html?utm_term=.1e23ef7eb539

preaching, hate-the-other teaching, and jihad glorification from blaring mosque loudspeakers and from radio and television.

4. US protection of the al-Sauds is also aided by various former senior Washington administration officials, captains of industry, media moguls, and professional lobbyists who act for the Saudi government, ruling family members, and private sector in return for hefty fees as lawyers, advisors, consultants, investment managers, business partners, etc. Furthermore, millions of dollars in Saudi contributions and endowments to leading US and Western universities and think tanks have silenced many professors, researchers, journalists, and politicians. Money turned others into active apologists or propagandists for the regime. The London *Independent* newspaper on March 12, 2016 stated that, "Arab oil states spread their power by many means in addition to religious proselytism, including the simple purchase of people and institutions which they see as influential. Academic institutions of previously high repute in Washington have shown themselves to be as shamelessly greedy for subsidies from the Gulf and elsewhere as predatory warlords and corrupt leaders in Iraq, Syria, Lebanon and beyond."[30]

In the interview Mr. Obama gave for the April 2016 issue of the *Atlantic* magazine, Jeffrey Goldberg wrote how an administration official describes Arab lobbying activities in Washington D.C. and how the media spreads views from "experts" on the pay of lobbyists: "One administration official refers to Massachusetts Avenue, the home of many think tanks, as 'Arab-occupied territory.' Television and newspapers happily quote supposed experts from such think tanks as if they were non-partisan academics of unblemished objectivity."[31]

5. Notwithstanding that Saudi Arabia was designated by the US State Department since 2004 as a Country of Particular Concern for its severe violations of religious freedoms, the US Secretary of State has waived the sanction that comes with such designation due to the important national interest of the US:

[30]Patrick Cockburn, "How Barack Obama turned his back on Saudi Arabia and its Sunni allies," *The Independent*, (March 12, 2016). http://www.independent.co.uk/news/world/middle-east/barack-obama-saudi-arabia-us-foreign-policy-syria-jihadism-isis-a6927646.html

[31]Goldberg, "The Obama Doctrine."

Since 2004, Saudi Arabia has been designated as a "Country of Particular Concern" (CPC) under the International Religious Freedom Act of 1998 for having engaged in or tolerated particularly severe violations of religious freedom. Most recently, on February 29, 2016, the Secretary of State re-designated Saudi Arabia as a CPC, and announced a waiver of the sanction that accompany designation as required in the important national interest of the United States pursuant to section 407 of the Act.[32]

When Might US Protection of the Al-Saud Regime End? Governments, investors, lenders, and workers in oil, gas, coal, car, and fossil fuel using power plants stand in the way of sustainable energy. They have been leading a fierce and effective crusade to discredit climate science and the scientists who attribute global warming to human expansion of the greenhouse effect. They have been lobbying politicians, especially in the US, to delay and water down, even repeal environmental protection laws, while propagating an image of themselves as being green and committed to renewable energy.

ExxonMobil, the world's biggest oil company, knew as early as 1981 of climate change—seven years before it became a public issue. However, the firm spent millions over the next 27 years to promote climate denial.[33] In Europe, topping the list of firms obstructing climate action is British Petroleum,[34] notwithstanding the very green logo, which it designed in 2000 to propagate a positive environmental image.[35] Also, Russia, a major oil and gas producer and exporter, has a vested interest in prolonging the life of oil and gas.

Despite environmentalists' campaigns against the use of fossil fuel and the successes in developing sustainable electricity generation from solar and wind technologies, global demand for oil between 1980 and 2015

[32]US Department of State, "International Religious Freedom Report for 2015, Saudi Arabia."

[33]Suzanne Goldenberg, "Exxon Knew of Climate Change in 1981, Email Says—But It Funded Deniers for 27 More Years," *The Guardian*, (July 8, 2015). https://www.theguardian.com/environment/2015/jul/08/exxon-climate-change-1981-climate-denier-funding

[34]"BP tops the list of firms obstructing climate action in Europe," *The Guardian*, (September 21, 2015). https://www.theguardian.com/environment/2015/sep/21/bp-tops-the-list-of-firms-obstructing-climate-action-in-europe

[35]"BP goes green," *BBC*, (July 24, 2000). http://news.bbc.co.uk/1/hi/business/849475.stm

increased by 56% from 61 million barrels per day to 95 million barrels per day.[36]

Multiple decades will elapse before renewable energy is allowed to replace oil. Saudi Arabia's Minister of Energy, said on October 24, 2017, "Energy demand is expected to rise by about 45% by the year 2050 ... [renewables] will only account for about 10% of the primary energy demand, and this is despite a very rapid growth rate... Petroleum, natural gas, and coal will continue to account for about 75% of the supply of energy by 2050.[37]

British Petroleum estimated in 2014 that based on global reserves of 1,688 billion barrels, the earth has enough oil left for about 53 more years at current production levels, but significantly more than that if new discoveries are made or drilling technologies improved.[38]

President Trump's Assault on Environmental Regulations: President Trump rolled back 23 environmental rules in his first 100 days in office.[39] The Trump administration issued its notification that the US intends to withdraw from the 2015 Paris Climate Agreement on August 4, 2017.[40] America is the only country in the world outside the Paris landmark agreement, while 197 countries are in support of the Agreement.[41] In the middle of 2017, the US Interior Secretary directed the Bureau of Land Management to ramp up sales of oil and gas leases on federal land in order to increase oil production on federal lands.[42] In a sign of what's to come, "Trump Digs Coal" placards are a common sight in Trump's rallies in America's coal states.

---

[36]YCHARTS, "World Oil Consumption Historical Data." https://ycharts.com/indicators/world_oil_consumption

[37]Anmar Frangoul, "Saudi Minister Says Global Energy Demand Expected to Jump 45% by 2050," *CNBC*, (October 25, 2017). https://www.cnbc.com/2017/10/24/saudi-minister-says-global-energy-demand-expected-to-jump-45-percent-by-2050.html

[38]McQueeney, "How Much Oil Is Left," *Zacks*, (December 27, 2017). https://www.zacks.com/stock/news/287141/how-much-oil-is-left-in-the-earth

[39]Nadja Popovich and Tatiana Schlossberg, "23 Environmental Rules Rolled Back in Trump's First 100 Days," *The New York Times*, (May 2, 2017). https://www.nytimes.com/interactive/2017/05/02/climate/environmental-rules-reversed-trump-100-days.html

[40]"US Notifies UN of Paris Climate Deal Pullout," *BBC*, (August 5, 2017). http://www.bbc.co.uk/news/world-us-canada-40829987

[41]Fiona Harvey, "Syria Signs Paris Climate Agreement and Leaves US Isolated," *The Guardian*, November 7, 2017. https://www.theguardian.com/environment/2017/nov/07/syria-signs-paris-climate-agreement-and-leaves-us-isolated

[42]Jim Lyons, "The Rush to Develop Oil and Gas We Don't Need," *The New York Times*, (August 28, 2017). https://www.nytimes.com/2017/08/28/opinion/trump-oil-public-lands.html?em_pos=small&emc=edit_ty_20170828&nl=opinion-today&nl_art=4&nlid=18135507&ref=headline&te=1

Resistance to Losing Trillions of Dollars Invested in the Oil and Related Industries: Investors, lenders, and politicians lead the war against sustainable energy. The oil, gas, car, fossil fuel power plants, and the myriad of supporting industries carry on their balance sheets trillions of dollars in equities, bonds, and bank loans.

According to the Bank for International Settlements, the oil industry had bonds outstanding in 2014 in the amount of $1.4 trillion and $1.6 trillion in syndicated loans, (excluding account repayments or loans that were never drawn).[43] Both numbers are likely to have increased since 2014, in part due to the boom in shale oil and gas extraction in the US.[44] As for equities, the world's top ten oil and gas companies are estimated to have had a combined equity of $2 trillion in 2015,[45] making the aggregate financial exposure of banks and investors to the oil and gas industry alone $5 trillion.[46]

To put the figure of $5 trillion in perspective, if the write-off period is 10 years, banks and investors must write-off $500 billion per year. If the period is 20 years, the annual write-off amount becomes $250 billion. If the period is 50 years, the annual write-off would still be a huge $100 billion. Additionally, it is necessary to add the bonds, loans, and equities extended to the hundreds of medium and small size oil and gas companies, and the independent oilfield and drilling service companies, pipeline companies, crude oil and product tankers companies, refining companies and the estimated 400,000 independent gasoline stations worldwide. When these are accounted for, the total would likely double, at least.

Sustainable energy will impact the auto industry's combustion engine and the thousands of fossil fuel burning electricity-generating plants. The combined financial impact on the oil and gas and auto industries and fossil fuel using power plants might reach $20 trillion, a gigantic exposure, well beyond the capital and reserves of exposed banks and investors, if the changeover is conducted too quickly. Further, the cost of building new green energy power plants and training millions of workers to replace the

---

[43]Phillip Inman and Rob Davies, "The Five Fears Stalking the Global Banking Industry," *The Guardian*, (February 10, 2016). https://www.theguardian.com/business/2016/feb/10/banking-shares-under-pressure-as-investors-fear-effects-of-global-downturn

[44]Ibid.

[45]Investopedia, "World's Top 10 Oil Companies," (January 7, 2015). http://www.investopedia.com/articles/personal-finance/010715/worlds-top-10-oil-companies.asp

[46]Syndicated loans (not all loans) of $1.6 trillion + bonds of $1.4 trillion + equities of $2 trillion = $5 trillion.

polluting technologies should be added to the estimated $20 trillion in fossil fuel and related industries' balance sheets.

The Hope: The expected demand for oil is not only a function of its physical availability. It is also a function of the speed through which the world's technologically advanced and big oil importing countries such as, China, continental Europe, India, and Japan would replace their importation of oil by sustainable sources of energy. Aside from environmental benefits, independence from US control over the oil imports of these countries must rank high on their national security priorities.

Potentially, fusion power could provide the world with limitless clean energy. The new technology could become a reality by December 2025,[47] with fusion plants coming on line as early as 2040. The European Union, China, India, Japan, Korea, Russia and the U.S. are contributing to International Thermonuclear Experimental Reactor (Iter), a £16-billion project, under construction at Saint-Paul-les-Durance in southern France.[48]

As the title to this book asserts, sustainable energy is a sharp weapon in the fight against Wahhabi terror. It is only when oil imports by US rivals is replaced by sustainable sources that Washington's protection of the Saudi regime will end, the al-Sauds' cash will dwindle, Wahhabi indoctrination and proselytization will falter, and Wahhabi terror will be defeated.

Should China, continental Europe, India, and Japan be successful in ending their importation of oil, they would have added to world peace a greater contribution than all the raids on terrorists' hideouts by the world's armies and air forces. The new technologies would also provide huge export revenues to the manufacturers of the new equipment.

Obama's Middle East Politics—The *Atlantic* Magazine Interview

There are a number of possible motives behind Mr. Obama's empowerment of Iran. The interview he gave to Jeffrey Goldberg for the April 2016 issue of the *Atlantic* magazine, nine months before leaving the White House shows one such motive. In the lengthy interview, Obama expressed

---

[47]John Von Radowitz, "Fusion power plants could provide energy for homes in just 20 years," *The Independent*, (December 30, 2017), http://www.independent.co.uk/news/world/fusion-power-plants-provide-energy-uk-homes-20-years-reactor-sun-iter-a8134946.html

[48]Ibid.

a jaundiced view of Sunni Arabs in general and outright hostility toward Saudi Arabia in particular. Goldberg wrote of Obama:

"He broke with what he calls, derisively 'the Washington playbook.' He has also questioned, often harshly, the role that America's Sunni Arab allies play in fomenting anti-American terrorism. He is clearly irritated that foreign policy orthodoxy compels him to treat Saudi Arabia as an ally.[49] In referring to Indonesia where he spent part of his childhood:

> In a meeting during APEC with Malcolm Turnbull, the new prime minister of Australia, Obama described how he has watched Indonesia gradually move from a relaxed, syncretistic Islam to a more fundamentalist, unforgiving interpretation; large numbers of Indonesian women, he observed, have now adopted the hijab, the Muslim head covering.
>
> Why, Turnbull asked, was this happening?
>
> Because, Obama answered, the Saudis and other Gulf Arabs have funneled money, and large numbers of imams and teachers, into the country. In the 1990s, the Saudis heavily funded Wahhabist madrassas, seminaries that teach the fundamentalist version of Islam favored by the Saudi ruling family, Obama told Turnbull. Today, Islam in Indonesia is much more Arab in orientation than it was when he lived there, he said.[50]

On the 9/11 terror attacks on New York and Washington D. C., Goldberg revealed:

> In the White House these days, one occasionally hears Obama's National Security Council officials pointedly reminding visitors that the large majority of 9/11 hijackers were not Iranian, but Saudi.[51]

On Saudi treatment of women:

> Obama himself rails against Saudi Arabia's state-sanctioned misogyny, arguing in private that "a country cannot function in the

---

[49]Goldberg, "The Obama Doctrine."
[50]Ibid.
[51]Ibid.

modern world when it is repressing half of its population." In meetings with foreign leaders, Obama has said, "You can gauge the success of a society by how it treats its women.[52]

On relations between Saudi Arabia and Iran:

> Saudis need to "share" the Middle East with their Iranian foes. "The competition between the Saudis and the Iranians—which has helped to feed proxy wars and chaos in Syria and Iraq and Yemen—requires us to say to our friends as well as to the Iranians that they need to find an effective way to share the neighborhood and institute some sort of cold peace.[53]

Additionally, two statements from Mr. Obama's speech at Cairo University on June 4, 2009 provide a helpful background to his ideas in the *Atlantic* magazine interview. In a conciliatory statement on Washington's future relations with Iran, Obama said:

> Rather than remain trapped in the past, I've made it clear to Iran's leaders and people that my country is prepared to move forward. The question now is not what Iran is against but, rather, what future it wants to build.[54]

Obama's patience with Saudi Arabia has always been limited. In his first foreign-policy commentary of note, that 2002 speech in Chicago, he said:

> Let's fight to make sure our so-called allies in the Middle East—the Saudis and the Egyptians—stop oppressing their own people, and suppressing dissent, and tolerating corruption and inequality.[55]

Mr. Obama's statements reveal hostility toward Saudi Arabia. The statements suggest that Obama's empowerment of Iran could have been a strategy to punish Saudi Arabia for culpability for 9/11, for manipulating

---

[52]Ibid.
[53]Ibid.
[54]"Barack Obama's Speech" *The Telegraph*.
[55]Goldberg, "The Obama Doctrine," *The Atlantic*, (April 2016 Issue).

the Washington Playbook, radicalizing Indonesia's Islam, state-sponsored misogyny, suppressing dissent, and tolerating corruption and inequality.

Obama's Three Strategies that Empowered Iran

Obama pursued three strategies that benefited Iran and ruined Iraq and Syria.

The First Strategy—Midwifing the Joint Comprehensive Plan of Action (JCPOA): In a sudden departure from previous US policy, the Obama administration announced on April 8, 2009, that the US would participate fully in the P5+1 talks with Iran.[56] In 1992, the US Congress had passed, the *Iran-Iraq Arms Nonproliferation Act of 1992.* The Act prohibited the transfer of technology that might contribute to Iran's proliferation of advanced weapons.[57] For seventeen years after the enactment of the law, successive US administrations required Iran to meet United Nations demands to suspend all enrichment and reprocessing related activities before Washington would negotiate incentives to halt Iran's nuclear program.

On July 14, 2015, negotiations between the P5+1 and Tehran were successfully concluded.[58] In return for a delay in its nuclear program for 15 years, Iran gained access to some $100 billion in frozen assets and became able to export oil, after forfeiting more than $160 billion in oil revenue since 2012 as a result of the sanctions.[59] Lifting economic sanctions on Iran shifted the balance of power in the Muslim Middle East in favour of Iran. It energized the Shi'ite Crescent and the March of Shi'ism.

In Obama's eagerness to smooth the negotiations toward the JCPOA, the White House derailed a law enforcement effort targeting the billion-dollar narcoterrorism enterprise run by Iran's surrogate, Hezbollah, even as the terror organization was funneling cocaine into the United States.[60]

---

[56]Arms Control Association, "Timeline of Nuclear Diplomacy with Iran." https://www.armscontrol.org/factsheet/Timeline-of-Nuclear-Diplomacy-With-Iran

[57]US Department of State, "Iran-Iraq Arms Nonproliferation Act of 1992," https://www.state.gov/t/isn/c15237.htm

[58]US Department of State," Joint Comprehensive Plan of Action." https://www.state.gov/e/eb/tfs/spi/iran/jcpoa/

[59]"Iran Nuclear Deal: Key Details," *BBC,* (January 16, 2016). http://www.bbc.co.uk/news/world-middle-east-33521655

[60]Josh Meyer, "The secret backstory of how Obama let Hezbollah off the hook," *Politico,* (December 18, 2017). https://www.politico.com/interactives/2017/obama-hezbollah-drug-trafficking-investigation/

The campaign was launched in 2008 after the Drug Enforcement Administration (DEA) amassed evidence that Hezbollah had become a crime syndicate dealing in drugs, weapon-trafficking, and money laundering.[61]

For eight years, American law enforcement followed Hezbollah's "cocaine shipments and tracked a river of dirty cash" from Latin America to the United States, West Africa, Europe, and the Middle East.[62] But, according to interviews with dozens of participants who in many cases spoke for the first time about events shrouded in secrecy, and a review of government documents and court records by a *Politico* magazine investigation published on December 18, 2017, Obama administration officials threw an increasingly insurmountable series of roadblocks in its way.[63] When project leaders sought approval for some significant investigations, prosecutions, arrests, and financial sanctions, officials at the Justice and Treasury Departments delayed, hindered or rejected their requests.[64]

Obama "really, really, really" wanted the nuclear agreement with Iran, a former CIA officer told *Politico*, and an Obama-era Treasury official, Katherine Bauer, in written testimony to the House Committee on Foreign Affairs, acknowledged that "under the Obama administration .... [Hezbollah-related] investigations were tamped down for fear of rocking the boat with Iran and jeopardizing the nuclear deal."[65]

Obama's eagerness for a successful JCPOA agreement may be gauged from the way the US transferred $1.7 billion to Iran. In the age of electronic money movement, the White House chose to transfer this huge amount in the form of banknotes. In January and February 2016, three planes, on three different dates, were used. The first planeload transferred $400 million, and the other two transferred another $1.3 billion.[66] The cash was first flown to Switzerland aboard an unmarked chartered aircraft, and then converted into Euros, Swiss Francs and other currencies. An Iranian transport aircraft flew the cash to Iran in January and February 2016 in three shipments. The first aircraft arrived in Tehran on Jan. 16, 2016,

---

[61]Ibid.
[62]Ibid.
[63]Ibid.
[64]Ibid.
[65]Ibid.
[66]Jay Solomon and Carol E. Lee, "U.S. Transferred $1.3 Billion More in Cash to Iran After Initial Payment," *The Wall Street Journal,* (September 6, 2016). https://www.wsj.com/articles/u-s-sent-two-more-planeloads-of-cash-to-iran-after-initial-payment-1473208256

with $400 million piled on wooden pallets.[67] Two other aircraft shipments of cash were sent on January 22, 2016, and February 5, 2016, totaling $1.3 billion.[68]

The transfer of $1.7 billion in cash, not through an electronic bank transfer, is odd. Obama's experts at the White House and Treasury Department should have suspected that the banknotes would be used to pay Iran's militias in Iraq, Syria, and Yemen. Indeed, in the two years since the cash was transferred, the US government traced some of the $1.7 billion to Hezbollah in Lebanon and Houthi rebels in Yemen.[69] White House officials were either gullible, or wanted to help Iran circumvent UN sanctions on Hezbollah's nefarious operations.

What Might Have Driven Obama to Embrace the JCPOA? Obama's keen interest in the nuclear deal might have been driven by his eagerness to produce some success as a legacy for his 44th presidency, given his lack of achievements domestically and internationally. The Noble Peace Prize he received in 2009 might have added to the pressure on him to justify the honor.[70]

The Second Strategy that Empowered Iran—Obama's Support of the Pro-Iran Sectarian Prime Minister of Iraq, Nouri al-Maliki (2006–2014). Maliki is a divisive, anti-Sunni, Iranian surrogate. Obama's indifference toward Maliki's maltreatment of Iraq's Sunnis engendered a deeper schism among Shi'ites and Sunnis than ever before in Iraq. For six years during Obama's eight-year presidency, Maliki committed gross acts of discrimination and violence against Iraq's Sunnis, while Obama looked the other way. US senators and American diplomats in Baghdad warned Obama about the danger to America's interest in Iraq and the region from his embrace of Maliki, but to no avail (see Chapter Seven: *Da'wa Party – Nouri al-Maliki*).[71]

Obama's decision to withdraw the last US soldier from Iraq at the end of 2011, left the door open to Iran to fill the gap left by the departing

---

[67]Bill Gertz, "Obama-era cash traced to Iran-backed terrorists," *The Washington Times*, (February 7, 2018). https://www.washingtontimes.com/news/2018/feb/7/inside-the-ring-obama-era-cash-traced-to-iran-back/

[68]Ibid.

[69]Ibid.

[70]"Nobel Secretary Regrets Obama Peace Prize," *BBC*, (September 17, 2015). http://www.bbc.co.uk/news/world-europe-34277960

[71]Peter Beinart, "Obama's Disastrous Iraq Policy: An Autopsy," *The Atlantic*, (July 23, 2014).

Americans. It allowed Maliki a free hand to further marginalize and abuse Iraq's Sunnis.

Nouri al-Maliki's pro-Iran credentials were well known. It is inconceivable that White House was ignorant of Iran's desire and capacity to fill the vacuum US' withdrawal would create. That US troops were withdrawn because Maliki rejected American demands for a Status of Forces agreement to shield US troops in Iraq from prosecution or lawsuits is a politically convenient excuse.[72] Maliki's insistence on rejecting the Status of Forces agreement was designed to hand Iran control of the Baghdad government under his stewardship. Indeed, if Obama refused to withdraw, what could Maliki and the Qom ayatollahs have done? Obama, Maliki, and Iran share the responsibility for the emergence of the so-called Islamic State.

Obama's premature withdrawal from Iraq and his keen interest in the success of the P5+1 negotiations with Iran energized the Qom ayatollahs. They acted as if Washington has given them the green light to encroach upon their Sunni neighbours. The destruction of much of Syria followed.

Obama's Third Strategy that Empowered Iran—Handing Syria to Iran: For six years, Obama not only refused to supply defensive anti-aircraft guns to Syria's anti-Assad forces, but also prevented other countries from supplying such weapons. He refused to punish the Assad regime for its use of chemical weapons on August 21, 2013 in Eastern Ghouta near Damascus, where 1,400 people were killed, repudiating his own infamous "red line."[73]

Syria was not going to be allowed to derail Obama's nuclear deal. Nor was Iran going to allow Obama to attack Assad, even if that meant walking away from the nuclear deal. Reportedly, Obama declined to enforce the red-line after Iran threatened to back out of the nuclear deal if Assad's forces were bombed.[74] According to *Wall Street Journal* reporter Jay Solomon, "When the president announced his plans to attack [the Assad regime] and then pulled back, it was exactly the period in time when American negotiators were meeting with Iranian negotiators secretly in

---

[72]Lara Jakes and Rebecca Santana, "Iraq Prime Minister: Immunity Issue Scuttled US Troop Deal," *The Washington Times*, (October 22, 2011).

[73]"Syria Chemical Attack: What We Know", *BBC*, (September 24, 2013). http://www.bbc.co.uk/news/world-middle-east-23927399

[74]Pamela Engel, "Obama reportedly declined to enforce red line in Syria," *Business Insider UK*.

Oman to get the nuclear agreement."[75] The timing of Obama's pull back is curious. On August 31, 2013, the US military strike against Syria for the chemical attack was unexpectedly put on hold, when Mr. Obama decided to first seek the approval of Congress. This approval never came.[76] Two days earlier, on August 29, 2013, Ed Miliband, leader of the Labor Party in the UK, scuttled a vote in parliament to bomb Assad's forces for the chemical attack.[77] Were the two events coordinated?

Risks Obama Ignored: In empowering Iran, Mr. Obama opened the gates of hell wider than ever before in the Muslim Middle East. He ignored the realities and fundamental religious, political, and historical facts of the Middle East and Islam. As a student of history, the son of a father who "came from a Kenyan family that includes generations of Muslims,"[78] Mr. Obama should have known that there was no realistic possibility of "sharing" the Middle East between an Iran ruled by extreme Shi'ite clerics and a Saudi Arabia ruled by an equally extreme Sunni Wahhabi regime. The theological plus ethnic differences are too wide and the long history of war that separates Shi'ite Persians from Arab Sunnis is deeply ingrained in their collective memories.

The so-called Islamic State in Iraq and Syria was created by the Systemic marginalization of Iraq's minority Sunnis by the Iran-controlled Shi'ite government in Baghdad during the eight-year reign of Prime Minister Nouri al-Maliki (2006–2014) and by Assad's 10% Alawite regime against most of Syria's 75% Sunni population since 1963.

Outcomes of Obama's Iran Policies: When Obama wrote his own version of the Washington Playbook, he set the stage for the restoration of relations with Iran after 38 years of estrangement since Ayatollah Khomeini deposed the Shah of Iran in 1979 and held 52 US diplomats and citizens as hostages for 444 days (November 4, 1979–January 20, 1981). In his rehabilitation of Iran, Mr. Obama's new playbook upended US strategy in the Middle East. His actions were a win for the United States:

[75]Ibid.

[76]Pau Lewis, "US attack on Syria delayed after surprise U-turn from Obama," *The Guardian*, (September 1, 2013). https://www.theguardian.com/world/2013/aug/31/syrian-air-strikes-obama-congress

[77]Nicholas Watt and Nick Hopkins, "Cameron forced to rule out British attack on Syria after MPs reject motion," *The Guardian*, (August 29, 2013). https://www.theguardian.com/world/2013/aug/29/cameron-british-attack-syria-mps

[78]"Barack Obama's Speech" *The Telegraph*.

a) It preoccupied Shi'ites and Sunni in wars thousands of miles away from the US in Iraq, Syria, and Yemen.

b) The confrontation with Iran left Riyadh with no option but to purchase more US weapons. The Obama administration sold Riyadh $112 billion in weapons and another $110 billion package was under negotiation before the Trump administration took office, which materialized when President Trump visited Riyadh on May 20, 2017.[79]

c) Saudi fear of the Shi'ite Crescent paved the way to seeking good relations with Israel. It is an open secret that senior officials from Saudi Arabia meet with Israeli officials in Israel and outside the Middle East with the aim of establishing cooperative relations.[80]

d) By lifting crippling economic sanctions on Iran, Obama opened Iran's markets to US companies, a market of eighty million consumers. Boeing agreed in December 2016 to sell 80 aircraft to IranAir while Obama was in office.[81] Since President Trump took office, Iran's Aseman Airlines announced on June 10, 2017 that it has signed an agreement to buy 30 Boeing-737 jets in Iran's first contract with an American company.[82]

The Snubbing of Obama in Riyadh: On January 20, 2017, when Obama left the White House, he left behind a Muslim Middle East on fire. He had dealt a severe blow to Arab Sunnis, brought them monumental losses and suffering, added gasoline to the fires of Sunni/Shi'ite wars that were started by G.W. Bush, and made the soil more fertile for big jihadist recruitment.

The *Atlantic* magazine's interview was a humiliating public rebuke of Saudi governance and values from top to bottom. It was the last straw that broke the Saudi back.[83] Despite their desperate need for US

---

[79]Bruce Riedel, "The $110 Billion Arms Deal to Saudi Arabia is Fake News," *Brookings*, (June 5, 2017). https://www.brookings.edu/blog/markaz/2017/06/05/the-110-billion-arms-deal-to-saudi-arabia-is-fake-news/

[80]Yoel Guzansky and Clive Jones, "Why Are Israelis and the Saudis Cozying Up?," *Newsweek*, (MAY 18, 2017). http://www.newsweek.com/why-are-israelis-and-saudis-cosying-611551

[81]"Iran Says It Sealed Boeing Plane Deal at Half Price," *Reuters*, (December 25, 2016). http://www.reuters.com/article/us-iran-boeing-discount-idUSKBN14E0AC

[82]"Iran's Aseman Signs Final Deal for 30 Boeing 737s: IRNA," *Reuters*, (June 10, 2017). https://www.reuters.com/article/us-iran-aseman-boeing-idUSKBN1910HT

[83]On March 10, 2016, the Atlantic published a summary of the forthcoming interview for the April issue; so when Obama visited Riyadh on April 20, 2017, Saudi officials must have known its contents.

protection, the King decided to say his farewell to a hostile president Obama, who was on his way out of the White House, with the biggest insult he knew how, in the hope that the next president would reverse course.

Obama was not welcomed at the airport by King Salman, as protocol provides, and not even by the foreign minister, but by a lowly governor of Riyadh, on his visit to Riyadh on April 20, 2016. The King snubbed the US president despite the fact that on the same day, Saudi state television showed King Salman personally greeting officials from Gulf States at the airport.[84] In terms of Arab culture, un-graciousness towards a guest is the ultimate insult.[85]

The RAND Corporation Report of 2008

Actions by the Bush and Obama administrations are consistent with rec-ommendations made in a RAND Corporation report funded by the US Army in 2008, titled, *Unfolding the Future of the Long War*.[86] The report sets the stage by outlining the risks facing an industrialized world dependent on oil from GCC lands, dominated by Wahhabi extremists, "The econo-mies of the industrialized states will continue to rely heavily on oil ... The geographic area of proven oil reserves coincides with the power base of much of the Salafi-Jihadist network ....The use of alternative fuel sources and increased efficiency of use ... will not remove (and may not even reduce) it in the short or medium term."

The Report identified seven strategy options for the United States to pursue in order to protect its access to Gulf oil, but the first one is noteworthy:

---

[84]Andrew Buncombe, "Barack Obama Gets Diplomatic Snub as Saudi Arabia Shows Its Anger over 9/11 Bill," *The Independent*, (April 20, 2016). http://www.independent.co.uk/news/world/middle-east/barack-obama-gets-diplomatic-snub-as-saudi-arabia-shows-its-anger-over-911-bill-a6993171.html

[85]The Arabic proverb: Oh friend, if you visit with us, you will find us to be the guests and you being the host.

[86]Christopher G. Pernin, Brian Nichiporuk, Dale Stahl, Justin Beck, and Ricky Radaelli-Sanchez, "Unfolding the Future of the Long War—Motivations, Prospects, and Implications for the US Army," (RAND Corporation, 2008), PP. 171–172. https://www.rand.org/content/dam/rand/pubs/monographs/2008/RAND_MG738.pdf

Divide and Rule

A strategy that focuses on exploiting fault lines between the various Salafi-Jihadist groups to turn them against each other. This strategy would rely heavily on covert action, information operations, unconventional warfare, and support to indigenous security forces.

US leaders could also choose to capitalize on the "Sustained Shia-Sunni Conflict" trajectory by taking the side of the conservative Sunni regimes against Shiite empowerment movements in the Muslim world.

It is very likely that al-Qaeda might focus its efforts on targeting Iranian interests throughout the Middle East and Persian Gulf while simultaneously cutting back on anti-American and anti-Western operations. [87]

The birth of the so-called Islamic State and its war with al-Qaeda is consistent with the *Divide and Rule* recommendation.:

- October 2004: Abu Mus'ab al-Zarqawi's Tawhid and Jihad terror organization pledges allegiance to Bin Laden's al-Qaeda. It becomes known as al-Qaeda in Iraq (AQI).
- October 2006: AQI merges with a smaller Sunni group in Iraq to form Islamic State of Iraq (ISI).
- April 2013: ISI claims al-Nusra in Syria to be a part of Islamic State in Iraq and al-Sham (ISIS).
- February 2014: al-Qaeda and al-Nusra reject ISI claim, insisting that al-Nusra is a part of al-Qaeda, not ISIS. Al-Qaeda and al-Nusra abandon ISIS.
- June 2014: The so-called Islamic State (IS) was born. Al-Qaeda and al-Nusra are at war with IS.

The Trump Administration's Likely Politics in the Muslim Middle East

Previous US administrations played the "Washington Playbook" not for the love of Saudi Arabia's corrupt absolute monarchy, nor for the Wahhabi cult, or for state-sponsored misogyny or proselytizing the Wahhabi creed

---

[87]RAND Corporation, "Unfolding the Future of the Long War," pages XVI, 85–86 and 96–102.

worldwide. Rather, it was played to add oil to the two other non-lethal weapons of mass destruction in America's arsenal; namely, dominance over global food exports and trade and dominance of the US Dollar as the main reserve currency for world central banks.

The Red Carpet for Donald Trump in Riyadh: In contrast with the snub to Obama, King Salman accorded Mr. and Mrs. Trump lavish hospitality and splendid pomp and circumstance, such as had never before been presented to a visiting dignitary. He welcomed them at the foot of Air Force One upon their arrival to Riyadh on May 20, 2017 for a three-day visit. The King accompanied his guests for the duration of the visit. He organized meetings with all GCC leaders and an address to the Arab-Islamic-American summit, attended by the leaders of more than 50 Muslim countries. The King organized the signing of contracts worth $500-billion in military hardware and civilian projects over the next ten years, $110 billion in weapon contracts, increasing to $300 billion in ten years,[88] and $200 billion in non-military contracts.[89]

Saudi Arabia was President Trump's first stop on his first overseas trip as president. The scheduling of the trip underscores the new administration's strategy to place Riyadh at the top of its relationships in the Arab and Muslim world.[90] Mr. Trump claimed credit for Saudi Arabia's political shakeup which took place a month later and resulted on June 20, 2017 in the removal from office of Crown Prince, Muhammad bin Nayef bin Adbulaziz,[91] and the naming of his 30-year old son, Muhammad, to the position of crown prince on June 21, 2017, "We've put our man on top," Trump is said to have claimed to friends.[92]

Mr. Trump reduces complex multifaceted long-term balanced relationships with other countries into a balance of payment surplus for the United States. Saudi Arabia is no exception. Increased threats from Iran, thanks

---

[88]Steve Holland, "US nears $100 billion arms deal for Saudi Arabia."

[89]"US, Saudi Firms Sign Tens of Billions of Dollars of Deals as Trump Visits," *CNBC.*

[90]Ali Vitali and Saphora Smith, "Donald Trump Lands in Saudi Arabia on First Overseas Visit of Presidency," *NBC News*, (May 20, 2017). https://www.nbcnews.com/storyline/trump-s-first-foreign-trip/donald-trump-lands-saudi-arabia-first-overseas-visit-presidency-n762126

[91]"Addiction and intrigue—Inside the Saudi palace coup," *Reuters*, (July 19, 2017). https://uk.reuters.com/article/uk-saudi-palace-coup/addiction-and-intrigue-inside-the-saudi-palace-coup-idUKKBN1A41IR

[92]According to a book by Michael Wolff, titled *Fire and Fury: Inside the Trump White House*. "'We put our man on top', Trump said on MBS, book claims," *Al Jazeera* (January 6, 2018). http://www.aljazeera.com/news/2018/01/put-man-top-trump-mbs-book-claims-180105124054629.html

to G.W. Bush and Obama, allow Donald Trump to raise the premium the Saudi King must pay for US protection. He declared on April 27, 2017, that "Saudi Arabia has not treated us fairly, because we are losing a tremendous amount of money in defending Saudi Arabia."[93] The message to Riyadh was clear. Three weeks later, King Salman obliged. He performed an act of pre-emptive surrender.

Mr. Trump was even more blunt during the visit of Crown Prince Muhammad bin Salman to the White House on March 20, 2018. He told his guest in front of world media: "Saudi Arabia is a very wealthy nation, and they're going to give the United States some of that wealth."[94]

Mr. Trump's address in Riyadh on May 21, 2017 to the Arab-Islamic-American summit, attended by the leaders of more than 50 Muslim countries was conspicuously silent on American ideals and values. Instead, he gave his audience the green light to do the opposite: "We are not here to tell other people how to live, what to do, who to be, or how to worship."[95] Three weeks later, on June 16, 2017, in a speech in Miami, Florida on US policy toward Cuba, Trump expounded contradictory values: "We will not lift sanctions on the Cuban regime until all political prisoners are free, freedoms of assembly and expression are respected, all political parties are legalized and free, and internationally supervised elections are scheduled."[96]

What Does Donald Trump Expect from the Saudi King?

In addition to big business contracts, Mr. Trump wants Saudi Arabia to

1) Normalize Saudi relations with Israel.
2) Bring the Palestinians to yield to Israeli settlement terms.
3) Help destroy the so-called Islamic State.
4) Moderate Wahhabi teaching and preaching.

---

[93] Adler, Mason, and Holland, "Exclusive: Trump complains Saudis not paying fair share for US defense."

[94] Tim DiChristopher, "Trump asks Saudi crown prince to share kingdom's wealth by buying more American weapons," *CNBC*, (March 20, 2018). https://www.cnbc.com/2018/03/20/trump-asks-saudi-crown-prince-to-share-wealth-by-buying-us-weapons.html

[95] "Donald Trump's Saudi Arabia Speech: Eight Key Points," *The Telegraph*, (May 21, 2017). http://www.telegraph.co.uk/news/2017/05/21/donald-trumps-saudi-arabia-speech-eight-key-points/

[96] Adam Fisher, "Trump 'Canceling' Obama's Cuba Policy but Leaves Much in Place," *ABC News*, (June 16, 2017). http://abcnews.go.com/Politics/trumps-cuba-policy/story?id=48058622

The Saudi King shall do his very best to oblige. He has little alternative. Iran is knocking on his door and Washington is his only protection.

1) Normalize Saudi Relations with Israel: On normalizing relations between Saudi Arabia and Israel, the Saudi King will abide by Mr. Trump's wishes. He will take steps to normalize relations with Israel. He will also put pressure on his Arab allies to normalize relations with Israel.[97] After 70 years of non-recognition and coldness, normalization is expected to evolve gradually without fanfare. As an example of the future course of Saudi Arabia's thawing relations with Israel, Mr. Netanyahu announced on March 5, 2018 to Israeli reporters after meeting with Mr. Trump in Washington that Riyadh had granted Air India permission to fly over Saudi territory to and from Tel Aviv.[98] There was no immediate confirmation from Saudi officials.[99] On March 22, 2018, the first Air India flight from New Delhi to Ben-Gurion Airport flew over Saudi Arabia and other Gulf states.[100]

Mr. Trump's recognition of Jerusalem as Israel's capital on December 6, 2017,[101] complicated matters for King Salman. Inasmuch as the King realizes the importance of US protection, he also realizes the dangers of appearing too hypocritical. The Wahhabi agenda sanctifies the duty of all Saudi monarchs to protect Islam's holy sites in Mecca and Medina as well as Jerusalem. No Muslim would acquiesce to giving up control over Jerusalem's Islamic holy sites to Israel.

"My greatest wish before I die is to pray in Jerusalem,"[102] said King Faisal shortly before his assassination on March 25, 1975. These words resonate in the Arab street. At the Arab League Summit meeting on April 15,

---

[97]Zvi Bar'el, "Saudi Proposal to Israel Could Be the Stuff of Trump's Dream Deal in Mideast," *Haaretz*, (May 21, 2017). http://www.haaretz.com/middle-east-news/1.789953

[98]"Saudi Arabia gives Air India overflight rights for its Israel routes: Netanyahu," *Reuters*, (updated March 6, 2018). https://www.reuters.com/article/us-israel-india-saudi-flights/saudi-gives-air-india-overflight-rights-for-its-israel-routes-netanyahu-idUSKBN1GI035

[99]Middle East Eye, "Saudi Arabia allows Air India to fly over airspace to Israel: Netanyahu," (March 6, 2018). http://www.middleeasteye.net/news/saudi-arabia-grants-air-india-fly-over-its-airspace-israel-netanyahu-1443712794

[100]Noa Landau, "Making History, First Flight to Israel Overflying Saudi Arabia Lands in Tel Aviv," *Haaretz*, (March 21, 2018) https://www.haaretz.com/israel-news/historic-flight-to-israel-over-saudi-arabia-takes-off-from-india-1.5935687

[101]Steve Holland and Maayan Lubell, "Trump Recognises Jerusalem as Israel's Capital, in Reversal of Policy," *Reuters*, (December 6, 2017). https://uk.reuters.com/article/uk-usa-trump-israel/trump-recognises-jerusalem-as-israels-capital-in-reversal-of-policy-idUKKBN1DZ053

[102]William Tracey, "To Pray in Jerusalem," *Aramco World*, (July/August 1974). http://archive.aramcoworld.com/issue/197404/to.pray.in.jerusalem.htm

2018, in Dhahran, Saudi Arabia, King Salman announced a $150-million donation for the maintenance of Islamic heritage in East Jerusalem.[103]

2) Bring the Palestinians to Yield to Israeli Settlement Terms: This request is very challenging for the King to deliver. Mr. Trump, the "master" of the art of the deal, described the Israeli/Palestinian peace as "the ultimate deal."[104] During a joint news conference at the White House on May 3, 2017 with Mahmoud Abbas, president of the Palestinian Authority, Mr. Trump declared, "We will get this done."[105] Notwithstanding such confidence, there is no realistic hope for a durable settlement. Peace between Israel and the Palestinians is most unlikely to materialize because negotiations between a very powerful Israel and a very weak Palestinian Authority are futile. The Palestinians are under occupation. They are alone, aside from empty Arab gestures of solidarity.

Arab neighbors are either in peace treaties with Israel (Egypt and Jordan), or demolished (Iraq and Syria), or protectorates of Washington (GCC states). With unlimited American support, Israel holds all the cards. Nonetheless, despite seventy years of living in refugee camps, under occupation, and Israel's active and mighty war machine against them, the Palestinians have not surrendered.[106]

A future solution will not materialize unless:

1. Israel becomes magnanimous and gives back some of the land it has taken. Palestinians have not taken anything from Israel. Israel is unlikely to give back an inch. At the heart of the dispute is Palestine's scarcity of land. Additionally, satisfactory solutions to the difficult and important issues referred to in the Oslo Accords must be agreed: borders, security for Israel and Palestine, water rights, Jewish

---

[103]"Saudi king announces $150 million for East Jerusalem," *France 24*, (April 15, 2018). http://www.france24.com/en/20180415-saudi-king-announces-150-million-east-jerusalem

[104]Tovah Lazaloff, "Trump: Israeli-Palestinian Peace Would Be Ultimate Deal," *The Jerusalem Post*, (November 12, 2016). http://www.jpost.com/Israel-News/Trump-Israeli-Palestinian-peace-would-be-ultimate-deal-472404

[105]Joe Wagner and Ashley Parker, "Trump Expresses Confidence in Chances of an Israeli-Palestinian Peace Deal but Says US Can't Force It," *The Washington Post*, (May 3, 2017). https://www.washingtonpost.com/news/post-politics/wp/2017/05/03/trump-welcomes-palestinian-leader-abbas-to-white-house/?utm_term=.e02d4961a600

[106]Israeli wars and armed confrontations with Palestinians include: The war of 1948, the war of 1967, the first uprising (intifada) starting December 1987, the second intifada starting September 2000, battling Palestinian fighters in Lebanon in 2006, three wars against Hamas in 2008 and 2012 and 2014.

settlers, the status of the Palestinian Israelis, the right of return for the refugees. Last but not least, the most challenging issue is a just and satisfactory solution to the status of Jerusalem, particularly East Jerusalem, despite Mr. Trump's complicating recognition of Jerusalem as Israel's capital.

2. Washington compels Israel to become magnanimous. This scenario is unlikely; Israel's friends in Washington are powerful. The past seven decades have proven that no US administration can defy the Israeli lobby. Such pro-Israeli partiality is one of the main factors behind the growth of extreme Islam.

3. The Bible and the Qur'an must be de-politicized. Zionism and the old Testament of the Bible are organically attached. Without the Old Testament, there would be little Jewish interest in Palestine. As long as the Bible is politicized, the Qur'an will be politicized too. Religious wars never end.

3) Help in the Destruction of Al-Qaeda and the So-Called Islamic State: The Saudi King is earnest in his determination to eliminate the so-called Islamic State and al-Qaeda from Saudi Arabia. In fighting his Islamist rivals/enemies, his aim is not to save the world from terrorism, but rather, to save his own throne. Al-Qaeda and the so-called Islamic State are particularly threatening to the king's regime. They accuse the al-Sauds of corrupting "true" Wahhabism. Their declared aim is to remove the al-Sauds from power and change the name of the country.

As for the war outside Saudi Arabia against al-Qaeda and the so-called Islamic State, the prospects of Saudi troops killing Wahhabi brethren is slim. Al-Qaeda and the so-called Islamic State are Wahhabis who share the same ideology, teachings, and way of life as Saudis. A former imam of Islam's holiest shrine, the Grand Mosque of Mecca, confirmed that the so-called Islamic State follows the same brand of Wahhabism as that officially espoused by Saudi Arabia: "We follow the same thought [as IS] but apply it in a refined way, he said. They draw their ideas from what is written in our own books, from our own principles ... we do not criticize the thought on which it (IS) is based."[107] To Riyadh, al-Qaeda and so-called Islamic State must be eliminated, but not by Saudi soldiers. Troops from other

---

[107]"Leading Saudi Cleric Says IS and Saudi Arabia 'Follow the Same Thought,'" *Middle East Eye*.

countries, like Egypt, Jordan, Morocco, and Sudan will be sourced and funded by Saudi Arabia.

4) Moderate Wahhabi Teaching and Preaching: Fundamental religious and political reforms in Saudi Arabia are a necessity for the benefit of Islam, Saudi Arabia, the Middle East, and the wider world. However, neither religious nor political reform is expected to be fundamental as long as the world is addicted to oil and Saudi Arabia is the swing oil producer and biggest exporter.

On October 24, 2017, at the Riyadh Future Investment Initiative conference, Crown Prince Mohammed made two false statements. He first vowed to return Saudi Arabia to "a more moderate Islam."[108] The statement implies that the Saudi regime was moderate in the past. That claim is false. Saudi Arabia was never moderate. Wahhabism and moderation are contradictions in terms.

Since the early 1800s, when Muhammad bin Saud and Muhammad bin Abdulwahhab launched the first Wahhabi rebellion against the Istanbul Sultan, coercion and forceful brainwashing have been a way of life in Saudi Arabia (see below: *Manifesting Wahhabism in Saudi daily life*). The rebellion was launched in the name of the "true" Islam against the Sultans' moderate Hanafite rite. The first rebellion was crushed in 1818 by the ruler of Egypt, Muhammad Ali and his son, Ibrahim, on orders from the Ottoman Sultan, Mahmoud II. A second rebellion by Abdulaziz al-Saud and the Abdulwahhab clan was launched in 1902; again, in the name of the "true" Islam to "cleanse" it from Ottoman "innovations". The second rebellion, with determined assistance from the British government, succeeded in 1932 to produce the kingdom that bears the al-Saud family name.

The Crown Prince made a second false claim. He said, "after the Iranian revolution in 1979, people wanted to copy this model in different countries, one of them is Saudi Arabia. We didn't know how to deal with it. And the problem spread all over the world."[109] This claim is disingenuous. Wahhabism radicalized Islam and polarized Muslims. The Iranian Islamic revolution in 1979 was in part a reaction to Wahhabi hatred and abuse of Shi'ites.

---

[108]Sam Meredith, "Saudi Arabia Promises A Return to 'Moderate Islam,'" *CNBC*, (October 25, 2017). https://www.cnbc.com/2017/10/25/saudi-arabia-promises-a-return-to-moderate-islam.html

[109]Martin Chulov, "I will return Saudi Arabia to moderate Islam, says crown prince," *The Guardian*, (October 24, 2017). https://www.theguardian.com/world/2017/oct/24/i-will-return-saudi-arabia-moderate-islam-crown-prince

More than two hundred years ago, in 1801, the Saud/Abdulwahhab enmity of Shi'ites reached the unprecedented level of invading Karbala, Iraq and destroying the holiest of Shi'ites' holies, the venerated tomb of the Imam Hussein.[110] With the formation of the Saudi state in 1932, Wahhabi hatred Shi'ites in schools, mosques, and the media became a part of the cultural fabric of Saudi society (see below: *The Threat from Saudi Arabia's Own Internal Sectarian Divisions*). Wahhabism put an end to six hundred years of generally peaceful co-existence among the many religions and sects of the moderate Ottoman Sultans' Hanafite rite.

The first Saudi King, Abdualaziz, imposed on his minority Shi'ite subjects the Islamic *jizya*, a tax collected from non-Muslims.[111] The Wahhabi doctrine brands the Shi'ites as heretics.[112] During the reign of King Faisal (1964–1975), Wahhabi ulama declared that meat slaughtered by Shi'ite butchers was not fit for consumption by Muslims.[113]

Although the Crown Prince's vow to return Saudi Arabia to "a more moderate Islam" is long overdue, he will be limited in his quest to cosmetic changes, like easing the odd and harsh governmental and religious police edicts on the daily lives of women (see Chapter Six: *Daily Living Under Wahhabi Dictums in the Words of a Saudi Female Journalist*).

Obstacles in the Way of Moderating Wahhabism: It is unlikely that the Crown Prince's vow of reforms will become a reality:

1. Wahhabism is the Saudi Kings' legitimating ideology to rule over the tribes. King Abdulaziz replaced Bedouin discord and rivalries by the brotherhood of Islam. Wahhabism is the glue that keeps the tribes under control and supportive of the regime. It is difficult to imagine a different ideology that could keep the tribes at peace with each other. To water down the glue is to risk the collapse of the al-Saud reign. Without Wahhabism, the "exaggerated individualism, lack of cooperation, and extreme jealousy among different segments of a tribe"[114] could resurface and bring civil war and the potential division of Saudi Arabia (see Chapter Six: *Tribal Sheikhs*).

---

[110]Hitti, *History of the Arabs*, P. 740.
[111]Madawi al-Rasheed, *A History of Saudi Arabia*, P. 89.
[112]Ibid., P. 146.
[113]Ibid. PP. 146–147.
[114]Ibrahim Ezzidine, and D.P. Cole, *Saudi Arabian Bedouin* (Cairo Papers in Social Science, The American University in Cairo, 1978), PP. 11 and 18.

2. Wahhabism is a useful psychological weapon. It energizes the Saudi masses in the regime's confrontation with Iran and discrimination against Saudi Shi'ites and Isma'ilis (see below: *The Threat from Saudi Arabia's Internal Sectarian Divisions*).[115] But nationalism is not a viable alternative to Wahhabism in the confrontation with Iran. Saudi Arabia's Grand Mufti, Abdulaziz bin Baz (1963–1999), called nationalism "a movement of ignorance whose main purpose is to fight Islam and destroy its teachings and rules."[116] Saudi history textbooks teach that Arab nationalism is "a conspiracy promoted by the West and Zionism to undermine the unity of Muslims."[117] It will be generations before such values fade away.

3. Blind obedience to the king rests on the king's claim of divine rule. Obedience by the masses does not flow from democratic principles. The palace ulama made Verse 4:59 a religious duty, an act of piety. It is inconceivable that the teaching and preaching of Verse 4:59 would be weakened.

4. Genuine religious reforms will not happen. Saudi Arabia is challenged today by two opposing religious extremes. The first is from the Muslim Brotherhood for representative democracy. The second is from the likes of al-Qaeda and the so-called Islamic State for more austere and violent Wahhabism. In reaction to these challenges, to maintain his Wahhabi credibility, the king will not abolish Shari'a courts and polygamy will not become illegal.[118] Saudi religious reforms will be limited to cosmetics only, like allowing women to drive cars, attend sporting event, and allow the opening of movie theatres. Al-Qaeda warned the Crown Prince that his cinemas and World Wrestling Entertainment event in Jeddah in April 2018 are sinful and opening the door for "corruption and moral degeneration."[119]

---

[115] Exploitation of religion for political purposes is age-old in the Middle East. Shah Ismail (1501–1524) forced the conversion of what was Sunni Persia to Shi'ite Islam in order to introduce Shi'ism's zeal into Persia's wars against the Sunni Ottoman Empire. Indeed, Wahhabism helped defeat the Soviet Union in the Afghanistan War (1979–1989).

[116] Al-Rasheed, *A History of Saudi Arabia*, P. 190.

[117] Ibid. P. 191.

[118] As if to capture the high religious ground, the holiday period in 2017 for the month of fasting, Ramadan, was lengthened for government employees to 23 days (June 16, 2017–July 8, 2017), from 11 days in 2016, CNN, *Saudi Arabia just gave government workers a very long vacation (23 days!)*, June 21, 2017, http://money.cnn.com/2017/06/21/news/saudi-arabia-vacation-government-workers/index.html

[119] Bethan McKernan, "Al-Qaeda warns Saudi Crown Prince his cinemas and WWE events are sinful," *The Independent*, (June 2, 2019). https://www.independent.co.uk/news/world/middle-east/al-qaeda-saudi-crown-prince-wwe-cinemas-sinful-mohammed-bin-salman-yemen-a8379021.html

5. Genuine political reforms will not happen either. Democracy and the king's absolute authority are a zero-sum game. The slightest gain for democracy represents a corresponding loss to the king's absolute authority. Representative democracy is frightening to the al-Sauds. It puts an end to their throne. Therefore, prospects for real democratic reforms is zero. The appointed Consultative Council will never become a democratically elected law-making assembly with powers to enact laws outside the king's instructions.

6. Societal customs, habits, and values do not get erased or reversed by fiat. Arabia's inhabitants have been under the control and constant indoctrination of the al-Sauds and their Wahhabi clerics for the past two centuries. It would require generations to erase common beliefs such as, Shi'tes and Isma'ilis are not Muslims, Christians and Jews are heretics (kuffar), women are light on faith and brains, and only Wahhabis go to paradise.

7. Today's reforms could be reversed tomorrow by the same ruler or by a new one. Furthermore, popular culture is difficult to change.

Notwithstanding the Crown Prince's celebrated easing of certain harsh edicts, unique to the Wahhabi way of life, seven women activists who campaigned for years for the right to drive were arrested in mid-May 2018. They were charged with "suspicious contacts with foreign entities" and labelled by state-controlled media as "traitors" and "agents of embassies."[120] The arrests are a warning to other would-be reform advocates to refrain from considering unsanctioned societal discourse (see Chapter Six: *Daily Living Under Wahhabi Dictums in the Words of a Saudi Female Journalist*).

What Does the Saudi King Expect from the US President?

The Saudi King's list includes five wishes:

- Reversal of Washington's Empowerment of Iran Since 9/11.
- Declaring the Muslim Brotherhood as a Terrorist Organizations.
- Punishing Turkey and Qatar for supporting the Muslim Brotherhood.
- Shutting down Qatar's Al Jazeera media network.
- Protection from the Justice Against Sponsors of Terrorism Act (JASTA).

---

[120]Sarah Dadouch, "Saudi Arabia expands crackdown on women's rights activists," Reuters, (May 22, 2018). https://uk.reuters.com/article/uk-saudi-arrests/saudi-arabia-expands-crackdown-on-womens-rights-activists-idUKKCN1IN223

Except for the repeal of JASTA, the King's five wishes are covered in the 13 demands Saudi Arabia and Bahrain, UAE, and Egypt made of Qatar on June 5, 2017.[121] The group blockaded Qatar's land, air, and sea ports. They expelled Qatar's diplomats and ordered Qatari citizens to leave their countries within 14 days.[122] Kuwait has been trying to use its goodwill and good offices with all parties, including Iran, to end the blockade. At the time of this writing, almost a year later, the blockade is still in effect.

The blockade came only two weeks after Mr. Trump's visit to Riyadh. Former US Secretary of State Rex Tillerson called on the Saudi bloc on June 9, 2017 to immediately ease their blockade of Qatar and urged all involved to quickly resolve their differences.[123] However, less than an hour later, Mr. Trump contradicted Mr. Tillerson. He said that the Saudi-led action against Qatar was "hard but necessary," that he had been consulted in advance "about confronting Qatar," a country he said had historically been a "funder of terrorism at a very high level," and that the time had come to call on Qatar to end that funding ... and its extremist ideology.[124]

Trump's support of the Qatar blockade was reportedly linked, to Qatar's refusal to finance Trump's son-in-law, Jared Kushner's property at 666 Fifth Avenue in New York City on March 2, 2018.[125] On March 5, 2018, the BBC obtained leaked emails that show a lobbying effort to get US Secretary of State Rex Tillerson sacked for failing to support the United Arab Emirates against Qatar.[126] On May 22, 2018, it was reported that the

---

[121]"Saudi Arabia Insists Qatar Close al-Jazeera as Arab States Present List of 13 Demands to End Feud," *The Independent*, (June 23, 2017). http://www.independent.co.uk/news/world/middle-east/saudi-arabia-qatar-diplomatic-feud-latest-al-jazeera-demands-list-uae-egypt-bahrain-a7803981.html

[122]"UAE Accused of Hacking Qatar State Media and Sparking Middle East's Diplomatic Crisis," *The Telegraph*, (July 17, 2017). http://www.telegraph.co.uk/news/2017/07/17/uae-accused-hacking-qatar-state-media-publishing-comments-sparked/

[123]Karen DeYoung and Sudsaran Raghavan, "Trump Seems to Undercut Tillerson's Remarks on Qatar," *The Washington Post*, (June 9, 2017). https://www.washingtonpost.com/world/arab-countries-place-dozens-on-new-qatar-terror-list-deepening-dispute/2017/06/09/fd727fab-e750-4fdd-ac23-26256e8e0493_story.html?utm_term=.1699c9b9196a

[124]Ibid.

[125]Jessica Kwong, "Jared Kushner Backed Qatar Blockade a Month After Qataris Wouldn't Finance His Property: Report," *Newsweek*, (March 2, 2018). http://www.newsweek.com/jared-kushner-backed-qatar-blockade-after-qataris-wouldnt-finance-his-property-828847

[126]Suzanne Kianpour, "Emails show UAE-linked effort against Tillerson," *BBC*, (March 5, 2018). http://www.bbc.co.uk/news/world-us-canada-43281519

Crown Princes of Saudi Arabia and the United Arab Emirates have been seeking to alter US foreign policy and punish Qatar.[127]

If Saudi Arabia and its allies aim to diminish Iran's influence, blockading Qatar is not the way to do it. Iran promptly started daily food deliveries to Qatar by air and sea.[128] The confrontation with Qatar is a gift to Iran. The following will address the King's wish list.

1. Reversal of Washington's Empowerment of Iran Since 9/11: Obama's Iran politics presents three options for the Trump administration: A case for reversal, the case for siding with Iran, or the case for siding with Saudi Arabia and its GCC allies while simultaneously keeping the door to Iran ajar.

The Case for Reversal: Under this scenario, the empowerment of Iran was an unwise, short sighted Obama policy, and the Trump administration will revert to the traditional Washington Playbook. This playbook treats Saudi Arabia as an ally and Iran as an enemy. The view is based on the argument that Saudi Arabia and the other five GCC states are more valuable to American interests than Iran for the reason that they comprise the following:

1. Decades of master/client relationship between Washington and GCC states.
2. One third of global oil reserves.[129]
3. More than one third of global oil exports.[130]
4. Vast markets for US exports of weapons and civilian goods.
5. Huge investments in America by GCC central banks and the private sector.
6. Denominating oil and gas exports in US dollar.
7. Support for the US dollar as the world's dominant reserve currency.
8. A combined Sunni majority of 70% in the Arabian Peninsula, the Levant, and Iraq.

---

[127]Desmond Butler and Tom LoBianco, "Emails reveal secret lobbying effort to alter U.S. policy in Middle East," *Chicago Tribune*, (May 22, 2018). http://www.chicagotribune.com/news/nationworld/ct-trump-saudi-uae-princes-20180521-story.html

[128]"Iran Flies Food to Qatar amid Concerns of Shortages," *Reuters*, (June 11, 2017). https://www.reuters.com/article/us-gulf-qatar-iran-idUSKBN1920EG

[129]Worldatlas.com, "The World's Largest Oil Reserves by Country." http://www.worldatlas.com/articles/the-world-s-largest-oil-reserves-by-country.html

[130]Index Mundi, *Oil—exports > TOP 20.*

The reversal of Obama's playbook is most likely to aim at changing the regime of the Qom ayatollahs. The warning shot came on May 8, 2018, when Mr. Trump announced the withdrawal of the US from the Iran nuclear deal (see below: *President Trump's politics behind the P5+1 Nuclear Agreement*). The appointment in April 2018 of John Bolton as Mr. Trump's national security advisor raises this likelihood. Bolton was one of the loudest voices urging G.W. Bush to occupy Iraq in 2003 and change the Baghdad regime. The Bush project might have also included a hidden plan to change the Tehran regime (see Chapter Seven). However, the failure of the Bush adventure empowered the ayatollahs instead. In Trump's White House, Bolton has his opportunity to work on changing the ayatollahs' regime.

In a speech on May 21, 2018, Secretary of State, Mike Pompeo, revealed White House intentions toward the ayatollahs. He ordered Iran to "stop all uranium enrichment; halt launches of nuclear-capable ballistic missiles; end support for Hamas, Hezbollah and Palestinian Islamic Jihad; withdraw all forces under Iranian command from Syria; and end support for Houthi rebels in Yemen.[131] If Iran does not comply, Pompeo said in remarks following the speech: "The Iranian people will get to make a choice about their leadership. If they make the decision quickly that will be wonderful. If they choose not to do so, we will stay hard at this until we achieve the outcomes that I set forth."[132]

Even, if the Tehran regime will be overthrown, the confrontations between Iran and Saudi Arabia will not end. Age-old ethnic rivalries between Arab and Persian would sooner or later fuel new confrontations and, US protection of Saudi Arabia would continue to be needed, if the al-Saud regime is to survive.

The Case for Siding with Iran: This scenario may be envisioned under two time horizons. The first is during the time of dependence on oil imports by America's rivals (China, continental Europe, India, and Japan). Mr. Trump inherited a Muslim Middle East shaped by the Obama playbook—Shi'ites and Sunnis killing each other far away from America and a Saudi King buying more American weapons than ever before and seeking normal relations with Israel for the first time. Trump also inherited from Obama an open door to trade with Iran's 85 million consumers without

---

[131]Julian Borger and Heather Stuart, "Iran told: comply with US demands or face 'strongest sanctions in history'," *The Guardian*, (May 21, 2018). https://www.theguardian.com/us-news/2018/may/21/iran-nuclear-deal-mike-pompeo-us-sanctions

[132]Ibid.

sacrificing an ounce of Saudi and GCC business. With such advantages, Trump and/or future administrations might see benefits in siding with Iran.

The second time horizon will be after America's rivals (China, continental Europe, India, and Japan) have achieved independence from oil imports. It is a matter of when, and not if, that national security concerns of America's rivals will replace their oil imports by renewable energy. Whenever that happens, Washington will abandon Riyadh to face its bigger and more powerful Iranian enemy on its own.

President Trump's Politics Behind the P5+1 Nuclear Agreement: While a candidate in the 2016 presidential election, Donald Trump was an outspoken critic of Iran's regime and the Obama P5+1 nuclear deal (JCPOA).[133] He fiercely criticized the agreement, calling it "the worst deal ever."[134] He complained that it limited Iran's nuclear activities for only a fixed period of time; failed to stop the development of ballistic missiles; and handed Iran a $100 billion windfall that it used "as a slush fund for weapons, terror, and oppression" across the Middle East.[135]

Under the terms of JCPOA, Iran agreed to limit the size of its stockpile of enriched uranium for 15 years, and the number of centrifuges for 10 years, and agreed to modify a heavy water facility so it could not produce plutonium suitable for a bomb.[136]

On May 8, 2018 Mr. Trump announced that he will withdraw the United States from the Iran nuclear deal and restore sanctions aimed at isolating Iran from the global financial system.[137] "We will be instituting the highest level of economic sanction," Mr. Trump declared. "Any nation that helps Iran in its quest for nuclear weapons could also be strongly sanctioned by the United States," he continued.[138] The US Treasury stated that

[133]"Iran Nuclear Deal: Trump Administration Approves Agreement but Review Looms," *The Guardian,* (April 19, 2017). https://www.theguardian.com/world/2017/apr/19/iran-nuclear-deal-trump-administration-approves-agreement-but-review-looms

[134]Max Greenwood, "Trump Called for End to Iran Deal Before Recertifying It: Report," *The Hill,* (July 18, 2017). http://thehill.com/homenews/administration/342475-trump-spent-most-meeting-calling-for-end-to-iran-deal-before

[135]"Is the Iran nuclear deal about to collapse?," *BBC,* (May 1, 2018). http://www.bbc.co.uk/news/world-middle-east-43888265

[136]"Iran nuclear deal: Powers seek to save agreement after US exit," *BBC,* (May 9, 2018). http://www.bbc.co.uk/news/world-us-canada-44049532

[137]Tom DiChristopher, "Trump announces he will withdraw US from Iran nuclear deal and restore sanctions," *CNBC,* (May 8, 2018). https://www.cnbc.com/2018/05/08/trump-to-announce-he-will-withdraw-us-from-iran-nuclear-deal.html

[138]Ibid.

the sanctions would target Iran's oil sector, aircraft exports, precious metals trade, and Iranian government attempts to buy US dollar banknotes.[139] Recall that the Obama administration transferred to Iran $1.7 billion in January and February 2016 in the form of banknotes, only to trace some of the banknotes two years later to Iranian-backed Hezbollah and Houthi rebels (see above: *Obama's Three Main Tactics in Support of JCPOA*).

European companies will have 90 to 180 days to wind down their operations in Iran, or they will run foul of the American banking system.[140] Given that all Eurodollar interbank transactions are settled in New York's *Clearing House Interbank Payment System*, the US can capture all dollar denominated international transactions that violate US sanctions against foreign countries. France, Germany, and the UK said they "will work with all remaining parties," while Russia and China stressed their continuing support for the agreement.[141]

Likely Consequences from Abandoning the JCPOA—The Case to Keep the Door Ajar to Iran: Donald Trump's business focus, carrots, sticks, bluster, threats, and ambiguities might ultimately leave the door ajar with Iran. Change(s) to JCPOA's terms to assuage Trump's ostensible concerns might reduce the intensity of US sanctions and allow a level of trading relationship with Iran. Even a simmering pot will drive the Saudi King to pay more protection money.

Mr. Trump has been sending positive messages to Iran. He tried to meet with Iranian President Rouhani at the United Nations in New York in September 2017, but Rouhani rebuffed the request.[142] The Kuwaiti newspaper *al-Jarida* reported (in Arabic) on February 21, 2018 that the Trump White House suggested to Tehran to hold secret negotiations in either Muscat or Geneva that would cover all matters of disagreement between the two countries.[143] Further, Mr. Trump handed Iran a gift on July 20, 2017, when he discontinued a program of arming and training

[139]"Iran nuclear deal: Powers seek to save agreement after US exit," *BBC*, (May 9, 2018).

[140]Mark Landler, "Trump Abandons Iran Nuclear Deal He Long Scorned," *The New York Times*, (May 8, 2018). https://www.nytimes.com/2018/05/08/world/middleeast/trump-iran-nuclear-deal.html

[141]Ibid.

[142]Zaid Sabah, "Iran Says Its President Turned Down a Meeting with Trump, *Bloomberg*," (October 29, 2017). https://www.bloomberg.com/news/articles/2017-10-29/iran-s-rouhani-said-to-reject-trump-s-request-to-meet-at-un

[143]Ferzad Kasimi, "Washington Suggests to Tehran Secret Negotiations," *Al-Jarida (in Arabic)*, (February 21, 2018). http://www.aljarida.com/articles/1519149629334600900/

anti-Assad rebels in Syria.[144] By March 29, 2018, the gift became bigger when he declared in a speech that the US would "be coming out of Syria, like, very soon."[145] Statements following the strikes by the US, UK, and France on April 14, 2018 against the Assad regime's chemical weapons sites must be reassuring to Assad, the Ayatollah, and Putin. US Defense Secretary described them as a "one time shot."[146] UK Prime Minister Theresa May said the strikes were not about "regime change."[147] Two days after withdrawing from JCPOA, President Trump said that he wants to pursue a new accord with Tehran that is better for the US and "better for them."[148]

Whether Ayatollah Khamenei would agree to keep the door ajar with Mr. Trump is not entirely up to him. Mr. Putin has a say in the matter. Russia protects the Assad regime, which keeps the Shi'ite Crescent's highway to the Mediterranean Sea clear, to safeguard the viability of Hezbollah in Lebanon. To guarantee the survival of the Shi'ite Crescent the Supreme Ayatollah will heed Mr. Putin's command.

It is difficult to see how US withdrawal from the JCPOA would contain Iran's power in the Muslim Middle East. While a serious drop in Tehran's export earnings and foreign investments are expected, Iran's military threat will not diminish. Anticipating a restart of Iran's nuclear development, Saudi Arabia's Crown Prince said, "if Iran developed a nuclear bomb, we would follow suit as soon as possible."[149]

Likely Consequences from Abandoning the JCPOA—The Case of War: A pre-emptive strike against Iran might succeed in destroying Iran's nuclear, rockets, and other military offensive capabilities and in

---

[144]Euan McKirdy and Laura Smith-Spark, "CIA No Longer Arming Anti-Assad Rebels, Washington Post Reports," *CNN*, (July 20, 2017). http://edition.cnn.com/2017/07/20/politics/cia-syria-anti-assad-rebels/index.html

[145]Ryan Browne and Barbara Starr, "Trump says US will withdraw from Syria 'very soon'," *CNN*, (March 29, 2018). https://edition.cnn.com/2018/03/29/politics/trump-withdraw-syria-pentagon/index.html

[146]Steve Holland and Tom Perry, "U.S., Britain, France launch air strikes in Syria," *Reuters*, (April 13, 2018). https://uk.reuters.com/article/uk-mideast-crisis-syria/u-s-britain-france-launch-air-strikes-in-syria-idUKKBN1HK16M

[147]"Syria air strikes: US and allies attack chemical weapons sites," *BBC*, (April 14, 2018). http://www.bbc.co.uk/news/world-middle-east-43762251

[148]Jonathan Allen, "Trump says he's aiming for new Iran deal that is 'better for them'," *AOL/NBC News*, (May 10, 2018). https://www.aol.com/article/news/2018/05/10/trump-says-hes-aiming-for-new-iran-deal-that-is-better-for-them/23432116/

[149]"Saudi Arabia pledges to create a nuclear bomb if Iran does," *BBC*, (March 15, 2018). http://www.bbc.co.uk/news/world-middle-east-43419673

crippling its retaliation capacity. If not successful, however, Saudi oil fields and water desalination plants will become targets for Iranian bombardment.

Meanwhile, absent simultaneous pre-emptive strikes against Hezbollah that would cripple its capacity to retaliate, destruction in Israel from Hezbollah's missiles and in Lebanon from Israeli bombings would be huge. It may be said that destroying Hezbollah's arsenal is more difficult than neutralising Iran's armoury. In 2016, Hezbollah had some 21,000 men under arms and 24,000 reservists, equipped with 130,000 rockets, hundreds of drones, and thousands of anti-tank missiles.[150] It may be said that Hezbollah is Iran's weapon of mass destruction on Israel's border with Lebanon (See Chapter Nine: *The Roots of the Iran/Hezbollah Axis*).

How Likely Is the Case for War Against Iran? Military and political realities dampen the possibility of an all out conflagration. While massive destruction would befall Iran, the damage to Israel, Lebanon, and Saudi Arabia would be high, too (see Chapter Nine: *Why Is Israel Anti-Iran?* Also see: *Why Is Iran Anti-Israel?*). Additionally, Russia's reaction must not be ignored.

US abandonment of the JCPOA is unlikely to trigger an all-out war. However, Israeli bombing raids of the past seven years on Iranian/Hezbollah related targets in Syria might intensify. Since the start of the Syrian revolution in March 2011, Israel has launched some 100 strikes in Syria[151] without retaliation.

An Alternative to an All Out War: If the US and its allies are truly and genuinely committed to breaking-up the Shi'ite Crescent, strangling Hezbollah, and rolling back Iran, a far more efficient strategy than war, or withdrawal from the JCPOA, would be to help Syria's own citizens overthrow the Assad regime. A new anti-Assad army to be recruited from amongst the more than ten million Syrian refugees, equipped with anti-warplane missiles, could result in a replay to the USSR's defeat in the war in Afghanistan (December 1979–February 1989). Syrians alone, with US weapons and advisors from America and, possibly, Jordan, could put an end to Assad's minority rule, and with it Iran's dominance over the Sunni Middle East plus Russia's control over Syria (see Chapter Nine).

---

[150]"Hezbollah, "From Terror Group to Army," *Haaretz*, (December 7, 2016). http://www.haaretz.com/st/c/prod/eng/2016/07/lebanon2/

[151]"Syria war: Israel 'strikes Damascus military complex'," *BBC*, (February 7, 2018). http://www.bbc.co.uk/news/world-middle-east-42973662

Saudi Arabia's Reaction to Mr. Trump's Politics in the Middle East: Mr. Trump's mercurial intentions must worry Riyadh. The Saudi King will not be satisfied unless the US eliminates Iran's military threat completely. He wants to see the American door shut tightly on the ayatollahs. He dreams of a Washington treating Tehran as a serious enemy.

What can Riyadh do if the White House refuses to fulfil the king's dreams? Absolutely nothing. An example of Mr. Trump's total disregard of the Saudi King is his recognition of Jerusalem as Israel's capital. The nine US presidents since the 1967 war in the Middle East respected the special status of East Jerusalem. They found it to be in the interest of the US to avoid offending Saudi and other Arab rulers and Muslims. Mr. Trump, however, handed Jerusalem to Israel on December 6, 2017 and moved the US embassy to Jerusalem on the symbolic day of May 14, 2018 to coincide with the 70th anniversary of Israel's formation. It is noteworthy that since 1948, the Palestinians commemorate May 15th as their day of catastrophe (nakba).

Trump not only demeaned the Saudi King, but also unceremoniously scuttled Saudi Arabia's heralded plan for a resolution to the Palestinian and Arab dispute with Israel (see: Chapter Eight, *The Arab Peace Initiative*). The plan was approved by Arab leaders at their summit in Beirut on March 28, 2002. It was re-endorsed at the 2007 Arab League Summit in Saudi Arabia[152] and again at the 2017 Arab League Summit in Jordan.[153] The plan was endorsed in June 2002 by the 57 member states of the Organization of Islamic Cooperation and earned the support of the Quartet members, and in April 2003, it was noted in the Roadmap for Peace in the Middle East.[154]

2. Declaring the Muslim Brotherhood as a Terrorist Organizations: Democratic rule frightens the al-Saud regime. Free multi-political party elections, coalition governments, modern laws, transparency, accountability, freedom of the press and speech, and human rights are all anathema to Wahhabi values.

---

[152]Avi Issacharoff, "Arab States Unanimously Approve Saudi Peace Initiative," *Haaretz*, (March 28, 2007). https://www.haaretz.com/1.4813455

[153]Adam Rasgon, "Arab Leaders at Summit Endorse Two-State Solution," *The Jerusalem Post*, (March 29, 2017). http://www.jpost.com/Arab-Israeli-Conflict/Arab-leaders-at-summit-endorse-two-state-solution-485572

[154]Lior Lehrs, "A Comparative Analysis of the 'Saudi Initiative'," *Jerusalem Institute for Israel Studies*, (August 2011). http://en.jerusaleminstitute.org.il/.upload/Peace%20Initiatives-English-%20last%20version.pdf

The Muslim Brotherhood was formed in Egypt in 1928. It is the oldest and largest Islamic political party in the Arab world.

It operates in all Arab countries and in scores of Muslim communities outside the Arab world.[155] The Muslim Brotherhood is an umbrella organization of independent chapters. The chapters do not report to each other or to a central authority. They reject Wahhabi extremism. They belong to the other three moderate Sunni rites (Hanafite, Malikite, and Shafe'ite).

The Muslim Brotherhood's commitment to free elections and representative democracy has been loud and clear. During the Arab Spring, the Brotherhood won free elections and formed coalition governments in Egypt, Morocco, and Tunisia.

In Jordan's September 2016 parliamentary elections, the Islamic Action Front (IAF), a Brotherhood chapter, won 16 out of 130 seats. Although executive power in Jordan resides with the King who has the right to appoint and dismiss the prime minister and cabinet and dissolve the National Assembly, IAF's participation reflects the Brotherhood's commitment to representative democracy. Significantly, the Brotherhood joined Christians and other candidates to form an alliance in the elections: the National Coalition for Reform.[156]

In Kuwait's November 2016 parliamentary elections, the Muslim Brotherhood dominated opposition won 24 of the 50 seats in the parliament. Like Jordan, most executive power remains in the hands of the ruling al-Sabah family.[157]

In Syria, the Brotherhood has had long democratic roots. Its officials were a part of democratically elected parliaments in 1954 (with eight other political parties) and in 1961 (with ten other political parties), until an air force decommissioned captain, Hafiz Assad and his comrades destroyed Syria's democracy on March 8, 1963 (see Chapter Nine).

Saudi Arabia's Kings and the Wahhabi palace establishment, worried over losing their legitimacy to rule to this credible Sunni, democratic-leaning institution, constantly paint democracy as a Western conspiracy to destroy Islam.

---

[155]Muslim Brotherhood Official English Website. http://www.ikhwanweb.com/index.php

[156]"Jordan Polls: Muslim Brotherhood and Women Make Gains," *BBC,* (September 23, 2016). http://www.bbc.co.uk/news/world-middle-east-37450259

[157]"Kuwait's Islamist Dominated Opposition Wins Near-Majority in Snap Elections," *DW,* (November 27, 2016). http://www.dw.com/en/kuwaits-islamist-dominated-opposition-wins-near-majority-in-snap-elections/a-36540834

To lump the Muslim Brotherhood with terrorist groups like al-Qaeda, the so-called Islamic State and Hezbollah is a distortion of the facts. The so-called Islamic State and al-Qaeda are Wahhabi terrorist organizations. Hezbollah is a Shi'ite terrorist organization under Iran's command. The Brotherhood is neither Wahhabi nor terrorist.

The Great Influence Egypt Has in Saudi Arabia: Egypt is the Arab world's center of gravity. It has a profound influence over the Arab world in general, but especially Saudi Arabia. With more than 90-million in population, 90% being Sunnis, Egypt has for more than fifty years supplied the Saudi labor market with talent. The supply accelerated greatly since the quadrupling of oil prices in 1973. Since that time, Saudi Arabia has been home to around a million Egyptians at any one time. Arabic language skill and Islamic culture enabled a good proportion of Egyptian expatriates to become school teachers. Supplemented by Cairo's al-Azhar, (the world's oldest university and the leading center for Sunni scholarship and authoritative fatwas), religious and literary influences have bonded Egyptians and Saudis in marriage, education, and culture. During the past fifty years, around two hundred billion dollars are estimated to have been transferred to Egypt in the form of workers' remittances, Saudi government financial aid, and Saudi private sector investments. Such financial flows cement relations between the people of the two countries.

Egypt's Muslim Brotherhood Is an Existential Risk to the al-Saud Regime: It is safer for the al-Saud regime to keep democracy away from Egypt. While the concept of a democratic Egypt under a secular government is frightening to Riyadh, a democratic Egypt under a Muslim Brotherhood government is far more frightening. As a result, the al-Sauds have supported military dictatorships in Cairo in order to deflect the wind of democratic and Islamic reforms from reaching Saudi Arabia.

A Brotherhood democratic Egypt could attract the Saudi masses to demand representative democracy as an alternative to the king's absolute Wahhabi rule. It would challenge the al-Sauds and the palace ulama's expropriation of the religious high ground, and the allegation for the past century that Wahhabism is the "true" Islam. It would refute the teaching that Islam is incompatible with democracy. It is the fear that a democratically elected Brotherhood parliament could undermine the al-Sauds' legitimating claim to authority. The harshness of Wahhabi dictates could turn young educated Saudi men and women in the age of the internet into supporters of the Brotherhood's less austere, less extreme, and less rigid way of life. Democracy and religious reforms in both Egypt and Saudi Arabia must wait until demand for oil by the world's big oil importing rivals of the US (China, continental Europe, India, and Japan) is replaced by sustainable sources of energy.

Egypt's cultural roots are anchored in its age-old progressive culture. Life in Egypt is rather gentle, less austere, and less extreme than the Wahhabi way of life. Egyptian thinkers in the modern age led the call to modernize interpretations of the Islamic script.[158] For economic development, a Brotherhood parliament needs to modernize Shari'a laws. As mentioned, dogmatic posturing produces neither jobs nor prosperity. To reduce unemployment and raise incomes, foreign investors should be welcomed, tourists encouraged, women employed, and religious studies reduced to give way to science and philosophy. The Brotherhood parliament would have to reverse Egypt's high population growth rates, including the possibility of limiting the number of children a family may have, even legalizing abortion. With Wahhabi inspiration and Saudi cash, anti-modernization Islamists would assault the new laws as un-Islamic edicts that should be scrapped. The Brotherhood's politicians, scholars, and ulama, all with credibility on Islamic legal and theological matters, would counter the attacks, citing impressive references from the Qur'an and the Sunna that the new laws are perfectly Islamic. The confrontations could open the door to examining the historicity of the Islamic script or debating theological issues like the belief in predestination. The debates could isolate the anti-modernization voices, cement democratic values, modernize Shari'a laws, and evolve a more tolerant, less austere, less extreme, and gentler way of life than the harsh Wahhabi rules.[159]

For years, the dangers posed by a democratic Muslim Brotherhood government in Cairo alarmed the al-Saud clan. The late Saudi Crown Prince and Interior Minister Prince Nayif bin Abdulaziz was intensely against the Muslim Brotherhood. He declared as far back as November 2002 in an interview with the Kuwaiti newspaper *al-Siyassah*, that, "all our problems come from the Muslim Brotherhood ... The Muslim Brotherhood has

---

[158]For example: Rifa'a Badawi Al-Tahtawi (1801–1873), Muhammad Abduh (1849–1905), Muhammad Farid Wajdi (1875–1954), Mustafa Abdulraziq (1885–1947), Qassim Amin (1865–1908), Ahmad Lutfi al-Sayyed (1872–1963), Ali Abd Al-Raziq (1888–1966), Taha Hussein (1889–1973).

[159]Elhadj, "The Arab Spring and the prospects for genuine religious and political reforms."

destroyed the Arab world.[160] The *New York Times* reported that a question in February 2011 about the improving prospects of Egypt's Muslim Brotherhood set Prince Nayif off on "a diatribe against both the treachery of the Brotherhood and the journalist who asked the question, with the prince labeling the journalist a terrorist sympathizer." [161] The Editorial Board of the *New York Times* explained in June 2017 the real reason behind the Saudi block's attacks on the Muslim Brotherhood aptly: "The real reason it's been labeled a terrorist group is that autocratic regimes see it as a populist threat."[162]

The relentless demonization and lobbying by the Saudi and Abu Dhabi ruling families to declare the Muslim Brotherhood organization a terrorist organization in Europe and the US are designed to protect the two clans from their own citizens who aspire to have democratic governance. The two clans are most eager to distract from their culpability for 9/11 (among the 19 terrorists of 9/11, 15 were Saudis and 2 were from the UAE).

The Muslim Brotherhood Transformation: The Brotherhood, having embraced in 2011 free elections, representative democracy, and coalition governments with secular political parties and non-Muslims in Egypt, is the one political force with the organization, credibility, and popularity to challenge Wahhabi teaching over the soul of Sunni Islam. The Muslim Brotherhood shares with Wahhabism the political circumstances of their birth. However, the two differ widely in the interpretation of the Islamic text. Both were born as a reaction to Kemal Ataturk's secularization of Turkey in the aftermath of the defeat and dismemberment of the Ottoman Empire in the First World War. While the Turks blamed the decline of their empire on a rigid Islam in a European world of the Enlightenment, Reformation, and the Industrial Revolution, the Brotherhood in Egypt and the al-Saud/Abdulwahhab partnership in the Arabian Peninsula claimed that the destruction of the Ottoman Empire was God's punishment for the sultans' abandonment and corruption of "true" Islam.

Even today, the Zogby survey shows this notion to be alive and well among Arabs. Like their great-great-grandfathers a century ago, the

---

[160]"Naif Says Muslim Brotherhood Cause of Most Arab Problems," *Arab News,* (November 28, 2002). http://www.arabnews.com/node/226291

[161]Neil MacFarquar, "Nayef bin Abdul Aziz, Saudi Crown Prince Who Led Crackdown on Al Qaeda, Dies at 78," *New York Times,* (June 16, 2012). http://www.nytimes.com/2012/06/17/world/middleeast/saudi-crown-prince-nayef-dies-led-crackdown-on-al-qaeda.html?pagewanted=all

[162]The Editorial Board, "Misguided Attacks on Al Jazeera," *The New York Times,* (June 21, 2017). https://www.nytimes.com/2017/06/21/opinion/misguided-attacks-on-al-jazeera.html

overwhelming majority of those surveyed disagreed with the notion that Islam "has been a major cause for the Arab world's decline in the social, political and economic realms in recent times."

Religion has been a major cause for the Arab world's decline in the social, political and economic realms in recent times.

	Morocco	Egypt	KSA	UAE	Bahrain	Kuwait	Jordan	Palestine
Agree	24	10	4	19	29	4	14	57
Disagree	76	90	96	81	71	96	86	43

Zogby Research Services, LLC, *Muslim Millennial attitudes on religion and religious leadership,* Tabah Foundation, 2015.

Former Brotherhood members abandoned the Brotherhood to form splinter groups of their own. To attract jihadi followers, they committed notorious acts of terrorism. The Egyptian Islamic Jihad, EIJ (Jama'at al-jihad) assassinated Egyptian President Anwar Sadat on October 6, 1981.[163] EIJ merged with Osama Bin Laden's Wahhabi al-Qaeda in February 1998. Ayman Zawahiri, EIJ leader, became the deputy to Osama Bin Laden. Another group, the Islamic Group (al-Jama'a al-Islamiyya), was blamed for most assassinations, bombings, shootings, and attacks against tourists and foreigners in Egypt during the 1990s. Other Brotherhood derivatives include Islamic Jihad and Hamas in the occupied Palestinian territories.

In Egypt's parliamentary elections of November-December 2005, members of the banned Muslim Brotherhood stood as independents. They won eighty-eight seats, or 20%, to become the major parliamentary opposition.[164] In 2012, the Brotherhood's candidate Muhammad Morsi won Egypt's first ever multi-party democratic election with 51.73% of the votes cast.

While the Wahhabi sword soaked the sands of the Arabian Desert with blood to install Saudi Arabia's absolute monarchy in 1932, Egypt's Muslim Brotherhood succeeded through the ballot box in 2005 to become a part of the Egyptian parliament, and in 2012, to legitimately rule Egypt. One year later, Riyadh and General Sisi contrived the coup d'etat that destroyed Cairo's first democratic experience.

---

[163]"Investigating Terror Organizations," *BBC.* http://news.bbc.co.uk/hi/english/static/in_depth/world/2001/war_on_terror/investigation_on_terror/organisation_2.stm

[164]"Egypt Islamists Make Record Gains," *BBC,* (December 8, 2005). http://news.bbc.co.uk/1/hi/world/middle_east/4509682.stm

A Spring in Egypt Cut Short: During the 66 years since the July 23, 1952 military coup that ended its monarchy, Egypt has endured 65 years of army dictatorships. During this period, four military presidents concocted nine un-contested referendums (between 1956 and 1999) and four contrived elections (between 2005 and 2018)—mere theatrics that produced 90%-100% approvals of the votes cast.

The one exception was the 2012 Arab Spring's democratically contested election of the Muslim Brotherhood's civilian candidate Muhammad Morsi. He was sworn in as Egypt's president on June 30, 2012 with 51.73%. He ran for the presidency against eight candidates. He formed a coalition government, including old regime figures.[165] He had a democratically elected parliament in which ten political parties shared 508 seats, with Morsi's Freedom and Justice Party winning 235 seats.[166]

It is notable that Mr. Obama did not protect Mr. Mubarak and did not stand in Mr. Morsi's way to the presidency. His hostility toward Saudi Arabia might explain his decision to let democracy be born in Egypt (see above: *Obama's Middle East Politics—The Atlantic Magazine Interview*). However, Riyadh had different plans.

During his one-year in office, President Morsi endured schemes and intrigues from Mubarak's old ruling group. His lack of good management skills and a profound ignorance of democratic values helped his enemies undermine his authority. He treated the 51.73% who elected him as if they were the 100%. Led by the media, judiciary, and business tycoons, the minority conspired against him.

Endless lines for bread at bakeries became the order of the day due to lack of flour. Public utilities services deteriorated. The *New York Times* reported that, "The state agencies responsible for providing electricity and ensuring gas supplies failed so fundamentally that gas lines and rolling blackouts fed widespread anger and frustration."[167] While Morsi was president, even the police refused to deploy fully. The police returned following Sisi's coup. The *New York Times* reported, "It is the police returning to the

---

[165]Abdel-Rahman Hussein, "Egypt Swears In First Post-Revolution Cabinet with Plenty of Old Guard," *The Guardian*, (August 2, 2012). https://www.theguardian.com/world/2012/aug/02/egypt-middleeast

[166]"Egypt's Islamist Parties Win Elections to Parliament," *BBC*, (January 21, 2012). http://www.bbc.co.uk/news/world-middle-east-16665748

[167]Ben Hubbard, "Anger at Egypt's Leaders Intensifies in Gas Lines," The *New York Times*, (June 26, 2013). http://www.nytimes.com/2013/06/27/world/middleeast/anger-at-egypts-leaders-intensifies-in-gas-lines.html?pagewanted=all

streets that offers the most blatant sign that the institutions once loyal to Mr. Mubarak held back while Mr. Morsi was in power.[168] Shortages and frequent electricity blackouts brought protests in cities across Egypt for weeks.

Democracy in Egypt did not endure. Opposition to the Muslim Brotherhood put a quick end to Morsi's presidency. By mid-June 2013, a group calling itself Tamarrod (meaning rebellion) claims to have collected 22 million signatures (no verification) calling on Morsi to resign. On June 30, 2013, the first anniversary of Morsi's inauguration, "millions" of protestors in dozens of Egyptian cities took to the streets demanding Morsi's departure. On July 3, 2013, General Sisi removed Morsi from office.[169]

On July 3, 2013, representative democracy was sacrificed on the altar of Saudi oil by General Abdul Fattah el-Sisi. He plunged Egypt back in the darkness of yet another non-representative military dictatorship.[170] As a reward to Sisi, Saudi Arabia immediately organized with Kuwait and United Arab Emirates a $12 billion aid package to Egypt.[171] President Morsi was jailed and accused of a long list of charges.[172] He was sentenced to death on the charge of taking part in prison breaks during the 2011 uprising prior to becoming president. The sentence was overturned in November 2016 by Egypt's Court of Cessation and ordered retrial.[173]

In the presidential elections a year later, Mr. Sisi managed to receive 96.91% of the vote cast, with a turnout of about 47% of the country's

---

[168]Ben Hubbard and David Kirkpatrick, "Sudden Improvements in Egypt Suggest a Campaign to Undermine Morsi," The New York Times, (July 10, 2013). http://www.nytimes.com/2013/07/11/world/middleeast/improvements-in-egypt-suggest-a-campaign-that-undermined-morsi.html

[169]Sarah Childress, "Timeline: What's Happened since Egypt's Revolution?," Frontline, (September 17, 2013). http://www.pbs.org/wgbh/frontline/article/timeline-whats-happened-since-egypts-revolution/

[170]Richard Spencer, "How Sisi Plotted to Save Army Rule Even While Hosni Mubarak Was in Power," The Telegraph, (June 1, 2014). http://www.telegraph.co.uk/news/worldnews/africaandindianocean/egypt/10866943/How-Sisi-plotted-to-save-army-rule-even-while-Hosni-Mubarak-was-in-power.html

[171]Rod Nordland, "Saudi Arabia Promises to Aid Egypt's Regime, The New York Times," (August 19, 2013). http://www.nytimes.com/2013/08/20/world/middleeast/saudi-arabia-vows-to-back-egypts-rulers.html

[172]The charges include: Inciting the killing of opponents, espionage for Hamas, Hezbollah, and Iran's Revolutionary Guards, escaping from prison during the 2011 revolution, leaking classified documents to Qatar, in addition to insulting the judiciary.

[173]Egypt's Mohamed Morsi Has Death Sentence Overturned," Al Jazeera, (November 15, 2016). https://www.aljazeera.com/news/2016/11/egypt-morsi-death-sentence-overturned-report-161115095201405.html

54 million voters, according to the election commission statement on June 2, 2014.[174]

For the March 26–28, 2018 elections, the two contenders who could have seriously threatened Sisi were sidelined by the regime. The first was former prime minister and former Commander of Egypt's air force Ahmad Shafik. He mysteriously retreated[175] five weeks after announcing his intention to run for president (November 29, 2017).[176] The second candidate was former military chief of staff Sami Anan. He was arrested shortly after announcing that he would challenge Sisi in the election. His arrest has "made it crystal clear" that the "election will be neither free nor fair", said *Foreign Policy* magazine on January 24, 2018.[177]

At the last minute, before the deadline for submitting candidacy documents (Monday January 29, 2018), a token challenger, an obscure politician who is a supporter of Sisi, submitted his candidacy documents to the election commission.[178]

In a joint statement, a coalition of opposition figures called on January 29, 2018 for a boycott of the elections after all real candidates were arrested, prosecuted, or intimidated out of the race.[179] "Threats, bribes and bullying at polls to bolster Sisi's legitimacy" said The London *Times* newspaper in an article on March 29, 2018.[180]

[174]Yasmin Saleh and Stephen Kalin, "Sisi Won 96.91 Percent in Egypt's Presidential Vote-Commission", *Reuters* (June 3, 2014). https://www.reuters.com/article/us-egypt-election-results/sisi-won-96-91-percent-in-egypts-presidential-vote-commission-idUSKBN0EE1UO20140603

[175]"Egyptian ex-PM Ahmed Shafik says won't run for presidency," *Reuters*, (January 7, 2018). https://uk.reuters.com/article/uk-egypt-politics/egyptian-ex-pm-ahmed-shafik-says-wont-run-for-presidency-idUKKBN1EW0MM

[176]Amina Ismail, "Former Egyptian premier Shafiq says intends to run in 2018 election," *Reuters*, (November 29, 2017), https://uk.reuters.com/article/uk-egypt-politics-exclusive/exclusive-former-egyptian-premier-shafiq-says-intends-to-run-in-2018-election-idUKKBN1DT20N

[177]Sara Khorshid, "Egypt's Undemocratic Election," *Foreign Policy*," (January 24, 2018). http://foreignpolicy.com/2018/01/24/egypts-undemocratic-election/

[178]"Obscure politician is face-saving challenger in Egypt vote," *Daily News*, (January 29, 2018). http://www.nydailynews.com/newswires/news/world/obscure-politician-face-saving-challenger-egypt-vote-article-1.3785514

[179]Abdallah Dalsh, "Egyptian opposition calls for boycott of elections after challengers are arrested and attacked," *The Telegraph*, (January, 29, 2018). http://www.telegraph.co.uk/news/2018/01/29/egyptian-opposition-calls-boycott-elections-challengers-arrested/

[180]Bel Trew, "Egypt election: Threats, bribes and bullying at polls to bolster Sisi's legitimacy." *The Times*, (March 29, 2018). https://www.thetimes.co.uk/article/egypt-election-threats-bribes-and-bullying-at-polls-to-bolster-sisi-s-legitimacy-b682krggv

On April 2, 2018, the results were announced: Mr. Sisi won 97% of the votes cast with a turnout of 41%.[181]

3. Punishing Turkey for Supporting the Muslim Brotherhood: In Turkey, secularism, democracy, and the moderate Hanafi Sunni Islam coexist. In the November 2015 general election, 16 political parties competed for the 550-seat parliament. President Recep Tayyip Erdogan's party, the Islamic Justice and Development Party (AKP), won 49.4% of the votes cast with 316 seats.[182] AKP was formed by Mr. Erdogan in 2001. It has been in power since the 2002 election.[183]

Turkish secularism, democracy and moderate Hanafi Sunni Islam represent a system of governance, which is frightening to the Saudi regime's propagation that Islam and democracy are contradictory and that democracy is the work of the devil. The Islam of Turkey and the Brotherhood represent an existential threat to the Saudi regime. It provides a credible, less austere, less harsh, less obtrusive way of life than the Wahhabi way of life. The Islam of Turkey and the Brotherhood appeal to the educated internet generation, especially women. Brotherhood women enjoy rights their sisters in Wahhabi Saudi Arabia are denied, like participation in public life, and freedom from male guardianship, which has for the past century controlled whether a Saudi wife, sister, or a mother can see a doctor, open a bank account, own a shop, or travel alone.

The Ottoman Empire ruled over most of the Arab world for four centuries (1517–1918). The Turkish Sultans belonged to the moderate Hanafi Sunni rite. In the Balkans, for example, they did not force their Christian subjects to convert to Islam in the sixteenth century. Had they done so, the savage sectarian wars in the former Yugoslavia four centuries later (1991–1999), would most probably not have happened. In 1492, the Ottoman Sultan, Bayezid-II (1481–1512) allowed Jews driven out from Spain and Portugal to settle in the Ottoman territories (see Chapter Eight: *Islam's Veneration of Judaism*).[184] The firm hand of the Sultans had kept

---

[181]John Davison and Ahmad Tolba, Egypt's Sisi wins 97 percent in election with no real opposition, Reuters, (April 2, 2018). https://www.reuters.com/article/us-egypt-election-result/egypts-sisi-wins-97-percent-in-election-with-no-real-opposition-idUSKCN1H916A

[182]"Turkey Election: Ruling AKP Regains Majority," *BBC*, (November 2, 2015). http://www.bbc.co.uk/news/world-europe-34694420

[183]"Erdogan Triumphs—With Plenty of Help from His Enemies," *The Economist*, (November 7, 2002). http://www.economist.com/node/1433284

[184]Bernard Lewis, *The Jews of Islam* (Princeton University Press, Princeton, New Jersey, 1987), P. 50.

religious extremism and hatred-of the–other culture in check.[185] This control was lost when the Ottoman Empire was dismembered in 1918 and separate states with different religious agendas were formed, especially Wahhabi Saudi Arabia in 1932.

Turkey was the first independent Muslim country to separate religion from the state, following the defeat of the Ottoman Empire in the First World War. Mustafa Kemal Ataturk (1881–1938) blamed Islam's rigidity during the previous four centuries for the decline and calamitous fall of the empire. While Europe was undergoing Christian reformation and progressing towards the industrial revolution, Ottoman modernization was impeded by the ulama's resistance to innovation.

Although Turkey's reforms evolved cautiously since the early 1800s under the reign of Sultan Mahmut II (1808–1839) and his son, Sultan Abdulmecit (1839–1861), their speed and depth became revolutionary under Ataturk. Between 1924 and 1935, Ataturk implemented a rapid and extensive program of fundamental change in Turkish society the likes of which the Islamic world had never seen.[186] Arabs, on the other hand, believed that the abandonment of Islam by the sultans was to blame for the Ottoman defeat. From such thinking, the Wahhabi state in Saudi Arabia was born in 1932 and the Muslim Brotherhood organization was formed in Egypt in 1928.

While it is true that Erdogan has been taking tough measures against his critics, especially the media, he has not repealed Ataturk's secular laws. Cosmetics aside, Erdogan has not altered any of Ataturk's basic reforms. The Swiss civil code and the Italian penal code, which replaced Shari'a laws and courts in 1926 are sacrosanct. Civil marriage, gender equality in divorce, custody, and inheritance continue to be the laws of the land. Polygamy is illegal. In fact, the changes Erdogan effected since AKP came to power in 2002 have been rather modest: construction of mosques, lifting the ban on wearing the hijab (scarf over a woman's hair), encouraging enrollment in Islamic schools, restricting the sale of alcohol, and the introduction of Islamic banking.

---

[185]The first Sunni empire was the Umayyad Empire (661–750) with its capital in Damascus, Syria. The second was the Abbasid Empire (750–1258) with its capital in Baghdad, Iraq.

[186]In addition to abolishing the Islamic caliphate on March 3, 1924, the Kemalist secular revolution included abolishing Shari'a laws and courts (1926), which was replaced by the Swiss civil code and the Italian penal code. It also replaced the fez by the Western-style hat or cap (1925), the Islamic calendar by Western calendar (1926), Latin alphabet instead of Arabic alphabet (1928), Western weights and measures (1931), and Sunday as the day of rest (1935) instead of Friday.

On the other hand, Erdogan has adopted judicial reforms to harmonize Turkey's legal system with that of the European Union as part of Turkey's interest in joining the EU. In January 2004, Turkey abolished the death penalty.[187] In 2009, the judicial provisions that allowed civilians to be tried in military courts were removed from the Turkish Constitution.[188] Judicial reforms were also adopted to restructure domestic judicial institutions in terms of their power and functions. The 2010 constitutional referendum expanded the Supreme Board of Judges and Prosecutors from 7 members to 22.[189] Also, it granted Turkish citizens the right to individually apply to the Constitutional Court if government decisions, laws or the implementation of laws violate their basic rights and fundamental freedoms.[190]

Ankara's contribution to a democratic Islam in the Arab world is a sharp ideological weapon to counter the Wahhabi ideology that grips Islamist terror organizations. For this alone, the US and its allies should give Turkey high marks. The US and its allies owe Turkey a debt of gratitude.

Turkey helped spread democracy in the Arab world through the Muslim Brotherhood. No other organization could be as effective as the Muslim Brotherhood in convincing the millions of Arab Sunni masses that democracy is compatible with Islam. The Brotherhood possesses the religious credibility to be an agent of change. The demonization of Mr. Erdogan and the Muslim Brotherhood by the US and Western politicians and media has wrecked the Arab Spring. In the confrontation between democrats and autocrats in the Arab world, the democratic West sides with the oil autocrats: A hypocritical and Machiavellian stance which brings into question whether the democratic West is truly interested in spreading democracy in Arab countries. Might it be that the democratic West, led by the US, is deliberately obstructing the development of democracy in the Arab Middle East?

4. Shutting Down Qatar's Al Jazeera Media Network: Silencing the Al Jazeera network, especially the Arabic service, is arguably the most important factor preoccupying and worrying the Saudi regime and its

---

[187]"Turkey Agrees Death Penalty Ban," *BBC*, (January 9, 2004). http://news.bbc.co.uk/1/hi/world/europe/3384667.stm

[188]Meltem Mü üler-Baç, *Judicial Reform in Turkey and the EU's Political Conditionality, (Mis)Fit between Domestic Preferences and EU Demands,* Maximizing the integration capacity of the European Union, MAXCAP Working Paper No. 18, January 2016, PP. 13–14. http://userpage.fu-berlin.de/kfgeu/maxcap/system/files/maxcap_wp_18.pdf

[189]Ibid. P. 15.

[190]Ibid. P. 16.

allies. For Wahhabi indoctrination to deliver blind obedience of the Saudi masses to the King, the masses must be insulated from the liberal and democratic values, and ideas of the modern age.

Qatar is certainly not a haven of democracy. It is as much of a non-representative non-participatory dictatorship as the rest of the GCC states. The Emir's authority is absolute. He controls the three branches of government. He is unaccountable to anyone. He serves for life, unless forcibly removed,[191] or abdicates.[192]

Qatar is a tiny peninsula with some 270,000 citizens and 2.04 million foreign workers (July 2017).[193] Qatari citizens enjoy the highest per-capita income in the world. Expatriate workers, on the other hand, are treated like slaves, similar to their treatment in the rest of the GCC. Dwarfed by neighbouring Saudi Arabia, steeped in tribal culture, Qatar's al-Thani rulers have been in a frustrating search for a regional role: A burning ambition that found expression in the creation of the Al Jazeera media network.

Since its launch on November 1, 1996, Al Jazeera's Arabic Television Network has been instrumental in opening the eyes of the Arab masses to the ills of their rulers' tyranny, to institutional corruption and mismanagement, to theft of public funds, human rights abuses, non-accountability, non-transparency, etc. Al Jazeera Arabic has been educating the oppressed downtrodden masses that, contrary to palace ulama preaching, democracy *is* compatible with Islam and that rebellion against unjust rulers is a part of its tenets. Al Jazeera Arabic opened the eyes of millions to the shining light of democracy, human rights, and the dignity of the citizen. It educated the masses that the three powers of government (legislative, executive, judicial) must be separate and independent of one another (though, not in the case in Qatar). The message was well received. According to audience data for the first quarter of 2013, Al Jazeera's daily viewership

---

[191]Emir Khalifa bin Hamad al-Thani, was deposed, while on vacation in Geneva, on June 26, 1995 by his son, crown Prince Hamad bin Khalifa al-Thani, in a bloodless palace coup, Patrick Cockburn, "Emir of Qatar deposed by his son," *The Independent,* (June 26, 1995). http://www.independent.co.uk/news/world/emir-of-qatar-deposed-by-his-son-1588698.html

[192]Ian Black, "Qatar's Emir Sheikh Hamad to Hand Power to Son, Crown Prince Tamim," *The Guardian,* (June 24, 2013). https://www.theguardian.com/world/2013/jun/24/qatar-emir-steps-down-son-tamim

[193]Central Intelligence Agency, "The World Factbook, Qatar." https://www.cia.gov/library/publications/the-world-factbook/geos/qa.html

across the Middle East and North Africa was 34% higher than all the other pan-Arab channels combined.[194]

Al Jazeera English has been successful as well. Since its launch in 2006, it has won prestigious awards from around the world. Among those were 18 awards in 2017 from The New York Festival, including Broadcaster of the Year, Best Short Documentary, five Gold World Awards, and eleven Silver World Awards. In 2016, Al Jazeera English won 31 awards from around the world; in 2015, 18 awards; in 2014, 13 awards; and in 2013, 8 awards.[195]

Despite Al Jazeera's silence on the dictatorship of the absolute authority of the Qatari al-Thani ruling family, which is similar to the rest of the autocracies in the GCC, the network has, nonetheless, been a catalyst of positive change in the Arab world. It has guided the Arab masses towards democratic enlightenment. Al Jazeera Arabic education and popularity frightens every Arab king and president. Al Jazeera's awakening of the Arab masses threatens to destroy the palace ulama's franchise. The culmination was the 2011 Arab Spring.

Even with the return of Sisi's dictatorship to Egypt and the destruction of Syria during years of war (started March 18, 2011) at the hands of the Assad family, Al Jazeera Arabic has planted the resilient seed of representative democracy in the heads of the Arab masses to the fury of the Saudi regime and the rest of the Arab dictators.

In 2002, Saudi Arabia tried to muzzle Al Jazeera. It withdrew its ambassador to Qatar for six years. In 2014, Qatar promised to stop "interfering" in its Gulf neighbors' domestic politics.[196]

In late May 2017, Egypt, Saudi Arabia, and the United Arab Emirates moved to block the websites of Al Jazeera and other Qatari media outlets. On June 7, 2017, Jordan closed Al Jazeera's Amman bureau and stripped it of its operating license. Saudi Arabia followed suit the next day, closing Al Jazeera's Riyadh bureau; then in yet a rather odd step, it ordered tourist hotels to block "all channels from the Al Jazeera Media Network."[197]

Al Jazeera is not alone in being targeted by Saudi Arabia's heavy hand. All media organizations that criticize Saudi policies invite Riyadh's wrath.

---

[194]Al Jazeera Arabic Tops Viewing Figures," *Al Jazeera*, (May 22, 2017). https://www.aljazeera.com/pressoffice/2013/05/201352291421900835.html

[195]"Awards won by Al Jazeera English," *Al Jazeera*, (October 6, 2015). https://www.aljazeera.com/pressoffice/2012/04/2012416161854868952.html

[196]Kevin Ponniah, "Qatar Crisis: Can Al Jazeera Survive?," *BBC*, (June 8, 2017). http://www.bbc.co.uk/news/world-middle-east-40187414

[197]The Editorial Board, "Misguided Attacks on Al Jazeera."

Hardly an Arab media outlet is independent of Saudi blackmail or cash. Even the BBC Arabic Television news channel had to close on April 21, 1996, after only a year and a half of operation, when the Saudi government attempted to suppress its programming. The *New York Times* put the reason for the closure of BBC Arabic Television as follows: "Nearly two years after the debut of BBC Arabic Television, Orbit Communications, a Rome-based media distribution company, and its Saudi financial backers had pulled the plug on the service they had helped to found and fund, labeling a recent BBC documentary on Islamic law in Saudi Arabia 'a sneering and racist attack.'"[198] The Editorial Board of the *New York Times* explained the real reasons behind the Saudi block's attack on Al Jazeera on June 21, 2017:

> By attacking Al Jazeera, the Saudis and their neighbors are trying to eliminate a voice that could lead citizens to question their rulers.
>
> Al Jazeera is hardly a perfect news organization: Critical reporting on Qatar or members of Qatar's royal family is not tolerated. But much of the rest of its reporting hews to international journalistic standards, provides a unique view on events in the Middle East and serves as a vital news source for millions who live under antidemocratic rule.
>
> Those are reasons enough for the monarchs and dictators attacking Qatar to silence Al Jazeera. And reason enough to condemn their action.[199]

The United Nations human rights chief said on June 30, 2017 that a "Demand by Saudi Arabia and three other Arab nations for Qatar to close down its Al Jazeera TV channel is an 'unacceptable attack' on the right to freedoms of expression and opinion."[200]

5. Protection from the Justice Against Sponsors of Terrorism Act (JASTA): On September 28, 2016, the US Congress enacted JASTA. It allows the Saudi government to be held responsible for any role in the 9/11/2001 assault on New York's World Trade Center and the Pentagon

---

[198]Erik Ipsen, "Demise of BBC Arabic TV: Nothing Lost in Translation," The *New York Times,* (May 6, 1996). http://www.nytimes.com/1996/05/06/news/demise-of-bbc-arabic-tv-nothing-lost-in-translation.html

[199]The Editorial Board, "Misguided Attacks on Al Jazeera."

[200]"Demand for Qatar to close down Al-Jazeera 'unacceptable': UN," *Reuters,* (June 30, 2017). https://www.reuters.com/article/us-gulf-qatar-un-idUSKBN19L18Z

in Washington D.C.[201] On March 21, 2017, families of 800 victims and 1,500 first responders filed a lawsuit accusing Saudi Arabia of involvement in the terror attacks.[202] The Saudi King wishes Mr. Trump's help to dismiss the case. On March 28, 2018, a US District Judge in Manhattan rejected Saudi Arabia's bid to dismiss lawsuits by the families of nearly 3,000 victims who were killed, roughly 25,000 people who suffered injuries, and many businesses and insurers claiming that Saudi Arabia "helped plan the September 11, 2001, attacks."[203]

If Saudi Arabia loses this case, it stands to possibly pay tens of billions of dollars in damages. As a guideline, on May 1, 2018, although no Iranian was involved in the 9/11 terror attacks, a federal judge faulted Iran, the Islamic Revolutionary Guard Corps, and the Iranian Central Bank. He ordered Iran to pay $12.5 million per spouse, $8.5 million per parent or child, and $4.25 million per sibling to the families of the more than 1,000 victims of 9/11 whose families joined the lawsuit.[204]

The Threat of "Alien" Ideas from the Internet

For Wahhabi indoctrination to be effective, the Saudi populace must be insulated from alien political, religious, and social ideas from the internet. The following is a description of how Saudi Arabia deals with the internet's undesirable influences, extracted from the US Bureau of Democracy, Human Rights and Labor, Country Reports on Human Rights Practices for 2015:[205]

> Security authorities actively monitored internet activity, both to enforce societal norms and to monitor recruitment efforts by organizations such as Da'esh [IS] ... The government coordinated with

---

[201]"Congress overrides Obama's veto of 9/11 bill letting families sue Saudi Arabia," *The Guardian.*

[202]Families of 800 Victims and 1,500 First Responders File a Lawsuit Against Saudi Arabia Accusing the Country's Officials of Aiding Hijackers in 9/11 Attacks," *DailyMail*, (March 21, 2017). http://www.dailymail.co.uk/news/article-4333512/Families-800-victims-sue-Saudi-Arabia-9-11.html

[203]Jonathan Stempel, "Saudi Arabia must face U.S. lawsuits over Sept. 11 attacks," Reuters, (March 28, 2018). https://www.reuters.com/article/us-usa-saudi-sept11/saudi-arabia-must-face-u-s-lawsuits-over-sept-11-attacks-idUSKBN1H43A1

[204]Max Greenwood, "Court orders Iran to pay billions to 9/11 victims and families," *The Hill*, (May 1, 2018). http://thehill.com/homenews/news/385769-court-orders-iran-to-pay-billions-to-9-11-victims-and-families

[205]US Department of State, Bureau of Democracy, Human Rights and Labor, "Country Reports on Human Rights Practices for 2016," https://www.state.gov/j/drl/rls/hrrpt/humanrightsreport/index.htm#wrapper

the Italian anti-threat software company Hacking Team to target Saudi citizens in Qatif with surveillance malware.

The government required internet access providers to monitor customers and since 2009, has made it mandatory for internet cafes to install hidden cameras and provide identity records of customers. Although authorities blocked websites offering proxies, persistent internet users accessed the unfiltered internet via other means.

The Press and Publications Law criminalizes the publication or downloading of offensive sites, and authorities routinely blocked sites containing material perceived as harmful, illegal, offensive, or anti-Islamic. The governmental Communications and Information Technology Commission (CITC) filtered and blocked access to websites it deemed offensive, including pages calling for domestic political, social, or economic reforms or supporting human rights.

According to the NGO Reporters without Borders, authorities claimed to have cumulatively blocked approximately 400,000 websites.

In November 2014, the Khobar Criminal Court sentenced human rights activist Mekhlef al-Shammary to two years in prison and 200 lashes after he commented on Twitter in support of Shia-Sunni reconciliation and attended a Shia religious gathering.

Raif Badawi, a Saudi blogger, was sentenced to 10 years in prison and 1,000 lashes, for allegedly "insulting Islam through electronic channels."[206]

The Threat from Saudi Arabia's Internal Sectarian Divisions

More dangerous than the liberal winds from the internet or Egypt are the Shi'ite and Isma'ili discontent facing Saudi Arabia in the Eastern Province and the Najran region to the Southwest bordering Yemen. Saudi Arabia's Shi'ites live in the towns and villages of the oil-rich Eastern

---

[206]Ensaf Haidar, "The First 50 Lashes: A Saudi Activist's Wife Endures Her Husband's Brutal Sentence," *The Guardian*, (May 17, 2016). https://www.theguardian.com/world/2016/may/17/raif-badawi-saudi-blogger-lashes-prison-ensaf-haidar

Province. They are estimated to be around 10% of the Saudi population (excluding foreigners).[207] Wahhabi discrimination against Shi'ites is fanatical. What follows is a description of the discrimination Shi'ites endure, extracted from the International Religious Freedom Report for 2012 of the US Bureau of Democracy, Human Rights and Labor:

> Shi'ites face discrimination in education, employment, the military, political representation, the judiciary, and the media. Shi'ites face employment discrimination in the private sector ... a "glass ceiling" existed and Shi'ites were passed over for less-qualified Sunni colleagues. Of the 20 appointed members to the Council of Senior Ulama, none is Shi'ite, with one representative of each of the three other Sunni Schools: Maliki, Hanafi, and Shafi'i. Of the Consultative Council's 150 members, only five are Shi'ite ... There were no Shi'ite ministers, deputy ministers, governors, deputy governors, or ministry branch directors in the Eastern Province, and only three of the 59 government-appointed municipal council members were Shi'ite. Shi'ites were significantly underrepresented in national security-related positions, including the Ministry of Defense, the National Guard, and the Ministry of Interior. A very small number of Shi'ites occupy high-level positions in government-owned companies and government agencies.
>
> In higher education the government discriminated against Shi'ites in the selection process for students, professors, and administrators at public universities. For example, Shi'ites constituted an estimated 5 percent of professors at a leading university in al-Ahsa, an area with a population that is at least 50 percent Shi'ite... At the primary and secondary levels of education in al-Ahsa, there continues to be severe underrepresentation of Shi'ites among school principals. There were no female Shi'ite principals in the 200 schools for girls in al-Ahsa, and 15 male Shi'ite principals in the 200

[207]Saudi statistics, especially population estimates, are unreliable political statistics. It serves the interest of the Saudi government to present the Shi'ites and Isma'ilis as being a tiny minority. According to the most recent data from Saudi General Authority for Statistics, Demography Survey 2016, P. 47, the Saudi population (excluding foreigners) in the Eastern Province was 3.09 million. Assuming that the Shi'ites are two thirds of the Saudis in the Province, the Shi'ite population becomes equal to 2.06 million, out of total population of 20.07 million = 10%, http://www.stats.gov.sa/sites/default/files/en-demographic-research-2016_3.pdf

schools for boys in Al-Ahsa. Shi'ites face significant employment discrimination in the public sector. The government did not officially recognize several centers of Shi'ite religious instruction located in the Eastern Province, provide financial support for them, recognize certificates of educational attainment for their graduates, or provide employment for their graduates, all of which it does for Sunni religious training institutions.

The Ministry of Islamic Affairs (MOIA) is financially and administratively responsible for Sunni mosques, which according to its 2012 estimates, number around 75,000, 15,000 of which are Friday mosques (larger mosques that host Friday prayers and include a sermon). The MOIA employs approximately 75,000 Sunni imams and 15,000 Sunni Friday khateebs (sermon leaders) to staff these mosques. Imams receive monthly MOIA salaries ranging from 2,500 to 5,000 riyals ($667 to $1,333), depending on the seniority and educational level of the individual... The government does not finance construction or maintenance of Shi'ite mosques, and the process of obtaining a government-required license for a Shi'ite mosque is reportedly unclear and arbitrary... Virtually all Shi'ite old mosques were unable to obtain licenses and faced the threat of closure at any time... Government religious authorities continue the practice of destroying ancient Shi'ite Islamic historical sites... Shi'ite mosques in mixed religious neighborhoods reportedly were required to recite the Sunni call to prayer, which is distinct from the Shi'ite call... Although Shi'ites combine two of the five daily Sunni prayers, Shi'ite businessmen often were forced to close their shops during all five prayer times, in accordance with the country's official Sunni practices... Public Shi'ite celebrations were restricted, even in some areas with large Shia population.

Qatif community leaders described zoning laws that prevent construction of buildings over a certain height in various Shi'ite neighborhoods. The leaders stated the laws prevented investment and development in these areas and aimed to limit the density of the Shi'ite population in any given area.

The one court of appeals on which Shi'ite judges sit has no real authority and only verifies documents ... The legal testimony of Shi'ite is either ignored or considered to have less weight than the testimony of Sunnis.

Anti-Shi'ite rhetoric persists in Sunni mosques. The government blocked access to some web sites with religious content it considered offensive or sensitive, including the Shia news web site Al-Rasid ... The government continues to exclude Shi'ite perspectives from the state's extensive religious media and broadcast programming. The government sporadically imposed bans on the importation and sale of Shi'ite books and audiovisual products.[208] The Department for Health Affairs in Eastern Province docked the monthly pay of a Shia Muslim hospital worker in Dammam after she reportedly played the Shia call to prayer on her mobile phone.[209]

Adding to Wahhabi/Shi'ite sectarian tension recently was the execution on January 2, 2016 of the influential Shi'ite sheikh Nimr al-Nimr. Sheikh al-Nimr was a vocal supporter of the mass anti-government protests that erupted in the Eastern Province in 2011 against Wahhabi marginalization of Shi'ites. Iran said Saudi Arabia would pay a "high price" for the execution.[210]

The Isma'ilis, a Shi'ite sect, are concentrated in Najran Province in Southwestern Saudi Arabia, bordering Yemen. They are estimated to be around 1.7% of the Saudi population (excluding foreigners).[211] Isma'ilis suffer as much discrimination as the Shi'ites the Eastern Province. The Islma'ilis plus the Shi'ites represent around 12% of Saudi citizens, around 2.5 million.

---

[208]US Department of State, Bureau of Democracy, Human Rights and Labor, "International Religious Freedom Report for 2012, Saudi Arabia," https://www.state.gov/j/drl/rls/irf/2012religiousfreedom/index.htm?year=2012&dlid=208398#wrapper

[209]US Department of State, Bureau of Democracy, Human Rights and Labor, "International Religious Freedom Report for 2015," https://www.state.gov/j/drl/rls/irf/religiousfreedom/index.htm#wrapper

[210]"Saudi Arabia Has Executed the Prominent Shia Cleric Sheikh Nimr al-Nimr," *BBC*, (January 2, 2016). http://www.bbc.co.uk/news/world-middle-east-35213244

[211]Bureau of Democracy, Human Rights and Labor, "International Religious Freedom Report for 2015,"

CHAPTER SIX

THE AL-SAUD WAHHABI GOVERNANCE

The Tool-Kit that Controls the Saudi Masses

Saudi governance is non-representative and non-participatory, mired in tribalism, cronyism, nepotism, and favoritism. Free press does not exist. Political parties, labor unions, and societal organization are banned. Control of Saudi society is performed by a ruling group composed of five constituencies: The al-Saud clan, the Wahhabi ulama, military and national guards, tribal Sheiks, and merchant families.

Thousands of Royals

In Saudi Arabia's patriarchal society, master/servant relationships dominate. Several thousand princes and their networks of servants and hangers-on bolster the forces of containment.

Estimated to be more than 11,000 direct descendants of King Abdulaziz, the founder of the dynasty, the al-Saud family is probably the largest ruling family in history (For a guesstimate of the number of the direct descendants of King Abdulziz, see Chapter Six – Appendix 1). When the families of Abdulaziz's brother and the half-dozen half-brothers are added, the extended family might be 15,000, possibly more. When the families of Abdulaziz's cousins, such as Saud al-Kabir and Abdallah bin Turki are added, the number becomes greater. When families into whom the al-Sauds married, such as al-Jiluwi, al-Sudairi and al-Thunayyan are added, the grand total will grow even further.

The king is an absolute ruler. He names and presides over the Council of Ministers, as well as the Consultative Council. He appoints the country's highest religious office, the grand mufti, and the 20 members of the Council of the Senior Ulama, headed by the grand mufti. He promulgates laws based on his own interpretation of the Saudi constitution, the Quran and the Prophetic Sunna. The palace ulama never fail to rubber stamp his edicts.

Since Abdulaziz al-Saud conquered the tribes with the sword, he and his descendants behave as if the wealth of the nation is their own property. The national budget is allocated at the king's sole discretion and therefore, government spending can appear to be a gift of the king's generosity, for which the people must be grateful.

The direct descendants of the patriarch, all of whom are addressed as their Royal Highness, occupy most of the important cabinet and security positions. The rest, addressed as their Highness, act as eyes and ears of the enterprise. Family members pull together at the slightest hint of discord. They realize that disagreement could mean forfeiting the throne and the fabulous riches that come with it. Money and compromise smooth over the rough edges that appear from time to time.

Among the major disruptions were the removal from office and replacement of King Saud by his half-brother Faisal in 1964, the rebellion of the Free Princes Movement led by Prince Talal from Cairo (August 1962-September 1963), the assassination of King Faisal on March 25, 1975 by his nephew, Faisal bin Musa'ed, whose own brother Khalid was killed in a confrontation with the police in Riyadh over his objection to the opening of the first Saudi television station, and King Salman's recent removal of two crown princes and the appointment of his own thirty-year old son, Muhammad, as Crown Prince (see below: *King Salman's Reign*).

The task of how to constructively occupy the time of thousands of idle, exceedingly wealthy, and authoritarian men and women poses a formidable challenge to the individuals involved, as well as to their immediate families, to the al-Saud clan, and to the state. No private business wants to employ a prince, because a prince would not conform to the discipline of office structures: A prince gives orders only.

There is little or no legal protection for anyone dealing with a prince in Saudi Arabia. His father, grandfather, or uncle is the king: The lawmaker.

A prince and his coterie of friends violate the law with impunity. It would be practically impossible to successfully sue a defaulting prince on a bank loan in a Saudi court of law, let alone enforce a court judgment against him—if a Saudi judge should dare to rule against a prince. Bad experiences in lending to even the highest ranking princes has resulted in most Saudi banks declining to lend to them.

The Financial Burden of the Al-Saud Clan on the Saudi Treasury: A sliding scale of monthly salaries is paid to al-Saud family members, according to their position in the genealogical hierarchy and proximity to the founding patriarch. A special department at the Ministry of Finance by the non-descript name of al-Idarat al-Aammah Li-lmuqarrarat Wal-Kawaed (General Administration for Allowances and Guidelines) administers these payments.

The burden of the ruling family on the national treasury is secret. It may be estimated, however, that the annual cost of the immediate family of King Abdulaziz is in the region of $11 billion, at the assumed low average of $1 million per descendant.[1] This estimate does not include lump-sum special handouts of cash or grants of public lands or crude oil allocation to certain members of the family.[2] It does not include costs beyond the immediate family of the patriarch.

Members of the al-Saud family have become extraordinarily wealthy. In addition to their official monthly stipend for life from the treasury, many royals engage in trading and construction businesses. They earn phenomenal commissions to get private sector companies billion-dollar government contracts. Out of the country's oil revenues between 1981 and 2016 of $3.22 trillion,[3] the surviving sons of King Abdulaziz, their children, and the descendants of his deceased children might have cost the Saudi Treasury $350 billion in the form of commissions/bribes on weapon purchases and infrastructure projects, in addition to monthly stipends,

---

[1]Ostentatious spending on palaces in Saudi Arabia and in European and American cities, on grand private jets, super-yachts, fleets of the most expensive luxury and sports cars, and on obscenely expensive Jewellery are the way of life of most of al-Sauds. It is common for a vacationing prince to carry a million dollars in banknotes for incidentals.

[2]In addition to cash, the King allocates crude oil for a certain period of time to certain princes. The recipient sells the bounty through an agent. These allocations are not reported in official Saudi oil export statistics. They raise OPEC's export quota for Saudi Arabia clandestinely.

[3]Saudi Arabian Monetary Agency (SAMA) paper annual reports: From 1981–2007, SAMA's electronic annual reports: From 2008–2016 http://www.sama.gov.sa/en-US/EconomicReports/Pages/AnnualReport.aspx?&&p_SortBehavior=0&p_SAMAFAQSortOrder=42%2e0000000000000&&PageFirstRow=1&View=e672847e-173c-4344-be1f-66280d034f46

special cash handouts, and land and oil grants of another $350 billion, for a total of $700 billion.

Legendary extravagance on palaces in Saudi Arabia and in European and American cities, on grand private jets, super-yachts, fleets of the most expensive luxury and sports cars, and on obscenely expensive jewellery are a typical way of life for most of the al-Sauds. It is common for a vacationing prince to carry a million dollars in banknotes and travellers checks for incidentals.

The 31-year old Crown Prince Muhammad bin Salman bought the Chateau Louis XIV, near Versailles, for over $300 million in 2015.[4] While he was holidaying in the South of France in October 2016, he paid $590 million (£452 million) for a 440 foot yacht.[5] Then, there was the Leonardo Da Vinci's "Salvator Mundi" painting. In mid-November 2017, it was purchased at a Christie's auction for $450 million by Badr bin Abdullah bin Mohammed bin Farhan bin Abdulaziz,[6] a fourth generation minor prince, on behalf of Muhammad bin Salman, according to U.S. intelligence officials.[7]

King Salman's Reign: Born in 1935, King Salman became King on January 23, 2015, and has effected political changes akin to a state coup d'etat. In 2015, he removed from office, the sitting Crown Prince, half-brother Muqrin bin Abdulaziz.[8] On June 20, 2017, he removed from office another Crown Prince, nephew Muhammad bin Nayef bin Adbulaziz.[9] On June 21, 2017, he made his 30-year-old son, Muhammad, next in line

---

[4]Nicholas Kulish, Michael Forsythe, "World's Most Expensive Home? Another Bauble for a Saudi Prince," The *New York Times*, (December 16, 2017). https://www.nytimes.com/2017/12/16/world/middleeast/saudi-prince-chateau.html

[5]Peter Walker, "Saudi Prince Mohammed bin Salman 'Buys £452m Yacht' but Slashes Public Spending," *The Independent*, (October 18, 2016). http://www.independent.co.uk/news/world/middleeast/saudi-prince-mohammed-bin-salman-yacht-france-new-york-times-a7365261.html

[6]Katya Kazakina, "A Saudi Prince Is the Mystery Buyer of the $450 Million Da Vinci," *Bloomberg*, (updated December 7, 2017). https://www.bloomberg.com/news/articles/2017-12-06/louvre-abu-dhabi-is-getting-the-450-million-da-vinci-painting

[7]Jackie Northam, "Mystery Solved: Saudi Prince Is Buyer of $450M DaVinci Painting," *NPR*, (December 7, 2017). https://www.npr.org/sections/thetwo-way/2017/12/07/569142929/mystery-solved-saudi-prince-is-buyer-of-450m-davinci-painting

[8]Nocole Chavez, Tamamra Qiblawi, James Griffith, "Saudi Arabia's King Replaces Nephew with Son as Heir to Throne," *CNN*, (June 21, 2017). https://edition.cnn.com/2017/06/21/middleeast/saudi-arabia-crown-prince/index.html

[9]"Addiction and intrigue—Inside the Saudi Palace Coup", *Reuters*, (July 19, 2017). https://uk.reuters.com/article/uk-saudi-palace-coup/addiction-and-intrigue-inside-the-saudi-palace-coup-idUKKBN1A41IR

to the throne, handing him sweeping powers.[10] On November 4, 2017, the Crown Prince, undoubtedly with the approval of his father, signaled the start of an ostensible anti-corruption campaign. He arrested 11 princes, 4 serving ministers, and dozens of Saudi Arabia's best-known business-men.[11] In reality, however, the young man terrified into submission his rival uncles, cousins, and whoever else in the family who might be tempted to claim the throne. Among the arrested was the long serving minister of the National Guard, 64-year old Mit'eb, son of the late King Abdallah bin Abdulaziz. He was stripped of his position.[12]

Among the arrested was Prince Turki bin Nasser bin Abdulaziz for his involvement in the contract when he served at the Defense Ministry.[13] The high profile al-Yamama arms deal between Britain's BAE Systems and Saudi Arabia, struck in 1985, received special attention. Yamama is an example of the scale of the endemic institutionalized corruption that pervades the senior members of the ruling family and their coteries.

Yamama was worth £43 billion.[14] The *Guardian* newspaper published on October 28, 2006 documents from the British Department of Trade and Industry showing that the cost of the airplanes had been inflated by nearly a third.[15] A few months later, the *Guardian* revealed that BAE secretly paid Prince Bandar bin Sultan bin Abdulaziz (son of the Saudi Minister of Defense at the time and later the Crown Prince) for his role in the contract the sum of £30 million every quarter for at least 10 years (£1.2 billion).[16] The payments were written into the arms contract in secret annexes, described

---

[10]Stephen Kalin and William Maclean, "Saudi King Empowers Young Reformer Son in Succes-sion Shake-up," *Reuters*, (June 21, 2017). https://www.reuters.com/article/us-saudi-succession-son/saudi-king-empowers-young-reformer-son-in-succession-shake-up-idUSKBN19C0AN

[11]Samuel Osborne, "Saudi Arabia Arrests 11 Princes and Four Ministers in Extraordinary 'Con-solidation of Power,'" *The Independent*, (November 5, 2017). http://www.independent.co.uk/news/world/middle-east/saudi-arabia-anti-corruption-arrests-consolidation-of-power-crown-prince-mohammad-bin-salman-a8038371.html

[12]Ibid.

[13]Richard Spencer, "Saudi Royal Behind al-Yamamah Arms Deal Held in Crackdown on Corrup-tion," *The Times*, (November 11, 2017). https://www.thetimes.co.uk/article/prince-turki-bin-nasser-saudi-royal-behind-al-yamamah-arms-deal-held-in-crackdown-on-corruption-s5h5jwthb

[14]"BAE and the Saudis: How Secret Cash Payments Oiled £43bn Arms Deal," *The Guardian*, (Febru-ary 5, 2010). https://www.theguardian.com/world/2010/feb/05/bae-saudi-yamamah-deal-background

[15]"The Secret Whitehall Telegram that Reveals Truth Behind Controversial Saudi Arms Deal," *The Guardian*, (October 28, 2006). http://politics.guardian.co.uk/foi/story/0,,1933764,00.html

[16]"BAE Accused of Secretly Paying £1bn to Saudi Prince," *The Guardian*, (June 7, 2007). https://www.theguardian.com/world/2007/jun/07/bae1

as "support services."[17] If the Yamama "commission" is applied on the estimated $500 billion in weapons procurement between 1981 and 2016, the sleaze in the Ministry of Defense alone becomes $150 billion.[18]

Prince Bandar told Public Broadcasting Service (PBS) in late September 2001, when he was ambassador to Washington, "So, what?" if corruption cost Saudi Arabia $50 billion out of $400 billion spent on development projects. He stressed that he and his clan "did not invent corruption," that corruption has "happened since Adam and Eve," and that corruption is a part of "human nature".[19] Such public uttering by a senior envoy of a regime that draws its legitimacy and laws from claiming the religious high ground is all the more astounding in light of the tradition in which the Prophet Muhammad reportedly "cursed the person who does the bribing as well as the person who accepts the bribe."[20]

Prince Mit'eb was released on November 29, 2017, without a trial in a court of law after paying a reported one billion dollars, maybe more.[21] Two of his brothers, Prince Mish'al and Prince Faisal were released on December 28, 2017, after reaching undisclosed settlements with the government. A third brother, Prince Turki, was not released with his brothers.[22] On January 30, 2018, the government announced that 56 suspects remained in custody out of the 381 detainees and that the total settlements "had topped $107 billion, which came in various forms of assets."[23] The absence of any due process of law reduces the anti-corruption drive to extortion.

Would the Crackdown End Corruption? No, as corruption is deeply rooted throughout the ruling family. In the future, corruption is

[17]"Saudi Prince 'Received Arms Cash,'" *BBC*, (June 7, 2007). http://news.bbc.co.uk/1/hi/business/6728773.stm

[18]According to the annual reports of the Saudi Arabian Monetary Agency (SAMA), defense and national security spending between 1981 and 2016 totaled the Saudi Riyal equivalent of $953 billion, representing, 30% of the $3.22 trillion in total revenues from oil exports during the same period. It is assumed here that weapons procurement was 50% of defense spending.

[19]To read the full Frontline interview: http://www.pbs.org/wgbh/pages/frontline/shows/terrorism/interviews/bandar.html

[20]*The Six Books*, Sunan Abi Dawood, tradition number 3580, P. 1488.

[21]Sam Meredith, "Saudi Prince Freed after Reportedly Paying More than $1 billion," *CNBC*, (November 29, 2017). https://www.cnbc.com/2017/11/29/saudi-prince-miteb-bin-abdullah-freed-after-1-billion-settlement-deal.html

[22]"Two Princes Accused of Corruption Freed from Detention," *Al jazeera*, (December 29, 2017). https://www.aljazeera.com/news/2017/12/princes-accused-corruption-freed-detention-171229073548719.html

[23]"Detainees held at Saudi Arabia's Ritz-Carlton released or Moved, 56 Remain in Custody: Attorney General," *Arab News*, (January 30, 2018). http://www.arabnews.com/node/1235891/saudi-arabia

expected to become concentrated in King Salman's progeny and, possibly, the families of his six full Sudairi brothers from his mother Hassa.[24] The anti-corruption drive was politically selective: the arrests involved only 11 princes. The fact that the Sudairis were exempted from arrest while four of the sons of the late King Abdallah were subjected to humiliation and extortion is curious. Certainly, Abdallah's sons are neither more corrupt nor richer than the Sudairis, especially the sons of the late King Fahd and Crown Prince Sultan.

Would the crackdown result in a family mutiny? This is unlikely. Even if the stipends and the handouts were eliminated, the royals are not likely to rebel. They fear that discord could cost the family not only the throne and their vast wealth, but their lives as well. On the other hand, given that the immediate family of King Abdulaziz number over 11,000, and that King Abdulaziz's children belong to many mothers from different tribes, and that tribal affiliations of the princes extend to the national guard and the military, armed confrontations with the Salman Sudairi branch and their allies, could turn bloody. If that were to happen, US forces would intervene to avert interruptions in oil exports and to keep Iran away. Washington's preferred faction would be the winner, if Salman and his son were to be removed in a palace coup.

The Al-Sauds' Claim to Legitimacy: More than two centuries ago, Muhammad bin Saud and Muhammad bin Abdulwahhab joined hands in a rebellion against their Sunni co-religionist Ottoman rulers in Istanbul. They constructed Wahhabism and proclaimed its tenets to be the "true" Islam. They accused the Ottoman Sultans of corrupting Islam. The new doctrine was heavily influenced by the Hanbali school of thought, the most austere and least followed among the four surviving Sunni rites due to its extremism. However, that rebellion failed. Mohammad Ali, Egypt's ruler, acting on behalf of the Ottoman Sultan, crushed the rebellion in 1817. In 1902, a second rebellion was launched by Abdulaziz al-Saud and the Abdulwahhab clan. On the ashes of the Ottoman Empire's defeat in World War I and with active help from London, the second rebellion succeeded. In 1932 the Wahhabi Kingdom that bears the al-Saud's name was formed.

The al-Saud kings' claim to legitimacy is not based on a connection to the family of the Prophet or His Quraish Tribe. Their family is often

---

[24]The Sudairi brothers are seven sons of King Abdulaziz with Hussa al-Sudairi: Fahd, Sultan, Abdulrahman, Nayef, Turki, Salman, and Ahmad.

alleged to be descended from the Masalikh of Banu Wa'el, a part of the northern Aniza tribe of camel herders.[25] The Prophet devised no criteria to choose a successor, nor established an outline of the successor's authority and duties. As mentioned, the Qur'an and the Sunna do not address these issues, either.

The al-Sauds claim to legitimacy derives from opinions of certain ulama, written a thousand years ago: Abu Hamid al-Ghazali (1058–1111) who taught obedience to unjust rulers, "Any ruler is better than chaos, no matter what the origin of his power."[26] Taki al-Din bin Taymiyya (1263–1328) who believed that, "The essence of government was the power of coercion ... The ruler could demand obedience from his subjects, for even an unjust ruler was better than strife and dissolution of society."[27] Badr al-Din bin Jama'a (1241–1333) who advocated that:

> The ruler is a necessity. Without him there can be no justice; he is the 'the shadow of God on the Earth' ... The community must accept him whoever he be ... The imam can either be chosen or can impose himself by his own power, and in either case, he must be obeyed, in order that the cohesion of the Muslims shall be maintained and their unity assured. If he is deposed by another, the other must equally be obeyed ... We are with whoever conquers ... He [the ruler] must obey God just as his officials obey him, and for this reason he should consult the ulama, the guardians of God's law.[28]

Urgings for obedience to the Muslim ruler by these scholars were a response to the political turmoil that prevailed during their lifetime. During the life of al-Ghazali (1058–1111), military commanders of the Seljuk Turks (1055–1153) dominated the Abbasid caliphs in Baghdad. Also, the Fatimid caliphs (909–1171), who challenged the authority of the Baghdad caliph, were well entrenched in Egypt, and the Crusaders had taken Jerusalem in 1099. Badr al-Din bin Jama'a (1241–1333) grew up during the turbulent period following the destruction of the Arab empire by the Mongols in 1258. Taki al-Din bin Taymiyya (1263–1328), a follower of

[25] Al-Rasheed, *A History of Saudi Arabia*, P. 15.
[26] Hourani, *Arabic Thought in the Liberal Age 1789–1939*, P. 10.
[27] Ibid. P. 19.
[28] Ibid. P. 15.

the extremist Hanbali rite, was born just after the Mongol invasion and served as an official of Mamluke sultans (1250–1517).[29]

In the modern age, however, following the abolishment of the Ottoman caliphate (March 3, 1924), in the religious and political confusion following Turkey's defeat in the First World War, Ali Abd al-Raziq, an al-Azhar scholar, contended in a short book entitled *Al-Islam Wa-Usul al-Hukm* (*Islam and the Principles of Political Authority*) that Islam is not concerned with the system of government, which is a secular affair, and that the caliphate is not an intrinsic religious element in Islam.[30]

It is interesting that to discredit the Islamic legitimacy of the al-Saud kingdom and its kings, the so-called Islamic State was designated as a caliphate, not a kingdom, and its ruler, as a caliph, not a king. The Qur'an takes a jaundiced view of kingships:

> Qur'an 27:34: *Surely when kings enter a city they destroy it and despoil the honor of its nobility.*

Wahhabi Ulama

In order to legitimize his rule, the founder of the al-Saud dynasty, King Abdulaziz, collaborated with the descendants of the eighteenth-century founder of Wahhabism, Muhammad Bin Abdulwahhab. The relationship between the al-Sauds and the Abdulwahhabs is a partnership, as presented by Riyadh. The reality, however, is that the relationship is a master (king)/servant (clerics) affiliation. The Wahhabi ulama are puppets. They do the king's bidding. They rubber stamp the king's dictates.

To ward-off Western governments' advice/pressure, the al-Sauds claim that they have little control over the clerics, or that the clerics are intractably anti-reformist. They contend that the clerics have huge control over the masses, and that reforms are happening at a pace suitable to local conditions.

---

[29]Interestingly, the Bible was invoked by US Attorney General, Jeff Sessions, to justify his government's action at US borders in June 2018 to separate children from illegal immigrant parents. "I would cite to you the Apostle Paul and his clear and wise command in Romans 13, to obey the laws of the government because God has ordained them for the purpose of order," Sessions said. This same justification was used, wrote the Telegraph, by defenders of slavery in the US South, Nazi rule in Germany, and apartheid in South Africa. Nick Allen, "Jeff Sessions says the Bible justifies separating children from illegal immigrant parents at US border," The Telegraph, (June 15, 2018). https://www.telegraph.co.uk/news/2018/06/15/jeff-sessions-says-bible-justifies-separating-children-illegal/

[30]For more on Abd al-Raziq's thesis, see Ali, *A Religion, Not a State.*

This claim contradicts reality. The king controls the wealth of the nation and its armed forces. He is the clerics' benefactor. He appoints the country's highest religious office, the grand mufti and the 20 members of the Council of the Senior Ulama, headed by the grand mufti. King Faisal established the Council in 1971. The appointments are for four years, renewable at the king's discretion. Prior to the creation of the Council, the grand mufti's power was considerable. The creation of the Council diluted his powers. His voice has become one of twenty-one voices.

In case of disagreement, the ulama prove to be flexible; should one of them hesitate to issue the "right" religious opinion (fatwa), others will oblige. In return for cooperation, the men of God and their families have enjoyed fabulous wealth. Saudi Kings have maintained a public display of unity with the Wahhabi establishment, to media fanfare.

The recent lifting of the ban on women driving cars shows the extent of the ulama's subordination. For decades, volumes were written and scores of religious opinions issued against women driving. No issue was as extensively covered in mosques, academia, and the media than the ills of women driving. Sheikh Saleh bin Saad al-Lohaidan, even ventured into the health dangers of women driving. He said that women who drive risk damaging their ovaries and bearing children with clinical problems.[31]

However, when on September 26, 2017, King Salman suddenly ordered that women be allowed to drive cars (by June 24, 2018),[32] the Council of Senior Scholars (ulama), promptly endorsed the King's decision.[33] Actually, in his order, the King referred to the approval of the Council of Senior Scholars: "We refer to the view of the majority of the members of the Council of Senior Scholars regarding women driving vehicles and which states that the religious ruling in this regard is permissibility."[34] Following the announcement of the decision, the Council posted on its Twitter account: "May God protect the Custodian of the Two holy Mosques, King Salman bin Abdul Aziz, who maintains the interest of his country and its people in the light of Islamic law."[35]

---

[31]"Saudi Cleric Says Women Who Drive Risk Damaging Their Ovaries," *Reuters*, (September 29, 2013). https://www.reuters.com/article/us-saudi-driving/saudi-cleric-says-women-who-drive-risk-damaging-their-ovaries-idUSBRE98S04B20130929

[32]Stephen Kalin and Yara Bayoumy, "Saudi King Decrees Women Be Allowed to Drive," *Reuters*, (September 26, 2017). https://uk.reuters.com/article/uk-saudi-women-driving/saudi-king-decrees-women-be-allowed-to-drive-idUKKCN1C12VY

[33]Habib Toumi, "Senior Saudi Scholars Support King's Decision Allowing Women to Drive," *Gulf News*, (September 27, 2017). http://gulfnews.com/news/gulf/saudi-arabia/senior-saudi-scholars-support-king-s-decision-allowing-women-to-drive-1.2096797

[34]Ibid.
[35]Ibid.

Obedience to the Saudi King by the clergy is as strong today as it has ever been. The founder of the Saudi Kingdom, Abdulaziz, destroyed his loyal, fanatic soldiers, known as the Ikhwan, or brothers, when they became a political liability. The Ikhwan were young tribal men indoctrinated in Wahhabi fervor to the point of martyrdom. They were the predecessors of the jihadists who crashed airplanes into buildings on 9/11. The Ikhwan were instrumental in conquering the tribes and bringing Abdulaziz to power. Their insistence on spreading Wahhabism to neighboring lands over the objections of Abdulaziz led to hundreds of Ikhwan being killed by Abdulaziz's forces in the battle of Sabilla in Zulfi, central Saudi Arabia, in March 1929.[36] Abdulaziz had agreed to a treaty with his British sponsors not to attack British protectorates of Kuwait, Qatar, and the Trucial States (today's UAE). Leading ulama from the Najd Region, the hotbed of Wahhabism, had issued a religious opinion (fatwa) allowing Abdulaziz to destroy his Ikhwan compatriots.

King Fahd dismissed in 1992 seven of the 17 members of the Council of the Senior Ulama for refusing to denounce a 46-page "Memorandum of Advice" signed by 107 clerics criticizing the government for corruption and human rights abuses and for allowing US troops on Saudi soil.[37]

Exploitation of Wahhabism to Claim Divine Rule: Since 1932, successive kings kept a tight embrace of Wahhabism in order to claim divine rule. They tailor Wahhabi dictums to suit the political agenda of the day. The palace clerics simply add their stamp of approval. The palace clerics have turned Wahhabism into a psychological security weapon to control the masses. They use the thousands of mosques, schools, and the media to accomplish the following:

1) Indoctrinate the populace that Islam is the perfect religion, Wahhabism is the most truthful representation of the true Islam, and the king is the most ardent protector, promoter, and devoted servant of the "Two Holy Mosques." The Wahhabi ulama brainwash the population into believing that Wahhabism is God's choice, superior to all other religions and sects. They question the purity of the other three Sunni rites (Hanafite, Malikite, Shafi'ite), which are followed by 97% of world Sunnis. They assert that only Wahhabis are eligible to inherit paradise.[38] Arabia's

---

[36]Iraq and Jordan were under British rule at that time, and Abdulaziz had signed a friendship and border recognition treaty with Britain, on December 26, 1915.

[37]"A Chronology: The House of Saud," *PBS FRONTLINE*. http://www.pbs.org/wgbh//pages/frontline/shows/saud/cron/

[38]The Prophet reportedly said that Islam would split into 73 sects but only one sect would go to heaven. This has spurred Wahhabi leaders to claim that theirs is the righteous sect and expropriate paradise.

Sunni rites were the first Wahhabi targets for conversion following the arrival of the Wahhabi warriors to Arabia.

Curiously, however, a conference to define who counts as a Sunni, attended by around two hundred senior Sunni scholars from 30 countries in Grozny, Chechnia on August 25–27, 2016, concluded that Wahhabism is "a dangerous deformation" of Sunni Islam.[39] Notably, among the attendees was Egypt's Grand Imam, Ahmad el-Tayeb of Cairo's al-Azhar, Islam's oldest and most important center for Islamic studies and issuance of Sunni opinions (fatwas).[40]

2) Invoke injunctions to order the faithful to blindly obey the king:

> Qur'an 4:59: *Obey God and obey God's messenger and obey those of authority among you.*

3) Invoke that the Prophet reportedly said, according to *Sahih Muslim,*

> *He who obeys me obeys God; he who disobeys me, disobeys God. He who obeys the ruler, obeys me; he who disobeys the ruler, disobeys me.*[41]

4) Brainwash the populace into believing that blind obedience to the king is a form of piety. By fusing God with blind obedience to the king, the slightest political opposition becomes a "deviation from the true path," a serious condemnation in a system based on religious dogma.

5) Dismiss calls for modernization, socialism, and Arab nationalism (in vogue in the Arab world since the advent of the socialist leftist Nasserite revolution and the Ba'th Party) as blasphemous innovation, which must be resisted. Al-Bukhari reported the Prophet as stating:

> *The most evil of all matters are those that get modernized.*[42]

The former Grand Mufti (1963–1999) and chairman of the committee of senior ulama, Abdulaziz bin Baz, called nationalism an atheist Jahiliyya

---

[39]Robert Fisk, "For the First Time, Saudi Arabia is Being Attacked by Both Sunni and Shia Leaders," *The Independent*, (September 22, 2016). http://www.independent.co.uk/voices/saudi-arabia-attacked-sunni-shia-leaders-wahhabism-chechenya-robert-fisk-a7322716.html

[40]Ibid.

[41]The Six Books, *Sahih Muslim*, traditions 4746 to 4763, PP. 1007–1008 and traditions 4782 to 4793, PP. 1009–1010.

[42]The Six Books, *Sahih Al-bukhari*, tradition 7277, P. 606.

(the pre-Islamic age of darkness), "a movement of ignorance whose main purpose is to fight Islam and destroy its teachings and rules."[43] Saudi history textbooks highlight that Arab nationalism is "European in origin, Jewish in motivation … [and] represented as a conspiracy promoted by the West and Zionism to undermine the unity of Muslims."[44]

6) Propagate that democracy is a Western conspiracy to destroy Islam, despite the fact that:

   a. Non-Arab Muslim-majority countries like Bangladesh, Indonesia, Malaysia, Pakistan, and Turkey (50% of the estimated 1.5 billion world Muslims) enjoy multi-party elections, representative democracy, even women presidents and prime ministers.

   b. The 90 year-old Muslim Brotherhood Organization is democratic.[45] It has been an integral part of the Arab Spring's three democratic governments in Morocco (2011), Tunisia (2011), and Egypt (2012), until Saudi Arabia helped General Abdulfattah al-Sisi to overthrow and imprison Egypt's first democratically elected President, Muhammad Morsi.

7) Inculcate the belief in predestination. The palace ulama preach that all good and bad in life is ordained by God. Even if a ruler is unjust or corrupt, his subjects must still accord him blind obedience unconditionally, for he is ordained by the will of God.

Wahhabism as a Security Weapon: In the hands of the al-Sauds and their palace clerics, Wahhabism has become a security tool to achieve three objectives:

1. Nullify Saudi women's role in public life. Women in Saudi Arabia suffer discrimination unknown to their sisters in other Arab and non-Arab Muslim societies. Dressed up in the garb of Wahhabism, the treatment of women is constructed for security reasons. It nullifies in one swoop the potential political opposition of 50% of society. Women are treated like chattel. Male guardianship means that a husband, father, son, or brother must grant his permission before a wife, mother, daughter, or a sister may undergo a medical procedure. The guardian of an errant woman

---

[43] Al-Rasheed, *A History of Saudi Arabia*, P. 190.

[44] Ibid. P. 191.

[45] Established in Egypt in 1928, the Brotherhood is the Arab world's oldest Sunni political party, with a large following, estimated at around two million.

must pledge in writing to the police his assurances and personal responsibility for the woman's future behavior. A man can marry four wives simultaneously and divorce any of them at will, a very common practice among the wealthy and the ruling elite. Two women equate to one man in inheritance and when serving as a witness in court. Severe gender segregation keeps the great majority of women out of the workforce.[46]

Since the formation of the al-Saud kingdom in 1932, palace clerics have been systematically preaching and quoting reported Prophetic sayings that "most of those in hell are women,"[47] women's "lack of intelligence" is the reason a woman's testimony in an Islamic court of law is equal to only half that of a Muslim male,[48] and that the reason women are prohibited from praying and fasting during menstruation is due to their being "deficient in religious belief."[49]

A form of marriage, called *misyar*, which is unique to Saudi Arabia, has proliferated in recent years. Some Saudi marriage officials say seven out of 10 marriage contracts they conduct are *misyar*.[50] Under the *misyar* contract, the couple live apart, with the man visiting the woman at her home without any obligations to her. The practice was legalized by former Grand Mufti and head of the Council of ulama of Saudi Arabia, Abdulaziz bin Baz (1963–1999).[51] The Egyptian Center for Women's Rights considers *misyar* as an insult to both men and women and a sanction for the trafficking of women.[52]

Such rules and attributions contradict what the ulama have informed us about the most celebrated woman of all, the Prophet's first wife, Khadija. We are told that she was the best born in Quraish, a wealthy and successful businessperson. We are told that Khadija employed young Muhammad in her business, that she proposed marriage to him when he was about twenty-five years old, and that she was about fifteen

[46]"Saudi Police 'Stopped' Fire Rescue," *BBC*, (March 15, 2002). http://news.bbc.co.uk/2/hi/middle_east/1874471.stm

[47]*The Six Books, Sahih Al-Bukhari*, traditions 304, P. 26; 3241, P. 263; 5197 and 5198, P. 450; 6449, P. 542; and, 6546, P. 549; and to *Sahih Muslim*, traditions 6938 to 6942, P. 1152; and to *Jame' Al-Tirmithi*, tradition 2613, P. 1915.

[48]Ibid.

[49]Ibid.

[50]Abdul Hannan Tago, "Misyar now 'a widespread reality'," *Arab News*, (October 12, 2014). http://www.arabnews.com/saudi-arabia/news/642991

[51]Syed Neaz Ahmad, "A proposal Saudis can't refuse," *The Guardian*, (August 16, 2009). https://www.theguardian.com/commentisfree/belief/2009/aug/16/saudi-arabia-marriage

[52]Ibid.

years his senior and twice a widow. We are told that for the twenty-five years of the Prophet's marriage to Khadija until her death in 620 he remained monogamous to her, that she was the one person to whom he turned for advice and comfort, and that Khadija was the first convert to Islam. This depiction of Khadija as an emancipated, commanding woman of high standing in Meccan society, a woman whom the Prophet treated with faithfulness and devotion does not reconcile with the perception and treatment of women in Saudi Arabia today.

The recent lifting of the ban on women driving cars or having sport classes in girl-schools is not a genuine sign of bringing about equality of the genders in the al-Saud kingdom. While lifting the ban on driving is a definite improvement, it is purely a cosmetic act of reform. In May 2018, in a warning to would-be advocates of reform, seven Saudi women activists who campaigned for the right to drive were arrested and labelled as "traitors."[53]

Popular culture is difficult to change by fiat. Societal attitudes toward women, as engendered by the Wahhabi ulama, are such that men, and even a proportion of women, accept that women's propagated "infirmities" are endowed by God, and therefore will not change.

2. In the hands of the al-Sauds and their palace clerics, Wahhabism has also become a psychological weapon to ensure domestic quietism. Religion supplements the regime's security forces. The two weapons together have kept five generations of Saudis under control. Wahhabism justifies the regime's absolute rule and the suppression of political dissent. It is the glue that keeps the al-Saud regime together. The fact that the holiest shrines are in Mecca and Medina, and that the Saudi Kings appointed themselves "servants of the two holy mosques" has been helpful in this enterprise.

3. Wahhabism not only justifies and bolsters the al-Saud regime, but this extreme, religious doctrine was also useful as a weapon against the spread of communism in the Arab and Muslim world. Wahhabism was an important tool used to recruit and energize the mujahideen (jihadists) who fought the Soviet Union in Afghanistan (1978–1989), with Washington's approval. In his interview with *The Washington Post* on March 23, 2018, the Saudi Crown Prince was asked about the Saudi-funded spread of Wahhabism. In reply, he said: "investments in mosques and madrassas overseas were rooted in the Cold War, when

---

[53]Sarah Dadouch, "Saudi Arabia expands crackdown on women's rights activists," *Reuters*, (May 22, 2018).

allies asked Saudi Arabia to use its resources to prevent inroads in Muslim countries by the Soviet Union."[54]

Wahhabism Boomeranged: On 9/11, Wahhabism boomeranged. Since 9/11, Wahhabi terror groups have metastasized, forming a more dangerous al-Qaeda in certain Arab countries, a more threatening Taliban in Afghanistan, Boko Haram in Nigeria, the so-called Islamic State in parts of Iraq and Syria, and al Shabab in Somalia. These terror groups are incarnations of Saudi Wahhabism. According to *the Economist* magazine, dissidents in the so-called Islamic State's capital of Raqqa, Syria report that "all 12 of the judges who now run its court system … [were] Saudis."[55] Raqqa was liberated in October 2017 by the U.S. supported Syrian Democratic Forces.[56]

The palace ulama deepened hatred towards Shi'ites. In reaction, Shi'ite extremism grew and the regime of the Qom ayatollahs was born in 1979. Today, the Muslim Middle East's two most powerful countries are ruled, on the one hand, by extreme Shi'ite ayatollahs in Iran and, on the other, by the partnership of the al-Saud and the extreme Wahhabi clerics in Saudi Arabia.

In a repeat of the al-Saud and Abdulwahhab partnership story against the Istanbul sultans, leaders of al-Qaeda and the so-called Islamic State are in rebellion against the al-Saud kings for corrupting the "true" tenets of Wahhabism. Al-Qaeda's chief Zawahiri has been at war against the Islamic State's caliph al-Baghdadi, and the two men are at war with Salman, the Saudi King. The confrontation is over power and wealth, not the purported purity of Wahhabism. Each commander is busy outdoing the other in savagery to claim the high Wahhabi ground in order to attract new recruits. Riyadh's war against al-Qaeda and the so-called Islamic State is a war for self-preservation, not for helping the world

---

[54]Karen Deyoung, "Saudi prince says relationship with Kushner is friendly but not improper," *Washington Post*, (March, 23, 2018). https://www.pressreader.com/usa/the-washington-post/20180323/281719795124454

[55]"Crime and Punishment in Saudi Arabia: The Other Beheaders," *The Economist*, (September 20, 2014). https://www.economist.com/news/middle-east-and-africa/21618918-possible-reasons-mysterious-surge-executions-other-beheaders

[56]Arwa Damon, Ghazi Balkiz, and Laura Smith, "Raqqa: US-Backed Forces Declare 'Total Liberation' of ISIS Stronghold," *CNN*, (October 20, 2017). http://edition.cnn.com/2017/10/20/middleeast/raqqa-syria-isis-total-liberation/index.html

eradicate the scourge of terrorism, which the Saudi Kings bred in the first place.

Manifesting Wahhabism in Daily Life: Saudi politics finds solutions to the challenges of modern living in Arabia's seventh century way of life. The following are some examples.

Education: The educational curriculum is overwhelmingly skewed toward Wahhabi theology, laws, and rituals. Starting with the first grade, young children are taught that Jews, Christians, and other non-Muslims are destined to 'hellfire.' As the children grow up, the same message is honed more explicitly. Of the sixteen core subjects that comprise the twelfth grade curriculum in high schools, nine are on Islam and related subjects.[57] The teaching of philosophy is prohibited. Wahhabi indoctrination aims at pre-occupying Saudis with religious dogma, belief in predestination, hatred of and jihad against the other, and promises of houris in paradise. Proselytization and conversion of non-Muslims to Wahhabism represent a very important mission to Saudi officialdom and Wahhabi clerics.

Proselytization Abroad: In foreign lands, Saudi-funded mosques, preachers, schools, teachers, students, charities, and the like propagate the Wahhabi message. Saudi-trained preachers in Britain denigrate their hosts, urge their congregations to avoid assimilation in their host culture, to reject women rights, to force child-age arranged marriages, and to view Western political systems as alien constructs. The Henry Jackson Society stated in a report revealed on July 5, 2017 that Saudi Arabia is the chief foreign promoter of Islamist extremism in the UK. It alleges that individuals and foundations have been heavily involved in exporting what it calls "an illiberal, bigoted Wahhabi ideology", quoting a number of examples.[58]

Speaking at a round-table debate in Parliament on July 14, 2017, Sir William Patey, former British Ambassador to Saudi Arabia from 2006 to 2010 and other countries in the Middle East (Afghanistan, Iraq, Sudan, and UAE) stated that, "Saudi Arabia funds ideologies which lead to extremist activity. They are not funding terrorism. They are funding something

---

[57]Qur'an, tafsir (interpretation of the Qur'an), Hadith (Sayings of the Prophet) and Islamic culture, tawheed (studies in monotheism), fiqh (Islamic jurisprudence), Arabic grammar, Arabic literature, history, and social studies.

[58]"Saudi Arabia Has 'Clear Link' to UK Extremism, Report Says," *BBC*, (July 5, 2017). http://www.bbc.co.uk/news/uk-politics-40496778

else, which may down the road lead to individuals being radicalized and becoming fodder for terrorism."[59]

The growth of extremism, is further fueled by expatriate workers who live in Saudi Arabia and become indoctrinated in Wahhabi way of life. In 2016, 10.4 million foreign nationals lived in Saudi Arabia out of a total population of around 31 million.[60] It may be estimated that since the quadrupling of oil prices in 1973, over 100 million foreigners have lived in Saudi Arabia.[61] If only 1% became Wahhabi, a million extremists could be roaming the world. The Rand Corporation's 2008 report put the danger of Wahhabi indoctrination of the foreign workers aptly:[62]

> A small percentage of these guest workers come to embrace radical Wahhabism while employed in Saudi Arabia or the Gulf states and, when they return to their home countries, they either attempt to spread the message of radical Islam or attempt to use violence against their home governments in the name of jihad.
>
> In the Philippines, for example, one of the more violent jihadist groups operating today, the Rajah Solaiman Movement (RSM), is a small group of former guest workers in Saudi Arabia who have vowed to launch a jihad in their home country similar to that being conducted by the Abu Sayyaf Group.

Religious Police: Brigades of religious police, known as mutawwa' (meaning coercers) fanatically and crudely enforce Wahhabi dictums. Although they were stripped recently of the authority to make arrests,[63] they ensure that government and business offices are closed for the five daily prayers (sunrise, noon, afternoon, sunset, and night). They empty

---

[59]"Saudi Arabia Funding Linked to Terror in UK by Britain's Former Ambassador to Riyadh," *The Independent*, (July 14, 2017). http://www.independent.co.uk/news/uk/home-news/saudi-arabia-terror-funding-uk-extremism-islamist-william-patey-former-ambassador-home-office-qatar-a7840406.html

[60]Rodolfo Estimo Jr., "KSA population: 21.1m Saudis, 10.4m expats, *Arab News*," (February 4, 2016). http://www.arabnews.com/saudi-arabia/news/875131

[61]Assuming that since 1973, an average of 7 million expatriate workers lived in Saudi Arabia and that the average stay per worker was 3 years, the number of foreigners who had lived in Saudi Arabia would be 102 million (44 years x 7 million per year = 308 million man year/3 years each = 103 million).

[62]RAND Corporation, "Unfolding the Future of the Long War."

[63]Will Worely, "Saudi Arabia Strips Religious Police of Powers of Arrest and Says They Must Be 'Kind and Gentle,'" *The Independent*, (April 14, 2016). http://www.independent.co.uk/news/world/middle-east/saudi-arabia-strips-religious-police-of-powers-of-arrest-and-says-they-must-be-kind-and-gentle-a6983816.html

shops, supermarkets, banks, and restaurants of customers during prayer time. They ensure that women are covered from head to toe in a black loose garment, and that women are not in the company of unrelated men, a serious offense. They enforce the ban on alcohol and prohibited foods, such as pork. They remove objectionable articles, photographs, and advertisements from foreign newspapers, magazines, and books. They raid shops, restaurants, cafes, supermarkets, hospitals, and other establishments without permission if they suspect a violation. They enforce a strict prohibition on religious activities by Christians, despite the fact that the Qur'an requires Muslims to hold Jesus and Mary in great reverence, and a million Christian expatriates live in the country. A Christian may not wear a cross pendant nor carry a Bible, for, if discovered, he will face imprisonment, lashings, and deportation.

The religious police are as old as the Saudi state. King Khalid (1975–1982) gave it the status of an independent agency of the government named, *The Commission for the Promotion of Virtue and the Prevention of Vice*. Numbering around 5,000 men, supported by approximately twice as many administrative staff, and operating out of around 500 police stations, the financial cost of the agency is not public. However, the agency's annual budget may be estimated to be in the region of a billion dollars, taking into account officers and staff salaries, office overhead, the cost of running the agency's fleets of distinctive SUVs, and other outlays.

Arts, Monuments and Idolatry: Fear of falling into idolatry or in love with anything that might distract from the love and adoration of God is prohibited. Wahhabi hatred of archaeological sites, historical monuments, and cultural heritage drove the Taliban to dynamite the 1,500-year old Buddhas of Bamiyan in Afghanistan in March 2001. The Islamic State destroyed much of Syria's Palmyra and the Mosul museum and the Ninevah ruins in Iraq in 2016.[64] In Saudi Arabia itself, 98% of the country's historical and religious sites have been destroyed since 1985, including the house of the Prophet's uncle in Mecca, which was flattened to make way for a hotel, and the house of the Prophet's first wife, Khadijah, in order to make way for public toilets. A Hilton Hotel has been built on the site where the house of the first caliph Abu Bakr once stood.[65]

---

[64]"Here Are the Ancient Sites ISIS Has Damaged and Destroyed," *National Geographic*,
[65]"Saudi Arabia Bulldozes Over Its Heritage," *Time magazine*,

Furthermore, for a Wahhabi, visiting the graves of family and relatives is sinful as is playing a musical instrument, drawing or acquiring a painting depicting the human figure, or sculpting or acquiring a statue of a man, let alone a woman. Moroccan sociologist Fatima Mernissi considers that Islamists see love between a man and a woman as a threat to the couple's allegiance to Allah.[66]

Penal Code: The Saudi Wahhabi agenda is demonstrated through Shari'a law with an archaic court system, complete with primitive, cruel seventh century penalties such as public severing of limbs, beheadings, and crucifixions, typically following the Friday noon prayers.[67] Flogging is a component of almost every prison sentence. The well-known Saudi blogger, Raif Badawi, convicted of insulting Islam, has been given 10 years in prison and 1,000 lashes. After Friday prayers on January 9, 2015, he was brought to a public square in Jeddah, feet and hands shackled, and flogged 50 times.[68]

Modern Saudi Arabian society is a paradox. While Wahhabism returns society to a seventh-century religious cult, Saudi Arabia is awash in glittering twenty-first century Western consumer products and tall glass buildings.

Daily Living Under Wahhabi Dictums in the Words of a Saudi Female Journalist: The following encapsulates the oddity of Wahhabi teaching, preaching, and way of life, written in *Arabic* by Saudi journalist Nadine al-Budayr, and *translated by Chiara Pellegrino.*

> I studied in public schools and read in my coursework that the other – Christian or Zoroastrian, Jew, Buddhist or Hindu – is a kafir, or nonbeliever. I also studied the rules of other faiths and schools within Islam – Shiite, Isma'ili, Twelver, Sufism – the followers of which are all considered nonbelievers and heretics. The same is true for thought. Those who indulge in thought and say what they think, breaking the doctrinal framework are nonbelievers, apostate

---

[66]Hisham Sharabi, *Neopatriarchy: A Theory of Distorted Change in Arab Society* (Oxford University Press, Oxford, UK, 1998), PP. 33–34.

[67]"When It Comes to Beheadings, ISIS Has Nothing Over Saudi Arabia," *Newsweek magazine,* (October 14, 2014). http://europe.newsweek.com/when-it-comes-beheadings-isis-has-nothing-over-saudi-arabia-277385?rm=eu

[68]"Saudi blogger receives first 50 lashes of sentence for 'insulting Islam'," *The Guardian,* (January 10, 2015). https://www.theguardian.com/world/2015/jan/09/saudi-blogger-first-lashes-raif-badawi

and heretic. The liberal, the leftist, the modernist ... they are all nonbelievers.

In schoolwork I learned that the woman is temptation, that her body is fitna (sedition) and that it is the cause of man's entry into the Gehennam (hell). I read that the man is a wolf that seduces women and therefore I must fear him. I mustn't leave the house or participate in the progress of the nation – that's how I am taught to protect my chastity. I studied that I was a gemstone to be preserved in a chest that can only be opened by its guardian, his Excellency, the man. Millions of women are unemployed, our economy is on the brink of the abyss and, yet, there are still those who urge women to stay home. I studied that it was prohibited to question and to have a personal thought. It is prohibited to innovate, invent and discover. All is written, illustrated and explained in religious books and all of my attempts to think differently are equal to leaving the community and detaching oneself from Muslims.

I studied that seventy-two beautiful women await men in paradise. And since having sex is prohibited in the earthly world, the shortcut to the afterlife is martyrdom through killing western nonbelievers. I studied that women's sports are prohibited, driving a car is haram (sinful/prohibited), traveling without the consent of the guardian is haram, democracy is haram, high heels are haram, the hairdryer is haram. Short dresses, even if worn in the presence of siblings is haram. Music, singing, dance, film, theater, festivals, promiscuity with men, philosophy, modern poetry are all haram, along with reading books that are not religious, liberty and the laws of personal status.[69]

Tribal Sheikhs

The way of life of Saudi Arabia's indigenous population is basically Bedouin, although the ratio of rural population as a percentage of total population

---

[69]OASIS, *The "J'Accuse" of a Saudi Journalist*, by Nadine al-Budayr, *translated from the original Arabic by Chiara Pellegrino*, (26 May 2016). http://www.oasiscenter.eu/articles/religions-and-the-public-sphere/2016/05/26/the-j-accuse-of-a-saudi-journalist

dropped from 69% in 1960 to 17% in 2016.[70] The shift should not mean that Bedouin social structures, customs, and values have been erased. Cultural traits do not change by moving houses. They evolve slowly over the generations. To put Bedouin traits in perspective, the Qur'an is helpful:

Verse 9:97: *The desert Arabians are most confirmed in unbelief and hypocrisy.*

Verse 49:14: *The Arabs of the desert say we believe, tell them: you do not believe ... for belief has not yet penetrated your hearts.*

The Prophetic Sunna too is revealing. In *Sahih al-Bukhari*, the Prophet is attributed as saying:

O Allah! Bestow Your blessings on our Sham [Syria]. O Allah! Bestow Your blessings on our Yemen ... The people said, O Allah's Apostle! And also on our Najd ... The Prophet said: there (in Najd) are earthquakes and insurrections and from it comes out the horn of Satan.[71]

Anthropologists and social researchers have analyzed Bedouin organization and personal characteristics. Sharabi considers Bedouin factionalism as, "The outstanding dynamic of the tribe-dominated structure ... It first separates the self from all others, then, on a higher level, divides the world into opposing pairs—kin and non-kin, clan and opposing clan, Islam and non-Islam, and so forth. For it, affiliation based on blood ties supersedes every other kind of relation."[72] Ibrahim and Cole believe that "The dynamics of tribal social structure ... can work in two different ways, each of which is contradictory to the other ... unity and cooperation, as well as exaggerated individualism, lack of cooperation, and extreme jealousy among different segments of a tribe."[73]

The formation of the tribe as an alliance among related clans was a pragmatic reaction to the perils of desert living. The belief in common ancestry, even when such commonality was imaginary, served as the cornerstone for

---

[70]The World Bank, *Rural population (% of total population)*. http://data.worldbank.org/indicator/SP.RUR.TOTL.ZS

[71]*The Six Books*, Sahih Aal-Bukhari, tradition 1037, P. 81 and tradition 7094, P. 592.

[72]Sharabi, *Neopatriarchy*, P. 28.

[73]Ibrahim Ezzidine, and D.P. Cole, *Saudi Arabian Bedouin* (Cairo Papers in Social Science, The American University in Cairo, 1978), PP. 11 and 18.

such a construction. Hitti explains that all members of a clan consider each other as of one blood, and blood relationships, whether real or invented, supply the adhesive element in tribal organization.[74] Tribesmen consider their clan or tribe as "a unit in itself, self-sufficient and absolute, and regard every other clan or tribe as its legitimate victim."[75] It is a world of 'us versus them' and of 'friend versus enemy.' This mentality is based upon the spirit of the clan (*asabiyyah*), which implies unconditional loyalty to fellow clansmen, generally similar to a passionate, chauvinistic patriotism. In the desert, a man without a tribe has no means of protection, has the status of an outlaw, and cannot survive.[76]

Following the creation of the new states in the Middle East after the First World War, roving tribes had to be settled. This was necessary if the new states—monarchies or republics, independent or under French or British mandates—were to assert their authority over all citizens within the new borders. By 1932, Abdulaziz al-Saud succeeded in forming Saudi Arabia after he had subjugated the tribes in parts of the east coast of the Arabian Peninsula, in the Najd Plateau in the center, in the Hijaz in the midwest, and in the Asir region along the Red Sea coast. To control the Bedouins, he imposed the bond of Islam, just as the Prophet and the first caliph, Abu Bakr (632–634), had done. For the defeated tribes, notwithstanding their indifference toward religion, acquiescing to the al-Saud's authority in the name of "true Islam," must have been less humiliating than acquiescing to the al-Saud's authority in surrender to his sword. As explained above, the bond of Islam, which Saudi Kings enforced since 1932 has kept the kingdom together. King Salman and his son's religious reforms could dilute this bond, which is why those reforms are expected to be superficial.

Abdulaziz al-Saud's success was due to other factors as well. First, active British assistance gave him the firepower and the financial muscle he needed. Second, his deliberate policy of marriage affiliations with famous Arabian tribes helped consolidate his authority. He took wives from the tribes of Banu Khalid, Shammar, Aniza, and Ajman, as well as from tribal nobility such as al-Shalan and al-Rasheed.[77]

---

[74]Hitti, *History of the Arabs*, P. 26.
[75]Ibid.
[76]Ibid.
[77]Al-Rasheed, *A History of Saudi Arabia*, P. 77.

Abdulaziz al-Saud's authority was personal. It was not due to the al-Sauds' tenuous tribal affiliation, nor to any nationalistic ideal. Over the ages, the stronger tribes raided the weaker tribes for booty. A weaker tribe would often buy protection from a more powerful tribe. As Abdulaziz conquered the tribes, he ended intertribal dependencies. He made himself the sole source of support, first from the spoils of raids, later from oil revenues.

Although the tribal leaders in modern Saudi Arabia have lost many powers, they continue to command considerable influence within their tribes and the Saudi system of governance. Within the tribe, such influence is not surprising. Coherence among members of the tribe and respect to hierarchical authority continue to give the tribal leader a position of strength.

Given the banning of political parties, labor unions, civil society organizations, student and women's associations, social clubs, etc. the tribal leader can help deliver the allegiance of his tribe to the regime. "The hereditary Bedouin leaders of the most powerful tribes ... have wielded political influence in the Saudi Kingdom since its founding."[78] Some tribal leaders become local governors. Others are advisors to the centers of power in the capital, Riyadh. Tribesmen hold government jobs in the armed forces and the civil service. "The National Guard ... recruited its personnel primarily from the Bedouin tribes and organizes its units by tribal affiliation."[79] The regime provides projects for clean water, sanitation, electricity, health, education, roads, and public amenities to cooperative tribe leaders.

Defense and National Security Establishment

The Saudi defense and national security machine has two arms. The first is the Ministry of Defense and Aviation, for decades under the leadership of the Sudairi side of the ruling family. The second is the Ministry of the National Guard for decades under the leadership of King Abdallah bin Abdulaziz. While the Defense Ministry protects against external threats, the National Guard protects the ruling family from domestic threats. The National Guard is a parallel army, a balance to avert a military coup, and vice versa.

---

[78]United States Library of Congress, Federal Research Division, "Country Studies—Saudi Arabia." http://countrystudies.us/saudi-arabia/55.htm
[79]Ibid.

Saudi Arabia has for decades allocated the highest proportion of its annual budget to defense and security. According to the annual reports of the Saudi Arabian Monetary Agency (SAMA), Saudi Arabia's Central Bank, defense and national security spending between 1981 and 2016 totaled the Saudi Riyal equivalent of $953 billion, representing, 30% of the $3.22 trillion in total revenues from oil exports during the same period.[80] On the procurement of arms from the US in recent years, the Obama administration sold Riyadh in a single deal in 2012 the huge amount of $112 billion in weapons over eight years. It also had another $110 billion package under negotiation before the Trump administration took office.[81] Mr. Trump's visit to Riyadh on May 20, 2017 yielded the $110 billion package, increasing to $300 billion in ten years.[82]

The National Guard: The National Guard finds its roots in the Ikhwan tribal fighters that helped Abdulaziz al-Saud subjugate Arabia's diverse tribes and form the al-Saud kingdom. The Ikhwan's leadership was crushed in 1929 for disobeying Abdulaziz' orders against invading the British protectorates of Kuwait, Qatar, and the Trucial States (today's UAE). The National Guard was built on the ashes of the Ikhwan. In 2014, the size of the National Guard was around 200,000 men.[83] By comparison, in 1960, its size was some 18,000 men.[84]

Light armored personnel carriers have met the operational needs of the National Guard's mission. In November 2009, General Dynamics Land Systems-Canada announced a contract for the sale of 724 such vehicles for $2.2 billion.[85] The company announced on February 14, 2014 that the contract is a part of a larger 14-year order worth up to $13 billion.[86] Helicopters have recently been added to the National Guard's arsenal.

---

[80]Saudi Arabian Monetary Agency (SAMA) paper annual reports: From 1981–2007, SAMA's electronic annual reports: From 2008–2016.

[81]Ridiel, The $110 Billion Arms Deal to Saudi Arabia."

[82]Steve Holland, "US nears $100 billion arms deal for Saudi Arabia: White House official."

[83]"Saudi national guard chief to seek more U.S. backing," *Al Arabiya*, (November 17, 2014). https://english.alarabiya.net/en/News/2014/11/17/Saudi-national-guard-chief-to-seek-more-U-S-backing.html

[84]"Saudi Arabian National Guard," *GlobalSecurity.org.* http://www.globalsecurity.org/military/world/gulf/sang.htm

[85]"Saudi Shopping Spree: A Hardened, Networked National Guard," *Defense Industry Daily*, (September 2, 2014). http://www.defenseindustrydaily.com/the-2006-saudi-shopping-spree-a-hardened-networked-national-guard-02462/

[86]Randall Palmer and Andrea Shalal-Esa, "General Dynamics Canada Wins Saudi Deal Worth up to $13 Billion," *Reuters*, (February 14, 2014). http://www.reuters.com/article/us-generaldynamics-canada-saudi-idUSBREA1D1EF20140214

Already, 36 aircrafts are on the ground in Saudi Arabia, a part of the plan to build a fleet of 156 aircraft.[87]

The Military: Saudi military personnel in 2017 numbered 256,000 men, equipped with 790 aircraft, 1,142 combat tanks, 5,472 armored fighting vehicles, and 55 navy assets, with a defense budget of $57 billion.[88]

Saudi Arabia's armed forces have not been effective on the battlefield. After spending $200 billion between 1981 and 1991 on sophisticated air, ground, and naval weapon systems,[89] in the 1991 Gulf War, Saudi Arabia needed over half a million US and other troops to defend itself against Iraq, a third-world developing country exhausted from an eight-year-war with Iran (September 1980-August 1989). However, the Saudi armed forces are capable of quelling domestic dissent.

Saudi defense depends mainly on US weaponry. Such weapons are beyond Saudi capabilities to maintain in good operating order. Saudi national security is dependent on American weapons, spare parts, and technicians. These realities make the Saudi defense strategy an exchange of US protection in return for billions of dollars in annual arms purchases, plus cooperation on oil politics and regional US interests. Post 9/11, fearing being held culpable by the United States for the involvement of fifteen Saudis in the horrors of that day, the al-Sauds have performed an act of preemptive surrender, becoming even more obsequious and obvious in their submissiveness to Washington than ever before.

The real danger to the Saudi monarchy is a military coup by its own soldiers. Modern Arab history must be disconcerting in this regard. The kings of Egypt (1952), Iraq (1958), Yemen (1961), and Libya (1969) were all deposed in military coups. To avert a similar fate, the Riyadh regime takes several measures. First, military and National Guard officers are recruited carefully from amongst loyal clans, tribes, and families, mainly those from the Najd Region. Secondly, generous salaries and benefits are paid to security personnel. Thirdly, an elaborate internal security apparatus with multi-security services operate, each watching the other. Fourthly, a Wahhabi state of mind requiring blind obedience to the ruler (waliy al-amr), is constantly nurtured by palace clerics. Fifthly, thousands of loyal

---

[87]Jen Judson, "Saudi Arabian National Guard Helicopter Force Takes Shape."
[88]"2017 Saudi Arabia Military Strength: Current Military Capabilities and Available Firepower for the Nation of Saudi Arabia," *Global Fire Power.* http://www.globalfirepower.com/country-military-strength-detail.asp?country_id=saudi-arabia
[89]SAMA annual paper report 2007, PP. 290–292.

royals keep a watchful eye, many serving in the air force. Finally, there has been effective nullification of the potential political opposition of one half of the Saudi society, namely its women.

Merchant families

Wealthy merchant families represent a powerful block in the Saudi power pyramid.[90] These families are generally engaged in importing and distributing the myriad of consumer goods, manufacturing light import-substitution items, constructing civilian and military projects for the government and the private sectors, and engaging in joint-venture partnerships with foreign companies. The Saudi business community supports the ruling family in return for a business environment conducive to making profits: a minimum of business regulations, protection from foreign competition, supportive monetary, fiscal, and foreign exchange policies, a ban on labor unions, a labor law with no minimum wage provisions, slavery rules on foreign workers, and easy terms on loans from government banks. These facilities are granted, while princes and government officials earn commissions (bribes) on government contracts and engage in insider trading practices with impunity.

The support of the business community is important to a regime that bans all forms of political, social, labor, civil, or civic organizations. Business leaders play a role similar to that of tribal leaders in helping the regime control dissent. They watch their employees and guard against political and labor unrest. This role is particularly important in view of the huge number of employees in the private sector, estimated to be around 10 million out of a total population of around 30 million. The following is an example of how the Saudi regime hands the big merchant families easy profits even at the cost of depleting the country's finite water resources.

Desert Agriculture—From Dust to Dust: Farming is alien to the desert habitat and also to the culture of its peoples. As Saudi Arabia became rich following the quadrupling of oil prices in 1973, however, some of the country's big merchant families were induced by huge

---

[90]Traditionally wealthy families include the Alireza, Ba Khashab, Bin Laden, Bin Mahfooz, al-Jumaih, Jameel, Juffali, Kaki, Olayan, al-Rajhi, Sulaiman, and the al-Zamil. Additionally, dozens of nouveau riche have been added since the quadrupling of oil prices in 1973.

government subsidies to invest in importing the equipment and the farm workers to implement a heavily propagated strategy of food self-sufficiency. Within twelve years, between 1980 and 1992, wheat production grew 29-fold to 4.1 million tons, making the Saudi desert the world's sixth-largest wheat exporting country.[91] To achieve this enormous growth, the wheat-producing areas were increased by 14-fold, to 924,000 hectares.[92]

Saudi Arabia's foray into desert irrigation confirms that money and water can make a desert bloom, until either the money runs out or the water is depleted.[93] Within 15 years, Saudi Arabia experienced shortages of both money and water. These shortages negatively impacted a heralded experiment in desert agriculture, in particular, growing wheat. In 1993, Saudi Arabia suffered financial strains under pressure from declining oil prices, so its cereal-growing program was scaled down drastically. Within four years, 76% of the new wheat-growing surface was abandoned, and wheat production cut by 70%.[94] Then, in early 2008, as the quality and quantity of non-renewable aquifers reached perilous levels, the government declared that purchases of wheat from local farmers would be reduced by 12.5% annually, with the aim of relying entirely on imports by 2016. This target was reached.[95]

The estimated financial cost of this venture between 1984 and 2000 was around $100 billion, or $500 per ton, excluding unquantifiable subsidies; if added, the overall spending might have doubled the cost of the wheat produced. The international price for wheat during that period averaged $120 a ton.[96]

As for the cost in terms of water, between 1980 and 1999, a gargantuan volume of water, 300 billion cubic meters were used, the equivalent

---

[91] Alan Richards and John Waterbury, *A Political Economy of the Middle East* (Westview Press, Boulder, Colorado, 1998), P. 160.

[92] Elie Elhadj, *Experiments in Achieving Water and Food Self-Sufficiency in the Middle East: The Consequences of Contrasting Endowments, Ideologies, and Investment Policies in Saudi Arabia and Syria*, London University, School of Oriental and African Studies, 2006, P. 72.

[93] Elie Elhadj, "Dry Aquifers in Arab Countries and the Looming Food Crisis," *Middle East Review of International Affairs (MERIA) Journal*, (December 7, 2008). http://www.rubincenter.org/2008/12/elhadj-asp-2008-12-07/#_ednref7

[94] Elie Elhadj, "Dry Aquifers in Arab Countries and the Looming Food Crisis."

[95] "Saudi Arabia Ends Domestic Wheat Production Program," *World-Grain.com*, (March 18, 2016). http://www.world-grain.com/articles/news_home/World_Grain_News/2016/03/Saudi_Arabia_ends_domestic_whe.aspx?ID=%7B50E0E390-7C3F-46A6-B832-54FA58F140B2%7D&cck=1

[96] Ibid.

of six-years flow of the Nile River into Egypt. This volume translates to around 15 billion cubic meters per annum, equivalent to the volume of water that Syria and Iraq combined receive from the Euphrates river. Two-thirds of the water thus used is regarded as non-renewable, according to estimates by the Saudi Ministry of Agriculture and Water.[97] At this rate, if the extraction does not stop, the non-renewable water reserves will sooner or later be depleted. The January 2008 announcement confirms this.

The dramatic rise and equally dramatic fall of Saudi cereal production reflected haphazard planning and a failed, politically determined economic and ecological policy created by a poorly informed elite enjoying rentier economic circumstances. This experience serves to prove that throwing money and water at the desert could make the desert bloom, until either the money or the water run out.

Food independence is impossible to achieve for a country like Saudi Arabia. An individual requires one cubic meter of drinking water per annum, between 50 and 100 m3 for other domestic uses, and about 1,000 m3 of water to raise the food requirement of that individual.[98] A Saudi population of about 30 million requires about 30 billion m3 of water annually to grow its food needs. However, Saudi Arabia extracts around 15 billion m3, or 50% of its needs. Eventually, the irrigated lands from non-renewable water sources will be abandoned and the investments written off. A country like Saudi Arabia would be better off to stop desert irrigation altogether in order to save its remaining ground water for drinking and household purposes for future generations. Saudi Arabia is fortunate in that oil revenues will enable it to import foodstuffs.

Deflecting Wahhabi Culpability for 9/11

Al-Qaeda was founded and led by a Saudi, Osama bin Laden (until his death in 2011), and fifteen of the nineteen terrorists on 9/11 were Saudis—an indictment of the Saudi regime and its Wahhabi way of life

---

[97] Ibid.

[98] Tony Allan, *The Middle East Water Question Hydropolitics and the Global Economy* (London: I.B. Tauris, 2000), P. 6.

from top to bottom: Political, religious, military, judicial, intellectual, and tribal. 9/11 is a blight on the al-Sauds' legitimating ideology, system of governance, educational system, indoctrination practices, and proselytization schemes.

Without a shred of convincing explanation, Saudi propagandists have brushed aside any connection between the Wahhabi way of life and 9/11. Vast amounts of money spent on Arab media, Madison Avenue barons, and influential American agents deflected the world's attention from Wahhabi culpability for 9/11.

The idea that politics, not Wahhabism was behind 9/11 is pure spin. Religious beliefs cannot be disregarded in human behavior, nor can they be neutralized. It is not possible to compartmentalize the human brain, then sanitize the religious compartment. Therefore, Riyadh stands morally accused of breeding the terrorists. Absurd fantasies like blaming Israel's Mossad, the CIA, or the American extreme right will not exonerate Wahhabism from causing the blood of 9/11. Saudi Arabia must admit moral responsibility for inflicting a great harm on the world. Saudi Arabia must apologize for blackening the name of Islam and provoking the international anger against 400 million Arabs, most of whom look down on Wahhabism with disdain.

Washington, too, must accept moral responsibility for what decades of protecting the al-Sauds' Wahhabi cult have inflicted upon the world. Saudi Arabia and the United States must share the responsibility for the destruction of much of Iraq and Syria and Yemen.

The fact that Saudi Arabia is painting an image of itself as the Good Samaritan fighting terrorist gangs is Machiavellian in the extreme, a ploy to deflect attention from moral Wahhabi culpability for 9/11, totalitarian rule, protection from the same terrorist groups it has engendered, and protection from the American Justice against Sponsors of Terrorism Act (JASTA).

To eliminate a terrorist cell or two, a hundred, or even a thousand will not root out terrorism. Not only must the material and the financial infrastructure of jihadism be dismantled, but also the religious foundation upon which jihadism rests, starting with Wahhabism. To be realistic, however, such a course of action will not be taken while the world is hooked on oil. It is only when renewable energy drives oil out of the global market that the US will abandon Saudi Arabia and the world will become a safer place.

Countering Wahhabi Ulama's Contention that Democracy Is Incompatible with Islam

Building blocks for the consensus of the ulama as the fourth source of Sunni Law may be found in Prophetic statements.[99]

According to *Jame' al-Tirmithi*, the Prophet said:

> God does not make my umma [community, nation], *Muhammad's umma, agree on a falsehood.*[100]

Also, according to *Sunan Ibn Majah*, the Prophet said:

> *My umma does not agree upon a falsehood, and if you see disagreement, you must follow the view of the majority.*[101]

The Qur'an accords consultation among the faithful a positive mention:

> Verse 42:38: *Those who submitted to their Lord, pray regularly, and their affairs are conducted through consultation among each other…*

Why has consensus of the Sunni ulama, not the consensus of the Sunni community/nation as a whole, or representatives of the community/nation, become a source of Sunni law?

Before the advent of electricity, computers, telecommunications, and modern polling techniques, gauging the community's opinion in far-flung lands of the Islamic nation (umma) was impossible. Thus, the opinion of a caucus of learned men was a practical choice. It made the Consensus of the Ulama a pragmatic approximation to the opinion of the majority of the Muslim nation.

In the modern age, however, electricity, computers, telecommunications, and modern polling techniques have made referendums on specific issues simple, just as they have made the election of representatives easy. Modern technology has enabled the prophecy, "My community reaches no agreement that is an error" to become a reality. Modern technology

---

[99]Ignaz Goldziher, *Muslim Studies*, P. 88.
[100]*The Six Books, Jame' Al-Tirmithi,* tradition 2167, P. 1869
[101]*The Six Books, Sunan Ibn Maja,* tradition 3950, P. 2713.

has rendered the consensus of a narrow and unelected caucus of appointees obsolete. The consensus of a regularly and periodically elected body, a parliament, would be more consistent with the word and spirit of the Prophetic tradition. For the religiously minded, democratic parliamentary and presidential elections–like those that took place in Arab Spring countries, should provide the comfort that their elected representatives would enact laws that are not in error.

The Prophetic tradition raises four issues: The first is concerned with who among the Muslims is eligible to vote in the referendums or run in the elections for a parliamentary seat. The answer is that every Muslim is eligible, the layperson as well as the clerics. The Prophet was reported as saying that all the faithful are as equal as the teeth of a comb in the sight of God.

The second issue relates to the degree of consensus required. Does consensus mean the agreement of every member of the community? Or, is it the agreement of the majority of the people in the community? Since a unanimous consensus of all the people is impossible, consensus must mean the agreement of the majority in a referendum or in parliament. Indeed, the Prophetic statement, according to ibn Maja, just mentioned above, specifies that in the event of disagreement, the opinion of the majority must prevail.

The third issue relates to the subject matter(s) that might be covered in the umma's agreement. Does "agreement" refer to a specific issue or to all issues? Since the Hadith did not specify a particular matter, nor did it exclude any matter, the "agreement" would apply to any and all matters— from the temporal to the spiritual, theological, and ritual.

The fourth relates to what constitutes "community." Is it the body of world's Muslims? Or, is it the Muslims of each country separately? The answer is that since Muslim peoples today live in 55 sovereign Islamic kingdoms and republics around the world, speaking dozens of languages and of many ethnicities, pragmatism and realism suggest that the word "community" signifies the Muslims of each country separately.

Further, replacing the consensus of a non-elected caucus such as the ulama by the consensus of the majority of elected representatives of the Muslim community would solve some of the weaknesses inherent in selecting caucus members, such as who appoints members of the caucus and who among the ulama may qualify for membership. Allowing the Muslim community as a whole to elect its representatives removes the political influences that typically plague nominations in small caucuses. It may be concluded that the Prophetic Hadith signifies that: 1) The truth lies in whatever the majority among the members of a parliament agrees on, and 2) Shari'a laws may be changed by the consensus of a parliamentary majority.

The Prophetic Hadith introduces, for the first time in Arab societies, a mechanism to replace a ruler peacefully. Arab dictators have typically remained in power until they die of natural causes, are killed or dethroned in palace intrigue, in military coups, or most recently, in popular uprisings. It may be said that Muslim countries that hinder the emergence of democratically elected parliaments are in violation of the Hadith: "My community reaches no agreement that is in error."

In non-Arab Muslim countries, free elections with active multi-party participation produce genuine and vibrant parliamentary democracy. In the Arab world, except for Morocco and Tunisia, representative democracy does not exist. Where elections are held, the dictator invariably rigs the process and parliamentarians are typically controlled by the security services. In Saudi Arabia, the king-appointed 150-member Consultative Assembly plays the role of an adviser to the king. It is a propaganda tool, a showcase devoid of democratic or legislative value, though housed in an impressive building with the latest electronic gadgets.

Certain Saudi Ulama as Agents of Change

Important Saudi modernist ulama and intellectuals such as Salman al-Awdah, Abdallah al-Hamid, Sulaiman al-Rushoudi, Muhammad al-Ahmari have been reinterpreting "Islamic political theology, especially that which provides justification for repressive government."[102] They have been reinterpreting the Islamic text "to create a modern state based on representation, accountability, and freedom" within a civil state that "reject theocracy."[103] The Saudi modernists seek to "consolidate a position that allows the Saudi state to move beyond legitimacy claims based on applying Shari'a and upholding tradition. A modern state is not necessarily an

---

[102]Madawi al-Rasheed, *Muted Modernists, The Struggle over Divine Politics in Saudi Arabia*, (Oxford University Press, 2015), P. 2.
[103]Ibid.

un-Islamic or secular project, but is in their opinion an outcome of engaging with tradition in novel ways that make processes such as democracy, the establishment of civil society, and political representation anchored in reconstruction in religious heritage."[104] The modernists are "committed to Islam and its teachings, but they offer alternative interpretations of the tradition in order to break the hegemony of salafi [devout ancestors] dogma, especially that which abhors politics, insists on total obedience to rulers, and outlaws political activism."[105]

Salman al-Awdah was imprisoned from 1994–1999 for agitating for political change. Significantly, in 2011, during the Arab Spring uprisings, he called for tolerance, democracy, elections, and separation of powers.[106] On September 10, 2017, Salman al-Awda and several prominent Saudi clerics were detained in an apparent crackdown on potential regime opponents.[107]

[104]Ibid. P. 5
[105]Ibid. P. 6.
[106]"Saudi Clerics Detained in Apparent Bid to Silence Dissent," *Reuters*, (September 10, 2017). https://www.reuters.com/article/us-saudi-security-arrests/saudi-clerics-detained-in-apparent-bid-to-silence-dissent-idUSKCN1BL129
[107]"Saudi Arabia: Prominent Clerics Arrested," *Human Rights Watch*, (September 15, 2017). https://www.hrw.org/news/2017/09/15/saudi-arabia-prominent-clerics-arrested

AN ESTIMATE OF THE NUMBER OF THE DIRECT DESCENDANTS OF KING ABDULAZIZ AL-SAUD

There are five generations of descendants of the founder of the Saudi dynasty, King Abdulaziz al-Saud (d. 1953). According to Leslie Mc Laughlin, the patriarch fathered "43 sons and many daughters."[108] Upon the patriarch's death, 35 sons were alive. These sons were born to seventeen wives and concubines (source: Various):

The wives: Wadha (King Saud) + Tarfah (King Faisal) + Jawhara (Muhammad, King Khalid) + Hassa al-Sudairi (King Fahed, Sultan, Abdulrahman, Nayif, Turki, King Salman, Ahmad) + Haya al-Sudairi (Badr, Abdulmajeed) + Jawhara al-Sudairi (Sa'ad, Abdelmuhsen, Musa'ed) + Noff (Thamer, Mamdouh, Mashhour) + Fahda (King Abdallah) + Bazza-I (Nasser).

The concubines: Bazza-II (Bandar, Fawwaz) + Shahida (Mansour, Mish'al, Mit'ab) + Manayer (Talal, Nawwaf) + Moudi (Sattam, Majid) + Bushra (Mishari) + Baraka (Miqrin) + Fatima (Hmoud) + Sai'ida (Hathloul).

Only the descendants of the male children who were alive at the time of the patriarch's death will be counted. The descendants of the daughters will not be counted. The al-Saud women marry their cousins and extended family.

At the time of this writing, 9 sons of Abdulaziz's first generation are alive, including the current king, Salman. The 35 first generation sons may have produced 525 second-generation children [35 sons at an assumed

---

[108]Leslie Mc Laughlin, *Ibn Saud: Founder of a Kingdom*, (Palgrave Macmillan, St Antony's Series)/1993), P. 206.

average of 15 children each (35 x 15 = 525)]. King Saud alone, for example, the eldest son of King Abdulaziz, had 53 sons and 54 daughters.[109]

The 263 second-generation sons (525/2) are assumed to have produced 8 children each, or 2,104 of third generation children (263 x 8 = 2,104). The younger generation is less likely to marry more than one or two wives at any one time, compared with up to four wives at any one time for many of the older generation. The three generations would total 2,638 princes and princesses (9 + 525 + 2,104 = 2,638).

Of the third generation, it is assumed that each of the 1,052 sons (2,104/2 = 1,052) has 6 children each, for a total fourth generation of 6,312 children (1,052 x 6 = 6,312). The four generations would total 8,950 (9 + 525 + 2,104 + 6,312 = 8,950).

Assuming that a third of the fourth generation male children are married and each has 2 children, the number of the fifth generation children would be 2,104 (6,312/2 = 3,156/3 = 1,052 x 2 = 2,104).

The grand total of the five generations of direct descendants of Abdulaziz al-Saud becomes 11,054 (9 + 525 + 2,104 + 6,312 + 2,104 = 11,054).

---

[109] Al-Rasheed, *A History of Saudi Arabia*, P. 76.

CHAPTER SEVEN

THE US INVASION OF IRAQ, THE EMPOWERMENT OF IRAN, AND THE OPENING OF SUNNI/SHI'ITE GATES OF HELL

C hapter Five discussed how Egypt was kept in the clutches of non-representative military dictators for 64 of the past 65 years in order to protect Saudi Arabia from the winds of democracy. Also, Chapter Five explained why the first democratically elected Egyptian president ever was sacrificed on the altar of Saudi oil and removed from office one year later in a military putsch with Saudi help.

This Chapter argues that Iraq, too, was sacrificed on the altar of Saudi oil. To avoid havoc in world's oil markets, Saudi Arabia escaped US retaliation for the heinous crimes committed by 15 of its citizens on 9/11. Although no Iraqi was among the nineteen Wahhabi terrorists, the G.W. Bush administration chose to invade Iraq (March 19, 2003), and remove the government of Saddam Hussein from power (April 9, 2003), an adventure that destroyed much of that country. Eight years later, on December 18, 2011, the last US soldier departed from Iraq, a gift to the ayatollahs of Qom, Iran.[1]

The Cost of Punishing the Wrong Party for 9/11

Two months before the war, while answering a question on January 18, 2003 on how much money the Department of Defense would need to pay for a war with Iraq, Secretary of Defense Donald Rumsfeld said, "Well, the

---

[1]A Timeline of the Iraq War, *ThinkProgress*, (March 17, 2006). https://thinkprogress.org/a-time-line-of-the-iraq-war-6622633720be#.p5bdlfcrn

Office of Management and Budget has come up with a number that's something under $50 billion for the cost. How much of that would be the US burden and how much would be other countries is an open question."[2]

Well, the Iraq war turned out to be more expensive than the Defense Secretary's prewar figures. It cost dozens of times as much as the Office of Management and Budget estimated: $3 trillion, according to a 2008 estimate by Joseph Stiglitz and Linda Bilmes.[3] Harvard University's Kennedy School estimated in 2013 that the wars in Iraq and Afghanistan cost the US between $4 trillion and $6 trillion.[4] Neta Crawford of Brown University's Watson Institute for International and Public Affairs estimated that the wars in Afghanistan and Iraq cost US taxpayers nearly $5.6 trillion.[5] President Trump said that the U.S. had "foolishly spent $7 trillion in the Middle East."[6] It is safe to say that the lion's share of this amount belongs to the Iraq war. Also, most of the trillions were not spent in the Middle East. Rather, they benefited the American military-industrial complex, which supplied fighter jets, tanks, guns, and bullets, in addition to soldiers' salaries, medical care, and transportation to and from the battle-fields. The American human cost in Iraq between March 2003 and the departure of the last soldier in December 2011, was heavy too: 4,484 soldiers killed (out of 4,802 coalition casualties) and many times this number wounded.[7]

Not only was the financial cost projected incorrectly, but the duration of the war and number of troops needed was badly planned. The US Central Command's war plan postulated in August 2002 that they would have only 5,000 troops left in Iraq by December 2006,[8] a far cry from the 141,000 US military personnel on the ground in Iraq at the end of December 2006, joined by another 30,000 additional soldiers in the "surge" of January 2007.

---

[2]"Interview Transcript, Rumsfeld Briefs Press," *CNN*, (January 19, 2003). http://transcripts.cnn.com/TRANSCRIPTS/0301/19/se.01.html

[3]Joseph Stiglitz and Linda Bilmes, *The Three Trillion Dollar War, The True Cost of the Iraqi Conflict*, (Allen Lane, an imprint of Penguin Books, 2008).

[4]Linda J. Bilmes, "The Financial Legacy of Iraq and Afghanistan: How Wartime Spending Decisions Will Constrain Future National Security Budgets," Harvard University: Faculty Research Working Paper Series, (March 2013). https://research.hks.harvard.edu/publications/workingpapers/citation.aspx?PubId=8956&type=WPN

[5]Neta Crawford, "US Budgetary Costs of Post-9/11 Wars Through FY2018: $5.6 Trillion."

[6]Alana Horowitz Satlin, "Trump Bemoans War Costs As Pence Promises Afghanistan To 'See This Through'," (December 22, 2017). https://www.huffingtonpost.co.uk/entry/trump-war-costs-afghanistan_us_5a3d0667e4b06d1621b3df68

[7]Simon Rogers, "War in Iraq: the cost in American lives and dollars," *The Guardian*, (December 15, 2011). https://www.theguardian.com/news/datablog/2011/dec/15/war-iraq-costs-us-lives

[8]The National Security Archive, *National Security Archive Electronic Briefing Book No. 214*, http://nsarchive.gwu.edu/NSAEBB/NSAEBB214/index.htm

As for Iraq, a rather small country of an estimated population of 25 million (in 2003), the losses were catastrophic. No one really knows the exact numbers of the dead and wounded in Iraq. Two million could be an understatement. Many Iraqi cities and towns were pulverized. Most damaging has been the sectarian civil war the US occupation engendered. In Baghdad, a city of seven million inhabitants, it was rather common for Shi'ite and Sunni families to intermarry. Today, members of the same family are enemies.

On April 27, 2005, two years after the occupation, the United Nations University International Leadership Institute stated that some 84% of Iraq's higher education institutions have been burnt, looted or destroyed.[9]

Four years after the occupation had started, Oxfam and Iraqi NGOs reported that, "Of Iraq's population, 70% was without adequate clean water, 80% had no access to effective sanitation, 15% regularly could not afford to eat, 92% of children suffered from learning problems, and nearly 30% of children were malnourished—a sharp increase from the situation four years earlier. The slide into poverty and deprivation since the coalition forces entered the country in 2003 has been dramatic."[10] Fourteen years after the occupation, a brutal civil war continues to consume Iraq. A UNICEF report released on June 27, 2017 stated that, "Over 3 million children don't attend school on a regular basis, while 1.2 million children are out of school. More than 5 million children are in need of urgent humanitarian assistance."[11]

America's Missed Opportunity: Had the United States supplemented brute force by a truly awe-inspiring program of reconstruction, they would have demonstrated to all Iraqis, and to the Arab masses everywhere not only what a powerful military giant America is, but also what a helpful friend America can be. Had the United States demonstrated its practically unlimited resources to build roads, hospitals, schools, water and sanitation networks, electricity generating plants, and other infrastructure, it would have not only improved the coverage and quality of these basic services, but it also would have helped tens of thousands of poverty-stricken Iraqis to be employed, especially the 400,000 soldiers and security men who lost

---

[9]The Current Status and Future Prospects for the Transformation and Reconstruction of the Higher Education System in Iraq, pdf download. http://www.unu.edu/news/ili/Iraq.doc

[10]For the full report: *Rising to the Humanitarian Challenge in Iraq*. http://news.bbc.co.uk/1/shared/bsp/hi/pdfs/18_07_07_oxfam_iraq.pdf

[11]"Nowhere to Go: Children in Iraq Trapped in Cycles of Violence and Poverty," *UNICEF*, (June 27, 2017). https://www.unicef.org/media/media_96529.html

their jobs as a result of the decision taken by Paul Bremer, the US civilian administrator (May 2003 to June 2004), to dissolve the Iraqi armed and security forces.[12]

Such a reconstruction program could have propelled America's democratic project in the Arab world to great heights. It could have given America's friends in the Arab and Muslim worlds the wherewithal to isolate their opponents. It could have replaced the war against the insurgency with a war against poverty and unemployment. It could have saved American and Iraqi lives, as well as a good proportion of the financial cost of the war.

The US occupation of Iraq failed to bring human rights to the Iraqi people. The violations of Arab and Muslim sensibilities and the horrifying images of abuse in the infamous Abu Ghraib prison in 2004 shocked the world. The image of American decency and fair play was shattered.

The Orange Kool-Aid

To make the war palatable to the American people, Vice President Dick Cheney said that Iraqis would receive America's troops with open arms. In a speech to the Veterans of Foreign Wars national convention in Nashville, Tennessee on August 27, 2002, Mr. Cheney said, "As for the reaction of the Arab 'street,' the Middle East expert Professor Fouad Ajami predicts that after liberation, the streets in Basra and Baghdad are sure to erupt in joy in the same way the throngs in Kabul greeted the Americans."[13] The administration propagated that Iraq had:

1) A connection to al-Qaeda.
2) Attempted to obtain uranium from the Central African country of Niger.
3) Attempted to acquire more than 100,000 high-strength aluminum tubes for gas centrifuges for use in enriching uranium.
4) Possessed stocks of chemical and biological weapons and continued the development of weapons of mass destruction.

---

[12]Mark Fineman, Warren Viethand, and Robin Wright, "Dissolving Iraqi Army Seen by Many as a Costly Move," *The Los Angeles Times*, (August 24, 2003). http://articles.latimes.com/2003/aug/24/world/fg-iraqarmy24

[13]"Full text of Dick Cheney's Speech," *The Guardian*, (August 27, 2002). https://www.theguardian.com/world/2002/aug/27/usa.iraq

Iraq vehemently denied these accusations. The first three charges were discredited before the start of the war. Examining the veracity of the fourth accusation had to wait until Iraq was occupied. In the event, that too proved to be false. The United States Senate's 145-page *Report of the Select Committee on Intelligence on Post War Findings about Iraq's WMD Programs and Links to Terrorism and How They Compare with Prewar Assessments with Additional Views (RSCI)* dated September 8, 2006 discredited all accusations in the clearest of terms.[14]

1) Connection to Al-Qaeda: Without proof, the Bush administration's message against Iraq, "honed for public consumption by Fox News and the *Weekly Standard*,[15] seemed to be that the hunt for al-Qaeda could not eradicate terrorism, because bin Laden and his Taliban hosts were mere puppets. The man pulling the strings was in fact Saddam Hussein."[16] The majority of Americans believed this message. In February 2003, just before the March 19, 2003 attack on Iraq, a CNN-Time poll found that 76% of those surveyed believed Saddam provided assistance to al-Qaeda.[17] President Bush stated in a speech on October 7, 2001 in Cincinnati, Ohio:

> We know that Iraq and al Qaeda have had high-level contacts that go back a decade. Some al Qaeda leaders who fled Afghanistan went to Iraq. These include one very senior al Qaeda leader who received medical treatment in Baghdad this year, and who has been associated with planning for chemical and biological attacks. We've learned that Iraq has trained al-Qaeda members in bomb making and poisons and deadly gases.
>
> Iraq could decide on any given day to provide a biological or chemical weapon to a terrorist group or individual terrorists. Alliance with terrorists could allow the Iraqi regime to attack America without leaving any fingerprints.[18]

---

[14]Select Committee on Intelligence, "Post War Findings About Iraq's WMD Programs and Links to Terrorism and How They Compare with Prewar Assessments with Additional Views," *United States Senate*, (September 8, 2006). https://fas.org/irp/congress/2006_rpt/srpt109-331.pdf

[15]Fox News and the Weekly Standard are both controlled by Rupert Murdoch.

[16]Giles Kepel, *The War for Muslim Minds. Islam and the West*, (Belknap/Harvard, 2004), P. 197.

[17]Bruce Morton, "Selling an Iraq–Al-Qaeda Connection," *CNN*, (March 11, 2003). http://www.twf.org/News/Y2003/0312-IraqalQaeda.html

[18]President George W. Bush, "Remarks by the President on Iraq: President Bush Outlines Iraqi Threat," *Official White House Transcript*, (October 7, 2002). https://georgewbush-whitehouse.archives.gov/news/releases/2002/10/print/20021007-8.html

Saddam's regime could be accused of a million crimes, but not the one of promoting Islamist extremism or of aiding jihadism. Under Saddam's regime, Iraq was the bulwark against Islamist fanaticism. The *New York Times* reported on October 27, 2001 that a senior Israeli official said: "We don't see any evidence of al-Qaeda in Iraq. Not as a base, not as financial support."[19] However, in an interview with NBC's *Meet the Press* on December 9, 2001, Vice President Dick Cheney said, "It's been pretty well confirmed that Atta [the leader of the September 11 attacks] did go to Prague, and he did meet with a senior official of the Iraqi intelligence service in (the Czech Republic) last April, several months before the attack."[20] Nevertheless, the *New York Times* reported on October 21, 2002 that the Czech president, Vaclav Havel, quietly told the White House he had concluded that there was no evidence to confirm earlier reports that Muhammad Atta, had met with an Iraqi intelligence officer in Prague just months before the attacks on New York and Washington.[21] The RSCI report concluded on this issue that, "Saddam Hussein was distrustful of al-Qaeda and viewed Islamic extremists as a threat to his regime, refusing all requests from al-Qaeda to provide material or operational support."[22] On the Iraqi regime's support of Abu Mus'ab al-Zarqawi (merged with al-Qaeda in 2004), RSCI said, "Saddam Hussein attempted, unsuccessfully, to locate and capture al-Zarqawi, and that the regime did not have a relationship with, harbor, or turn a blind eye toward Zarqawi."[23] It is notable that the president of the United States repeated in a speech as late as mid-August 2006 that, "Saddam Hussein … had relations with Zarqawi."[24]

2) Attempt to Obtain Uranium from the Central African Country of Niger: President Bush, in his January 28, 2003 State of the Union address,

---

[19]Patrick Tyler and John Tagliabue, "A Nation Challenged: The Investigation; Czechs Confirm Iraqi Agent Met with Terror Ringleader," The *New York Times*, (October 27, 2001). http://www.nytimes.com/2001/10/27/world/nation-challenged-investigation-czechs-confirm-iraqi-agent-met-with-terror.html

[20]Vice President Dick Cheney, "The Vice President Appears on NBC's Meet the Press," *Official White House Transcript*, (December 9, 2001). https://georgewbush-whitehouse.archives.gov/vicepresident/news-speeches/speeches/print/vp20011209.html

[21]James Risen, "Threats and Responses: The View from Prague; Prague Discounts an Iraqi Meeting," The *New York Times*, (October 21, 2002). http://www.nytimes.com/2002/10/21/world/threats-and-responses-the-view-from-prague-prague-discounts-an-iraqi-meeting.html

[22]Select Committee on Intelligence, "Post War Findings About Iraq's WMD Programs and Links to Terrorism and How They Compare with Prewar Assessments with Additional Views," P. 105.

[23]Ibid. P. 109.

[24]"Saddam 'Had No Link to al-Qaeda,'" *BBC*, (September 9, 2006). http://news.bbc.co.uk/1/hi/5328592.stm

declared that, "The British government has learned that Saddam Hussein recently sought significant quantities of uranium from Africa."[25]

Well before the president's speech, in February 2002, the CIA had dispatched US Ambassador Joseph Wilson to Niger to investigate. Joseph Wilson was a career foreign service officer and ambassador who in the mid-1970s had been a diplomat in Niamey, Niger's capital. Wilson advised the CIA and the State Department that the Niger story was bogus. Ambassador Wilson's findings were ignored. Ambassador Wilson published his findings on July 6, 2003 in the *New York Times* article entitled, "What I Didn't Find in Africa."[26]

3) Attempts to Acquire High-Strength Aluminum Tubes for Gas Centrifuges: In the weeks leading up to the war, Dick Cheney and National Security Advisor Condoleezza Rice repeatedly stated that Iraq had attempted to acquire more than 100,000 high-strength aluminum tubes for gas centrifuges to be used for enriching uranium. Dick Cheney and National Security Advisor Condoleezza Rice made this claim. President Bush declared at the UN General Assembly on September 12, 2002, "Iraq has made several attempts to buy high-strength aluminum tubes used to enrich uranium for a nuclear weapon."[27] He later repeated the accusation on several occasions, including the State of the Union Address on January 28, 2003: "Our intelligence sources tell us that he [Saddam Hussein] has attempted to purchase high-strength aluminum tubes suitable for nuclear weapons production."[28] The aluminum tubes story was also part of General Powell's case to the UN on February 5, 2003, when he asserted, "Saddam Hussein made repeated covert attempts to acquire high-specification aluminum tubes from eleven different countries."[29]

The CIA emphasized that the tubes were intended specifically for centrifuges. Experts at the Department of Energy's (DOE) Oak Ridge, Livermore, and Los Alamos National Laboratories disagreed because the tube dimensions were far from ideal for this purpose. The DOE pointed out that if these tubes were for centrifuges, there should be evidence of Iraqi

---

[25]Full Transcript, "Bush's State of the Union Speech," *CNN*, (January 29, 2003). http://edition.cnn.com/2003/ALLPOLITICS/01/28/sotu.transcript/

[26]Joseph C. Wilson, "What I Didn't Find in Africa," The *New York Times*, (July 6, 2003). http://www.nytimes.com/2003/07/06/opinion/what-i-didn-t-find-in-africa.html

[27]Full Transcript, "President Bush's Address to the United Nations," *CNN*, (September 12, 2002). http://edition.cnn.com/2002/US/09/12/bush.transcript/

[28]"Bush's State of the Union Speech," *CNN*.

[29]"Powell's Key Points on Iraq," *CNN*, (February 5, 2003). http://edition.cnn.com/2003/US/02/05/sprj.irq.key.points.txt/index.html

attempts to acquire hundreds of thousands of other very specific components, but no such evidence existed. This critique of the CIA interpretation was seconded by the State Department Intelligence Branch, and also by the international group of centrifuge experts advising the International Atomic Energy Agency (IAEA). Mr. Powell had even been briefed by the IAEA about its disagreement with the CIA analysis.[30]

4) Possessing Stocks of Chemical and Biological Weapons and Continued Development of Weapons of Mass Destruction: According to a CNN article, in the January 28, 2003 State of the Union Address, President Bush described Saddam Hussein's stockpile of hundreds of tons of deadly chemical and biological weapons:

> Saddam Hussein had the materials to produce as much as 500 tons of sarin, mustard, and VX nerve agent. In such quantities, the President continued, these chemical agents could also kill untold thousands, and added that, Iraq, in the late 1990s, had several mobile biological weapons labs designed to produce germ warfare agents, which can be moved from place to a place to evade inspectors. As for delivery munitions, the president disclosed, US intelligence indicates that Saddam Hussein had upwards of 30,000 munitions capable of delivering chemical agents.[31]

Secretary of State Colin Powell, at the UN Security Council on February 5, 2003, echoed the president's address. General Powell, a military expert, having been the chairman of the Joint Chiefs of Staff (October 1, 1989 to September 30, 1993), told the world that the United States had, "First-hand descriptions of biological weapons factories on wheels and on rails ... We know what the fermenters look like, we know what the tanks, pumps, compressors, and other parts look like. We know how they fit together. We know how they work. And we know a great deal about the platforms on which they are mounted."[32]

The General presented a video of a modified fuel tank for an F-1 Mirage jet obtained by UNSCOM some years before, noting that the spray coming from beneath the Mirage was 2,000 liters of simulated anthrax.[33] As if

---

[30]Scientific Integrity in Policy Making, *The Bush Administration's Misuse of Science. Misrepresenting Evidence on Iraq's Aluminum Tubes*, http://webexhibits.org/bush/9.html

[31]"Bush's State of the Union Speech," *CNN*.

[32]"Transcript of Powell's U.N. Presentation," *CNN*, (February 5, 2003). http://edition.cnn.com/2003/US/02/05/sprj.irq.powell.transcript.05/

[33]Ibid.

to strengthen his argument, Mr. Powell referred glowingly to a UK government report entitled: *Iraq, Its Infrastructure of Concealment, Deception, and Intimidation*, published one week earlier, on January 30, 2003, saying, "I would call my colleagues' attention to the fine paper that the UK distributed ... which describes in exquisite detail Iraqi deception activities."[34] The Downing Street authors claimed that they drew upon a number of sources, including intelligence material. In fact, they copied material from at least three different authors and gave no credit to them. Indeed, they plagiarized, directly cutting and pasting.[35] One of the sources was an essay by a graduate student at a US university, complete with spelling errors, published in the Middle East Review of International Affairs (MERIA), a professional journal published in Israel. Channel 4 UK TV reported that, "The student's work regarding the Iraqi intelligence structure was written in a historical perspective on pre-1991 Iraq and was used in the document as a description of today's Iraq. Apart from pages 6 to 16 that have been directly cut and pasted, other sections have had words altered to make it sound more sinister. Even typographic mistakes in the original article were repeated."[36]

Hans Blix, the UN chief weapons inspector, disputed Mr. Powell's evidence at the Security Council on February 5, 2003. Dr. Blix stated there was no evidence of mobile biological weapons laboratories or of Iraq trying to evade inspectors by moving equipment before his teams arrived. Dr. Blix said he had already inspected two alleged mobile labs and found nothing.[37] General Powell came to regret his performance. He described his presentation as "a blot" on his record: "It was painful. It's painful now."[38]

On March 7, 2003, the Director-General of the IAEA, Mohammad al-Baradei, presented to the UN the IAEA's findings regarding Iraq's nuclear activities during the previous decade. He said, "After three months of intrusive inspections, the Agency had found no evidence or plausible indication of the revival of a nuclear weapons program in Iraq. There was

---

[34]"Full text of Colin Powell's Speech," *The Guardian*, (February 5, 2003). https://www.theguardian.com/world/2003/feb/05/iraq.usa

[35]Glen Rangwala, "British Intelligence Iraq Dossier Relies on Recycled Academic Articles," *Center for Research on Globalisation*, (February 5, 2003). http://globalresearch.ca/articles/RAN302A.html

[36]Channel 4 UK TV, "Part of Colin Powell's Address to the UN Was Plagiarized: It Was Copied and Pasted from a Website!" (February 6, 2003). http://globalresearch.ca/articles/CHF302A.html

[37]Dan Plesch, "US Claim Dismissed by Blix," *The Guardian*, (February 5, 2003). http://www.guardian.co.uk/international/story/0,3604,889133,00.html

[38]Steven Weisman, "Powell Calls His UN Speech a Lasting Blot on His Record," The *New York Times*, (September 9, 2005). http://www.nytimes.com/2005/09/09/politics/powell-calls-his-un-speech-a-lasting-blot-on-his-record.html?_r=0

also no indication that Iraq had attempted to import uranium since 1990 or that it had attempted to import aluminum tubes for use in centrifuge enrichment."[39] However, Mr. Cheney contradicted the IAEA chief on March 16, 2005 on NBC Television, saying, "We believe Saddam Hussein has, in fact, reconstituted nuclear weapons. I think Mr. al-Baradei frankly is wrong. If you look at the track record of the International Atomic Energy Agency and this kind of issue, especially where Iraq is concerned, they consistently underestimated or missed what Saddam Hussein was doing."[40]

On the second accusation, possession and continued development of nuclear and chemical weapons of mass destruction (WMD) and the means to deliver them, this accusation proved to be false as well. The 1,000-page *Comprehensive Report of the Special Advisor to the Director of Central Intelligence Agency on Iraq's Weapons of Mass Destruction* (named the Duelfer Report), released on April 25, 2006, found no such weapons, despite the keen interest of the war managers in Washington and the vast expense and diligence of 1,200 inspectors for one-and-a-half years.[41] On January 12, 2005, the search for WMD in Iraq stopped and the inspectors returned home.[42] On April 26, 2005, the United States closed the book on the Iraq WMD hunt.[43]

How Might the Intelligence Failures Be Explained? The intelligence evidence was obtained from dubious sources, knowingly or gullibly, without proper verification, or plagiarized, possibly even invented, without fear of punishment. On those occasions when analysts voiced doubt, politicians simply ignored them.

Senator Angus King stated during the confirmation hearing of Mike Pompeo on January 12, 2017 for the position of Director of the Central Intelligence Agency: "The great foreign policy mistakes of my lifetime— Vietnam, the Bay of Pigs, and Iraq—all were based in one way or another

---

[39]United Nations, "United Nations Weapons Inspectors Report to Security Council on Progress in Disarmament of Iraq," (March 7, 2003). http://www.un.org/press/en/2003/sc7682.doc.htm

[40]"Transcript for Meet the Press with Dick Cheney," *NBC News*, (September 14, 2003). http://www.nbcnews.com/id/3080244/#.WHF9Qnecb6k

[41]US Government Publishing Office, *Comprehensive Report of the Special Advisor to the DCI on Iraq's WMD, with Addendums (Duelfer Report)*, (April 25, 2005). https://www.gpo.gov/fdsys/pkg/GPO-DUELFERREPORT/content-detail.html

[42]"US gives up search for Iraq WMD," *BBC*, (January 12, 2005). http://news.bbc.co.uk/2/hi/americas/4169107.stm

[43]"US Closes Book on Iraq WMD Hunt," *BBC*, (April 26, 2005). http://news.bbc.co.uk/2/hi/americas/4484237.stm

on bad intelligence or, more accurately, intelligence that was tailored to fit the demands of the policymakers. You can't read the histories of those decisions without coming to that conclusion."[44]

In his memoires, "My Life, Our Times" published in November 2017, Former British Prime Minister Gordon Brown, Chancellor of the Exchequer at the time, states that the UK was misled over former Iraqi dictator Saddam Hussein's access to weapons of mass destruction.[45] Mr. Brown says US intelligence, which challenged the extent of Iraq's WMD stockpile, was not shared with the UK before it joined the Iraq War and that, "We were not just misinformed, but misled."[46]

The Plan to Invade Iraq Well Before 9/11

On January 26, 1998, almost four years before September 11, 2001, regime change in Iraq had been on the minds of influential Washington politicians. Eighteen individuals, many of whom became senior officials in the first administration of President George W. Bush, sent an open letter to President Bill Clinton urging him to remove Saddam Hussein from power.[47] Part of the letter stated, "We urge you to seize [the] opportunity and to enunciate a new strategy that would secure the interests of the USA and our friends and allies around the world. That strategy should aim, above all, at the removal of Saddam Hussein's regime from power."[48] On October 31, 1998, the Congress passed and President Bill Clinton signed the Iraq Liberation Act. It declares that it should be the policy of the United States to:

---

[44]Full Transcript, "Confirmation Hearing of Mike Pompeo for CIA Director," *CNN*, (January 12, 2017). http://transcripts.cnn.com/TRANSCRIPTS/1701/12/ath.02.html

[45]"Iraq War: Gordon Brown Says UK 'Misled' over WMDs," *BBC*, (November 5, 2017). http://www.bbc.co.uk/news/uk-41872701

[46]Ibid.

[47]The authors of the letter included Richard Perle (head of the Pentagon's defense policy board), Richard Armitage (deputy secretary of state), John Bolton (under-secretary of state), Paula Dobriansky (under-secretary of state), Elliott Abrams (presidential advisor for the Middle East and a member of the US National Security Council), Peter W. Rodman (assistant secretary of defense for international security affairs), Zalmay Khalilzad (special envoy to the Iraqi opposition), Robert B. Zoellick (US trade representative), Paul Wolfowitz (deputy secretary of defense), and former CIA director James Woolsey.

[48]PNAC letters sent to President Bill Clinton, (January 26, 1998). http://www.informationclearinghouse.info/article5527.htm

Seek to remove the Saddam Hussein regime from power in Iraq and to replace it with a democratic government.

Authorizes the President, after notifying specified congressional committees, to provide to the Iraqi democratic opposition organizations: (1) grant assistance for radio and television broadcasting to Iraq; (2) Department of Defense (DOD) defense articles and services and military education and training (IMET); and (3) humanitarian assistance, with emphasis on addressing the needs of individuals who have fled from areas under the control of the Hussein regime. Prohibits assistance to any group or organization that is engaged in military cooperation with the Hussein regime. Authorizes appropriations.

Directs the President to designate: (1) one or more Iraqi democratic opposition organizations that meet specified criteria as eligible to receive assistance under this Act; and (2) additional such organizations which satisfy the President's criteria.

Urges the President to call upon the United Nations to establish an international criminal tribunal for the purpose of indicting, prosecuting, and imprisoning Saddam Hussein and other Iraqi officials who are responsible for crimes against humanity, genocide, and other criminal violations of international law.

Expresses the sense of the Congress that once the Saddam Hussein regime is removed from power in Iraq, the United States should support Iraq's transition to democracy by providing humanitarian assistance to the Iraqi people and democracy transition assistance to Iraqi parties and movements with democratic goals, including convening Iraq's foreign creditors to develop a multilateral response to the foreign debt incurred by the Hussein regime.[49]

The occupation of Iraq was consistent with the recommendations contained in a report written in September 2000 by the neo-conservative think-tank, Project for the New American Century (PNAC), entitled *Rebuilding America's Defenses: Strategies, Forces and Resources for a New Century*. The report states that, "The United States has for decades sought to play a more permanent role in Gulf regional security. While the unresolved

---

[49]US Congress, "Iraq Liberation Act of 1998," *Congress.gov*. https://www.congress.gov/bill/105th-congress/house-bill/4655

conflict with Iraq provides the immediate justification, the need for a sub-stantial American force presence in the Gulf transcends the issue of the regime of Saddam Hussein."[50]

The story of Iraq's weapons of mass destruction was a late invention. In 2001, the Bush administration spoke confidently of how effective the American policy of containment had been. Secretary of State Powell stated in Cairo on February 24, 2001 that, "Saddam Hussein has not developed any significant capability with respect to weapons of mass destruction."[51]

On May 15, 2001, Powell went further, saying that, "Saddam Hussein had not been able to rebuild his military or to develop weapons of mass destruction for the past ten years. America, he said, had been successful in keeping him "in a box.""[52] Two months later, National Security Adviser Condoleezza Rice described a weak, divided, and militarily defenseless Iraq, "Saddam does not control the northern part of the country, she said. We are able to keep his arms from him. His military forces have not been rebuilt."[53]

The 9/11 atrocities facilitated the realization of PNAC's objectives in *Rebuilding America's Defenses* to change Saddam Hussein's regime.[54]

Ostensible Motives behind the Occupation of Iraq

The Bush administration was in a hurry to invade Iraq despite the Blix and al-Baradei reports. That the two reports found "no evidence or plausible indication of the revival of a nuclear weapons program" suggests a hidden agenda to:

1) Change the regimes of Iran and Syria.
2) Control Iraq's vast oil reserves.

---

[50]Project for the New American Century, *Rebuilding America's Defenses, Strategy, Forces and Resources for a New Century*, (September 2000). http://www.informationclearinghouse.info/pdf/RebuildingAmericasDefenses.pdf

[51]"Powell '01: WMD Not 'Significant'," *CBS NEWS*, (September 28, 2003). https://www.cbsnews.com/news/powell-01-wmds-not-significant/

[52]"Colin Powell & Rice in 2001 says "Saddam Hussein was no threat"," *IN REVIEW*, (September 29, 2003). http://www.inreview.com/topic-10092.html

[53]Ibid.

[54]For the Iraq War timeline from the day George Bush went to the Pentagon for 'a top-secret session with the Joint Chiefs of Staff to review hot spots around the world' on January 11, 2001 to the day the US invaded Iraq, March 19, 2003, see: Public Interest Investigations, Powerbase, *Iraq War 2003 Timeline*, http://powerbase.info/index.php/Iraq_War_2003_Timeline

3) Hand US companies billions of dollars in re-construction contracts.
4) Bolster Israel's security.
5) Quench Mr. Bush's personal hatred of Saddam Hussein.
6) Spread democracy in the Arab world.
7) Replace the Cold War with a new enemy.

Change the Regimes of Iran and Syria: Changing the regimes of Iran and Syria could have been the strongest motive. The two countries were two of the three members of Mr. Bush's "axis of evil."[55] Regarding Syria's Assad regime, US policy intentions toward Damascus can be gleaned through a 1996 study entitled, *A Clean Break: A New Strategy for Securing the Realm*[56] conducted by the Likud-leaning Israeli think-tank, the Jewish Institute for National Security Affairs. Eight policy advisors to Israel authored the study.[57] *A Clean Break* advocates removing Saddam Hussein from power in order to weaken Syria. The study states that, "Israel can shape its strategic environment ... by weakening, containing, and even rolling back Syria. This effort can focus on removing Saddam Hussein from power in Iraq—an important Israeli strategic objective in its own right—as a means of foiling Syria's regional ambitions." The study also advocates "reestablishing the principle of preemption, rather than retaliation alone."

Changing Iran's ayatollahs' regime would change the political map of the Middle East. It could turn a hostile anti-US theocracy into a secular democratic pro-American country. It could complete US control over Middle East oil, and open a market of 70 million (in 2003) Iranians to US business. With Iran and Syria added to Iraq, a Middle East Pax-Americana involving Arabs, Iranians, and Israelis could become a reality—a tantalizing prospect, on paper, at least. In a speech to the Veterans of Foreign Wars (VFW) national

---

[55]Frank Gardner, "Who's Who in the 'Axis of Evil,'" *BBC*, (December 20, 2003). http://news.bbc.co.uk/1/hi/1988810.stm

[56]The Institute for Advanced Strategic and Political Studies, Study Group on a New Israeli Strategy Toward 2000, *A Clean Break: A New Strategy for Securing the Realm*, https://www.sourcewatch.org/index.php/Study_Group_on_a_New_Israeli_Strategy_Toward_2000

[57]Richard Perle (head of the defense policy board), Douglas Feith, (undersecretary of defense for policy), James Colbert (Jewish Institute for National Security Affairs, Israel), Charles Fairbanks, Jr. (Johns Hopkins University/SAIS), Robert Loewenberg (President, Institute for Advanced Strategic and Political Studies), Jonathan Torop (The Washington Institute for Near East Policy), David Wurmser (Institute for Advanced Strategic and Political Studies), Meyrav Wurmser (Johns Hopkins University).

convention in Nashville, Tennessee on August 27, 2002, Cheney said, "Our ability to advance the Israeli-Palestinian peace process would be enhanced."[58]

Control of Iraq's Vast Oil Reserves: Estimated to have been 112 billion barrels in 2002[59] (in 2016, reserves grew to 143 billion barrels),[60] Iraq possesses one of the world's largest oil reserves. The cluster of super-giant fields of Southeastern Iraq forms the largest known concentration of such fields in the world, accounting for 70% to 80% of the country's proven oil reserves, or around 100 billion barrels.[61] Adding Iraq's oil reserves to those of Saudi Arabia, Kuwait, Qatar, and the UAE would have effectively completed America's control over Arab oil resources, estimated at more than half of the world's proven oil reserves.

US intentions toward Iraq's oil may be detected from documents secured by the public interest group Judicial Watch in July 2003, which stated:

> "Vice President Dick Cheney has been plotting the conquest of Iraq since he was Secretary of Defense in President George H.W. Bush's administration—a plan then considered insane aggression. On July 17, 2003, Judicial Watch announced that Cheney's Energy Task Force had developed a map of Iraq dated March 2001, as well as maps of the neighboring United Arab Emirates (U.A.E.) and Saudi Arabia, which show that Cheney knew precisely how much the conquest of Iraq would be worth. The map, which shows oilfields, pipelines, tanker terminals, and refineries, includes eight "blocks" for exploration near the border with Saudi Arabia."[62]

It is noteworthy that President Trump stated on January 21, 2017 that the US should have taken Iraq's oil.[63]

---

[58]"Full text of Dick Cheney's Speech," *The Guardian*, (August 27, 2002). https://www.theguardian.com/world/2002/aug/27/usa.iraq

[59]Gal Luft, "How Much Oil Does Iraq Have?," *Brookings*, (May 12, 2003). https://www.brookings.edu/research/how-much-oil-does-iraq-have/

[60]Central intelligence Agency, The World Factbook, *Country Comparisons: Crude Oil—Proved Reserves*, https://www.cia.gov/library/publications/the-world-factbook/rankorder/2244rank.html

[61]Patrick Avis, "The Outlook and Challenges for Oil in Iraq," *Energy Analyst*, (October 31, 2016). https://energyanalyst.co.uk/the-outlook-and-challenges-for-oil-in-iraq/

[62]Scott Thompson, "Dick Cheney Has Long Planned to Loot Iraqi Oil," *by Scott Thompson, Executive Intelligence Review*, (August 1, 2003). http://www.larouchepub.com/other/2003/3030cheney_oil.html

[63]Matt Fuller, "President Trump Just Told The CIA The US Should Have Stolen Iraq's Oil," *The Huffington Post*, (January 21, 2017). http://www.huffingtonpost.com/entry/trump-cia-iraq-oil_us_5883ccf5e4b096b4a23243b2

Hand US Corporations Billions of Dollars in Reconstruction Contracts: Hundreds of billions of dollars would potentially go to U.S. companies for reconstructing Iraq's invasion-ravaged cities and towns, oil and gas production and refining infrastructure, water and sanitation facilities, electricity and telecommunication networks, roads, harbors, airports, and so forth.

Bolster Israel's Security: Destroying Iraq's armed forces and infrastructure is one way to work toward the goal of bolstering Israel's security. The other way is to carve Iraq into separate states for Kurds, Arab Shi'ites, and Arab Sunnis. The breakup of Iraq would be a prelude, Arabs believe, to similar breakups in Lebanon and Syria into enclaves for Alawites, Christians, Druzes, Shi'ites, and Sunnis.

Quench Mr. Bush's Personal Hatred of Saddam Hussein: Saddam was accused of plotting to assassinate former President George H.W. Bush during his ceremonial visit to Kuwait in April 1993. Mr. Bush kept a gun that Saddam Hussein was holding when US forces caught him. The president "really liked showing it off," and "was really proud of it,"[64] suggesting that Mr. Bush's animosity toward Saddam Hussein was personal.

Spread Democracy in the Arab World: In 2005, the Bush administration embarked on a program to steer Arab countries to hold democratic elections. This strategy was without regard to the explosion that would have erupted from lifting the lid on religious and sectarian pressures. The results were not encouraging for US policies.

Palestinian Authority (PA): Washington, the European Union, Israel, and the Palestinian Authority tried to derail Hamas in the January 2006 elections. The PA was threatened with financial aid cut-off if Hamas prevailed.[65] It was revealed three days before the elections that the Bush administration had been spending foreign aid money to increase the popularity of the PA and to campaign against the Hamas candidates.[66] In the event, Hamas, who participated in elections for the first time, won

---

[64]"Bush Has Saddam Gun as Souvenir," *BBC*, (May 30, 2004). http://news.bbc.co.uk/1/hi/world/middle_east/3762641.stm

[65]GolobalSecurity.Org, "Palestinian Parliamentary Elections 2006". http://www.globalsecurity.org/military/world/palestine/pa-elections2006.htm

[66]Scott Wilson and Glenn Kessler, "US Funds Enter Fray in Palestinian Elections," *Washington Post*, (January 22, 2006). http://www.washingtonpost.com/wp-dyn/content/article/2006/01/21/AR2006012101431.html

74 of the 132 seats in parliament[67] or, 56%. In reaction, the US demanded the return of $50 million in aid funds Washington had given to the PA in 2005 for infrastructure development in Gaza, to which the PA agreed promptly.[68] Almost twelve years later, in October 2017, Tony Blair, Prime Minister at the time, said that he and other world leaders were wrong to yield to Israeli pressure to impose an immediate boycott on Hamas after Hamas won the 2006 elections.[69]

Iraq: In the January 30, 2005 elections for the Transitional National Assembly, the United Iraqi Alliance list of candidates (UIA) was approved by Grand Ayatollah Ali al-Sistani. He is the leader of Shi'ism's preeminent 950-year old Najaf Hawza (Shi'ite scholarly center). The list was known as the *Sistani List*. Dominated by Shi'ite clerics, the *Sistani List* won 140 of the 275 seats.[70] In the December 15, 2005 elections, the UIA won 128 out of 275 seats.[71] Sunnis were sidelined in both elections.

Saudi Arabia: The 2005 municipal elections were farcical theatrics of no democratic value. Nonetheless, one-half of the 178 councilors were government appointed. Women were barred from running for office and from voting. Saudi democracy meant that when the councils were finally announced in December 2005, ten months after the first round was held, the municipal affairs minister declared that the councils would have largely advisory roles on local affairs.[72]

Egypt: A constitutional amendment was made to allow a sort of contested presidential election with restrictions on President Mubarak's opponents. A nine-page Egyptian judges' report described the referendum on constitutional reform as "marred by widespread fraud."[73] On September 7, 2005, President Mubarak was re-elected by a majority of 88.6% of the

---

[67]"CEC Announces Final Results of Second PLC Elections," *Independent Media Review Analysis (IMRA)*, (January 29, 2006). http://www.imra.org.il/story.php3?id=28320

[68]"Israel to Consider Palestinian Sanctions," *CNN*, (February 18, 2006). http://edition.cnn.com/2006/WORLD/meast/02/18/hamas.abbas/index.html

[69]Donald Macintyre, "Tony Blair: 'We Were Wrong to Boycott Hamas after its Election Win,'" *The Guardian*, (October 14, 2017). https://www.theguardian.com/world/2017/oct/14/tony-blair-hamas-gaza-boycott-wrong

[70]"Iraqi Shia Unite to Contest Poll," *BBC*, (October 27, 2005). http://news.bbc.co.uk/1/hi/world/middle_east/4382640.stm

[71]"Guide to Iraqi Political Parties," *BBC*, (January 20, 2006). http://news.bbc.co.uk/1/hi/world/middle_east/4511450.stm

[72]"Saudi Councils Finally Announced," *BBC*, (December 15, 2005). http://news.bbc.co.uk/1/hi/world/middle_east/4531862.stm

[73]"Egyptian Judges Allege Vote Fraud," *BBC*, (July 2, 2005). http://news.bbc.co.uk/2/hi/middle_east/4644503.stm

votes cast. Turnout was low—23% of Egypt's 32 million registered voters.[74] Opposition groups alleged voter intimidation, people casting more than one vote, and busing voters to polling stations to vote for Mr. Mubarak.[75] The difference between Mubarak's performance in the September 7, 2005 election and his four previous non-contested farcical referendums was minimal; 88.6% as compared with 98.5% in 1981; 97.1% in 1987; 96.3% in 1993; and 93.8% in 1999.

Also, in Egypt's parliamentary elections in November-December 2005, members of the banned Muslim Brotherhood stood as independents. They became the major parliamentary opposition, winning 88 seats, or 20%. They could have won more seats had they been recognized as a legal party and allowed to campaign freely.

With such poor experience, the Bush administration's faith in Arab democracy quickly vanished.

Replace the Cold War Against the Former Soviet Union with a New Enemy: During the decades of the Cold War, the Soviet "Evil Empire" maintained the good health of the US military-industrial complex. The end of the Cold War could not be allowed to hinder the viability of the US military-industrial complex. The United States has invested too many financial and human resources in military-production infrastructure. According to the 2004 DSB report, the Global War on Terrorism replaced the Cold War as a national security meta-narrative.[76] It explains that the new development is increasingly viewed by the overwhelming majority of Muslims as a threat to the survival of Islam itself. As evidence, the report refers to three polls conducted one year after the invasion of Iraq that showed an overwhelming conviction by Muslims that the US seeks to "dominate" and "weaken" the Muslim World.[77]

To promote the new war, its proponents had to find common denominators between the ideologies, aims, and methods of Marxism/Leninism and radical Islam. In a speech at the National Endowment for Democracy in Washington, D.C. in October 2005, President G.W. Bush outlined

---

[74]"Landslide Win for Egyptian Leader," *BBC*, (September 9, 2005). http://news.bbc.co.uk/2/hi/middle_east/4231338.stm

[75]"Egypt Challenger to Seek Re-run," *BBC*, (September 8, 2005). http://news.bbc.co.uk/2/hi/middle_east/4225912.stm

[76]Office of the Under Secretary of Defense For Acquisition, Technology, and Logistics, *Report of the Defense Science Board Task Force on Strategic Communication (DSB)*, (September 2004), P. 17. https://fas.org/irp/agency/dod/dsb/commun.pdf

[77]Ibid. P. 35.

the similarities between America's fight against "the murderous ideology of the Islamic radicals" and the "struggle against communism in the last century."[78]

The following examines the reaction of Iraq's Arabs Sunnis, Kurds, and Shi'ites to the American invasion and occupation. It also examines the reaction in Tehran and its surrogates, the Assad regime in Syria, and Hezbollah in Lebanon.

Arab Sunnis' Resistance to the US Occupation of Iraq

Qur'anic injunctions to fight non-Muslim occupiers inspired Arabs, Sunnis and Shi'ites alike to liberate their lands from European colonizers. The mosque has always served as a podium to wage "holy" wars of liberation. Led by Najaf Seminary clerics, Sunni and Shi'ite Iraqis rose in 1920 in response to the call of jihad against British occupation.

Iraqis learned liberation lessons from Algeria, Egypt, Lebanon, Libya, Tunisia, Sudan, and Syria who liberated themselves from British, French, and Italian occupiers. These lessons were also fueled by the anti-imperialist rhetoric that engulfed the Arab region since the dawn of the nationalist Nasserite era in 1953 and the Ba'th regimes in Iraq and Syria in 1958. Since the early 1950s, support for the Palestinian refugees and the liberation movements from Vietnam to anti-apartheid South Africa have been constants in Arab national discourse. A poll conducted by an Iraqi university research team for the UK Ministry of Defense in August 2005 showed that 82% of Iraqis are "strongly opposed" to the presence of coalition troops in Iraq.[79]

The US occupation of Iraq turned the life of Iraqi Sunnis upside down. If the occupation were a knife in the Sunnis' back, the anti-Sunni sectarianism and divisiveness of Nouri al-Maliki's eight-year premiership twisted the knife. Thus, Iraq's Arab Sunnis led the insurgency against the occupation.

On May 23, 2003, one month after the occupation, Paul Bremer, the US civilian administrator (May 2003 to June 2004), dissolved Iraq's Armed

---

[78]"Bush: Islamic Radicalism Doomed to Fail," *CNN*, (October 6, 2005). http://edition.cnn.com/2005/POLITICS/10/06/bush.transcript/

[79]Andrew Robathan, "Secret MoD Poll: Iraqis Support Attacks on British Troops," *The Telegraph*, (October 23, 2005). http://www.telegraph.co.uk/news/worldnews/middleeast/iraq/1501319/Secret-MoD-poll-Iraqis-support-attacks-on-British-troops.html

Forces, its Ministries of Defense and Information, and other security institutions. As a result, 400,000 Iraqi soldiers immediately became unemployed.[80] Unemployment and poverty drove many of them to join the resistance.

Sunni resistance included Saddam-era Ba'th Party activists ranging from soldiers and security personnel to Iraqi nationalists and Islamists, plus foreign al-Qaeda Wahhabi fighters.[81] According to US military figures, 45% of foreign militants were from Saudi Arabia, 15% from Syria and Lebanon, and 10% from North Africa.[82] Estimates of the size of the Sunni insurgency vary. In January 2005, the head of Iraq's intelligence service, General Muhammad Shahwani, put the number of hard-core insurgents at 40,000, with another 160,000 of active supporters.[83]

Kurds Welcome the US Invasion

Iraq's Kurds are a non-Arab minority living in northern Iraq. They are mainly Sunni Muslims. There are no official and reliable statistics on the number of the Kurdish people. The Institut Kurd of Paris estimates that there are about 8 million Iraqi Kurds (CIA World FactBook puts the number at 15%–20% of Iraq's 38 million population, or between 5.7 million and 7.6 million).[84] Iraq's Kurds are a part of a Kurdish nation that aspires to statehood and has minorities scattered in three adjacent countries: Iran (about 10 million, or roughly 15% of the population), Turkey (around 20 million, or about 25% of the population), and Syria (2.5 million, or about 10% of the population). Another two million Kurds are scattered around the world.[85]

Iraq's Kurds welcomed the US occupation. The American occupation meant more than autonomy; it brought the hope of independence and,

---

[80]Rory McCarthy, "Saddam's Army and Apparatus Sacked," *The Guardian*, (May 24, 2003). https://www.theguardian.com/world/2003/may/24/iraq.rorymccarthy1

[81]Brian Whitaker and Ewen Macaskill, "Report Attacks 'Myth' of Foreign Fighters," *The Guardian*, (September 23, 2005). https://www.theguardian.com/world/2005/sep/23/iraq.ewenmacaskill

[82]Ned Parker, "Saudis' Role in Iraq Insurgency Outlined," *The Los Angeles Times*, (July 15, 2007). https://web.archive.org/web/20090223180041/http://fairuse.100webcustomers.com/fairenough/latimesA98.html

[83]Paul Reynolds, "Blistering Attacks Threaten Iraq Election," *BBC*, (January 10, 2005). http://news.bbc.co.uk/1/hi/world/middle_east/4145585.stm

[84]Central Intelligence Agency, The World FactBook, *Iraq people and Society*. https://www.cia.gov/library/publications/the-world-factbook/geos/iz.html

[85]"The Kurdish Population," *Institut Kurd de Paris*, (January 12, 2017). http://www.institutkurde.org/en/info/the-kurdish-population-1232551004

ultimately, the dream of a state for all Kurds. Iraqi Kurds held a non-binding referendum on independence in January 2005 in which 99% voted in favor of eventual statehood.[86] On September 25, 2017, another referendum was held. 92% of those who cast their ballots supported secession; the turnout was 72.61%.[87]

There are two main Kurdish political parties in Iraq, the Kurdistan Democratic Party (KDP), led by Massud Barazani, and the Patriotic Union of Kurdistan (PUK), headed by its founder Jalal Talabani until his death on October 3, 2017. After almost a decade of intra-Kurdish fighting between the two parties, the KDP and the PUK formed a coalition in the early 1990s. The coalition was agreed in order to govern the Kurdish region after it gained self-rule following the 1991 Gulf War.

In the January 30, 2005 election for the Transitional National Assembly, the Kurdish coalition won 75 seats of the 275-seat assembly.[88] In the December 15, 2005 election, the Kurdish coalition won 75 seats[89] of the 275-seat parliament. In the 2010 election, the Kurdish coalition won 51 seats. In the 2014 election, the Kurdish coalition won 62 seats.[90] Jalal Talabani was selected by parliament to be president of Iraq from 2005 to 2014. He was the first non-Arab President of Iraq. On July 24, 2014, the parliament selected Fouad Massoum, a cofounder of PUK to be president, succeeding the ailing Talabani.[91] Although there is no legal text that mandates the presidency should go to Kurds, it was agreed that Kurds hold the presidential office, while the prime minister is a Shi'ite, and the speaker of the parliament a Sunni Arab.

Iraq's 2005 constitution recognizes an autonomous Kurdish region governed by the Kurdistan Regional Government (KRG), with its capital

---

[86]Carol Williams, "Iraqi Kurds Signal Intent to Hold Independence Referendum," *Los Angeles Times*, (July 3, 2014). http://www.latimes.com/world/middleeast/la-fg-iraq-kurds-independence-referendum-20140703-story.html

[87]"Iraqi Kurds Back Independence in Referendum," *BBC*, (September 27, 2017). http://www.bbc.co.uk/news/world-middle-east-41419633

[88]CNN, World/Election Watch—Iraq, http://edition.cnn.com/WORLD/election.watch/meast/iraq3.html

[89]House of Commons Library, "The Parliamentary Election in Iraq, March 2010," (May 11, 2010). researchbriefings.files.parliament.uk/documents/SN05380/SN05380.pdf

[90]Suadad al-Sahly and Cathy Otten, "Uncertainty as Iraq Election Results Revealed," *Al Jazeera*, (May 26, 2014). https://www.aljazeera.com/news/middleeast/2014/05/uncertainty-as-iraq-election-results-revealed-201452611145311548.html

[91]Mohammed Salih, "Kurds Decide on New Iraqi President," *Al Jazeera*, (July 24, 2014). https://www.aljazeera.com/news/middleeast/2014/07/iraqi-kurds-divided-over-presidential-pick-201472462141842494.html

in Erbil. Kurdistan is a parliamentary democracy with its own regional parliament that consists of 111 seats.[92] The Kurdistan Democratic Party (KDP) holds the office of president and prime minister. Since the first session of the Kurdish parliament in Irbil in June 2005, KDP leader, Massoud Barzani, has been president of the Kurdish autonomous region.

The Kurdistan Regional Government gained control of the oil rich region of Kirkuk in June 2014 as Iraqi soldiers fled the onslaught on nearby Mosul by the so-called Islamic State men. The men and women of Kurdistan's Peshmerga army protected the oil wells and processing facilities in the Kirkuk region. Kurdistan Regional Government President Massoud Barzani made it clear that Irbil would retain control of Kirkuk and its assets. Kurdish Peshmerga and Iraqi special-forces, with US help, liberated Mosul from the clutches of the so-called Islamic State in mid July 2017.

Kurdish Referendum on September 25, 2017 for Independence: Kurdistan Regional Government President Masoud Barzani announced on June 7, 2017 that an independence referendum would be held on September 25, 2017 in the Kurdish region, as well as the disputed areas currently under Kurdish military control, including the oil-rich province of Kirkuk.[93] Kirkuk has been a disputed region between Irbil and Baghdad for decades, especially since the regime of Saddam Hussein changed its ethnic composition in favor of Arabs. Two days after the announcement of the referendum, Turkey called the referendum a "terrible mistake," saying that Iraq's territorial integrity and political unity was a fundamental principle for Ankara.[94] On July 14, 2017, the US envoy to the coalition confronting the so-called Islamic State said that the US is against holding the referendum.[95] A resolution by the Iraqi parliament on September 12, 2017 considered the referendum a "threat to … the civil peace and regional security," and authorizes Iraq's prime minister to take any measures necessary

---

[92]Kurdistan Regional Government, The Kurdistan Parliament. http://cabinet.gov.krd/a/d.aspx?r=160&l=12&s=04070000&a=15057

[93]"Iraqi Kurds Set Date for Independence Referendum," *Al Jazeera*, (June 8, 2017). https://www.aljazeera.com/news/2017/06/iraqi-kurds-set-date-independence-referendum-170608044202182.html

[94]"Turkey Says Iraqi Kurdish Independence Vote a 'Terrible Mistake,'" *Reuters*, (June 9, 2017). https://www.reuters.com/article/us-mideast-crisis-iraq-turkey/turkey-says-iraqi-kurdish-independence-vote-a-terrible-mistake-idUSKBN1900WP

[95]Donna Abu-Nasr, "US Against Kurds Holding Referendum in September, Envoy Says," *Bloomberg*, (July 14, 2017). https://www.bloomberg.com/news/articles/2017-07-14/u-s-against-kurds-holding-referendum-in-september-mcgurk-says

to preserve Iraq's existing borders.[96] The Arab League council unanimously adopted a resolution on September 12, 2017, rejecting the Kurdistan independence referendum.[97]

Russia has not called on Iraq's Kurds to cancel the referendum. Russian state oil Rosneft was reported on September 20, 2017 to have announced an investment worth more than $1 billion to help Iraqi Kurdistan develop its natural gas industry.[98] Despite this, on a visit by President Putin to Turkey on September 28, 2017, Russia and Turkey agreed that the territorial integrity of Iraq and neighboring Syria must be preserved.[99] Prime Minister Benjamin Netanyahu said on September 13, 2017 that Israel, on the other hand, supports the establishment of a Kurdish state.[100]

On September 25, 2017, the referendum was held. The electoral commission declared that 92% of the 3.3 million who cast their ballots supported secession and that the turnout was 72.61% among those eligible to vote.[101] In a televised address on September 26, 2017, Kurdish leader Barzani called on Iraq's central government in Baghdad to engage in "serious dialogue" instead of threatening the Kurdish Regional Government with sanctions.[102]

On September 29, 2017, US Secretary of State Tillerson stated that the United States does not recognize the Kurdistan Regional Government's unilateral referendum.[103] On October 16, 2017, in the aftermath

---

[96]"Iraq Parliament Rejects Kurdish Independence Referendum," *Al Jazeera*, (September 12, 2017). https://www.aljazeera.com/news/2017/09/iraq-parliament-rejects-kurdish-independence-referendum-170912132652290.html

[97]"Arab League Rejects Iraq's Kurdish Independence Referendum," *New China*, (September 14, 2017). http://news.xinhuanet.com/english/2017-09/14/c_136607440.htm

[98]Dmitry Zhdannikov, "Russia Becomes Iraq Kurds'Top Funder, Quiet about Independence Vote," *Reuters*, (September 20, 2017). https://uk.reuters.com/article/uk-mideast-crisis-kurds-referendum-russi/russia-becomes-iraq-kurds-top-funder-quiet-about-independence-vote-idUKKCN1BV1IX

[99]"Erdogan and Putin Agree Iraqi Kurdish Referendum Has No Legitimacy," *Al-Arabiya*, (September 28, 2017). https://english.alarabiya.net/en/News/middle-east/2017/09/28/Erdogan-and-Putin-agree-Iraqi-Kurdish-referendum-has-no-legitimacy.html

[100]Jeffrey Heller, "Israel Endorses Independent Kurdish State," *Reuters*, (September 13, 2017). https://www.reuters.com/article/us-mideast-crisis-kurds-israel/israel-endorses-independent-kurdish-state-idUSKCN1BO0QZ?il=0

[101]"Iraqi Kurds decisively back independence in referendum," *BBC*, (September 27, 2017). http://www.bbc.co.uk/news/world-middle-east-41419633

[102]Maher Chmaytelli and Ahmed Rasheed, "Iraqi Kurdish Leader Says 'Yes' Vote Won Independence Referendum," *Reuters*, (September 26, 2017). https://in.reuters.com/article/mideast-crisis-kurds-referendum/iraqi-kurdish-leader-says-yes-vote-won-independence-referendum-idINKCN1C112C

[103]US Embassy and Consulate in Egypt, "Secretary Tillerson on Iraqi Kurdistan Regional Government's Referendum," September 29, 2017. https://eg.usembassy.gov/secretary-tillerson-iraqi-kurdistan-regional-governments-referendum/

of the referendum, the Iraqi army of the federal government in Baghdad backed by Iran-dominated Shi'ite militias took control of Kirkuk.[104] On October 29, 2017, Barzani announced his resignation as Kurdistan Regional Government President, effective on November 1, 2017.[105]

Iraqi Shi'ite Leaders Welcome the US Invasion, but Are Divided on Loyalty toward Iran

Shi'ites represent an estimated 60% of Iraq's population. They are concentrated in the central and southern parts of the country. Iraq's Shi'ite leaders, secular and religious, supported the Bush administration's invasion to put an end to Saddam Hussein's regime and democratize Iraq's governance system. They helped in the preparation and administration of the invasion. They were tantalized by the expectation of power and wealth and majority rule. However, while they hailed the invasion, they did not support the occupation. They desired the removal of Saddam Hussein's regime and hoped for a quick departure of US forces thereafter.

When on May 1, 2003, three weeks after the occupation of Baghdad, Mr. Bush delivered his "mission accomplished" speech from the flight deck of the USS Lincoln declaring an end to major combat in Iraq, Shi'ite political leaders expected US troops to start going home.[106]

All Shi'ite leaders saluted the American invasion to remove Saddam's regime. They were well aware of Iran's power and interest in dominating a disarmed powerless Iraq. Their allegiance to Iran, however, ranged and continue to range from the strong to the lukewarm, to the nonexistent:

1) Strong allegiance to Iran: the organizations of Abdulaziz al-Hakeem (died August 26, 2009), Ahmad Chalabi (died November 3, 2015), and the Da'wa Party's leaders Ibrahim al-Jaafari and Nouri al-Maliki.

---

[104]"Baghdad: Iraqi Forces in Full Control of Kirkuk," *Al Jazeera*, (October 16, 2017). http://www. AlJazeera.com/news/2017/10/baghdad-iraqi-forces-full-control-kirkuk-171016133409720.html

[105]Raya Jalabi and Maher Shmaytelli, "Kurdish Leader Barzani Resigns after Independence Vote Backfires," *Reuters*, (October 29, 2017). https://uk.reuters.com/article/uk-mideast-crisis-iraq-kurds-barzani/kurdish-leader-barzani-resigns-after-independence-vote-backfires-idUKKBN1CY0JS

[106]Full Text, "Bush Makes Historic Speech Aboard Warship," *CNN*, (May 1, 2003). http://edition. cnn.com/2003/US/05/01/bush.transcript/

2) Lukewarm allegiance to Iran: Haidar al-Abadi, Grand Ayatollah Ali al-Sistani.

3) Apprehension over Iran: Muqtatda al-Sadr, Iyad Allawi.

Strong Allegiance to Iran

Abdulaziz al-Hakeem (died August 26, 2009): The late Abdulaziz al-Hakeem was a leading champion of the American invasion. He was the head of the powerful Supreme Council of Islamic Revolution in Iraq (name was changed in 2007 to the Supreme Islamic Iraqi Council) and its military arm, the notorious Badr Brigade, a militia of more than 10,000 men equipped, trained, and financed by Iran's Revolutionary Guard. *Time* magazine reported in 2005 that they obtained documents from Iranian Revolutionary Guard Corps files that included pay records from August 2004 that appear to indicate that Iran was paying 11,740 members of the Badr Brigade.[107] Badr fought alongside the Iranians in the Iran-Iraq war (1980–1988). Soon after the US occupation, the Badr Brigade became the Badr Organization for Development and Reconstruction.

Abdulazizi al-Hakeem was born in Najaf in 1953. He was a son of Grand Ayatollah Muhsin al-Hakeem, leader of the Najaf Hawza from 1955 to 1970. In 1980, he and his older brother, Muhammad Baqir, fled Saddam's persecution to Iran. In 1983, 18 members from the al-Hakeem family were executed by Saddam.[108] With the support and funding of the Iranian government, the brothers established SCIRI in November 1982. Ayatollah Mahmoud Shahroudi, former head of Iran's powerful judiciary was briefly the chairman of SCIRI.[109]

Soon after the fall of Saddam Hussein's regime, Abdulaziz al-Hakeem returned in April 2003 to Iraq from Iran. He represented SCIRI on the American-appointed Iraqi Governing Council. His name was at the top of the al-Sistani-approved United Iraqi Alliance List (UIA) of candidates in

---

[107]Michael Ware, "Inside Iran's Secret War for Iraq," *TIME magazine*, (August 22, 2005). http://www.mickware.info/Past/2005/files/1ed99bba67b6c013794d8844a97615ab-11.php

[108]Ijtihad.ir, Hakim, *Ayatollah Sayyed Muhammad Baqer*, http://ijtihad.ir/ScholarDetailsen.aspx?itemid=305

[109]Mahan Abedin, "The Supreme Council for the Islamic Revolution in Iraq (SCIRI)," *Middle East Intelligence Bulletin. 5*, No. 10, (October 2003). https://www.meforum.org/meib/articles/0310_iraqd.htm

the January 30, 2005 elections. Abdulaziz's brother, Ayatollah Muhammad Baqir al-Hakeem returned to Iraq from Iran on May 10, 2003. He had been Ayatollah Khomeini's choice to head a future Islamic Republic of Iraq.[110] He was assassinated by a car bomb in Najaf on August 29, 2003. Iran declared three days of official mourning following his assassination.[111]

As mentioned, Abdulaziz al-Hakeem welcomed the American invasion, but not the occupation. Two months after the US occupation, he told a large gathering in Najaf in May 2003 upon his return from Iran, "Let them [the Americans] leave Iraq to its own people … the Iraqis are capable of providing security and protecting Iraq."[112] Two months later, in early July 2003, Hakim called on the United States to hand control of Iraq to the United Nations: "If the goal was to free Iraq—not exploit it afterwards—why not let the UN handle it as was done in Bosnia and elsewhere?"[113]

The Iran-loyal Shi'ite leadership in Iraq wanted the American military to destroy as much of Iraq's Sunnis and Sunni infrastructure as possible, then leave Iraq. Following a meeting with President Bush at the White House on December 4, 2006, Abdulaziz al-Hakeem said, "The only way to stave off civil war in Iraq is for US forces to strike harder against Sunni-led insurgents."[114]

Ahmad Chalabi (died November 3, 2015): Chalabi was leader of the Iraqi National Congress (INC). Supposedly a secular Shi'ite, he was educated at M.I.T and the University of Chicago where he earned a Ph.D. in mathematics. In 1977, he founded and managed Petra Bank in Amman, Jordan. In 1992, Chalabi was sentenced in absentia by a Jordanian court to twenty-two years in prison after being convicted of fraud, embezzlement, and breach of trust over the insolvency of Petra Bank that left over $300 million missing.

Charismatic, Chalabi was well connected to some of the senior-most officials of the Bush administration. Yet, he was among the five members

---

[110]Kenneth Katzman, "Iraq: US Regime Change Efforts and Post-Saddam Governance," *Congressional Research Service, Library of Congress*, (October 2003): P. 6. i.cfr.org/content/publications/attachments/RL31339_2006Jan13.pdf

[111]Jim Muir, "Iran Mourns Shia leader," *BBC*, (August 30, 2003). http://news.bbc.co.uk/1/hi/world/middle_east/3193361.stm

[112]Mahan Abedin, "The Supreme Council for the Islamic Revolution in Iraq (SCIRI)," *Middle East Intelligence Bulletin*. 5, No. 10, (October 2003).

[113]Ibid., quoting *The Associated Press*, 7 July 2003.

[114]"Bush Meets Iraqi Shia Leader," *Al Jazeera*, (December 4, 2005). https://www.aljazeera.com/news/middleeast/2006/12/20085251301060527.html

of the Iraqi Governing Council who embarrassed the US by refusing to show up on March 5, 2004 to sign the Iraqi interim constitution.[115] The 1998 Iraq Liberation Act authorized $97 million in aid for Iraq's opposition, which benefited the INC substantially.[116] Chalabi promoted the claim that Saddam possessed weapons of mass destruction.

With the full knowledge of the US State Department, the INC maintained an office in Iran.[117] The justification for this presence was that the Iraqi National Congress identified Tehran as a key location that would allow them access to Iraqis living inside Iran. The INC used US government money in the Tehran office ostensibly to help lay the foundation for the US government's plan for regime change in Iraq.

The payment to INC stopped in June 2004, presumably, because Chalabi and his organization provided what later proved to be false information regarding Iraq's WMD development. In the spring of 2004, rumors circulated in Washington that Chalabi had been duping the Americans all along while spying for Iran, and US news organizations accused Chalabi of alerting Iranian intelligence that the United States had cracked Iran's cryptography.[118] On May 24, 2004, American soldiers and the Iraqi police raided Chalabi's home and offices.[119] According to *Forward* magazine's Marc Perelman, "Officials at the CIA, as well as at the State Department, have long held a skeptical view of Chalabi, who is often cited as the main source for the notion that Hussein was developing weapons of mass destruction and [that] US forces would be welcome as liberators by the Iraqi people."[120] Former Clinton administration aide Sidney Blumenthal further stated that, "The Iraqi neocon favorite ... has been identified by the CIA and the Defense Intelligence Agency as an Iranian double agent ... Either Chalabi perpetrated the greatest con since the Trojan horse, or he

---

[115]The Council on Foreign Relations, "Q&A: Iraq's Constitution," The *New York Times*, (March 5, 2004). http://www.nytimes.com/cfr/international/slot3_030504.html?pagewanted=print& position=&_r=0

[116]Kenneth Katzman, "CRS Report for Congress, Iraq's Opposition Movements," *Library of Congress, Congressional Research Services*, Order Code 98-179 F, (Updated June 27, 2000): P. CRC-5. http://www.au.af.mil/au/awc/awcgate/crs/98-179.pdf

[117]Romesh Ratnesar, "From Friend to Foe," *TIME magazine*, (May 22, 2004). http://content.time.com/time/magazine/article/0,9171,641077,00.html

[118]Paul Reynolds, "Breaking Codes: An Impossible Task?" *BBC*, (June 21, 2004). http://news.bbc.co.uk/1/hi/technology/3804895.stm

[119]"US Under Fire over Chalabi Raid," *BBC*, (May 21, 2004). http://news.bbc.co.uk/1/hi/world/middle_east/3734443.stm

[120]Marc Perelman, "Intel Agencies Fear Iran Used Chalabi to lure US into Iraq," *Forward*, (June 4, 2004). http://forward.com/culture/5758/intel-agencies-fear-iran-used-chalabi-to-lure-us-i/

was the agent of influence for the most successful intelligence operation conducted by Iran, or both."[121]

The enigmatic Chalabi's résumé raises questions as to whether he was a patriot delivering his people from oppression, a CIA agent promoting America's interests in the Middle East, an Iranian agent promoting Qom's interests in Iraq and the Shi'ite Crescent, or an opportunist enhancing his personal power and wealth.

The Da'wa Party

The Islamic Da'wa Party (IDP) was founded in 1958 by the eminent scholar and philosopher, the Grand Ayatollah Muhammad Baqir al-Sadr. Muqtada al-Sadr is his nephew and son-in-law. Da'wa is the oldest Shi'ite political party in Iraq. It aims to establish a theocratic state. The word Da'wa in the name describes its mission: converting non-Muslims and non-Shi'ite Muslims to Shi'ism, in other words, proselytization.

Muhammad Baqir al-Sadr was executed, along with his sister, Bint al-Huda, by Saddam Hussein's regime in April 1980. The executions followed a series of violent acts by Da'wa Party activists against senior government officials. Also, they might have been intended to thwart Iran's attempts to export the 1979 Khomeini revolution to Iraq. Khomeini lived in exile in Najaf from September 5, 1965 until the Iraqi government deported him on October 3, 1978.[122] Khomeini and Baqir al-Sadr were colleagues at the Najaf seminary where Khomeini taught Islamic jurisprudence (fiqh) and refined his thoughts on the concept of wilayat al-faqih.

Al-Sadr envisioned a generation of revolutionaries who would one day seize power to establish a Shi'ite state. In his book in 1975, *Islamic Political System*, he formulated IDP's political ideology in four principles:

I. Absolute sovereignty belongs to Allah.
II. Shari'a law is the basis of legislation. The legislative authority may enact any law not in contravention of Islam.

---

[121]Ibid.

[122]Iran Chamber Society, *Ayatollah Khomeini*, http://www.iranchamber.com/history/rkhomeini/ayatollah_khomeini.php

III. The people, as vice-regents of Allah, are entrusted with legislative and executive powers.

IV. The Jurist holding the highest religious authority is Islam's representative. By confirming legislative and executive actions, he gives them legality.[123]

Muhammad Baqir al-Sadr essentially constructed what later became known as wilayat al-faqih, or the rulership of the senior-most specialist in Islamic jurisprudence, as the basis for future Shi'ite governance.

IDP represents a radical departure from the culture of political quietism that has traditionally characterized the Shi'ite ulama. In 1979, four years after the publication of al-Sadr's book, the Khomeini wilayat al-faqih revolution in Iran was born.

The Islamic Da'wa Party received substantial support from the Khomeini regime. Like SCIRI's leaders, Da'wa's leaders are well connected to the Iranian religious and political leadership. It is believed that exiled Da'wa Party activists in Iran, Lebanon, and Syria helped Iran create Hezbollah (Party of God) in Lebanon in 1984.[124] Hezbollah is an Iranian proxy, whose senior leaders are closely linked to Tehran.

The Da'wa Party has ruled Iraq since 2005. Ibrahim al-Ja'fari was Prime Minister in the Transitional Government (May 2005–May 2006), Nouri al-Maliki was Prime Minister (May 2006–September 2014), and Haidar al-Abadi (September 2014–). It is thought that Da'wa's accession to power is a compromise between Iraq's two leading rival Shi'ite families: al-Hakim and al-Sadr.

Ibrahim Al-Ja'fari: A physician, Ja'fari spent twenty years in exile in Iran and London. Ja'fari became Iraq's prime minister in the Transitional Government in April 7, 2005. Earlier, in June 2004, he was one of the two vice presidents in the US-appointed interim Iraqi government, and before that, he was appointed to the Iraqi Governing Council.[125] He became Iraq's foreign minister in 2014.

---

[123]Rodger Shanahan, "The Islamic Da'wa Party: Past Development and Future Prospects," *Middle East Review of International Affairs Journal (MERIA)* 8, no 2, (June 2004). http://www.rubincenter.org/2004/06/shanahan-2004-06-02/

[124]Juan Cole, "Saving Iraq: Mission Impossible," *Salon*, (May 11, 2006). https://www.salon.com/2006/05/11/maliki_4/

[125]"Iraq Profile—Timeline," *BBC*, (October 26, 2017). http://www.bbc.co.uk/news/world-middle-east-14546763

Nouri al-Maliki: Maliki, spent more than two decades in exile in Iran and Syria. Maliki, a hardline activist was approved as Iraq's first full-term prime minister by the Iraqi parliament in May 20, 2006 after five months of political deadlock, following the December 15, 2005 parliamentary elections.[126] To demonstrate US approval and bolster Maliki, President Bush visited Maliki in Baghdad a month later, June 13, 2006.[127]

Maliki Usurped the 2010 Elections While Obama Watched: Maliki was approved for a second term as prime minister on December 22, 2010, this time after nine months of haggling and confusion. He refused to recognize the results of the March 7, 2010 parliamentary elections. His list, State of Law, won 89 seats in the 325-seat parliament, two seats less than the 91 seats won by his arch rival, the secular Iyad Allawi's list, Iraqiya. A vote recount involving 2.5 million ballots in Baghdad reaffirmed the original result.[128] Nonetheless, under pressure from Maliki, an Iraqi judge allowed him to form a government. According to Emma Sky, chief political adviser to General Raymond Odierno, who commanded US forces in Iraq, American officials knew this violated Iraq's constitution. But, they never publicly challenged Maliki's power grab, which was backed by Iran.[129] A few months before the 2010 elections in Iraq, according to the New Yorker magazine, "American diplomats in Iraq sent a rare dissenting cable to Washington, complaining that the US, with its combination of support and indifference, was encouraging Maliki's authoritarian tendencies."[130] Obama ignored the complaint.

Iran had adamantly refused to allow Allawi to become prime minister. Finally, it was pressure from Iran on Muqtada al-Sadr that made possible the return of his old arch enemy, Maliki,[131] to head the cabinet. At that time, Sadr had been living in Iran for about four years (early

[126]"Maliki Endorsed as New Iraqi PM," *BBC*, (April22, 2004). http://news.bbc.co.uk/1/hi/4933026.stm

[127]Jonathan Finer and Michael Abramowitz, "In Baghdad, Bush Pledges Support to Iraqi Leader," *Washington Post*, (June 14, 2006). http://www.washingtonpost.com/wp-dyn/content/article/2006/06/13/AR2006061300432.html

[128]Khalid Al-Ansary, "Iraq Election Recount Over, No Fraud Found," *Reuters*, (May 14, 2010). http://www.reuters.com/article/us-iraq-election-idUSTRE64D3Y220100514

[129]Peter Beinart, "Obama's Disastrous Iraq Policy: An Autopsy," *The Atlantic*, (July 23, 2014).
[130]Ibid.
[131]In March 2008, Muqtada led a civil disobedience movement to protest arrests of his followers by Maliki. Bitter fighting between Maliki's security forces and supporters of Muqtada's militia in the southern city of Basra spread to several Baghdad districts. "Peaceful Iraq Protests Spark Clashes, 50 Reported Dead," CNN, (March 25,2008). http://edition.cnn.com/2008/WORLD/meast/03/25/iraq.main/index.html

2007–January 5, 2011) in a self-imposed exile, after the US army wanted him dead or alive.[132] Sadr delivered his bloc of 39 seats in the 2010 parliament in return for eight ministries in Maliki's cabinet.[133] He returned to Iraq two weeks after Maliki became prime minister.[134]

Maliki's Sectarianism: A sectarian divisive figure, Maliki failed the political reconciliation test. On August 1, 2007, the main Sunni bloc the Iraq Accord Front, pulled out its five ministers from the Maliki cabinet.[135] A week earlier, five Shi'ite ministers loyal to former Prime Minister Ayad Allawi began a boycott, and the six Shi'ite ministers of Muqtada al-Sadr's bloc withdrew earlier.[136] On September 15, 2007, Muqtada al-Sadr withdrew his parliamentarians from the governing Shi'ite grouping.[137] In all, nearly half of the al-Maliki cabinet, or, at least seventeen ministries, became empty.

On August 16, 2007, a new parliamentary alliance was made up of two Shi'ite parties, the Da'wa Party and SCIRI, and two Kurdish parties.[138] The new alliance excluded the Arab Sunnis. Adnan al-Dulaimi, leader of the Iraq Accord Front, criticized Maliki and Iran. In an email to the Associated Press, Dulaimi wrote that there was against Sunnis, "An unprecedented genocide campaign by the militias and death squads that are directed, armed and supported by Iran."[139]

Maliki's sectarian and corrupt reign was described aptly in *Foreign Policy*:

> The security sector, which had an annual budget greater than the budgets for education, health, and the environment combined, was subject to minimal oversight. Soldiers were enrolled and paid

---

[132]Patrick Cockburn, "The Secret US Plot to Kill Sadr," Counterpunch, (May 21, 2007). https://www.counterpunch.org/2007/05/21/the-secret-us-plot-to-kill-sadr/

[133]Charles McDermid with Nizar Latif, "Iraq: Preparing for the Return of Moqtada al-Sadr," *Time*, (December 20, 2010). http://content.time.com/time/world/article/0,8599,2037986,00.html

[134]Khalid Farhan, "U.S. foe, Sadr, returns to Iraq after exile," *Reuters*, (January 11, 2007). https://uk.reuters.com/article/uk-iraq-politics-sadr/u-s-foe-sadr-returns-to-iraq-after-exile-idUK-TRE7042M820110105

[135]Mariam Karouny and Peter Graff, "Sunni bloc quits as bombs kill over 70," *Reuters*, (August 1, 2007). https://www.reuters.com/article/us-iraq/sunni-bloc-quits-as-bombs-kill-over-70-idUSYAT71 336220070801?src=080107_1109_TOPSTORY_dozens_dead_in_iraq

[136]"Iraqi PM calls for crisis summit," *BBC*, (August 12, 2007). http://news.bbc.co.uk/1/hi/world/middle_east/6943120.stm

[137]"Sadr Group Quits Iraq Ruling Bloc," *BBC*, (September 15, 2007). http://news.bbc.co.uk/1/hi/world/middle_east/6996942.stm

[138]"Iraqi Leaders Form New Alliance," *BBC*, (August 16, 2007). http://news.bbc.co.uk/1/hi/world/middle_east/6949890.stm

[139]"Iraqi PM calls for Crisis Summit," *BBC*,

monthly salaries without reporting for duty. Overpriced and faulty equipment was procured using the laxest [sic] standards. Training sessions were financed on paper but never took place in practice. Appointments were politicized. Officers close to the prime minister's office who failed to investigate leads on terrorist attacks were almost never held accountable for their actions. Even the most grotesque failures, including the military's passivity in the face of regular attacks against Christians in Nineveh over a period of years, went unpunished. Morale among the rank and file was low, and there was very little desire to take risks on behalf of political elites who were viewed as wildly corrupt.[140]

The Awakening Forces: In early 2007, American forces in Iraq were increased by 27,000 soldiers. The increase was known as the "surge." General David Petraeus was made US commander of Multi-National Force in Iraq. Concurrently with the surge, Petraeus pursued a new tactic—training and arming about 100,000 Sunni tribesmen in the Anbar province, extending to Salaheddin, Diyala, Nineveh, and Tamim Provinces. Named Sah'wa (Awakening) Councils Forces, many were former soldiers in Saddam Hussein's military and members of the ruling Ba'th Party. As a result of the previous disbanding of the military and the Ba'th party in May 2003 by Paul Bremer, many of the 400,000 men who had suddenly become jobless joined al-Qaeda, not only to fight the US occupation, but also to feed their families. Awakening fighters were paid by Petraeus US $300 per month each. They switched sides from fighting alongside al-Qaeda against US forces and Iraqi government Shi'ite troops (plus the militias of the Badr Brigade and the Mahdi Army) to instead fight against their old al-Qaeda compatriots.[141]

Within a few months, the Awakening forces had reduced the level of violence considerably. In the *Report to Congress* dated September 26, 2008, *Measuring Stability and Security in Iraq*, it was stated that "Civilian deaths across Iraq have declined dramatically. During this reporting period, according to Coalition and Iraqi reports, there were 77% fewer deaths than during the same period one year ago."[142]

---

[140]Zaid Al-Ali, "How Maliki Ruined Iraq," *Foreign Policy*, (June 19, 2014). http://foreignpolicy.com/2014/06/19/how-maliki-ruined-iraq/

[141]"Q&A: Iraq's Awakening Councils," *BBC*, (July 18, 2010). http://www.bbc.co.uk/news/world-middle-east-10677623

[142]Department of Defense, Report to Congress, "Measuring Stability and Security in Iraq," (September 26, 2008). http://archive.defense.gov/news/d20080930iraq.pdf

The decline in violence was not entirely due to the Awakening project. The success was made possible through the cooperation of Iran. Tehran's interest in calming matters down in Iraq during the remaining few month of the Bush administration's term in office was designed to deflect a possible attack by the US over the Iran's nuclear program. In October 2007, US military officials began noticing a decrease in the supply of Iranian weapons and assistance. Spokesman Col. Steven Boylan said General Petraeus observes that Iran is following through on promises it made to Iraqi and US officials not to provide aid to extremists in Iraq, adding, "we are ready to confirm the excellence of the senior Iranian leadership in their pledge to stop the funding, training, equipment and resourcing of the militia special groups."[143] In a related development, on August 29, 2007, Muqtada al-Sadr suddenly ordered his Mahdi Army militia to suspend all acts of violence for six months and on February 23, 2008, Sadr extended the cease-fire for six additional months.[144]

US pressure made the Iraqi government agree to pay the salaries of the Awakening fighters[145] and to absorb up to 20% of the fighters into the Iraqi security forces, with others to be given government jobs.[146] However, the Maliki government reduced the monthly salary to $250 and absorption of Awakening fighters into the security forces was well below 20%. Maj. Gen. Mike Ferriter, deputy operations commander of the American-led forces, conceded at a press briefing that in the past year (2008), only 5,000 fighters had been integrated into the Iraqi security forces, mostly in the police. That was well short of Maliki's pledge of 20,000 fighters.[147]

Maliki's intention to dismantle the Awakening project became public knowledge. Defense Minister Abdul-Qadir al-Obaidi said at a news conference, "We completely, absolutely reject the Awakening becoming a third military organization ... The groups would also not be allowed to have any infrastructure, such as a headquarters building, that would give

[143]Sara A. Carter, "Iran No Longer Aids Iraq Militants," *Washington Times*, (January 3, 2008). http://www.washingtontimes.com/apps/pbcs.dll/article?AID=/20080103/NATION/498097125/1001

[144]Sudarsan Raghavan and Amit R. Paley, "Sadr Extends Truce In Iraq. U.S. Officials Hail Cleric's Decision," *Washington Post*, (February 23, 2008). http://www.washingtonpost.com/wp-dyn/content/article/2008/02/22/AR2008022200495.html?nav=rss_world

[145]Liz Sly, "Iraq Plans to Cut Sunni Fighters' Salaries," *Chicago Tribune*, (November 3, 2008). http://articles.chicagotribune.com/2008-11-03/news/0811020469_1_awakening-leader-sunni-awakening-awakening-members

[146]Ibid.

[147]Rod Norland and Alissa Rubin, "Sunni Fighters Say Iraq Didn't Keep Job Promises," *The New York Times*, (March 24, 2009). http://www.nytimes.com/2009/03/24/world/middleeast/24sunni.html

them long-term legitimacy."[148] Christopher Hill, US ambassador in Baghdad between 2009 and 2010 recalled how Maliki resisted paying Sunni Awakening fighters and how he doubted the entire project, "I had to go to him, sometimes on a weekly basis, just to make sure the check was indeed in the mail ... Just looking at his body language, he didn't believe in the whole venture ... Nothing was squared away in 2007."[149] Sheikh Awad al-Harbousi, who lost a son, a father and four other relatives to al-Qaeda, said, "The Iraqi Army considers us members of al-Qaeda, not Awakening Council leaders. We sacrificed to kick out al-Qaeda, and this is their thank-you?"[150]

As long as US forces were in Iraq, Maliki camouflaged his true sectarian spots. Immediately after US forces left Iraq on December 18, 2011, he embarked upon an aggressive program of marginalization of Sunnis. The next day, on December 19, 2011, Maliki ordered the arrest of Iraq's Sunni vice president, Tariq al-Hashimi. He accused Hashimi of running a death squad that assassinated Shiite officials.[151] Hashimi was sentenced to death in absentia on September 9, 2012. He had fled first to the largely autonomous Kurdish north, and from there to Qatar and on to Turkey.[152]

In public remarks after a meeting on December 12, 2011 with Maliki at the White House, Obama praised Maliki for leading "Iraq's most inclusive government yet." Iraq's Sunni Deputy Prime Minister, Saleh al-Mutlaq, told *CNN* he was "shocked" by the president's comments. "There will be a day," he predicted, "whereby the Americans will realize that they were deceived by al-Maliki ... and they will regret that."[153]

Six senators sent the White House a letter before Maliki visited with Obama on November 1, 2013 warning that, "by too often pursuing a sectarian and authoritarian agenda, Prime Minister Maliki and his allies are

---

[148]Diaa Hadid, "Iraq Defense Minister: Disband Sunni Allies," *ABC News*, (December 22, 2007). http://abcnews.go.com/International/wireStory?id=4043559

[149]Warren Strobel, Missy Ryan, David Rohde, and Ned Parker, "Special Report: How Iraq's Maliki Defined Limits of US Power," *Reuters*, (June 30, 2014). http://uk.reuters.com/article/us-iraq-security-maliki-specialreport-idUKKBN0F51HK20140630

[150]Rod Norland and Alissa Rubin, "Sunni Fighters Say Iraq Didn't Keep Job Promises."

[151]Jack Healy, "Arrest Order for Sunni Leader in Iraq Opens New Rift," The *New York Times*, (December 19, 2011). http://www.nytimes.com/2011/12/20/world/middleeast/iraqi-government-accuses-top-official-in-assassinations.html

[152]"Iraq VP Tariq al-Hashemi Sentenced to Death," *BBC*, (September 9, 2012). http://www.bbc.co.uk/news/world-middle-east-19537301

[153]Peter Beinart, "Obama's Disastrous Iraq Policy: An Autopsy," *The Atlantic*, (July 23, 2014).

disenfranchising Sunni Iraqis … This failure of governance is driving many Sunni Iraqis into the arms of Al-Qaeda."[154]

The Fall of Mosul to IS: Maliki filled Iraq's reconstituted army, disbanded in May 2003 by Paul Bremmer, with Shi'ite officers short on ability and professionalism, but long on loyalty to himself. Corruption became the glue that kept the Maliki regime together.

On June 10, 2014, two and a half years after US troops left Iraq, about 1,000 lightly armed men from the so-called Islamic State in Iraq and al-Sham (ISIS) riding in Toyota pick-ups forced 30,000 Maliki soldiers with tanks, helicopters, and heavy guns to flee the city of Mosul, Iraq's second largest city of two million inhabitants.[155] The sectarian genie released by the American occupation starting in 2003, nurtured by eight years of Maliki's sectarianism and corruption, meant that his armed forces demonstrated little military prowess, discipline, or professionalism. The Sunni soldiers did not want to risk their lives for Maliki's crooked government. The Shi'ite soldiers did not want to risk their lives to defend Mosul's Sunni citizens. A just and fair-minded prime minister was needed for reconciliation and protection of the rights of all citizens, but Maliki's pro-Iran policies and extreme sectarianism stood in the way. In reaction, Awakening's tribesmen re-embraced al-Qaeda as if the Awakening project had never happened. When Obama entered the White House on January 20, 2008, he inherited a momentum of improving security in Iraq and a narrowing of the Shi'ite Sunni divide. Obama squandered a great opportunity to build on the fruits of the Awakening project. Instead, he tolerated Maliki's extreme sectarianism, ignored his divisiveness, empowered Iran, and helped breed the so-called Islamic State.

Lukewarm Allegiance to Iran

Haidar Al-Abadi

In the April 30, 2014 election, the Maliki List won comfortably. However, the fall of Falluja to ISIS in January 2014 and the calamitous fall of Mosul in June 2014 led to sharp criticism by both Iraqi political leaders and Washington of the Maliki years that had led to the Mosul disaster. A member of

---

[154]Ibid.

[155]"Mosul: Iraq's beleaguered second city," *BBC*, (October 18, 2016). http://www.bbc.co.uk/news/world-middle-east-37676731

the Islamic Da'wa Party since 1967, Haidar al-Abadi was the Party's coordi-
nator in the UK since 1977. He replaced Maliki to the premiership on September 8, 2014, despite Maliki and Iran's vehement objection and insistence
on a third term for Maliki. Grand Ayatollah Ali al-Sistani was instrumental
in forcing Maliki out of the premiership.[156] The US supported the removal
of Maliki as well.[157] Abadi's task was to recover Mosul, end Maliki's years of
sectarianism and divisiveness, and bring about national reconciliation.

By mid-July 2017, a devastated ancient Mosul was liberated after a
nine-month battle by the Iraqi army, Popular Mobilization Forces militias,
US-led international military coalition, and Iran.[158] Whether Abadi will
be able to reconcile Iraq's Shi'ites and Sunnis remains to be seen. Iran will
do its best to stoke sectarian divisions in Iraq and install a surrogate prime
minister.

An electrical engineer, Abadi completed a Ph.D. at the University of
Manchester in 1981. He worked in the UK until his return to Iraq after
the US occupation in 2003.

Grand Ayatollah Ali Al-Sistani

Millions of Shi'ites in Iraq and outside Iraq obey the religious opinions
(fatwas) and emulate the 86-year old Grand Ayatollah. They provide him
annually with several hundred million dollars in religious tax, the khums
(fifth) on a Shi'ite's annual saving, which he spends on charity and religious education of thousands of students.[159]

The Ayatollah was born in Mashhad, Iran and moved to the holy city
of Najaf in 1950.[160] He is the senior-most among the four Grand Ayatollahs who lead the 960 year-old leading center for Shi'ite scholarship. Najaf
is the burial shrine of Ali bin Abi Taleb, the Prophet's cousin, son-in-law,
and the fourth caliph (656–661). Sistani acceded to the supreme religious

---

[156]For the ayatollah's statement on the removal of Maliki from office (in Arabic), the Website
of Grand Ayatollah Ali al-Sistani, (August 18, 2014). https://www.sistani.org/arabic/in-news/24950/

[157]Martin Chulov, Luke Harding, and Dan Roberts, "Nouri al-Maliki Forced from Post as
Iraq's Political Turmoil Deepens," *The Guardian*, (August 18, 2014). https://www.theguardian.com/
world/2014/aug/11/nouri-al-maliki-iraq-forced-out-prime-minister

[158]Mehdi Jedinia, "Analysts: Tehran Sees Liberation of Mosul as Victory for Iraq and Iran," *Voice of
America (VOA)*, (July 15, 2017). https://www.voanews.com/a/analyst-says-tehran-sees-liberation-of-
mosul-as-victory-for-iraq-iran/3945363.html

[159]Nader, "Iran's Role in Iraq," Rand Corporation, P. 4.

[160]Al-Sayyid Ali al-Hussainin Al-Sistani official Website, http://www.sistani.org/english/

authority in 1992, following his mentor, the Iranian born Grand Ayatollah Abu Gharib al-Qassim al-Khoei (1970–1992).

Grand Ayatollah Sistani's Political Influence: In dealing with the United States since the invasion in March 2003, the Ayatollah clashed with Washington policies on several occasions and prevailed.

In June 2003, when the Ayatollah issued a religious ruling stating that the framers of Iraq's constitution had to be elected, not appointed by US officials and the Iraqi Governing Council, (as the United States had wanted), the Ayatollah prevailed.[161] When he issued a statement in November 2003 declaring that elections would be the proper way to select a transitional government, not a system of regional caucuses as envisioned by the United States, and demanded UN involvement in overseeing the election process, the Ayatollah prevailed. When al-Sistani called for a transitional assembly to ratify an interim constitution and to define the terms under which US troops would remain in Iraq after sovereignty was handed over, the Ayatollah again prevailed.[162] The Grand Ayatollah was instrumental in reaching a ceasefire agreement in June 2004 to stop the fighting in Najaf between Muqtada al-Sadr's Mahdi Army militia and US forces. He also brought an end to the second round of fighting between the two sides in August 2004.[163]

On October 1, 2004, Sistani issued a fatwa, ordering Iraq's Shi'ites to vote in the upcoming elections.[164] The Ayatollah's followers entered the January 30, 2005 election under a unified list of candidates, the United Iraqi Alliance (UIA), approved by the Ayatollah. Dominated by Shi'ite clerics, the list also included parties and individuals from different ethnic and religious groups. Fear of violence kept the identity of the great majority of the candidates concealed. Until the last minute, voters did not know the names of most of the candidates, let alone their backgrounds or views. Voters chose the UIA because al-Sistani had approved its candidates. The list became known as the "Sistani List." The UIA won 140 seats out of the 275-seat assembly.[165] In the December 15, 2005 election for the full-term four-year parliament, the UIA won 128 seats.[166]

---

[161]Sharon Otterman, "Iraq: Grand Ayatollah Ali al-Sistani," *Council on Foreign Relations*, (September 1, 2004). http://www.cfr.org/iraq/iraq-grand-ayatollah-ali-al-sistani/p7636

[162]Ibid.

[163]"Sistani Ends the Siege," *The Economist*, (August 30, 2004). http://www.economist.com/node/3146701

[164]The Website of Grand Ayatollah Ali al-Sistani.

[165]Mohamed El-Anwar, "New Beginning?" *Al-Ahram Weekly on Line, no 730*, (February 23, 2005). http://weekly.ahram.org.eg/Archive/2005/730/re3.htm

[166]"Iraqi Shias Win Election Victory," *BBC*, (January 21, 2006). http://news.bbc.co.uk/1/hi/world/middle_east/4630518.stm

Under Ayatollah Sistani's guidance, the Draft Permanent Constitution, approved in the December 15, 2005 referendum, specified in Article 2(a) that, "No law can be passed that contradicts the undisputed rules of Islam." The parliamentary majority, which the Ayatollah controls, defines the undisputed rules of Islam. Reflecting their governments' gratitude, the US Secretary of State together with the British Foreign Secretary were both full of praise during their joint visit to Iraq on April 2, 2006 for the Ayatollah's "guidance and restraint."[167]

Ali al-Sistani is no friend of the American occupation. While consolidating Shi'ite control over Iraq, he cooperated with the occupiers. No sooner than Iraq Shi'ites achieved the upper hand, Sistani demanded the departure of US troops. An objective of the election platform of the Sistani-approved list of candidates in the January 30, 2005 elections was a timetable for the withdrawal of the US led multinational forces from Iraq.

Ending months of political deadlock, the Ayatollah was instrumental in getting Ibrahim al-Ja'fari, the transitional prime minister, and the UIA's selection for the full-term premiership, to step aside.[168] The Ayatollah paved the way for Nouri al-Maliki to become the full-term prime minister.[169] Eight years later, in June 2014, Sistani was also instrumental in removing Prime Minister Nouri al-Maliki from office.[170] Maliki was blamed for the collapse of the Iraqi army and the fall of Mosul to the so-called Islamic State. Maliki's divisiveness, sectarianism, and marginalization of Iraq's Sunnis created fertile ground for Mosul's calamity. On June 13, 2014, the Ayatollah issued a call to arms to liberate Mosul and the other towns lost on Maliki's watch.[171]

It is clear that the Ayatollah has been heavily involved in Iraq's political affairs since the start of the US invasion. Ayatollah Sistani will continue to be active in Iraqi politics. Given his discreet nature, he will shape, from

---

[167]"US and UK Try to Break Iraq Delay," *BBC*, (April 3, 2006). http://news.bbc.co.uk/2/hi/middle_east/4871148.stm

[168]Roger Hardy, "Iraq Conflict Thwarts PM Jaafari," *BBC*, (April 21, 2006). http://news.bbc.co.uk/1/hi/world/middle_east/4932692.stm

[169]"Iraqi Leaders Discuss Militia Problem," *Al Jazeera*, (April 27, 2006). https://www.aljazeera.com/archive/2006/04/200849161751921423.html

[170]Harith Hasan Al-Qarawee, "From Maliki to Abadi: The Challenge of Being Iraq's Prime Minister," *Brandeis University, Crown Center for Middle East Studies*, (June 2016). https://www.brandeis.edu/crown/publications/meb/MEB100.pdf

[171]"Iraq conflict: Shia Cleric Sistani Issues Call to Arms," *BBC*, (June 13, 2014). http://www.bbc.co.uk/news/world-middle-east-27834462

behind the scenes, the direction taken by his handpicked officials in the Iraqi government.

Apprehension over Iran

Muqtada Al-Sadr: Muqtada belongs to a prominent Arab Shi'ite dynasty. The al-Sadrs trace their lineage to the Prophet Muhammad. Muqtada is a son of the highly respected and revered Grand Ayatollah Muhammad Sadiq al-Sadr. In 1993, following the death of the supreme religious authority of the Najaf Seminary, Grand Ayatollah al-Khoei (1970–1992), Saddam Hussein's regime eased the appointment of Sadiq al-Sadr as a grand ayatollah in the Najaf Seminary."[172] Saddam was concerned over the influence Iranian ayatollahs commanded over Shi'ism's most illustrious seminary. To appreciate Muqtada's political thinking, a look at his father's politics is enlightening.

Muhammad Sadiq al-Sadr preached national unity and sought to straddle the Shi'ite/ Sunni divide.[173] Significantly, he once called on his followers to pray in Sunni mosques, a call that brought throngs of followers to do so.[174] Saddam's regime became concerned over Sadiq's growing popularity among Shi'ites and Sunnis. His sermons often began with the words "no, no to America; no, no to Israel; no, no to the Devil" along with attacks on the West and Qom's claims to Shi'ite leadership.[175] Sadiq al-Sadr advocated wilayat al-faqih concept to govern Iraq. He rejected Ayatollah Ali Khamenei's claim to supreme pan-Shi'ite leadership, a stand that led to a serious straining of relations with Khameini and the Qom establishment.[176] Sadiq al-Sadr made himself a rival to both Saddam Hussein and Ali Khameini. He and two of his sons were assassinated in Najaf in February 1999.

Senior politicians and ayatollahs in Iraq and Iran disregarded the young (thirty years of age in 2003) Muqtada who lacked the high religious scholarly qualifications to be a senior cleric. However, his family's high religious

---

[172]"Iraq's Muqtada Al-Sadr: Spoiler or Stabilizer? Middle East Report N°55," *International Crisis Group*, (July 11, 2006).
[173]Ibid.
[174]Ibid.
[175]Ibid.
[176]Ibid.

scholarly standing, noble bloodline to the family of the Prophet, and staunch posture of Iraqi nationalism against American and Iranian influences earned him the undivided loyalty of the estimated two million downtrodden inhabitants in Baghdad's shanty town of Sadr City. He organized thousands of his followers into a political movement, including a military wing known as the Mahdi Army, estimated to be 60,000-man militia, according to BBC (2006) and Council on Foreign Relations (2007).[177]

Muqtada al-Sadr called for a jihad against the US occupation soon after Baghdad fell and Saddam Hussein was removed from power in 2003. Al-Sadr's anti-American stand was an anti-occupation, not a pro-Iran policy. He engaged in bloody fighting against US forces in April 2004 and again in August 2004 in Najaf, Karbala, and Sadr City.[178] Muqtada al-Sadr made himself a prime enemy of the United States. On April 13, 2004, Lieutenant General Ricardo Sanchez, America's most senior general in Iraq declared on television that "the mission of US forces is to kill or capture Muqtada al-Sadr."[179] He was never apprehended.

To further his political aims of resisting the American occupation, Muqtada al-Sadr stood ready to accept assistance from Tehran. Reciprocally, Sadr's Mahdi Army was useful to Iran to harass US forces in Iraq. By the spring of 2004, when al-Sadr directed violent uprisings around Najaf and Karbala, Iran had reportedly supplied up to $80 million to al-Sadr and was establishing camps along the Iran-Iraq border to provide basic military training to Mahdi fighters.[180] A senior American intelligence official said on November 27, 2006 that Hezbollah, Iran's proxy in Lebanon, had been training Mahdi Army fighters and other Shiite militias, and that Iran had facilitated the link with Hezbollah.[181]

In 2007, Muqtada went into self-imposed exile in Qom, Iran, where he resumed his religious studies to become an ayatollah. It is doubtful whether he attained the high scholarly recognition, given that his time

---

[177]Stanford University, "Mapping Militant Organizations, Mahdi Army." http://web.stanford.edu/group/mappingmilitants/cgi-bin/groups/view/57

[178]Ibid.

[179]Rory McCarthy, Owen Bowcott, and Sarah Ball, "US Pledge to Arrest or Kill Shia Cleric," *The Guardian*, (April 13, 2004). https://www.theguardian.com/world/2004/apr/13/usa.iraq

[180]Joseph Felter and Brian Fishman, "Iranian Strategy in Iraq Politics and "Other Means"," *Occasional Paper Series, West Point*, (October 13, 2008), P. 30. https://web.archive.org/web/20100621081229/http://ctc.usma.edu/Iran_Iraq/CTC_Iran_Iraq_Final.pdf

[181]Michael R. Gordon and Dexter Filkins, "Hezbollah Said to Help Shiite Army in Iraq," The *New York Times*, (November 28, 2006). http://www.nytimes.com/2006/11/28/world/middleeast/28military.html?_r=1&oref=slogin

in Iran was dedicated not only to study, but also to managing the Mahdi army. He returned to Najaf in January 5, 2011. His Sadrist bloc won 39 seats in the Iraqi parliament and was given eight ministries by the prime minister, Nouri al-Maliki, whose return as leader was made possible in November 2010 by Sadr's backing, brokered by Iranian officials.[182]

Muqtada's ideas evolved. In 2015, he started calling for a "civic state, not a religious state, as Iran's Shi'ites have done."[183] He revealed that he "wants Iranian revolutionary guards and advisers to go just as much as he wants American troops to leave."[184] Mahmoud Mashhadani, a former speaker of the Iraqi parliament, described Sadr as "the Shia who is closest to Sunnis."[185]

In loud defiance to Iran's protection of the Assad Alawite regime in Syria, Muqtada al-Sadr condemned the killing on April 4, 2017 of 87 people, including 31 children, in a chemical attack on the Syrian town of Khan Shaykhoon. Sadr, in a statement, urged Assad to resign: "I would consider it fair for President Bashar al-Assad to resign and leave power, allowing the dear people of Syria to avoid the scourge of war and terrorist oppression."[186]

In a significant step, Muqtada al-Sadr paid a rare visit to Iran's archenemy Saudi Arabia on July 30, 2017 and met with Crown Prince Muhammad bin Salman.[187] He visited Abu Dhabi on August 13, 2017 and met with the anti-Iran crown prince of Abu Dhabi.[188] He also visited with anti-Iran King Abdullah of Jordan on October 23, 2017.[189]

In an unprecedented move, on March 11, 2018, *Agence France Press* (AFP), reported that Muqtada al-Sadr decided to campaign for the May 12, 2018 parliamentary elections alongside former enemies,

---

[182]Martin Chulov, "Moqtada al-Sadr Returns to Iraq after Exile," *The Guardian*, (January 5, 2011). https://www.theguardian.com/world/2011/jan/05/moqtada-al-sadr-returns-iraq

[183]Jonathan Steele, "Sectarian militias have no place in Iraq, says Muqtada al-Sadr," *Middle East Eye*, (March 20, 2017). http://www.middleeasteye.net/news/muqtada-al-sadr-iraq-1637609574

[184]Ibid.

[185]Ibid.

[186]"Moqtada al-Sadr urges Assad to Quit," *Middle East Eye*, (April 8, 2017). http://www.middleeasteye.net/news/controversial-shiite-iraqi-cleric-sadr-urges-assad-step-down-1344377597

[187]"Saudi Crown Prince Meets with Iraq's Moqtada Al-Sadr," *Arab News*, (July 31, 2017). http://www.arabnews.com/node/1137151/saudi-arabia#photo/2

[188]"Iraqi Shia Leader Sadr Visits UAE, Boosts Ties with Sunni States," *Middle East Eye*, (August 14, 2017). http://www.middleeasteye.net/news/iraqi-shia-leader-sadr-visits-uae-boosting-ties-sunni-states-749395211

[189]"Iraqi Shiite leader Meets with Jordan King in Rare Visit," *Voice of America (VOA)*, (October 23, 2017). https://www.voanews.com/a/iraqi-shiite-leader-meets-with-jordan-king-in-rare-visit/4082950.html

Communists who demand a secular state.[190] On election day, voters handed Muqtada al-Sadr's coalition the most parliamentary seats—54 of the 328 seats, while the pro-Iran alliance came second with 48 seats, followed by Prime Minister Abadi with 42 seats.[191] Sadr will play a major role in shaping Iraq's next government, which requires 165 seats.

Ayad Allawi: A secular Shi'ite, born to a prominent merchant family, Ayad Allawi was a former member of the Ba'th Party. He fell out with Saddam Hussein in the early 1970s. He went into exile in the UK where he became a neurosurgeon. He was seriously wounded in an assassination attempt in London in 1978, believed to have been ordered by Saddam Hussein. So serious were his injuries, that he spent a year in hospital to recover.[192]

Upon the removal of Saddam Hussein in April 2003, Mr. Allawi was appointed by the US-led coalition authorities as a member of the Iraqi Governing Council. With the US handover of sovereignty on June 28, 2004, Allawi was elected unanimously by the Governing Council to be prime minister of the interim government until national elections, scheduled for early 2005.[193] In the 2005 election, the Da'wa Party formed the government and Ibrahim al-Jaafari became prime minister.

In the March 2010 parliamentary elections, the secular anti-Iran Allawi won 91 seats, two seats more than his rival, Maliki. Allawi drew support from Sunni Arabs, who saw in him hope for an end to their marginalization by the Maliki sectarian government.[194]

Despite the fact that Allawi won more seats than Maliki, Maliki became prime minister, thanks to Iranian manipulation, maneuvering, pressure, and threats. It was nine months of haggling and confusion, including a vote recount in Baghdad that reaffirmed the original count,

---

[190]"Iraq's Sadr and Communist Sickle Join Forces for Election," *Agence France Press (AFP)*, (March 11, 2018). https://www.afp.com/en/news/826/iraqs-sadr-and-communist-sickle-join-forces-election-doc-1297iv1

[191]Dalila-Johari Paul and Hamdi Alkhshali, "Populist cleric Muqtada al-Sadr's coalition wins Iraq's election," *CNN*, (May 19, 2018). https://edition.cnn.com/2018/05/19/middleeast/iraq-elections-parliament-intl/index.html

[192]"Profile: Iyad Allawi," *BBC*, (March 27, 2010). http://news.bbc.co.uk/1/hi/world/middle_east/3757923.stm

[193]"US Hands Over Power in Iraq," *The Guardian*, (June 28, 2004). https://www.theguardian.com/world/2004/jun/28/iraq.iraq1

[194]*Leila Fadel and Karen DeYoung*, "Ayad Allawi's Bloc Wins Most Seats in Iraqi Parliamentary Elections," *Washington Post*, (March 27, 2010). http://www.washingtonpost.com/wp-dyn/content/article/2010/03/26/AR2010032602196.html

before a coalition behind Maliki was cobbled together, but not before Iran delivered Muqtada al-Sadr's support to Maliki.

The Importance of Iraq to Iran

Iraq was a gift from the gods to Iran. The ayatollahs hailed the US invasion of Iraq, although, not the occupation. Iran had reasons to love and hate America's project in Iraq. Tehran cherished the opportunity to finally see the end of the regime of their archenemy, Saddam Hussein and install a submissive Shi'ite regime in Baghdad. Tehran treasured the prospects of controlling the oil politics of the more than 100 billion barrels of oil reserves in the Shi'ite dominated Southern Iraq.[195] On the other hand, Tehran feared US forces might use Iraq as a launch pad to change the regimes in Tehran and its surrogate in Damascus, the Assad regime. Eight years later, however, by December 18, 2011, an obsequious Shi'ite government under Nouri al-Maliki was ruling over Baghdad and the last US soldier departed Iraq.

Iran and Iraq share a nearly 1,000-mile-long border. Seven holy shrines of the Shi'ite Imams are in Central and Southern Iraq. The holy city of Najaf is where Imam Ali is thought to be buried, and the nearby city of Karbala, is where Imam Ali's son, Imam Hussein, is buried. The two shrines are the holiest sites for Shi'ites. There are also the holy shrines of the seventh and the ninth Imams in Kazimayn (a suburb of Baghdad), the tombs of the tenth and eleventh Imams as well as the highly venerable Mosque of the Occultation in the nearby city of Samarra. By comparison, in Iran, only one Imam is buried: the eighth Imam, Ali al-Rida in Mashhad. Additionally, southern Iraq contains more than 100 billion barrels of proven crude oil reserves.[196] Control over Iraq's oil strategies is important to Tehran's influence within the Organization of the Petroleum Exporting Countries.

Shi'ites are drawn together by shared memories of suffering. As a 15% minority among world Muslims, Shi'ites feel solidarity against the Sunni majority. They share common cultural and religious ties. The shrines in Iraq are the focal points of annual pilgrimage for millions of Shi'ites. A high

---

[195]Patrick Avis, "The Outlook and Challenges for Oil in Iraq," (October 31, 2016). https://energyanalyst.co.uk/the-outlook-and-challenges-for-oil-in-iraq/

[196]"Iraqi Hydrocarbon Reserves and Production," *Open Oil*, (2012). http://wiki.openoil.net/Iraqi_Hydrocarbon_Reserves_and_Production

proportion of the pilgrims come from Iran. Many pilgrims never return home: They remain near the holy shrines to live and die. Over the centuries, a colorful tapestry of Shi'ite ethnicities that exists in southern Iraq today, has been fused into an inseparable mix. In the cemeteries of the holy cities, many of the most illustrious and senior Shi'ite clerics and other Shi'ite men of religion are buried.

Some of the most prominent Shi'ite ulama families in Najaf (Sahibuljawahir, Ashshaykh Radi, Bahrululoom, al-Jawahiri, and Tabatabai al-Hakeem) and Karbala (such as al-Hujja al-Haeri, Tabatabai al-Haeri, Tabatabai Burujurdi, and Shahrastan) trace their genealogical roots to long lines of intermarriages with notable Iranian families in Burjurid, Isfahan, Kirmanshah, and Tehran.[197]

During the years of persecution under Saddam Hussein, many Shi'ite ulama fled from Najaf and Karbala to the seminaries of Qom and Mashhad.

The March of Shi'ism: The G.W. Bush administration, wittingly or unwittingly, handed Iraq to Iran. Former US Ambassador to Iraq, Zalmay Khalilzad, one of the architects of the ill-conceived and badly executed project in Iraq said, "The 2003 toppling of Saddam Hussein's regime had opened a 'Pandora's Box' of volatile ethnic and sectarian tensions."[198] Khalilzad described a "worst-case scenario in which religious extremists could take over sections of Iraq and begin to expand outward."[199] Khalilzad's prophesy came true in 2014. The so-called Islamic State was born.

Former President Obama further empowered Iran. The nuclear agreement signed on July 14, 2015 lifted UN economic sanctions against Tehran and released tens of billions of dollars in frozen Iranian assets in return for a reduction in Iran's nuclear facilities for 15 years. Mr. Obama's refusal to supply or allow other countries to supply anti-aircraft weapons to Syria's revolutionaries gave Assad the freedom to kill hundreds of thousands of defenseless Sunni civilians and destroy their towns and villages. In handcuffing Syria's Sunnis, Mr. Obama handed Syria to Iran. His actions multiplied Wahhabi jihadists all around the Middle East and beyond, helped breed the so-called Islamic State, polarized the Sunni/Shi'ite divide, and deepened the Sunni/Shi'ite hatred of one another more than ever before.

---

[197]For a lineage tree showing intermarriages among Shi'ite ulama families in Iran and Iraq from the late 17th to the early 19th centuries, see Momen, (1985), PP. 132–134.

[198]Borzou Daragahi, "Envoy to Iraq Sees Threat of Wider War," *Los Angeles Times,* (March 7, 2006), http://articles.latimes.com/2006/mar/07/world/fg-envoy7

[199]Ibid.

In handing Iraq and Syria to the ayatollahs, the US transferred the political and economic control of the Levant from Arab Sunnis to Iran's ayatollahs after a thousand years of Sunni control dating back to 1055, when the Sunni Seljuk Turks ended the rule of the Shi'ite Buyid Persians in Baghdad, and Salaheddin al-Ayyoubi (1138–1193) ended the rule of the last Shi'ite state, the Isma'ili Fatimids in Egypt (969–1171).

While Mr. Bush might have handed Iraq to Iran unwittingly, Mr. Obama's actions suggest that he knew what he was doing when he handed Syria to Iran. By doing so, he opened the gates of hell in the Muslim Middle East far wider than Mr. Bush had. The Bush and Obama administrations enabled the creation and growth of a Shi'ite crescent from Iran, to Iraq, Syria, and Lebanon. An overconfident Supreme Leader, Ayatollah Khamenei, quickly launched an aggressive march of Shi'ism, a crusade against Sunni neighbors. Today, 16 years after 9/11, Sunnis and Shi'ites in Iraq, Syria, and Yemen are killing each other with vengeance.

The Bush and Obama administrations precipitated the destruction of much of modern Iraq and Syria, plus Yemen, with millions of dead and injured and millions of refugees, let alone the hundreds of demolished cities and towns. The General Commander of the Iranian Revolutionary Guard Corps, Major General Mohammad Ali Jafari said in a speech in January 2016, that Iran has equipped nearly 200,000 young men with arms in Yemen, Iraq, Syria, Afghanistan and Pakistan, in order to face terrorism.[200]

When on January 20, 2017, Obama left the White House, he left behind a Muslim Middle East on fire. He left Arab Sunni masses seething with anger over America's empowerment of Iran.

Iraq's Challenge to Iran

Just because a much bigger and more powerful Iran has oil, political and religious interests in Iraq, does not mean that Iraqi Shi'ites would submit to Iran's designs. Differences in ethnicities and languages are deep. Memories of wars between Arabs and Persians before and since the advent of Islam fuel distrust among Arab Shi'ites and Iranian Shi'ites. It is safe to

---

[200]"Iran's Revolutionary Guards: We Have Armed 200,000 Fighters in the Region," *Middle East Monitor*, (January 15, 2016). https://www.middleeastmonitor.com/20160115-irans-revolutionary-guards-we-have-armed-200000-fighters-in-the-region/

say that the bond between a major proportion of Iraq's Shi'ites and Sunnis is stronger than the bond between Iraq's Shi'ites and Iran's Shi'ites. It is noteworthy that Iraqi families generally refrain from marrying into Iranian families who live in Iraq's holy cities.[201]

Iraq is the spiritual heart and soul of Shi'ites everywhere, especially Arab Shi'ites. Iraq is home to most of the world's Shi'ite holy shrines. Arab Shi'ites and Sunnis alike, in Iraq and in the wider Arab world, are proud of the Qur'an's designation of Arabs as "the finest umma evolved to the human kind" (3:110). Iraq is the cradle of Shi'ism. In addition to the mausoleums of seven of the twelve infallible Imams, events of monumental impact on the shaping of Shi'ite Islam have taken place in Iraq.[202]

Al-Kufah, Central Iraq, was caliph Ali bin Abi Talib's capital city. Outside Basra, Southern Iraq, the Battle of the Camel took place on December 9, 656. The battle was between the caliph Ali and the opponents who refused to acknowledge his caliphate and was led by Talha and al-Zubayr and Aisha, the Prophet's favorite wife. On the plain of Siffin, South of al-Raqqa (in today's Syria), on the west bank of the Euphrates river, the armies of caliph Ali and the Damascus Governor, Muawiyah (later, the first Umayyad caliph), met on July 28, 657. In Karbala, Central Iraq, about twenty-five miles northwest of al-Kufah, arguably the most significant battle in Islamic history took place. On October 10, 682, Hussein, son of Ali and the grandson of the Prophet was killed with his family and companions. Hussein's head was sent to Yazid, successor son of Muawiyah in Damascus. Hussein is buried in Karbala.

The ayatollahs have universal followings. An Iraqi ayatollah would, for example, have followings not only in Iraq but also in Iran and other countries. Likewise, Iran's ayatollahs have followings not only in Iran but also in Iraq and other countries. Cross boundary followings unite the Shi'ites. The senior-most grand ayatollah of the Najaf Seminary has traditionally enjoyed the widest following among Shi'ites.

The millennia-old seminaries of Najaf and Karbala are the most famous and revered in the world of Shi'ite Islam for scholarship and the issuance of authoritative religious opinions (fatwas). From the famous shrines and seminaries of Najaf and Karbala, the most illustrious Shi'ite scholars study and teach. It is safe to say that every important Iraqi and non-Iraqi Shi'ite

---

[201]Over the generations, these families came from Iran to perform the pilgrimage to the Imam's tombs and decided to made the holy cities their home.

[202]Hitti, *History of the Arabs*, PP. 179–180 & 190.

religious personality spent years in Najaf or Karbala. Since 1970, two Grand Ayatollahs from Iran led the Najaf Hawza—Abu Gharib al-Qassim al-Khoei (1970–1992) and Ali al-Sistani (1992-present). Al-Sistani was born near Mashhad in Iran. He moved to Najaf in 1952 for further education. The Ayatollah speaks Arabic with a Persian accent.[203] The leader of the Iranian Revolution, Grand Ayatollah Khomeini, lived in exile in Najaf for thirteen years, from September 5, 1965 until the Iraqi government forced him out of Iraq on October 3, 1978. In Najaf, at the Sheikh Murtada Ansari seminary (Madrasa), Khomeini taught Islamic jurisprudence (fiqh) and refined his thought on the concept of wilayat al-faqih.[204]

Iraq and Saudi Arabia have been attempting to reconcile their political differences. On October 21, 2017, Iraqi Prime Minister Haider al-Abadi met with the Saudi King in Riyadh to establish a joint Saudi-Iraqi coordination council. US Secretary of State, Rex Tillerson arrived in Riyadh to take part in the meeting.[205]

Warming Relations Between Iraqi Shi'ite Religious and Political Leaders and Sunni Neighbors

On August 14, 2017, the Iraqi land port of Ar'ar was permanently reopened to trade with Saudi Arabia after 27 years of closure.[206] On August 8, 2017, Iraq's oil minister visited Saudi Arabia at the invitation of the Saudi minister of oil.[207] Muqtada al-Sadr paid a rare visit to Saudi Arabia on July 30, 2017 and met with Crown Prince Muhammad bin Salman.[208] The meeting drew severe criticism from Iran's proxies in Iraq and Lebanon's Hezbollah.[209] Al-Sadr visited Abu Dhabi on August 13, 2017 and met

---

[203]Dilip Hiro, "Iran's Influence in Iraq," *BBC*, (April 15, 2004). http://news.bbc.co.uk/2/hi/middle_east/3629765.stm

[204]Iran Chamber Society, "Historic Personalities: Ayatullah Khumayni," http://www.iranchamber.com/history/rkhomeini/ayatollah_khomeini.php

[205]"King Salman Receives Iraqi PM in Riyadh," *Arab News*, (October 22,2017). http://www.arabnews.com/node/1181461/saudi-arabia

[206]Iraq's Economic Center, "The Ar'ar Border Crossing Between Iraq and Saudi Arabia Has Been Reopened," (August 14, 2017). http://en.economiciraq.com/2017/08/14/the-arar-border-crossing-between-iraq-and-saudi-arabia-has-been-reopened/

[207]"Iraqi Oil Minister Visits Saudi Arabia," *Egypt Oil & Gas*, (August 9, 2017). http://www.egyptoil-gas.com/news/iraqi-oil-minister-visits-saudi-arabia/

[208]"Saudi Crown Prince Meets with Iraq's Moqtada al-Sadr," *Arab News*, (July 31, 2017).

[209]"Abadi Will Form a New Political Grouping with Sunnis and Kurds to Contest Next Parliamentary Elections," *Al-Quds al-Arabi (in Arabic)*, (August 4, 2017), http://www.alquds.co.uk/?p=765295

with the anti-Iran crown prince of Abu Dhabi.[210] He also visited with anti-Iran King Abdullah of Jordan on October 23, 2017.[211] On July 17, 2017, Iraqi interior minister visited Saudi Arabia at the invitation of his Saudi counterpart and met with Saudi Arabia's Crown Prince.[212] Iraq's prime minister, Haider al-Abadi, visited Saudi Arabia and met with King Salman on June 19, 2017 to "establish a coordination council to upgrade relations."[213] Saudi Arabia reopened its embassy in Baghdad in December 2015 following a 25-year break and the Saudi Foreign Minister visited Baghdad on February 25, 2017.[214] King Salman met with Prime Minister Abadi in March 2017 on the sidelines of an Arab summit in Jordan.[215] Iraqi Parliament Speaker visited Riyadh on March 14, 2016 at the invitation of the Speaker of the Saudi Consultative Assembly.[216]

A decade ago, in May 2005, the Yemeni Zaydi leader, Badr al-Din al-Houthi (d. 2010), reportedly sent an appeal to Iraq's Ayatollah Ali al-Sistani and to the Muslim Council of Najaf asking them to intervene and support the Zaydi sect, which he claimed was the victim of genocide. He also sought the intervention of the Arab League and the Organization of the Islamic Conference. Significantly, he did not seek help from Iran's ayatollahs at that time.[217]

The Houthis are supported by Iran in the war against Saudi Arabia and its allies that started on March 25, 2015. This does not necessarily mean genuine allegiance exists between the Yemeni Houthis and Iran. The Houthis need help; Iran offered to help (to challenge Saudi Arabia), and the Houthis accepted Iran's help.

[210]"Iraqi Shia Leader Sadr Visits UAE, Boosts Ties with Sunni States," *Middle East Eye*, (August 14, 2017). http://www.middleeasteye.net/news/iraqi-shia-leader-sadr-visits-uae-boosting-ties-sunni-states-749395211

[211]"Iraqi Shiite Leader Meets with Jordan king in rare visit," *Voice of America (VOA)*.

[212]"Iraq's interior minister meets with Saudi Crown Prince," *The National*, (July 17, 2017). https://www.thenational.ae/world/gcc/iraq-s-interior-minister-meets-with-saudi-crown-prince-1.610401

[213]"Iraq, Saudi Arabia Aim to Upgrade Diplomatic Relations," *Jerusalem Post*, (June 20, 2017), http://www.jpost.com/Breaking-News/Iraq-Saudi-Arabia-aim-to-upgrade-diplomatic-relations-497396

[214]Maher Chmaytelli, "Saudi FM Visits Baghdad to Bolster Sunni-Shi'ite Reconciliation Post Islamic State," *Reuters*, (February 25, 2017). http://www.reuters.com/article/us-iraq-saudi-diplomacy/saudi-fm-visits-baghdad-to-bolster-sunni-shiite-reconciliation-post-islamic-state-idUSKBN1640AR

[215]"Iraq, Saudi Arabia Aim to Upgrade Diplomatic Relations," *Jerusalem Post*.

[216]Saudi Press Agency, "Iraqi Parliament Speaker Arrives in Riyadh," (March 14, 2016). http://www.spa.gov.sa/viewfullstory.php?lang=en&newsid=1477746

[217]Nasser Arrabyee, "Yemeni Religious Scholars Reject Repression Charges of Zaidis," *Gulf News*, (May 8, 2005). http://gulfnews.com/news/gulf/yemen/yemeni-religious-scholars-reject-repression-charges-of-zaidis-1.286981

CHAPTER EIGHT

THE BIBLE FACES THE QUR'AN IN PALESTINE

Introduction

For most Arabs, the Palestine issue is bound to the Arab identity. Arab frustration over the Israel-Palestine conflict can be gauged from the fact that thirty-nine years after the signing of a peace treaty between Egypt and Israel (March 26, 1979), and twenty-four years after the signing of a similar treaty between Jordan and Israel (October 26, 1994), despite the goodwill of the Egyptian and Jordanian governments, relations with Israel have been limited to small diplomatic missions, with minor or no cultural, educational, or economic exchanges.

Arab Opinion Index, a poll conducted in 12 Arab countries in 2016 by the Arab Center for Research and Policy Studies in Doha, Qatar, found that 89% of the 18,310 respondents believed that Israel poses a threat to the region's stability.[1] Ten years earlier, matters were not much different. A poll conducted by the Egyptian government in August/September 2006 found that 92% of Egyptians regard Israel as the greatest threat to Egypt.[2]

Israeli policies in the Middle East have been driving otherwise moderate Muslims toward orthodoxy and the orthodox toward jihadism. Israeli

---

[1] Devon Haynie "Poll: Arabs See US as a Threat," *US News*, (April 11, 2017). https://www.usnews.com/news/best-countries/articles/2017-04-11/poll-arabs-believe-israel-us-are-biggest-threat-to-the-region

[2] "Denmark 'Egypt's Foe,' Says Poll," *BBC*, (November 1, 2006). http://news.bbc.co.uk/2/hi/middle_east/6107160.stm

denial of any connection between humiliating Arabs and Palestinians and the growth of jihadism is similar to Saudi Arabia's denial of any connection between its Wahhabi way of life and 9/11.

The victory of Hamas in the January 25, 2006 parliamentary elections in the West Bank and the Gaza Strip and the control that Hamas imposed over the Gaza Strip in June 2007 should be a reminder that this conflict is driving the Palestinians and Arabs into the hands of radicals. As the Palestinian problem festers, downtrodden Palestinians and Arabs will turn to God for deliverance. Despair, belief in predestination, jihad injunctions, martyrdom, and paradise will continue to be a jihadist factory.

This chapter focuses on the root causes of the Arab-Israeli conflict. It will show that Arab antagonism toward Israel is not against Judaism as a religion. Rather, it is against Zionism, a political movement. It proposes a one-state solution instead of the two-state solution, envisioned in the 1993 failed Oslo Accords between Israel and the Palestine Liberation Organization (PLO).

Islam's Veneration of Judaism

Islam venerates Judaism. Arabs believe that they share a common ancestry with the Jewish people, and regard the Jewish people as their Semitic cousins. Arabs believe that their ancestry goes back to Ismail (Ishmael), the son of Abraham by the Egyptian slave woman Hagar, and the half-brother of Ishaq (Isaac), the son of Abraham with Sarah, to whom the Jewish people trace their descent.

The Qur'an praises Abraham as the first Muslim, and describes Islam as the "religion of Abraham." Muslims believe that Islam was revealed in order to restore the religion of Abraham to its original tenets:

> Qur'an 2:130: *And who, unless he be weak of mind, would want to abandon Abraham's creed, seeing that We have indeed raised him high in this world, and that, verily, in the life to come he shall be among the righteous?*
>
> Qur'an 3:33: *God did choose Adam and Noah, the family of Abraham, and the family of Imran above all people.*
>
> Qur'an 3:95: *Say God speaks the truth. Follow the Religion of Abraham the upright, who was not of the idolaters.*

Qur'an 4:125: *Who can be better in religion than the one who submits himself to God, does good, and follows the way of Abraham the true in faith? For God did take Abraham for a friend.*

Today, names like Dawoud (David), Ibraheem (Abraham), Ishaq (Isaac), Mousa (Moses), Sara (Sarah), Sulaiman (Solomon), Yacoub (Jacob), Yousef (Joseph), Zakariyya (Zakaria), and Sham'oun (Shimon) are common in Arab societies. Until the Zionist-led Jewish migrations into Palestine started in earnest, Jews in the Arab and the Muslim worlds had centuries of generally peaceful relations.

Arabs and Jews enjoyed a generally tranquil coexistence for centuries. Notwithstanding the intolerant Verses of the Qur'an and the claimed stories about the harsh treatment of the Jewish tribes in Medina, the majority of Muslims have generally been, over the centuries, moderate and tolerant of other faiths. Tolerance can be seen through the mostly peaceful treatment that the "People of the Book," Christians and Jews, received in Muslim lands. Except for short periods during the long sweep of Islamic history, primarily during the reigns of four Arab caliphs, out of a total of ninety-one Muslim rulers—fifty-five Arab caliphs (632–1258) and thirty-six Ottoman Sultans (1280–1924)—Christians and Jews were generally treated decently. Discrimination, when it happened, included the display of distinctive markings on their homes and clothes, exclusion from public office, and demolition of places of worship.

The four caliphs who discriminated against Jews and Christians were the Umayyad Omar-II in Damascus (717–720), the Abbasid Haroun al-Rasheed (786–809) and al-Mutawakkil (847–861) in Baghdad, and the Fatimid al-Hakim in Cairo (996–1021). Another period of discrimination followed the final expulsion of the Crusaders from Syria. In the early 1300s, two Mamluk sultans, Qalawoon and al-Nasir, discriminated against not only People of the Book, but also against Muslim sects that helped the European Christian Crusades during the eleventh and twelfth centuries, including the Isma'ilis, and the Nusayris (today's Alawites).

During the Umayyad dynasty (661–750), Christians and Jews enjoyed considerable tolerance upon the payment of land and poll taxes.[3] During the Abbasid dynasty (750–1258), they filled important financial, clerical, and professional positions.[4] Hitti describes how the Jews fared under Muslim rulers:

---

[3]Philip Hitti, *History of the Arabs*, 10th ed. (MacMillan Press Ltd London), 1970. P. 233.
[4]Ibid, P. 353.

In 985, al-Maqdisi found most of the money-changers and bankers in Syria to be Jews ... Under several caliphs, particularly al-Mu'tadid (892–902), we read of more than one Jew in the capital and the provinces assuming responsible state positions. In Baghdad itself, the Jews maintained a good-sized colony, which continued to flourish until the fall of the city [1258]. [Rabbi] Benjamin of Tudela, who visited the colony about 1169, found it in possession of ten rabbinical schools and twenty-three synagogues; the principal one, adorned with variegated marble, was richly ornamented with gold and silver. Benjamin depicts in glowing colors the high esteem in which the head of the Babylonian Jews was held as a descendant of David and head of the community.[5]

In 1492, the Ottoman Sultan, Bayezid-II (1481–1512) allowed Jews driven out from Spain and Portugal to settle in the Ottoman territories, where they were able to rebuild their lives after being expelled from Iberia.[6] In Mesopotamia, Spain, North Africa, Egypt, and Ottoman Turkey, Jews lived peacefully under the moderate Hanafi rite of the Ottoman Sultans.[7] Indeed, had the sultans forced their Christian subjects in the Balkans in the sixteenth century to convert to Islam, the sectarian wars that devastated the former Yugoslavia in the 1990s would probably not have happened.

Here, a further quotation from the novel *Coningsby* written by British Prime Minister Benjamin Disraeli, Britain's first and so far only prime minister of Jewish parentage (1868 and 1874–1880) is relevant. On the golden age of Muslim Spain, Disraeli wrote,

"That fair and unrivaled civilization in which the children of Ishmael rewarded the children of Israel with equal rights and privileges with themselves. During these halcyon centuries, it is difficult to distinguish the followers of Moses from the votary of Mohamet. Both alike built palaces, gardens, and fountains, filled equally the highest offices of the state, competed in an extensive and enlightened commerce, and rivaled each other in renowned universities."[8]

---

[5]Ibid, PP. 356–357.

[6]Bernard Lewis, *The Jews of Islam* (Princeton University Press, Princeton, New Jersey, 1987), P. 50.

[7]John Garraty and Peter Gay, editors, *The Columbia History of the World*, (New York: Harper & Row, 1981, PP. 289–290).

[8]Benjamin Disraeli, *Coningsby, or The New Generation*, (Kessinger Publishing, Whitehish, MT, 2004), P. 179, http://www.amazon.com/Coningsby-Generation-Benjamin-Beaconsfield-Disraeli/dp/1419113887/ref=reader_auth_dp/102-7296008-3005735

The fact that around 850,000 Jews migrated from the Arab world around the time of Israel's creation in 1948 and shortly after suggests that the Jews of the Arab world must have found it sufficiently agreeable to live among Arabs for centuries.[9] In 1917, a third of the population of Baghdad were Jewish.[10] That Arab maltreatment of Jews caused the Jewish migration from Arab lands should be taken within the context of the events leading up to 1948. By the early part of the twentieth century, Zionism had transformed Judaism into a divine crusade to justify the occupation of Palestine, which Palestinians and their Arab brethren resisted. David Ben-Gurion, Israel's first prime minister (1948–1953 and 1955–1963) reportedly told Nahum Goldmann, the president of the World Jewish Congress, "If I were an Arab leader, I would never make terms with Israel. That is natural: We have taken their country ... We come from Israel, but two thousand years ago, and what is that to them? There has been anti-Semitism, the Nazis, Hitler, Auschwitz, but was that their fault? They only see one thing: We have come here and stolen their country. Why should they accept that?"[11]

Genesis of the Arab-Israeli Dispute

Two events during the first half of the twentieth century humiliated and embittered the Arab peoples. The first was the Sykes-Picot Agreement, struck in the middle of the First World War (May 19, 1916) between London and Paris, two years and five months before the allies had actually won the war against the Ottoman Empire (November 11, 1918).

---

[9] In a BBC report on Israeli Jews from Iraq published in May 2007, Yakov Reuveni remembered his youth in the 1940s: "We used to eat with them, sleep with them, go to school with them; the Arabs and the Jews went to the same high school. During the Shi'ite festival of Muharram we would take part in the procession and along with our Arab friends, beat our chests to remember the epic battle of Karbala ... After school we would go out to the date palm grove with the freshly caught fish from the river Hidekel, which we would barbeque in the fields over an open fire ... Jews shared almost all aspects of life with their Arab neighbors". Another interviewee, Eli Mizrakhi, whose family came from northern Iraq said, "Most of us still feel connected to the country where we or our ancestors came from. Our parents and our grandparents still remember many things from their Iraqi past and they bring them to us, with food, music, language." Lipika Pelham, "Israelis from Iraq Remember Babylon", *BBC*, (May 7, 2007), http://news.bbc.co.uk/1/hi/world/middle_east/6611667.stm

[10] Julian Worricker, "BBC WS Claims Israeli 'Pressure' and 'Incentives' Led Jews to Flee Iraq," *BBC*, (November 21, 2017). https://bbcwatch.org/2017/11/21/bbc-ws-claims-israeli-pressure-and-incentives-led-jews-to-flee-iraq/

[11] Paul Craig Roberts, "The Genocide of a Land," *Foreign Policy Journal*, (August 22, 2016). https://www.foreignpolicyjournal.com/2016/08/22/the-genocide-of-a-land/

The Agreement carved up and divided the Levant between Britain (Iraq, Palestine, and Jordan) and France (Syria and Lebanon). That the Agreement was concluded secretly behind the back of the Sharif of Mecca, Hussein bin Ali, is all the more painful. Sharif Hussein had declared the Arab Revolt on June 10, 1916 against his Muslim Sunni Ottoman co-religionists to fight on the side of Christian Britain and France in return for hazy promises of Arab independence after the war (see Chapter Nine).

The second event that embittered the Arab world was the Balfour Declaration (November 2, 1917). The British Foreign Secretary, Lord Balfour, offered lands Britain never owned in Palestine to the Zionist Federation. The offer was made well before winning the First World War against Istanbul (November 11, 1918). The fact that the Declaration could not wait until Britain and the allies had actually won the war and Palestine became mandated by the League of Nations to Britain opens to speculation the reason(s) that lurked behind London's rush to promise Lord Rothschild a home in Palestine.

That the Sykes-Picot Agreement and the Balfour Declaration took place within eighteen months from one another and were one year before the end of the First World War suggests a possible exchange of benefits relating to the war effort between Britain and Lord Rothchild. The letter reads:[12]

> Dear Lord Rothschild,
> I have much pleasure in conveying to you, on behalf of His Majesty's Government, the following declaration of sympathy with Jewish Zionist aspirations, which has been submitted to, and approved by, the Cabinet:
> "His Majesty's Government views with favour [sic] the establishment in Palestine of a national home for the Jewish people, and will use their best endeavours [sic] to facilitate the achievement of this object, it being clearly understood that nothing shall be done which may prejudice the civil and religious rights of existing non-Jewish communities in Palestine, or the rights and political status enjoyed by Jews in any other country."

---

[12]Jewish Virtual Library, "Balfour Declaration: Text of the Declaration," (November 2, 1917). http://www.jewishvirtuallibrary.org/text-of-the-balfour-declaration

> I should be grateful if you would bring this declaration to the knowledge of the Zionist Federation.
>
> Yours sincerely,
> Arthur James Balfour

That the part of the Declaration which specified: "nothing shall be done which may prejudice the civil and religious rights of existing non-Jewish communities in Palestine," was ignored and resulted in 1948, according to Palestinian sources, in "over 800,000 Palestinians … expelled from 531 towns and villages, in addition to 130,000 from 662 secondary small villages and hamlets became refugees"[13] turned Arab frustration to fury. Jewish sources put the number of the refugees at around 650,000.[14]

Palestinian Population's Size Since 1893

Had Palestine been uninhabited in the nineteenth century, a refugee problem would not have arisen. To justify Palestine as a Jewish home, Zionist leadership promoted the slogan: *A land without people to a people without a land*. However, as far back as 1893, the lowest estimate of the number of Palestinians, Muslims and Christians, was 410,000.[15] According to the 1922 census, Mandatory Palestine had a population of 673,000 Palestinians (589,000 Muslims plus 84,000 Christians) and 71,000 Jews.[16] In 1948, there were 1,415,000 Palestinians and 700,000 Jews.[17] Most recently, on New Year's Day 2017, of Israel's population of 8.63 million, included 1.8 million (20.8%) Palestinian Israelis.[18] The Palestinian Israelis are the Palestinians who remained in what became Israel in 1948. Their number in 1948 was about 156,000, according to the Israeli Central Bureau of Statistics.[19]

---

[13]Palestine Land Society, "Al-Nakba Anatomy." http://www.plands.org/en/books-reports/books/right-of-return-sacred-legal-and-possilble/from-refugees-to-citizens-at-home

[14]Michael Bard, "The Exodus of 1947–48" *Jewish Virtual Library*, (updated August 2015). http://www.jewishvirtuallibrary.org/jsource/History/refugees.html

[15]MidEastWeb, "Population of Ottoman and Mandate Palestine, The Population of Palestine Prior to 1948," http://www.mideastweb.org/palpop.htm

[16]Ibid.

[17]Sami Hadawi, *Palestinian Rights & Losses in 1948: A Comprehensive Study*. (Saqi Books, London, 1988).

[18]Jewish Virtual Library, "Vital Statistics: Latest Population Statistics for Israel," (May 2017). http://www.jewishvirtuallibrary.org/latest-population-statistics-for-israel

[19]MidEastWeb, "Population of Ottoman and Mandate Palestine.

Palestinian Israelis increased by 11.5 times in three generations. At the end of 2016, the Palestinian population worldwide was estimated to be 12.7 million living under the Palestine Authority (4.9 million), Israel (1.53 million), the Arab world (5.6 million) and foreign countries (0.7 million).[20]

The number of Jews who migrated from the Arab world was estimated to be 850,000 and of this number, 586,000 went to Israel.[21] That the number of Palestinian refugees in 1948 was rather close to the size of the Jewish migration from the Arab world is notable. It is as if there was a deliberate plan to exchange Palestinians for Jews from Arab countries.

The exodus of 850,000 Jews from Arab countries within a relatively short period of time must have been accomplished with the acquiescence of Arab rulers. The exodus raises questions over Arab rulers' cooperation with their British Mandate masters in Egypt, Iraq, and Jordan as well as with Zionist leaders to let their Jewish citizens go to Israel, or cause them to go.

Politicizing the Bible and the Qur'an

Israel's founding on a biblical covenant in the *Old Testament* precipitated a vexing religio-political conflict between Muslims and Jews. After thirteen centuries of generally tranquil coexistence, Arab political and religious leaders, particularly in Arab countries bordering Israel, were faced with a politicized Bible to encourage migration to Palestine; namely,

> Genesis 15:18: *The Lord made a covenant with Abraham, saying, 'unto thy seed have I given this land from the river of Egypt unto the great river, the river Euphrates.*

However, the time to lay claim to the Promised Land is in dispute. Elon Gilad describes the timing as possibly the biggest theological question in modern-day Judaism. Gilad wrote in Haaretz:[22]

---

[20]State of Palestine, Palestinian Central Bureau of Statistics, "Palestine in Figures 2016," (March 2017). http://www.pcbs.gov.ps/Downloads/book2261.pdf

[21]Jewish Virtual Library, "Fact Sheet: Jewish Refugees from Arab Countries." http://www.jewishvirtuallibrary.org/jewish-refugees-from-arab-countries

[22]Elon Gilad, "If the Messiah Isn't Here Yet, Does Israel Belong to the Jews?," *Haaretz*, (March 24, 2017). https://www.haaretz.com/jewish/features/.premium-1.779154

The Land of Israel was promised to the Jews, and yes, God will one day, in his own time, return the Jews to their land and give them control of it, but this will only happen in the future when the Messiah arrives.[23]

Jerusalem is Islam's third holiest sanctuary after Mecca and Medina. It is yet another religious cause that pulls the Muslim world together in the conflict with the Bible. Muslims believe that the Prophet Muhammad put his foot on the Rock inside the Dome of the Rock Mosque in Jerusalem before He ascended to Heaven on His Night Journey (Isra'). Chapter (Surat) 17 of the Qur'an is named *The Journey by Night* (Surat al-Isra):

Qur'an 17:1: *Glory to Him Who transported His servant by night from the Sacred Mosque to the Farthest Mosque, whose environs We have blessed.*[24]

Arab and Palestinian Reaction to Genesis 15:18: Since 1948, three generations of Palestinian refugees have existed in primitive, squalid, and overcrowded camps in abject poverty, ill health, and hopelessness, relying on meager United Nations handouts. The number of Palestinian refugees eligible for United Nations Relief and Works Agency (UNRWA) services is five million.[25] Arab countries have been unwilling to settle these refugees within their own borders, partly, in order to maintain their Palestinian identity.

To Arabs, the affliction of the Palestinian refugees represents a warning of the fate that could be awaiting millions of Arabs who live in the land *from the river of Egypt unto the great river, the river Euphrates.* The two parallel blue lines across Israel's flag are seen by Arabs as if they represent the Nile and the Euphrates.

Arab fears are compounded by the apocalyptic beliefs of some influential American fundamentalist Christian evangelicals who fantasize about a second coming of Christ and who see the Jewish settlements in the West Bank and the future rebuilding of the Jerusalem Temple on the sacred Dome of the Rock Mosque, as steps in God's unfolding plan.

[23]Ibid.
[24]The "Sacred Mosque" is believed to be at Mecca. The "Farthest Mosque" is believed to be at Jerusalem.
[25]United Nations Relief and Works Agency for Palestine Refugees in the Near East (UNRWA), *Palestine Refugees.* https://www.unrwa.org/palestine-refugees

Helpless, Arab religious and political leaders counter, by invoking divine covenants of their own, which have been dormant for centuries. Intolerant Verses have been resurrected to arouse Arab and Muslim passion. Also, tales of the troubled relationship the Prophet had with the Jewish tribes of Medina following his migration from Mecca in 622 are now recounted. Arabs drew lessons from the symbolism of substituting Friday for the Sabbath, and changing the direction of *Qiblah* during prayer from Jerusalem to Mecca.

In the confrontation between the Bible and the Qur'an, Islam pulls Muslims of different nationalities together. Muslims belong to the universal nation of Islam (*umma*). Islam supersedes nationalism and ethnicities. The Qur'an demands that Muslims aid each other as if they were one body:

> Qur'an 3:103: *And hold fast, all together, unto the bond with God, and do not draw apart from one another.*
> Qur'an 103:1–3: *Enjoin one another to truth and enjoin one another to endurance.*

The Prophet reportedly said that Muslims are brothers,[26] that the relation of one believer to another is like a building whose parts support one another,[27] and that the solidarity among Muslims in their mutual love, mercy, and sympathy, is like that of a body; if an organ aches, the whole body sympathizes with it with sleeplessness and fever.[28]

President Trump Hands Jerusalem to Israel: The recognition of Jerusalem as Israel's capital by President Donald Trump on December 6, 2017 adds immeasurably to the humiliation, anger, and despair of Palestinians and Arabs.[29] Jerusalem is the third holiest Muslim sanctuary after Mecca and Medina. On December 10, 2017, Arab foreign ministers called on Mr. Trump to rescind his decision, warning that the move threatens to plunge the whole region into "more chaos, violence, bloodshed and

---

[26] *The Six Books, Sahih Muslim*, traditions 6526 to 6540, PP. 1126–1127.
[27] *Sahih al-Bukhari*, traditions 481, P. 40 and tradition 6026, P. 510; and *Sahih Muslim*, tradition 6585, P. 1130.
[28] *Sahih Muslim*, traditions 6582 and 6585 to 6589, P. 1130.
[29] Steve Holland and Maayan Lubell, "Trump Recognises Jerusalem as Israel's Capital, in Reversal of Policy," *Reuters*, (December 6, 2017). https://uk.reuters.com/article/uk-usa-trump-israel/trump-recognises-jerusalem-as-israels-capital-in-reversal-of-policy-idUKKBN1DZ053

instability."[30] Palestinian Authority President Mahmoud Abbas, speaking to Palestinian faction leaders in Ramallah on January 14, 2018, described Mr. Trump's "deal of the century" as "the slap of the century."[31] The European Union's foreign policy chief assured President Mahmoud Abbas at a meeting in Brussels on January 22, 2018 that the European Union supported his ambition to have East Jerusalem as the capital of a Palestinian state.[32] In their closing statement, Arab leaders at the Arab League Summit meeting on April 15, 2018, in Dhahran, Saudi Arabia rejected Trump's decision on Jerusalem as "null and illegitimate."[33] Saudi Arabia renamed this year's summit "Quds [Jerusalem] Summit" and King Salman said: "We confirm that East Jerusalem is an inseparable part of the Palestinian land."[34]

Muslim and Christian leaders protested against the Jerusalem move. The Grand Sheikh of Cairo's al-Azhar Mosque, Ahmed al-Tayeb, issued a statement on December 8, 2017 rejecting a meeting request by U.S. Vice President Mike Pence during his visit to Cairo on December 20, 2017.[35] Similarly, the Pope of the Coptic Church in Egypt, Tawadros II, announced on December 9, 2017 the cancellation of his scheduled meeting with the U.S. Vice President over the same issue.[36] In the event, Mr. Pence's visit was postponed until January 20, 2018. He met in Cairo with the President of Egypt only.[37]

Grand Ayatollah Ali al-Sistani, leader of the preeminent Shi'ite seminary, the Najaf Hawza, said this about Trump's action: "This decision is denounced and condemned. It has hurt the sentiments of hundreds

[30]Andrew England, "Arab ministers sound warning on Trump's Jerusalem decision," *Financial Times*, (December 11, 2017). https://www.ft.com/content/91e5b398-ddb6-11e7-a8a4-0a1e63a52f9c

[31]"Jerusalem Embassy: Abbas Says Trump Plan 'Slap of the Century'," *BBC*, (January 15, 2018). http://www.bbc.co.uk/news/world-us-canada-42684082

[32]Robin Emmot,"Abbas wins EU backing for Palestinian capital in East Jerusalem,"*Reuters*,(January 22, 2018). https://uk.reuters.com/article/uk-usa-israel-abbas/abbas-wins-eu-backing-for-palestinian-capital-in-east-jerusalem-idUKKBN1FB1NM

[33]"Arab leaders mute on Syria strikes at Saudi summit," *Al Jazeera*, (April 15, 2018). https://www.aljazeera.com/news/2018/04/arab-leaders-mute-syria-strikes-saudi-summit-180415174014924.html

[34]Ibid.

[35]"Egypt's al-Azhar Head Rejects Meeting with US Vice President over Jerusalem," *Egypt Independent*, (December, 9, 2017). http://www.egyptindependent.com/egypts-al-azhar-head-rejects-meeting-us-vice-president-jerusalem/

[36]"Egypt's Coptic Pope Rejects Pence Meeting over Jerusalem," *The Times of Israel*, (December 9, 2017). https://www.timesofisrael.com/egypts-coptic-pope-rejects-pence-meeting-over-jerusalem/

[37]Jeff Mason, "Pence Tells Egypt's Sisi that U.S. Still Backs Two-State Solution," *Reuters*, (January 20, 2018). https://uk.reuters.com/article/uk-usa-egypt/pence-tells-egypts-sisi-that-u-s-still-backs-two-state-solution-idUKKBN1F90YT

of millions of Arabs and Muslims, but it will not change the fact that Jerusalem is an occupied land that should return to the sovereignty of its Palestinian owners no matter how long it takes.[38]

To add insult to injury, the U.S. President tweeted on January 2, 2018:

> *We have taken Jerusalem, the toughest part of the negotiation, off the table, but Israel, for that, would have had to pay more.*[39]

Jerusalem is not a Trump property to take off the table. Jerusalem is an existential issue to Palestinians and Arabs, just as it is to the Jewish people. The future of Jerusalem, must be decided by the Arabs and the Jews. In handing the entirety of Jerusalem to Israel, Mr. Trump did not take "the toughest part of the negotiation off the table". He aggravated the conflict greatly. He put, possibly, the final nail in the coffin of the Oslo Accords and the two-state solution. He abdicated America's role as a fair honest mediator.

Mr. Trump stated that Israel "would have had to pay more" in future negotiations in return for his recognition of Jerusalem as Israel's capital.[40] The statement is naive, if not cynical. Mr. Netanyahu's Likud party was quick to unanimously urge legislators on December 31, 2017, albeit, in a non-binding resolution, to move well beyond Jerusalem and annex Israeli settlements in the occupied West Bank, lands that Palestinians want for a future state.[41] Given the history of the proliferation of the settlements since the Oslo Accords, the non-binding resolution today is a short distance from becoming binding tomorrow.

The US President lacks the right to give Jerusalem to Israel. United Nations Security Council resolutions 242 (1967), 338 (1973), 446 (1979), 452 (1979), 465 (1980), 476 (1980), 478 (1980), 1397 (2002), 1515 (2003), 1850 (2008), and 2334 (2016) condemn *all measures aimed at altering the*

---

[38]Al-Sayyid Ali al-Hussainin Al-Sistani official Website.

[39]Jeff Mason, "Pence Tells Egypt's Sisi that U.S. Still Backs Two-State Solution," *Reuters*, (January 20, 2018).

[40]Amir Tibon and Noa Landau, "Trump Threatens to Cut Palestinian Aid; Says Israel Would Have 'Had to Pay' for Jerusalem Recognition," *Haaretz*, (January 3, 2018). https://www.haaretz.com/us-news/.premium-trump-threatens-to-cut-palestinian-aid-israel-would-have-had-to-pay-for-jerusalem-move-1.5630315

[41]Rami Amichay,"Likud Party Calls for De-Facto Annexation of Israeli Settlements,"*Reuters*,(December 31, 2017). https://uk.reuters.com/article/uk-israel-palestinians-likud/likud-party-calls-for-de-facto-annexation-of-israeli-settlements-idUKKBN1EP0M4

demographic composition, character and status of the Palestinian Territory occupied since 1967, including East Jerusalem.[42] Specifically, resolution 2334 of December 23, 2016:

> *1. Reaffirms that the establishment by Israel of settlements in the Palestinian territory occupied since 1967, including East Jerusalem, has no legal validity and constitutes a flagrant violation under international law and a major obstacle to the achievement of the two-State solution and a just, lasting and comprehensive peace,*
>
> *2. Reiterates its demand that Israel immediately and completely cease all settlement activities in the occupied Palestinian territory, including East Jerusalem, and that it fully respects all of its legal obligations in this regard,*
>
> *3. Underlines that it will not recognize any changes to the 4 June 1967 lines, including with regard to Jerusalem, other than those agreed by the parties through negotiations,*
>
> *4. Stresses that the cessation of all Israeli settlement activities is essential for salvaging the two-State solution, and calls for affirmative steps to be taken immediately to reverse the negative trends on the ground that are imperiling the two-State solution.*[43]

President Trump Starves UNRWA of US Funds: Coinciding with Mr. Trump's threat to cut off funds to the Palestinian Authority on January 2, 2018, the U.S. Ambassador to the United Nations threatened to stop funding the United Nations Relief and Works Agency (UNRWA). On January 16, 2018, the U.S. said it would provide $60 million to UNRWA while withholding a further $65 million.[44] On January 17, 2018, UNRWA said it would launch a global fundraising appeal in hopes of making up for funding cuts announced by the United States.[45] At the Arab League

---

[42]14 delegations (out of 15) voted in favor of Resolution 2334 and one abstention (U.S.). United Nations, Security Council, "Israel's Settlements Have No Legal Validity, Constitute Flagrant Violation of International Law, Security Council Reaffirms," (December 23, 2016). https://www.un.org/press/en/2016/sc12657.doc.htm

[43]Ibid.

[44]Arshad Mohammed, "U.S. Withholds $65 Million in Palestinian Aid After Trump Threat," *Reuters*, (January 16, 2018). https://www.reuters.com/article/us-israel-palestinians-usa/u-s-withholds-65-million-in-palestinian-aid-after-trump-threat-idUSKBN1F52GA

[45]"After US Cuts, Palestinian Refugee Agency Seeks Donations," *TheNewArab*, (January 17, 2018). https://www.alaraby.co.uk/english/news/2018/1/17/after-us-cuts-palestinian-refugee-agency-seeks-donations

Summit meeting on April 15, 2018, in Dhahran, Saudi Arabia, King Salman announced a $50 million donation to UNRWA.[46]

US Senator Bernie Sanders, comparing the $50 million donation to the extravagance of the Saudi Crown Prince, Muhammad bin Salman said: "So I say to the crown prince and the other multi-billionaire leaders in the region, stop just talking about the poverty and distress in Gaza, do something meaningful about it … I heard the other day that the Saudi king pledged $50 million to UNRWA, the UN agency that works with Palestinian refugees. Fifty million dollars is not a small sum of money, but let us not forget that it is ten percent of what the crown prince paid for a yacht."[47]

UNRWA is funded almost entirely by voluntary contributions from UN member states.[48] Out of a $668-million budget in 2016, the U.S. contributed over $130 million, and the European Union, with over $106 million, was second in funding size.[49] The agency provides humanitarian assistance to some five million Palestinian refugees in education (515,000 students in 677 schools, costing 54% of the agency's budget), healthcare (143 primary health facilities, with 9 million annual patient visits, costing 17% of the agency's budget), and relief and social services (9% of the agency's budget). Additionally, the agency provides emergency response help to 460,000 refugees impacted by the conflict in Syria. It also made a total of 437,000 micro loans aggregating $494 million.[50]

Lurking behind the American threats is the notion that pressuring the host countries of the UNRWA camps, Jordan, Lebanon, and Syria, plus GCC and other countries that employ Palestinian workers might lead

---

[46]"Saudi king announces $150 million for East Jerusalem," *France 24*, (April 15, 2018). http://www.france24.com/en/20180415-saudi-king-announces-150-million-east-jerusalem

[47]Amir Tibon, "Bernie Sanders Slams Netanyahu and Saudi Crown Prince, Says Israel 'Overreacted' to Gaza Protests," *Haaretz*, (April 16, 2018). https://www.haaretz.com/us-news/bernie-sanders-slams-netanyahu-says-israel-overreacted-in-gaza-1.6009159

[48]UNRWA was established following the 1948 Arab-Israeli conflict by the United Nations General Assembly Resolution 302 (IV) of December 8, 1949 to carry out direct relief and works programmes for Palestine refugees. The Agency began operations on 1 May 1950. In the absence of a solution to the Palestine refugee problem, the General Assembly has repeatedly renewed UNRWA's mandate. United Nations Relief and Works Agency (UNRWA), "Who We Are?". https://www.unrwa.org/who-we-are

[49]United Nations Relief and Works Agency (UNRWA), "Frequently Asked Questions". https://www.unrwa.org/who-we-are/frequently-asked-questions

[50]United Nations Relief and Works Agency (UNRWA), "How We Spend Funds." https://www.unrwa.org/how-you-can-help/how-we-spend-funds

to permanently settling them where they reside, something which Israel would applaud.

However, the Palestinians' right-of-return was enshrined in the United Nations General Assembly resolution number 194 of December 11, 1948:

> *The United Nations General Assembly adopts resolution 194 (III), resolving that "refugees wishing to return to their homes and live at peace with their neighbours should be permitted to do so at the earliest practicable date, and that compensation should be paid for the property of those choosing not to return and for loss of or damage to property which, under principles of international law or equity, should be made good by the Governments or authorities responsible."[51]*

President Trump Threatens the Palestinian Authority: Mr. Trump's threat in tweets on January 2, 2018 to withhold aid payments to the Palestinian Authority for being "no longer willing to talk peace" with Israel,[52] leaves the Palestinian Authority with the option to dissolve itself and hand the Israeli government the responsibility of providing security and municipal services to the occupied territories. Created in 1994, following the signing of the Oslo Accords, the Authority has been reduced to a mere service provider for the Israeli government in the occupied Palestinian cities, towns, and villages.

Failed Attempts for a Solution

The Oslo Accords: As part of the Oslo Accords, letters were exchanged on September 9, 1993 between the Chairman of the PLO, Yasser Arafat, and the Israeli Prime Minister, Yitzhak Rabin. In Mr. Arafat's letter, he accepted Israel's right to exist. In return, Mr. Rabin recognized the PLO as the sole representative of the Palestinian people.[53] (For the letters,

---

[51]United Nations Relief and Works Agency (UNRWA), "Resolution 194." https://www.unrwa.org/content/resolution-194

[52]Rodrigo Campos, "U.S. Threatens to Withhold Aid Cash to Palestinians," *Reuters*, (January 2, 2019). https://uk.reuters.com/article/uk-usa-palestinians-aid/u-s-threatens-to-withhold-aid-cash-to-palestinians-idUKKBN1ER1WV

[53]Jewish Virtual Library, "Israel-Palestinian Peace Process: Declaration of Principles On Interim Self-Government Arrangements ("Oslo Accords")," (September 13, 1993). http://www.jewishvirtual-library.org/declaration-of-principles

see Appendix 1 to this chapter). In the *Declaration of Principles*, the Oslo Accords envisioned an interim period of five years of negotiation, starting no later than May 1996, with the aim of agreeing on serious issues including the status of Jerusalem, Palestinian refugees, Israeli settlements, security, and borders.

Twenty-five years later, the Accords are effectively dead. On the twentieth anniversary of the Oslo Accords, Ron Pundak, one of the two Israelis who conducted the negotiations with PLO representatives in Oslo (the other was Yair Hirschfeld), "blamed Rabin and his foreign minister … Shimon Peres for the fact that the process did not yield a final-status agreement." In an interview with *The Times of Israel* on September 15, 2013, Pundak said that he had "no doubt whatsoever" that "Arafat truly sought peace with Israel."[54]

Among the reasons behind the failure is Israel's insistence on adding the condition of a "Jewish state" to Israel's "right to exist," notwithstanding that the *Declaration of Principles* was silent on such a condition.[55] Similarly, the peace treaties between Israel and Egypt (March 26, 1979) and Israel and Jordan (October 26, 1994) were also silent on this issue.

This new condition, is seen by Palestinians as filibustering the peace process to death. The Palestinians reject the new condition because it represents an existential risk to the Palestinians in Palestine. A purely "Jewish state" would jeopardize the rights of the more than 1.5 million Palestinian Israelis. A purely "Jewish state" is impossible to create unless the Palestinian Israelis vanish. A "Jewish state" would put an end to the right of return of the refugees, a serious issue. The Arab League Summit in Kuwait on March 26, 2014, rejected the notion of Israel as a Jewish state: "We express our absolute and decisive rejection to recognizing Israel as a Jewish state."[56]

The Arab Peace Initiative (API): When the two sides failed to reach agreement on the "serious issues" of the Oslo Accords during the five-year interim period, Saudi Arabia promoted The Arab Peace Initiative (API). The Arab League summit in Beirut on March 28, 2002 proposed to the

---

[54]Raphael Ahren, "No Regrets, Many Laments, from the Architect of Oslo," *The Times of Israel*, (September 15, 2013). https://www.timesofisrael.com/no-regrets-many-laments-from-the-architect-of-oslo/

[55]"Text: 1993 Declaration of Principles", *BBC*, (Last updated: November 29, 2001). http://news.bbc.co.uk/1/hi/in_depth/middle_east/israel_and_the_palestinians/key_documents/1682727.stm

[56]Khoury, "Arab League Rejects Israel as Jewish State."

Israeli Government a resolution for the Palestinian and Arab dispute with Israel on the following terms:

In return for:

a) Full Israeli withdrawal from all the territories occupied since 1967.
b) Achievement of a just solution to the Palestinian refugee problem in accordance with UN General Assembly Resolution 194.
c) The establishment of a Sovereign Independent Palestinian State on the Palestinian territories occupied since the 4th of June 1967 in the West Bank and Gaza strip, with east Jerusalem as its capital.

The Arab countries affirm the following:

a. Consider the Arab-Israeli conflict ended, and enter into a peace agreement with Israel, and provide security for all the states of the region.
b. Establish normal relations with Israel in the context of this comprehensive peace.

The Initiative was agreed by the 22 member states of the Arab League. It was re-endorsed at the 2007 Arab League Summit in Saudi Arabia[57] and again at the 2017 Arab League Summit in Jordan.[58] It was also endorsed in June 2002 by the 57 member states of the Organization of Islamic Cooperation and earned the support of the Quartet mediators' *Roadmap for Peace in the Middle East*, composed of the United Nations, European Union, United States and Russia.[59]

Successive Israeli governments rejected the Initiative's terms. In June 2016, the Israeli newspaper *Haaretz* quoted Benjamin Netanyahu as saying, "Arab nations must revise the deal to reflect Israeli demands … If they bring the proposal from 2002 and define it as 'take it or leave it'—we'll choose to leave it."[60] However, Israeli business and security leaders found merits in the Initiative. On November 20, 2008, a group of over 500 former

---

[57] Avi Isaccharoff, "Arab States Unanimously Approve Saudi Peace Initiative," *Haaretz*, "March 28, 2007". http://www.haaretz.com/news/arab-states-unanimously-approve-saudi-peace-initiative-1.216851

[58] Adam Rasgon, "Arab Leaders at Summit Endorse Two-State Solution."

[59] "The roadmap: Full text," *BBC*, (April 30, 2003). http://news.bbc.co.uk/1/hi/world/middle_east/2989783.stm

[60] Barak Ravid, "Netanyahu: Israel Will Never Accept Arab Peace Initiative as Basis for Talks with Palestinians," *Haaretz*, (June 13, 2016). http://www.haaretz.com/israel-news/1.724725

Israeli security elites and diplomats, led by retired Major General Danny Rothschild launched a campaign in the Israeli media endorsing the API and urging the Israeli government to take advantage of the proposal and not miss an opportunity for peace and security.

In April 2011, leaders from Israel's business sector, civil society, academia, and security establishment, including former Shin Bet heads Yaakov Peri and Ami Ayalon, former Mossad chief Danny Yatom, retired IDF General Amram Mitzna, and former Minister of Public Security Moshe Shahal launched a proposed response to the API known as the Israeli Peace Initiative (IPI). Though unaffiliated with the Israeli government, this was the first major effort by a group of Israelis to seriously engage with the API. It did not garner the support and traction it needed amongst Israeli politicians to be implemented.[61]

The Difficulties with the Two State Solution

A long list of intractable thorny issues stands in the way of the two-state solution. The list includes Jerusalem, borders, security for Israel and Palestine, water rights, Jewish settlers, the status of the Palestinian Israelis, and the right of return for the refugees. Twenty-five years since the signing of the Oslo Agreement on September 13, 1993, the two-state solution proved to be illusionary. None of these issues has been resolved. When President Bill Clinton, Prime Minister Ehud Barak, and President of the Palestinian Authority Yasser Arafat attempted to tackle these issues at Camp David in July 2000, the negotiations collapsed, paving the way for the second intifada.

Even if a miracle could patch-up a two-state agreement, an emasculated and an impoverished Palestinian state sitting next to the most powerful and prosperous country in the Middle East would eventually prove unsustainable. And, the extremists on both sides would ruin the agreement. Armed with the Bible's Genesis 15:18, emboldened by Israel's military might, Zionist extremists would want the entirety of Palestine, even the "*land from the river of Egypt unto the great river, the river Euphrates.*" In reaction, Palestinians would again turn to God. They would engage in holy

---

[61]S. Daniel Abraham Center for Middle East Peace, "Arab Peace Initiative." http://www.center-peace.org/explore/arab-peace-initiative/

jihad, driven by the belief in predestination, tantalized by the promise of paradise, and "instructed" by God in the Qur'an *to fight those who wage war against Muslims* (2:190), *slay them … and drive them out of the places whence they drove Muslims out* (2:191), *fight them until there is no more oppression* (2:193), and … [to] *strike terror into the enemies of God* (8:60).

Even if a two-state agreement were to be signed, the masses in Arab countries, and Muslims in general, would continue to shun a Zionist Israel. Judging from Israel's peace treaties with Egypt and with Jordan, relations failed to develop beyond small diplomatic missions. For a two-state solution to be credible, it must be part of a process that would lead to a single-state solution.

A Single State Solution

A single, democratic, and secular state for Palestinians and Jews based on equal citizenship and constitutional protection of religious and ethnic identities promises a more realistic solution. With a single Arab/Jewish state, Arabs in neighboring countries will no longer have an excuse to boycott their Jewish cousins. A single state would commingle Arabs and Jews into an inseparable mix, paving the way for recognition by Arab governments. More important than governmental acceptance, however, would be the acceptance by the masses in the Arab world and Muslims everywhere. Economic, cultural, educational, and social interaction would follow. The two sides would quickly learn how much they could benefit from one other.

In addition, a single state would eliminate the key obstacles to a two-state solution—the aforementioned issues of Jerusalem, security, settlements, refugees, Palestinian-Israelis, water, and borders—and would allow Arabs and Jews access to the entirety of Palestine. The Jews would realize their dream of living in all of Palestine, and the Palestinians would feel that they, too, inhabit the entirety of the country.

The advantages of a single-state solution are not naïve fantasies. If history is any indication, Arabs and Jews can live together in peace, as hundreds of thousands of Jews lived in Arab countries for centuries before migrating to Israel around 1948. The Jews of the Arab world who had lived in Morocco, Algeria, Libya, Tunisia, Egypt, Lebanon, Syria, Iraq, and Yemen and who settled in Israel could be a positive link with the Arab world, today and in the future. The Jews of the Arab world represent a good proportion of the Jewish population of Israel today. They share with the Arab peoples many cultural traits, customs, habits, food, music, dance, and, for the older generation, the Arabic language.

The Jewish population in settlements, estimated in 2016 to be 756,000 in 148 settlements (406,000 in 128 locations in the West Bank plus 350,000 in 20 locations in East Jerusalem)[62] could become instruments of integration between Palestinians and Jews, not segregation; a mixture of Jews among Arabs would be as difficult to unscramble as removing the Palestinian Israelis from Israel.

The contention that since the Qur'an contains intolerant Verses against the Jews, conflict between Muslims and Jews is unavoidable, does not stand the test of time. Except for relatively short periods under the reign of four out of ninety-one Muslim rulers since the advent of Islam, these Verses remained effectively dormant for thirteen centuries until the Zionists declared their mission.

A Blurred Vision: Creating a Zionist state instead of having a home for the Jewish people in the holy land invited the hostility of the Palestinian people, the Arab masses, and Muslims everywhere. Had Zionism limited its ambitions to Jews living among the Arabs of Palestine, and adhered to the Balfour Declaration's stipulation that, *nothing shall be done which may prejudice the civil and religious rights of existing non-Jewish communities in Palestine*, the vicious Muslim and Arab/Jewish conflict of the past seventy years may not have occurred.

A hundred years after the Balfour Declaration, Lord Roderick Balfour, a great-great-nephew of foreign secretary Balfour, said that Israel, by mistreating Palestinians, is failing to honor the terms of the document. "I have major reservations," he said in an interview with the London *Telegraph* newspaper on October 22, 2017. There is this sentence in the Declaration, "Nothing shall be done which may prejudice the civil and religious rights of existing non-Jewish communities in Palestine. Well, that's not being adhered to. That has somehow got to be rectified."[63]

---

[62]"Israel Report: More than 400,000 Settlers in West Bank," *Middle East Monitor*, (February 19, 2016). https://www.middleeastmonitor.com/20160219-israeli-report-more-than-400000-settlers-in-west-bank/

[63]Stuart Winer, "Current Lord Balfour Says Israel Failing to Live up to 1917 Declaration," *The Times of Israel*, (October 22, 2017). https://www.timesofisrael.com/current-lord-balfour-says-israel-failing-to-live-up-to-1917-declaration/?utm_source=current-lord-balfour-says-israel-failing-to-live-up-to-1917-declaration&utm_medium=desktop-browser&utm_campaign=desktop-notifications#

In provoking the enmity of Muslims, Zionism has done a disservice to the Jewish people. Islam shares much in common with Judaism (see above: *Islam's Veneration of Judaism*). Muslims and Jews do not have fundamental religious conflicts, such as the issue of the blood of Jesus, which stands between Christians and Jews. Arabs are bewildered as to why Zionism has rewarded them with occupation, dispossession, and humiliation.

In Christian Europe, centuries of maltreatment of Jews culminated in the horrors of the Holocaust. Today, American evangelical Christianity acts as if exploiting Zionism would expedite the return of Christ. Evangelical support of Zionism, however, must not obscure the fact that dispensationalist dogma predicts the mass slaughter of Jews by the Antichrist and the conversion of the few surviving Jews to Christianity.[64] Absurdities such as premillennial dispensationalism, the Rapture, the Tribulation, the Antichrist, and the Millennium will not bring peace to the Middle East. Meanwhile, it is morally flawed for Zionism to take advantage of evangelical dogma.

Smart bombs and nuclear weapons cannot force a genuine acceptance of a Zionist Israel. Seventy years and nine wars later failed to deliver Palestinian surrender.[65] The long-term prosperity of the Jewish people in the Middle East require the genuine welcome of Israel by its neighbors. For Israel to be welcomed, it must become a good neighbor.

Harmonizing Prosperity: The gulf between impoverished Palestinian neighborhoods sitting next door to prosperous Israeli garden cities and villages must be remedied. Mountains of investment dollars will be required to harmonize this unpleasant scene. Not only Israel must underwrite the cost. The United Kingdom, which enabled the Zionist project in the first place and the United States, which empowered Israel since 1948, must bear a major proportion of the cost.[66] The lifting of East Germany out of relative poverty by West Germany since their unification in October 1990, is a good precedent.

Whether it would be a good bargain to exchange an unstable two-state solution for a single durable state embracing Jews, Muslims, and Christians is a question Israel's Jewish people alone can answer.

---

[64]Paul S. Boyer, "When US Foreign Policy Meets Biblical Prophecy," *Alternet*, (February 20, 2003), http://www.alternet.org/waroniraq/15221/

[65]1948, 1956, 1967, 1973, Lebanon wars in 1982 and 2006, and three wars against Hamas in Gaza (2008, 2012, 2014).

[66]In the integration of East and West Germany an example.

What if the Stalemate Persists?

Arabs resent the labeling of their struggle against the occupation as terrorism while the occupier's actions are considered self-defense. Originally the victims, the Arab masses have been portrayed as the villains. For Israel and the US to deny responsibility for having helped create the sparks of anger and humiliation felt by the Arabs is deluded and dangerous. A just solution to the Palestinian-Israeli conflict would be an important weapon in the fight against jihadism and terrorism.

With huge military superiority and Washington's unlimited support, Israel is the hegemonic power in the Middle East. Palestinians and the Arab states are underdeveloped, weak, and divided. The Arab peoples are ruled and abused by non-representative tyrannical kings and rulers-for-life presidents. As the Palestinian problem festers, Arabs will continue to turn to God for deliverance. What was al-Qaeda a few years ago has metastasized into a variety of more extreme strands of jihadists in many countries.

The Jewish people, having suffered persecutions and injustices over the long sweep of history more than any other peoples, should appreciate the plight of the subjugated Palestinians. The fact that he Palestinian Authority is demonized because it refuses to surrender to Israeli terms is unfair propaganda. The Palestinians did not take anything from Israel. It is Israel who should return a part of what it took.

Israel's hegemonic power should not be used to stonewall the Oslo Accords and the Arab Peace Initiative. For a durable long-term peace, the Bible cannot be at war with the Qur'an. Unless the Bible's is depoliticized, the Qur'an will not be depoliticized, and wars between Arabs and Jews could go on for a thousand years.

Mr. Trump escalated the religious nature of the conflict between Muslims and Jews further. Religious wars often defy political solutions. Had it not been for politicizing the Bible and the Qur'an, the Arab-Israeli conflict would have been a political conflict open to political solutions. Future protests against Trump's decision will become fodder for the likes of *Fox News* and *Breitbart*. Mr. Trump's action will fan the fires of Islamophobia and add vitality to Samuel P. Huntington's Clash of Civilizations hypothesis.

Men and women of conscience and wisdom in Israel must prevail over Zionist extremists who want to force the occupation through helicopter gunships in the name of the Old Testament. Israel should pursue ethical policy toward the Palestinian people. As long as Israeli society fails to reach a just solution with the Palestinians, the Zionist project will remain morally lacking.

The following is how Avraham Burg, former speaker of Israel's Knesset (1999–2003) and a former chairman of the Jewish Agency sees the challenges facing Israel. Fifteen years later, with three wars against Gaza plus a land, sea and air blockade, and a frozen peace process, Avraham Burg's vision and wisdom are more needed today than ever.

The End of Zionism[67]
Israel must shed its illusions and choose between racist oppression and democracy

The Zionist revolution has always rested on two pillars: a just path and an ethical leadership. Neither of these is operative any longer. The Israeli nation today rests on a scaffolding of corruption, and on foundations of oppression and injustice. As such, the end of the Zionist enterprise is already on our doorstep. There is a real chance that ours will be the last Zionist generation. There may yet be a Jewish state here, but it will be a different sort, strange and ugly.

There is time to change course, but not much. What is needed is a new vision of a just society and the political will to implement it. Diaspora Jews for whom Israel is a central pillar of their identity must pay heed and speak out.

The opposition does not exist, and the coalition, with Ariel Sharon at its head, claims the right to remain silent. In a nation of chatterboxes, everyone has suddenly fallen dumb, because there's nothing left to say. We live in a thunderously failed reality. Yes, we have revived the Hebrew language, created a marvelous theatre and a strong national currency. Our Jewish minds are as sharp as ever. We are traded on the Nasdaq. But is this why we created a state? The Jewish people did not survive for two millennia in order to pioneer new weaponry, computer security programs or anti-missile missiles. We were supposed to be a light unto the nations. In this we have failed.

It turns out that the 2,000-year struggle for Jewish survival comes down to a state of settlements, run by an amoral clique of corrupt lawbreakers who are deaf both to their citizens and to their enemies. A state lacking justice cannot survive. More and more Israelis are coming to understand

---

[67]Avraham Burg, "The End of Zionism," The *Guardian*, (September 15, 2003). Reprinted with permission of *The Forward*, which translated and adapted the essay from an article that originally appeared in *Yediot Aharonot*. http://www.guardian.co.uk/israel/comment/0,10551,1042071,00.html

this as they ask their children where they expect to live in 25 years. Children who are honest admit, to their parents' shock, that they do not know. The countdown to the end of Israeli society has begun.

It is very comfortable to be a Zionist in West Bank settlements such as Beit El and Ofra. The biblical landscape is charming. You can gaze through the geraniums and bougainvilleas and not see the occupation. Travelling on the fast highway that skirts barely a half-mile west of the Palestinian roadblocks, it's hard to comprehend the humiliating experience of the despised Arab who must creep for hours along the pocked, blockaded roads assigned to him. One road for the occupier, one road for the occupied.

This cannot work. Even if the Arabs lower their heads and swallow their shame and anger forever, it won't work. A structure built on human callousness will inevitably collapse in on itself. Note this moment well: Zionism's superstructure is already collapsing like a cheap Jerusalem wedding hall. Only madmen continue dancing on the top floor while the pillars below are collapsing.

We have grown accustomed to ignoring the suffering of the women at the roadblocks. No wonder we don't hear the cries of the abused woman living next door or the single mother struggling to support her children in dignity. We don't even bother to count the women murdered by their husbands.

Israel, having ceased to care about the children of the Palestinians, should not be surprised when they come washed in hatred and blow themselves up in the centres [sic] of Israeli escapism. They consign themselves to Allah in our places of recreation, because their own lives are torture. They spill their own blood in our restaurants in order to ruin our appetites, because they have children and parents at home who are hungry and humiliated. We could kill a thousand ringleaders a day and nothing will be solved, because the leaders come up from below—from the wells of hatred and anger, from the "infrastructures" of injustice and moral corruption.

If all this were inevitable, divinely ordained and immutable, I would be silent. But things could be different, and so crying out is a moral imperative.

Here is what the prime minister should say to the people: the time for illusions is over. The time for decisions has arrived. We love the entire land of our forefathers and in some other time, we would have wanted to live here alone. But that will not happen. The Arabs, too, have dreams and needs.

Between the Jordan and the Mediterranean there is no longer a clear Jewish majority. And so, fellow citizens, it is not possible to keep the whole thing without paying a price. We cannot keep a Palestinian majority under an Israeli boot and at the same time think ourselves the only democracy in the Middle East. There cannot be democracy without equal rights for all who live here, Arab as well as Jew. We cannot keep the territories and preserve a Jewish majority in the world's only Jewish state—not by means that are humane and moral and Jewish.

Do you want the greater land of Israel? No problem. Abandon democracy. Let's institute an efficient system of racial separation here, with prison camps and detention villages.

Do you want a Jewish majority? No problem. Either put the Arabs on railway cars, buses, camels and donkeys and expel them en masse—or separate ourselves from them absolutely, without tricks and gimmicks. There is no middle path. We must remove all the settlements—all of them—and draw an internationally recognised [sic] border between the Jewish national home and the Palestinian national home. The Jewish law of return will apply only within our national home, and their right of return will apply only within the borders of the Palestinian state.

Do you want democracy? No problem. Either abandon the greater land of Israel, to the last settlement and outpost, or give full citizenship and voting rights to everyone, including Arabs. The result, of course, will be that those who did not want a Palestinian state alongside us will have one in our midst, via the ballot box.

The prime minister should present the choices forthrightly: Jewish racism or democracy. Settlements, or hope for both peoples. False visions of barbed wire and suicide bombers, or a recognized [sic] international border between two states and a shared capital in Jerusalem.

Why, then, is the opposition so quiet? Perhaps because some would like to join the government at any price, even the price of participating in the sickness. But while they dither, the forces of good lose hope. Anyone who declines to present a clear-cut position—black or white—is collaborating in the decline. It is not a matter of Labour versus Likud or right versus left, but of right versus wrong, acceptable versus unacceptable. The law-abiding versus the lawbreakers. What's needed is not a political replacement for the Sharon government but a vision of hope, an alternative to the destruction of Zionism and its values by the deaf, dumb and callous.

Israel's friends abroad—Jewish and non-Jewish alike, presidents and prime ministers, rabbis and lay people—should choose as well. They must reach out and help Israel to navigate the road map toward our national destiny as a light unto the nations and a society of peace, justice and equality.

CHAPTER 8—APPENDIX 1

L etters from PLO Chairman Yasser Arafat to Israeli Prime Minister Yitzhak Rabin, from Israeli Prime Minister Yitzhak Rabin to PLO Chairman Yasser Arafat, and from PLO Chairman Yasser Arafat to Norwegian Foreign Minister Johan Holst.[68]

Letter from PLO Chairman Yasser Arafat to Israeli Prime Minister Yitzhak Rabin

Mr. Prime Minister,

The signing of the Declaration of Principles marks a new era in the history of the Middle East. In firm conviction thereof, I would like to confirm the following PLO commitments:

- The PLO recognizes the right of the State of Israel to exist in peace and security.
- The PLO accepts United Nations Security Council Resolutions 242 and 338.
- The PLO commits itself to the Middle East peace process, and to a peaceful resolution of the conflict between the two sides and declares that all outstanding issues relating to permanent status will be resolved through negotiations.
- The PLO considers that the signing of the Declaration of Principles constitutes a historic event, inaugurating a new epoch of peaceful coexistence,

---

[68]Jewish Virtual Library, "Israel-Palestinian Peace Process: Letters of Mutual Recognition," (September 9, 1993). https://www.jewishvirtuallibrary.org/israel-palestinian-letters-of-mutual-recognition-september-1993

free from violence and all other acts which endanger peace and stability. Accordingly, the PLO renounces the use of terrorism and other acts of violence and will assume responsibility over all PLO elements and personnel in order to assure their compliance, prevent violations and discipline violators.

In view of the promise of a new era and the signing of the Declaration of Principles and based on Palestinian acceptance of Security Council Resolution 242 and 338, the PLO affirms that those articles of the Palestinian Covenant which deny Israel's right to exist, and the provisions of the Covenant which are inconsistent with the commitments of this letter are now inoperative and no longer valid. Consequently, the PLO undertakes to submit to the Palestinian National Council for formal approval the necessary changes in regard to the Palestinian Covenant.

Sincerely,
Yasser Arafat
Chairman, Palestine Liberation Organization

Letter from Israeli Prime Minister Yitzhak Rabin to PLO Chairman Yasser Arafat

Mr. Chairman,
In response to your letter of September 9, 1993, I wish to confirm to you that, in light of the PLO commitments included in your letter, the Government of Israel has decided to recognize the PLO as the representative of the Palestinian people and commence negotiations with the PLO within the Middle East peace process.

Yitzhak Rabin
Prime Minister, Israel

Letter from PLO Chairman Yasser Arafat to Norwegian Foreign Minister Johan Holst

Dear Minister Holst,

I would like to confirm to you that, upon the signing of the Declaration of Principles, the PLO encourages and calls upon the Palestinian people in the West Bank and Gaza Strip to take part in the steps leading to the normalization of life, rejecting violence and terrorism, contributing to peace and stability and participating actively in shaping reconstruction, economic development and cooperation.

Sincerely,
Yasser Arafat
Chairman, Palestine Liberation Organization

THE ARAB PEACE INITIATIVE—FULL TEXT[69]

The text of the Agreement reached at the Arab League Summit in Beirut on March 28, 2002.

The Council of the League of Arab States at the Summit Level, at its 14th Ordinary Session,

- Reaffirms the resolution taken in June 1996 at the Cairo extraordinary Arab summit that a just and comprehensive peace in the Middle East is the strategic option of the Arab countries, to be achieved in accordance with international legality, and which would require a comparable commitment on the part of the Israeli government.
- Having listened to the statement made by his royal highness Prince Abdullah Bin Abdullaziz, the crown prince of the Kingdom of Saudi Arabia in which his highness presented his initiative calling for full Israeli withdrawal from all the Arab territories occupied since June 1967, in implementation of Security Council Resolutions 242 and 338, reaffirmed by the Madrid Conference of 1991 and the land for peace principle, and Israel's acceptance of an independent Palestinian state, with East Jerusalem as its capital, in return for the establishment of normal relations in the context of a comprehensive peace with Israel.
- Emanating from the conviction of the Arab countries that a military solution to the conflict will not achieve peace or provide security for the parties, the council:

---

[69] Arab Peace Initiative: Full Text, *The Guardian*. https://www.theguardian.com/world/2002/mar/28/israel7

1. Requests Israel to reconsider its policies and declare that a just peace is its strategic option as well.
2. Further calls upon Israel to affirm:
   a) Full Israeli withdrawal from all the territories occupied since 1967, including the Syrian Golan Heights to the lines of June 4, 1967, as well as the remaining occupied Lebanese territories in the south of Lebanon.
   b) Achievement of a just solution to the Palestinian refugee problem to be agreed upon in accordance with UN General Assembly Resolution 194.
   c) The acceptance of the establishment of a Sovereign Independent Palestinian State on the Palestinian territories occupied since the 4th of June 1967 in the West Bank and Gaza strip, with east Jerusalem as its capital.
3. Consequently, the Arab countries affirm the following:
   a) Consider the Arab-Israeli conflict ended, and enter into a peace agreement with Israel, and provide security for all the states of the region.
   b) Establish normal relations with Israel in the context of this comprehensive peace.
4. Assures the rejection of all forms of Palestinian patriation which conflict with the special circumstances of the Arab host countries.
5. Calls upon the government of Israel and all Israelis to accept this initiative in order to safeguard the prospects for peace and stop the further shedding of blood, enabling the Arab Countries and Israel to live in peace and good neighborliness and provide future generations with security, stability, and prosperity.
6. Invites the international community and all countries and organizations to support this initiative.
7. Requests the chairman of the summit to form a special committee composed of some of its concerned member states and the secretary general of the League of Arab States to pursue the necessary contacts to gain support for this initiative at all levels, particularly from the United Nations, the security council, the United States of America, the Russian Federation, the Muslim States and the European Union.

CHAPTER NINE

SECTARIANISM, DICTATORSHIP, AND THE DESTRUCTION OF MOST OF SYRIA

The Assads' Quasi Islamic/Quasi Secular Agenda

The Assad regime propagates that Syria is a secular state. The reality, however, is different. Islam and the Syrian state have been inseparable. The constitution of 1973 made Islam the religion of the president [Article 3 (1)] and enshrined the Islamic Shari'a as a main source of legislation [Article 3 (2)].[1] Thirty-nine years later, the constitution of 2012 repeated the same provisions:

> Article 3: Religion of the President of the Republic is Islam; Islamic jurisprudence shall be a major source of legislation.[2]

Shari'a laws and courts regulate Muslims' personal status affairs. The Druze community follows their doctrinal courts. Christians follow the rules of their own churches.

In "secular" Syria, the law allows a man to marry four wives simultaneously and divorce any of them at will. A Muslim woman is prohibited from marrying a non-Muslim (unless he converts to Islam), while a Muslim

---

[1]International Constitutional Law, "Syria—Constitution, Adopted on March 13, 1973." http://www.icla.up.ac.za/images/un/use-of-force/asia-pacific/SyrianArabRepublic/Constitution%20Syrian%20Arab%20Republic%201973.pdf
[2]UNHCR. "Syrian Arab Republic: Constitution, 2012," http://www.refworld.org/docid/5100f02a2.html

man is allowed to marry a Christian woman (she does not need to change her religion). A Syrian woman cannot pass her nationality on to her foreign husband and children, however, the Syrian man married to a foreign woman can do so. The punishment for "honor killings" of women by a male relative is a light sentence. Two women equate to one man in inheritance and when serving as witness in a Shari'a court.

Religious events are national holidays. During the month of Ramadan, government offices have short working hours. Special religious programming takes over the airwaves on government radio and television. More mosques, larger congregations, and a greater number of veiled women than ever before have become the order of the day. On Sunni feast days, the president performs prayers and rituals publically to media fanfare. He typically attends the Umayyad Mosque in Damascus, one of Sunni Islam's most revered mosques after the mosques in Mecca, Medina, and Jerusalem. During periods of drought, special rain prayers are staged in mosques across the country by order of the president, who is supposed to be an ophthalmologist, and thus, a scientist.

Syria's elementary, middle, and high schools teach Sunni Islam regardless of the Islamic sect to which a pupil belongs. The religious textbooks are discriminatory, divisive, and intolerant of non-Muslims. The textbooks propagate the regime's political agenda.

The Damascus Sunni palace ulama surround Assad with a religious protective halo similar to that exploited by the al-Sauds' palace ulama. Syria's Grand Mufti, Ahmad Kuftaro, the highest Sunni Islamic authority (1964–2004) and his successor, Ahmad Hassoun, found it rewarding to make a career out of imploring the Sunni masses to obey the Assad presidents blindly in order to accord with the Verse 4:59.[3] Sunni palace ulama also promote the regime's agenda. In December 2016, the imam of the Grand Umayyad Mosque in Damascus, Sheikh Ma'moun Rahme, exhorted the country during a televised Friday prayer to join the Fifth Corps, a military force formed on November 22, 2016,[4] which is commanded by Russian officers.[5]

---

[3] *Obey God and the Prophet and those in authority amongst you.*

[4] Abdulrahman al-Masri, "Analysis: The Fifth Corps and the State of the Syrian Army," *Syria Deeply*, (January 11, 2017). https://www.newsdeeply.com/syria/articles/2017/01/11/analysis-the-fifth-corps-and-the-state-of-the-syrian-army

[5] "Russia Says General Killed in Syria Held Senior Post in Assad's Army," *Reuters*, (September 27, 2017). https://ca.reuters.com/article/topNews/idCAKCN1C22TW-OCATP

Under the regime of the two Assads, Syria has become more Islamic than it was in 1963 when the democratically elected parliament and government were toppled by the Assad coup. Nonetheless, the regime and its apologists constantly propagate that theirs is a secular regime.

Islamism to Control the Home Front and Frighten the West: The Assads' religious credentials contradict the ruling Ba'th Party's secular constitution. The Party's holy trinity is Arab unity, freedom, and socialism. There is no mention of religion in the Ba'th constitution.[6]

Since the Assad clan belongs to the Alawite minority sect, seen by Sunnis as a heterodox sect, appeasement of the Sunni majority works in the regime's favor. Instead of wading in the muddy waters of Shari'a reform or secularization, as called for in the Ba'th Party constitution, the regime has chosen to be neither secular nor sincere in its Islam.

For the past five decades, the regime has played the Islamist card skillfully in a strategy of blackmail legitimacy, allowing the Islamist threat to remain alive to threaten Western interests, but too weak to pose a serious threat to the Assad clan. Islamists are regularly rounded up. Since 1980, membership in the Muslim Brotherhood has been punishable by death.

Blackmail legitimacy was an effective weapon against the 2011 revolution. By releasing hardened Islamists from prisons, the regime allowed jihadists to hijack the revolution and Islamitize it. This had the intended effect of scaring the world into choosing between tyranny in Damascus or the barbarism and criminality of the so-called Islamic State.

The Alawites

Since the tenth century, the Alawites have inhabited Syria's northern Mediterranean coast. The Alawites represent about 10% of Syria's estimated population of around 20 million. Three quarters, maybe slightly more of Syria's population, are Sunnis, followers of the moderate Hanafi school of jurisprudence. There are minorities of Christians, Druze, and Ismailis, accounting for the rest. Arabs make up about 90%. Ethnic

---

[6]The Ba'th Party. "The Constitution of the Ba'th Arab Socialist Party," (published on August 31, 2015) http://www.baath-party.org/index.php?option=com_content&view=category&id=307&Itemid=327&lang=en

minorities of Kurds, Armenians, and others make up the remaining 10%. Arabic (official), Kurdish, Armenian, Aramaic, and Circassian languages are spoken in addition to English and French.[7]

The original name of Alawites is Nusayris. They are one of the extreme Isma'ili sects. Around the end of the ninth century, Muhammad bin Nusayr, a Persian partisan of the eleventh imam, al-Hassan al-Askari (d. 874), formulated the Nusayris' doctrine.[8] The name Alawite first appeared during the French mandate (1920–1946), possibly because Alawites consider Ali bin Abi Talib, the Prophet's cousin, son-in-law, and the fourth caliph as the "incarnation of the deity."[9]

The Alawites say their ancestors come from the Makhzum tribe in Arabia. There are four main Alawite tribal confederations—the Haddadin, the Matawira, the Khaiyatin, the Kalbiya (Assads' confederation) and three smaller tribes, the Darawisa, the Mahaliba and the Amamira.[10] Alawites believe that the Prophet was Ali's visible veil and that the Prophet's companion, Salman al-Farisi, was Ali's proselytizer. The three men formed a divine triad, akin to Christianity's holy trinity.[11] Transmigration of souls figured in their cosmology.[12] Unlike other Muslim sects, Alawites have a liturgy in their religious rituals.[13] Other similarities to Christianity include the consecration of the sacrament, the celebration of the mass, and the celebration of Christmas and Easter.[14]

The famous eleventh-century scholar Muhammad bin al-Hassan al-Tusi (d. 1067) accused the Alawites of heresy.[15] Al-Tusi, a leading Shi'ite authority from Persia, wrote two of the four early four Shi'ite canonical Hadith collections. While Twelver Shi'ite heresiographers regard the Alawites as exceeding all bounds in their deification of Ali, the Alawites

---

[7]Central Intelligence Agency, "The World Factbook." https://www.cia.gov/library/publications/the-world-factbook/geos/sy.html

[8]Hitti, *History of the Arabs*, P. 448.

[9]Ibid, P. 449.

[10]Patrick Seale, *Assad, the Struggle for the Middle East* (Berkeley, California: University of California Press, 1995), P. 9.

[11]Martin Kramer; Editor, *Shi'ism, Resistance, and Revolution*, (Westview Press, Boulder, Colorado, 1987), PP. 237–254.

[12]Ibid.

[13]Hitti, *History of the Arabs*, P. 449.

[14]Matti Moosa, *The Nusairi mass, Extremist Shi'ites*, (Syracuse University Press, 1987), P. 405.

[15]Barak Barfi, "The Real Reason Why Iran Backs Syria," *The National Interest*, (January 24, 2016). http://nationalinterest.org/feature/the-real-reason-why-iran-backs-syria-14999

hold Twelve Shi'ites to fall short of fathoming Ali's divinity. Sunni heresiographers view the Alawites as disbelievers and idolaters.[16]

Due to their age-old difficulties with Sunnis, Nusayris learned to practice their rituals in secrecy. The sect is hierarchical and esoteric.[17] They have a three-class hierarchy of initiates, consisting only of males, while the rest of the community remains uninitiated. They meet at night in secluded places.[18]

The Shi'ite Fatimid dynasties in Egypt and Syria between the tenth and the thirteenth centuries were helpful to the Nusayris. However, as the Fatimid reign was ended in 1171, the Alawites suffered persecution for the next eight centuries.[19] The orthodox theologian ibn Taymiyya (1263–1328), the inspiration behind the Wahhabi ideology of Saudi Arabia, condemned the Nusayris as being more dangerous than the Christians. Ibn Taymiyya encouraged Muslims to conduct jihad against them.[20]

How Was Alawism Anointed as a Part of Shi'ism in 1973? When Hafiz Assad (1971–2000) revealed his new constitution on January 31, 1973, he excluded the clause that required the president of the republic to be a Muslim. Demonstrations erupted in protest. To avert bloody confrontations, he instructed his rubber-stamp parliament to return the clause back into the constitution.

To confirm that an Alawite can legitimately be called a Muslim, Hafiz obtained in 1973 from Imam Musa al-Sadr, head of the Higher Shi'ite Council in Lebanon, a religious opinion (fatwa) that made the Alawites a community of Shi'ite Islam.[21]

The opinion was politically expedient for al-Sadr during the turbulent period in Lebanon that led to the civil war (April 1975–October 1990). The fatwa was not assented to by Shi'ites' senior-most ayatollahs, Grand Ayatollah Abol Qasem Kho'i of the Najaf Seminary, or Grand Ayatollah Kazem Shariatmadari of the Qom Seminary in Iran.[22] Alawite senior clerics then refused to submit to the authority of the grand ayatollahs in Najaf or Qom.

---

[16]Ibid.

[17]Philip Hitti, *Syria: A Short History*, (MacMillan & Co. Ltd., London, 1959), P. 172.

[18]Ibid, P. 173.

[19]Momen, Moojan, *An Introduction to Shi'i Islam* (Yale University Press, New Haven, CT, 1985), P. 58.

[20]Patrick Seale, *Assad, the Struggle for the Middle East*, P. 10.

[21]Ibid, P. 173.

[22]Martin Kramer; Editor, *Shi'ism, Resistance, and Revolution*, PP. 237–254.

In July 2005, an international Islamic conference in Amman convened by King Abdullah II, attended by 200 leading Islamic scholars from 50 countries unanimously recognized that:

> Whosoever is an adherent to one of the four Sunni schools of Islamic jurisprudence (Hanafi, Maliki, Shafi'i and Hanbali), the two Shi'iite schools of Islamic jurisprudence (Ja'fari and Zaydi), the Ibadi school of Islamic jurisprudence and the Thahiri school of Islamic jurisprudence, is a Muslim.[23]

The Amman Message did not recognize the Alawites as Muslims.

The Poverty and Maltreatment of the Alawites: Until 1963, when a 33-year old decommissioned former air-force captain, Hafiz al-Assad and compatriots seized power in a military coup, the Alawites' mountainous region was destitute. Poverty was so abject that many Alawite families were compelled to send their daughters, sometimes as young as ten years of age, to live and work for paltry wages as housemaids in the homes of affluent non-Alawite families in nearby cities. While other parts of rural Syria were also poor, the Alawite region was worse: Villages had no electricity, running water, or sanitation. Elementary schools were scarce, intermediate schools were rare, and high schools were only available in large urban centers. Hospitals were nonexistent. Most villages were accessible only by horse or donkey. The region's main source of income was tobacco, but the high brokerage fees charged by wholesalers in the largest coastal city of Latakia left little profit for the growers.

The Assads' Regime's Legitimacy Ideology

Notwithstanding the fatwa from Musa al-Sadr that the Alawite sect is a part of Shi'ite Islam, the Sunni masses disagree. Consequently, Arab Socialist Ba'th Party's slogan of Arab unity and socialism became the Assads'

---

[23]The Royal Aal al-Bayt Institute for Islamic Thought, "The Amman Message," P. 16. https://docs. google.com/viewer?a=v&pid=forums&srcid=MDE5NTA5NDY4NTM4NDk1OTU5MjkBMDI5 OTAxNzQwNDQxNDUwNzg1MzIBc1ZMZEdQSEVGMklKATAuMQEBdjI Over 500 leading Muslim scholars world-wide adopted The Amman Message, including the Organization of the Islamic Conference summit at Mecca in December 2005, six other international Islamic scholarly assemblies, and the International Islamic Fiqh Academy of Jeddah, in July 2006.

mantra. The 2012 Constitution, like the 1973 Constitution, enshrined Arab unity in the preamble[24] and socialism in Article 14.[25]

Despite these lofty aims, fifty years later, neither Arab unity nor socialism was achieved. The Arab nation is more divided in 2018 than in many centuries. Even the two branches of the one and same Ba'th Party that ruled Iraq (under Saddam Hussein) and Syria were the bitterest of enemies. Syria was the only Arab Sunni-majority country to have sided with Persian Shi'ite Iran against Ba'thist Arab Iraq in the long Iran/Iraq war (1980–1988). As for socialism, it is a contradiction in terms, in such a lawless police state where rampant corruption is the glue that keeps the regime together, and which has frayed the fabric of Syria's society.

Arab nationalism has been a reaction to two major events in the modern Middle East. The first was the Sykes-Picot Agreement and the Arab Revolt. The second was the 1948 war between Arabs and Israel.

The Arab Revolt and the Sykes-Picot Agreement: Sharif Hussein Bin Ali (1854–1931) was appointed on November 24, 1908 by the Ottoman caliph/Sultan, Abdulhameed-II, to the coveted position of Emir of Mecca. The religious standing of this position in the world of Islam is immense. On June 10, 1916, Sharif Hussein[26] declared the Arab Revolt from Mecca in support of Britain and the allies against his Sunni Turkish co-religionist rulers in the middle of the First World War. With his allegiance to Britain, he effectively stabbed Istanbul in the back.

Arab leaders in the Levant joined Sharif Hussein's Revolt after agreeing that if WWI were to end in victory for the allies, they would be granted independence within a unified Arab state. The borders of the new state were outlined in the Damascus Protocol in May 1915. Sharif Hussein assured his Levant compatriots of his commitment to the bargain and of his ability to get British agreement to the Damascus Protocol terms. In the first of the five letters the Sharif sent to Sir Henry McMahon, the British high commissioner in Cairo on July 14, 1915, eleven months before the revolt

---

[24]In the Preamble: "The Syrian Arab Republic embodies this belonging in its national and pan-Arab project and the work to support Arab cooperation in order to promote integration and achieve the unity of the Arab nation." Voltairenet.org, "Constitution of the Syrian Arab Republic—2012." http://www.wipo.int/wipolex/en/text.jsp?file_id=429791

[25]Article 14: "Natural resources, facilities, institutions and public utilities shall be publicly owned, and the state shall invest and oversee their management for the benefit of all people, and the citizens' duty is to protect them." Ibid.

[26]In Arabic, Sharif means honorable, honest, and truthful. The Sharif of Mecca was the honorific title of the ruler of the holy cities of Mecca and Medina and their environs.

254 Oil and God

was launched, he communicated the borders as outlined in the Damascus Protocol. According to these letters, Sharif Hussein must have been aware at the time of declaring the Revolt on June 10, 1916, that he did not get a definite and clear agreement from Britain on the Damascus Protocol borders. He should have known that his reward was going to be limited to a rather small piece of northwest Arabia in the Hijaz, not the Arab state his Levant compatriots had demanded in the Damascus Protocol.

London tantalized a parochial, ambitious man who did not speak English or French with vague promises of a kingdom.[27] The Sharif's siding with Christian Britain against the Muslim caliph was of crucial importance to London, given the large Muslim population in British colonies, especially India. Three weeks before Sharif Hussein declared the Arab Revolt on June 10, 1916, London and Paris had agreed behind the Sharif's back, on May 19, 1916, to mandate Syria and Lebanon to France, and Palestine and Iraq to Britain. To add insult to injury, Sharif Hussein and his Arab compatriots learned about the Sykes-Picot Agreement, not from their British and French partners but from the Russian press on November 23, 1917, following the Russian Revolution against the tsar.

In joining the Revolt, the Arabs of the Levant thought that their allies would grant them independence. Instead, Britain and France simply took the place of the Turks. In his haste to declare the Revolt, under urgings from Sir Henry, the Sharif sacrificed the interests of his Levantine Arabs compatriots without even notifying them. Sir Henry was anxious for the Sharif to join the war as soon as possible. 13,300 British soldiers with their commander, General Townshend, had surrendered to Turkish forces in Kut, Iraq on April 29, 1916.[28] Only weeks earlier, on January 9, 1916, after suffering more than 250,000 casualties, including some 46,000 dead, British and Allied forces had to be withdrawn after failing to take Gallipoli from the Turks in a strategy to keep open the sea route from Europe to Russia.[29]

Britain made Iraq a kingdom in 1921 under King Faisal (August 23, 1921–September 8, 1933), Sharif Hussein's son. It also made Jordan a

---

[27]Sharif Hussein was reliant on his son, Abdullah, in dealing with the British High Commission in Cairo.

[28]Al Jazeera, "Kut 1916: How the Ottomans Defeated the British Army," https://interactive. aljazeera.com/ajt/2016/kutul-amare/en/index.html

[29]History.com, "Battle of Gallipoli," https://www.history.com/topics/world-war-i/battle-of-gallipoli

kingdom in 1921 under King Abdullah (April 1, 1921–July 20, 1951), another son of Sharif Hussein. However, Britain helped Abdulaziz al-Saud oust Sharif Hussein from Mecca in 1924. Al-Saud created Saudi Arabia in 1932. France divided Syria into five semi-autonomous regions.

The 1948 Arab/Israeli War: The second event that engendered a rise in Arab nationalism in the Levant was the founding of Israel in 1948. This event created hundreds of thousands of Palestinian refugees and led to the defeat of the Arabs in their first war against the new state, and in every subsequent confrontation. Before the Syrian revolution erupted in March 2011, 500,000 Palestinian refugees lived in Syria. The confrontations with Israel humiliated and frustrated the Arab masses, particularly those in the Arab republics near or bordering Israel. The fear grew, that if the Zionist dream of all Jews in the world migrating to Palestine were to materialize, Israel would inevitably have to expand into the Arab lands between the Nile River in Egypt and the Euphrates river deep in Syria, in accordance with Genesis 15:18 of the Old Testament.[30] Arabs see the two parallel blue lines across Israel's national flag as representations of the Nile and Euphrates rivers. Further, apocalyptic calls for Israeli hegemony by influential US Christian fundamentalist evangelicals, who fantasize about a second coming of Christ, compound Arab fears.

The turning point for Arab officers was the 1948 war. They blamed civilian politicians for losing the war. Syria's army in 1948 was comprised of only 2,500 soldiers, reduced from 7,500 men two years earlier when Syria obtained its independence from the French mandate on April 17, 1946.[31] The reduction in force was for domestic reasons. Syrian troops went into battle in 1948 with small amounts of ammunition. The officers felt that corruption, profiteering, and mismanagement rose to the level of criminal negligence, and saw themselves as the sole champions of the country's welfare, on guard against the enemy on the frontier, and also against the incompetence, or perhaps treachery, of the politicians at home.[32]

The 1948 defeat led to the assassination of King Abdullah of Jordan on July 20, 1951 at the gateway of the al-Aqsa Mosque. Three days earlier, on July 17, 1951, Lebanese politician Riyad al-Solh, prime minister from

---

[30] *The Lord made a covenant with Abraham, saying, unto thy seed have I given this land, from the river of Egypt unto the great river, the river Euphrates.*

[31] Philip Khoury, *Syria and the French Mandate: The Politics of Arab Nationalism, 1920–1945,* (Princeton University Press, 1987), P. 629.

[32] Patrick Seale, *The Struggle for Syria.* P. 33.

1943 to 1945, and again from 1946 to 1951, was assassinated in Amman, Jordan.

The 1948 defeat was among the main events that led to the series of military coups in Syria, Egypt and Iraq in 1949 and in the 1950s. Army leaders used the national mantra of "avenging 1948" to legitimize the seizure of power. They also adopted a posture of rhetorical attack on colonialism, imperialism, and Western powers for their unlimited support of Israel.

The Change in Syria's Power Structure in the Twentieth Century: For centuries, Syria's wealthy urban families and notables enjoyed a privileged position under the highly stratified society of Ottoman rule (1517–1918). The French mandate (1920–1946) changed all that. Syria's urban elite wanted to govern an independent Syria after the defeat of the Ottoman Empire in the First World War. For this reason, they supported the Arab Revolt. However, France and Britain had secretly agreed in the 1916 Sykes-Picot Agreement to govern Iraq and natural Syria, which includes today's Syria, Lebanon, Palestine, and Jordan. So, Syria's embittered urban elite led the nationalist resistance against French rule, driving France to rely on Syria's ethnic and religious minorities. The French recruited infantry and cavalry units composed exclusively of Alawites, Christians, Circassians, Druze, Isma'ilis, and Kurds.[33] France divided Syria into five semi-autonomous regions—Aleppo, Alexandretta (France transferred it to Turkey on July 13, 1939), Damascus, Druze Mountain, and Latakia.

After the nationalists forced France out of Syria in 1946, Damascus' early governments were mainly composed of the urban notables. The new leaders resented a Syrian army composed of ethnic and religious minorities, left behind by the French. Between 1946 and 1948, they reduced the size of the army from 7,500 men to 2,500 men.[34] Army commanders reciprocated the resentment. The army became politicized, leading to the military coups that followed. During the next fifteen years, young Alawites, most of whom could not afford a university education, sought careers in the military. The military academies offered free education and board.

Serious change in Syria's power pyramid was started in earnest during the union between Egypt and Syria (February 1, 1958–September 28, 1961) under the presidency of Gamal Abdul Nasser. During this relatively

---

[33]Philip Khoury, *Syria and the French Mandate*. P. 81.
[34]Ibid, P. 629.

short period of time, the Nasser government pursued a socialist agenda that destroyed the base of the centuries-old power structure in Syria (and Egypt as well). In 1958, Nasser nationalized factories and promulgated the Land Reform Act, which redistributed/expropriated feudalists' land, ostensibly, to improve the living conditions of non-farm workers and the peasantry after centuries of neglect by the ruling elites of feudalists, capitalists, and urban notables of the Ottoman era.

The leaders of the 1963 military coup maintained Nasser's land reform and industrial nationalization policies. The new strategies were self-serving. They made the sons and relatives of the new ruling military and intelligence officers and Ba'th Party mangers wealthy.

The Regime's Power Pyramid

The Assad regime's power pyramid is composed of four layers. At the top is the Assad family, followed by the armed forces, Arab Ba'ath Socialist Party, and peasants and farmers.

The Power Pyramid—The Assad Family: On March 8, 1963, Hafiz Assad, at that time, a 33-year old decommissioned air-force Captain, joined two other Alawite decommissioned officers, Muhammad Umran and Salah Jdeid, and three active-duty pro-Egypt's President Nasser Colonels, Rashid Quttaini, Muhammad al-Sufi, and Ziad al-Hariri, in a military putsch that deposed Syria's democratically elected parliament, president, and coalition cabinet.

On that day, legitimate representative governance in Syria was extinguished. President Nazim al-Qudsi was arrested and kept in the hospital of the infamous Mazzeh Prison in Damascus for seven months before he was released in late November 1963. In mid-December 1963, the coup leadership allowed Dr. Qudsi to leave Syria. He left for Beirut, Lebanon, never to return to Syria again. He died in Amman, Jordan on February 6, 1998.[35]

By 1970, following bloody confrontations among the 1963 coup organizers that eliminated the Nasserite elements, Hafiz Assad managed to eliminate the Ba'th Party's founding fathers and its national leadership, and his own Alawite army comrades. Most prominent among his targets was fellow Alawite, Salah Jdeid. Between 1966 and 1970, Jdeid was Syria's

---

[35]Source: President Qudsi's son, Faisal.

strongman. Upon seizing power in 1970, Assad jailed Jdeid in the notorious Mazzeh Prison in Damascus without trial.[36] He kept him there until shortly before his death in 1993. Umran was assassinated in 1972 during exile in Lebanon under mysterious circumstances, rumored to have been accomplished at the instigation of Hafiz' brother, Rif'at.[37]

Hafiz Assad consolidated his authority in March 1971. He became president in an uncontested, farcical referendum with near 100% of the votes cast in his favor. Four more referendum theatrics of near 100% approvals of the votes cast made Assad president until his death in 2000. To allow Hafiz's 34-year old son, Bashar, to inherit the throne, a constitutional amendment to lower the minimum age eligibility from forty to 34 years was forced upon the rubber-stamp parliament by Assad's army surrogates. The son, true to the father's legacy, organized an uncontested referendum that made him president with, again, near 100% approval of the votes cast. A repeat referendum and a contrived election with full marks are the son's claim to legitimacy. Realistically, the father and the son may count on around a third of Syria's eligible votes, a far cry from those fabricated embarrassing performances.[38]

An obsession with referendums and near 100% approvals must be a sign of personality disorder. Today, after seven years of revolution, two million dead and injured, two million homes destroyed, and two thirds of the 20 million-population displaced internally and in refugee camps in Jordan, Lebanon, and Turkey, Assad could count on around 20% of the votes, if un-rigged. March 8, 1963, started a process of failures that culminated fifty-years later in the destruction of much of what was once a rather well-to-do country.

The Assad family is small. Hafiz Assad had five brothers and five children. Hafiz was not well-educated. He had a high school degree (1951), followed in 1952 by three years at the Homs military academy and the air force academy in Aleppo. He spent less than a year of pilot training (1958/1959) in the former Soviet Union. Aside from technical and basic Russian, he spoke no foreign languages and rarely travelled out of Syria. Hafiz was reckless. He was punished by an air-force inquiry panel because he overshot the Nayrab Airbase runway near Aleppo and crash-landed

---

[36]Patrick Seale, *Assad, the Struggle for the Middle East*, P. 164.

[37]Ibid, P. 184.

[38]90% of the 10% Alawi population (9%) + 2/3 of the other 15% of minorities (10%) + 20% of the 75% Sunni population (15%) = 34%.

his Mercer Airplane on its belly (late 1956). After admitting that before taking off, "he knew his brakes were defective, he was reprimanded, fined and given a suspended jail sentence."[39]

His eldest son, Basil, died in a car accident in 1994. Another son, Majd, died in 2009. Bushra, the first child and the only daughter, left Syria with her five children to Dubai[40] shortly after her husband, Asef Shawqat, deputy defense minister, was killed in a bomb blast in Damascus on July 18, 2012.[41] In defiance of her family, Bushra married Asef in 1995, after her brother Basil's death (1994).[42] Basil had jailed Asef in 1993 to keep him away from his sister, according to security sources and to US diplomatic cables published by Wikileaks.[43]

Maher, the youngest surviving of Hafiz's children, has a reputation for being violent and emotionally unstable.[44] Diplomats say Maher shot and wounded Asef, his brother-in-law, in 1999.[45] As commander of the Republican Guard and the army's best-equipped division, his cruelty is unmatched. In 2005, Maher and Shawkat were both mentioned in a preliminary report by UN investigators as one of the people who might have planned the assassination of the former Lebanese Prime Minister, Rafiq Hariri.

Within a few months after the 1963 coup, Hafiz and coup comrades orchestrated a wholesale retirement of the majority of Sunni officers. Even cadets in military schools were dismissed and replaced by Alawite high school graduates. Since that time, trusted Alawite officers known for their loyalty to the Assad family, fill the ranks of the armed forces and the

---

[39]Ibid, PP. 52 & 53.

[40]"Assad's Sister Defect Amid 'Disputes' Between Ruling Alawites," *Al-Arabiya*, (September 18, 2012). https://english.alarabiya.net/articles/2012/09/18/238771.html

[41]The blast hit the headquarters of the National Security Bureau during a meeting of cabinet ministers and senior security officials. John Hall, "Brother-in-law of Syrian President Killed in Bomb Blast as Rebels Close in on Assad Regime," *The Independent*, (July 18, 2012). http://www.independent.co.uk/news/world/middle-east/brother-in-law-of-syrian-president-killed-in-bomb-blast-as-rebels-close-in-on-assad-regime-7956389.html

[42]"Assad Loses Assef Shawkat, Syria's Shadowy Enforcer," *Al-Arabia*, (July 18, 2012). https://english.alarabiya.net/articles/2012/07/18/227058.html

[43]Abdulrahman al-Rashed, "Visit of Assad's sister to Dubai," *Arab News*, (September 26, 2012). http://www.arabnews.com/columns/visit-assad's-sister-dubai

[44]"Bashar al-Assad's Inner Circle," *BBC*, (June 30, 2012). http://www.bbc.co.uk/news/world-middle-east-13216195

[45]Nour Ali and Esther Addley, "At Home with the Assads: Syria's Ruthless Ruling Family," *The Guardian*, (October 11, 2011). https://www.theguardian.com/world/2011/oct/11/assads-syria-ruling-family

security machine. Every important army unit in and around the capital Damascus is commanded and manned by trusted Alawite officers. No Sunni is in a sensitive security post. Sunnis can be generals, but not in the tanks brigades, artillery regiments or the intelligence units in or near the capital city. Sunnis may hold top administrative positions, from the prime minister to cabinet ministers, but not in the security units.

Hafiz's formula for the art of survival is adhered to by his son. Paraphrasing French diplomat Alain Chouet, Van Dam wrote,

> President al-Assad has since 1970 surrounded himself with Alawi military loyalists originating in particular from three specific Alawi family or tribal circles, one closer to the president than the others. Each circle is, in turn, composed of three different elements in such a manner that specific subtle tribal-confederational balances and rivalries are carefully maintained and respected. On those rare occasions when a member of one of the circles of Alawi intimi was substituted by someone else, replacements were, according to Chouet, effected in such a way that the succeeding person had a family or tribal-confederational profile as close and as similar as possible to that of his predecessor.[46]

The cult of personality around the Assad dynasty is everywhere; huge portraits of father and son are at major city intersections and public buildings. Projects are named after the two men—Lake Assad, Assad City, Assad Library, Assad Stadium, Assad this, Assad that ... The government-controlled media exalts the president's every action as a great achievement for Syria, for the Arab cause, even for the world. Zealots preach that Assad is inspired by God. Criticism of the regime means jail, torture, or death. Even refraining from praising Assad's every policy could lead to loss of a job and harassment by the regime's security torturers.

The President and His Senior Commanders: Hafiz Assad was deceitful, cruel, and devoid of empathy. A master manipulator, he played one sycophant commander against the other. He struck a balance among rival

---

[46]Nikolas Van Dam, *The Struggle for Power in Syria. Politics and Society under Assad and the Ba'th Party* (I. B. Taurus, London, 1997), P. 124.

officers, and among competing security and intelligence services, creating a situation where he alone would hold the strings.

Hafiz Assad's brutality was legendary. It served as a reminder of what would be in store for those who provoked his ire. His younger brother Rif'at, commander of the notorious Defense Companies and Vice President learned this the hard way. He tried to overthrow Hafiz from power in 1984 while the president was sick. Rif'at was defeated and exiled, living between Paris, London, and Marbella.[47] Rif'at was purportedly spared Hafiz's viciousness by their mother, Na'isa.

Having no legitimacy or support among most of the 75% Sunni majority, the ruling minority of Alawite officers must cling together. The relationship between the president and his military commanders is one of mutual dependency. The allegiance of the commanders to the president is personal and total, based on fear, uncertainty, and the promise of riches. The officers protect the regime in return for wealth and power. The president has no choice but to tolerate the sleaze of his protectors.

Characteristics of Assad's Rule—Corruption: The Assad regime is dictatorial, sectarian, and corrupt. Lacking in majority support, a narrow ruling group consisting of religious minorities plus Sunni merchant families is cobbled together. The modest salaries of the military and security commanders are boosted, by allowing the officers enrich themselves illegally. For a business to flourish, the owner must join hands with some middle to high-ranking Alawite officer, preferably, in the intelligence services. Ordinary citizens, too, must bribe their way up and down the bureaucracy for government services, be it expediting the issuance of a passport, or avoiding a traffic ticket.

The president is the patron-in-chief. Patron-client associations cascade down through all ranks of society. Among the chief offenders was Hafiz Assad's brother Rif'at. From poverty he accumulated enormous wealth in just a few years. In June 2013, it was reported that he sold a 12,000-foot apartment in the most exclusive part of Paris for 70 million euros ($100 million), "after it had been on the market for 100 million Euros, apparently fearing it could be seized by police."[48] An investigation into

---

[47] Claude Salhani, "Machiavellian Levantine Politics," *United Press International (UPI)*, (June 30, 2000). http://www.upi.com/Archives/2000/06/30/Machiavellian-Levantine-politics/1662962337600/

[48] Henry Samuel, "Bashar al-Assad's Uncle Sells Paris Mansion for 70 Million Euros," *The Telegraph*, (June 25, 2013). http://www.telegraph.co.uk/news/worldnews/europe/france/10141461/Bashar-al-Assads-uncle-sells-Paris-mansion-for-70-million-euros.html

Rif'at's finances was triggered in France in 2013 accusing him of stealing his fortune from Syria.[49] He was placed under formal investigation on June 9, 2016, in an indication that the evidence against him is building and that he is likely to face charges.[50]

On April 4, 2017, it was reported that police in Spain raided 15 properties belonging to Rif'at, and some of his children as part of a money laundering investigation. Spanish police are investigating six of his sons, some of his daughters-in-law and two of his four wives. The judge overseeing the case blocked 16 bank accounts held by individuals suspected of being connected to Rif'at and also deposit accounts belonging to 76 companies. The judge ordered the seizure of more than 500 properties worth £590 million (over $800 million) owned by Rif'at and his relatives, a court statement said. Investigators believe that, more than £250 million ($350 million) in Syrian public funds, has been siphoned into these accounts by Rif'at and his family.[51]

Rami Makhlouf, a cousin of Bashar Assad, is the supreme crooked wheeler-dealer. Foreign companies cannot do business in Syria without his consent—in return for commissions and kickbacks. In 2008, the US Treasury Department banned US firms and individuals from doing business with Makhlouf, and froze his US-based assets. The US accused him of, "corrupt behavior, disadvantaging innocent Syrian businessmen and entrenching a regime that pursues oppressive and destabilizing politics. Makhlouf has manipulated the Syrian judicial system and used Syrian intelligence officials to intimidate his business rivals. He employed these techniques when trying to acquire exclusive licenses to represent foreign companies in Syria and to obtain contract awards."[52]

There are hundreds of Rif'ats and Makhloufs in Syria. The disease is a consequence of a minority, sectarian, totalitarian regime in need of broadening its support-base to survive by promising self-enrichment to

---

[49]Josie Ensor and David Chazan, "Syrian President's Uncle Under Investigation for Corruption and Money Laundering in France," *The telegraph*, (June 28, 2016). http://www.telegraph.co.uk/news/2016/06/28/syrian-presidents-uncle-charged-with-corruption-and-money-launde/

[50]Ibid.

[51]James Badcock, "Spanish Police Seize Property Worth £590m from Assad Family," *The Telegraph*, (April 4, 2017). http://www.telegraph.co.uk/news/2017/04/04/spanish-police-seize-property-worth590m-assad-family/

[52]"Bashar al-Assad's Inner Circle," *BBC*, (July 30, 2012).

its supporters through illicit means.[53] Just before the 2011 revolution, the World Bank's 2010 study of Worldwide Governance Indicators, Control of Corruption, shows Syria's poor score. Of the 213 countries in the study, Syria ranked 189, among the lowest 12% along with Afghanistan, Angola, Chad, Haiti, Somalia, and Zimbabwe.[54]

Huge disparities in wealth, income, and political power between the ruling group in Damascus and Aleppo and the rest of the country, created a stratified society akin to apartheid. On March 18, 2011, the pressure cooker exploded in the Southern city of Dar'a (see blow: *The Syrian Revolution*).

Dubious Oil Accounting: Corruption also manifests itself also in bad accounting for oil revenues and spending. Reporting by Syria's Central Bureau of Statistics (CBS) of the country's oil revenues in the national budget and balance of payments is confusing, inconsistent, and ambiguous. The IMF report finds that "Government finance statistics (GFS) suffer from major deficiencies with respect to definitions, coverage, classification, methodology, accuracy, reliability, and timeliness that generate severe inconsistencies with monetary and balance of payments statistics."[55] In other words, government budget data left billions of dollars unaccounted for, as will be shown next.

Syria's Statistical Abstract reveals (Table 5/5) that 21,425,000 cubic meters of oil per day were extracted on average during 2007, 2008, and 2009, equivalent to 152 million barrels per annum (at 7.15 barrels = 1 m3), or around 420,000 barrels per day. Of this volume, the Banyas refinery (capacity of 133,000 bbl./day) and Homs refinery (capacity of 107,000 bbl./day) use a total of some 240,000 bbl./day. Assuming full capacity refining, Syria's oil exports must have been 180,000 bbl./day.[56]

The average price for crude oil between 2007 and 2009 was US$75/bbl. Assuming that Syria's share after royalties to foreign companies and

---

[53]Corruption manifests itself in a non-monetary form, too. In the Damascus region, 87% of water wells in 1998 were non-licensed, a far higher ratio of illegal wells than in the rest of the country of 38%. The concentration of senior military officers, ruling party functionaries in the capital, many of whom own farms for business and recreation, may explain the variance. Illegal water extraction of that period contributed to ruining the Damascus Barada Basin aquifer. Elie Elhadj, *Experiments in Achieving Water and Food Self-Sufficiency in the Middle East*, (Dissertation.com, 2006) P. 155. http://www.dissertation.com/book.php?book=1581122985&method=ISBN

[54]The World Bank, "Worldwide Government Indicators," (2016). http://info.worldbank.org/governance/wgi/index.aspx#home

[55]The International Monetary Fund, *Country Report on Syria, No. 10/86*, (March 2010), P. 30.

[56]420,000 bbl./day—240,000 bbl./day = 180,000 bbl./day.

operating expenses was $50/bbl., the dollar revenues from oil exports should have been in the region of US$3.28 billion for each of the three years,[57] or S£164 billion.[58] But, the national budget (Table 4/14) shows Government Royalty of Joint Oil Fields to be an average of S£43.6 billion for each of the three years, not S£164 billion. The question is, what happened to the annual difference of S£120 billion or, $2.4 billion?[59] Additionally, there is no mention of revenues from the 240,000 bbl./day crude oil deliveries to the Banyas and Homs refineries. Certainly, the refineries do not get their crude oil free of charge. At a discount of, say, 30%, the government budget should show the Syrian Lira equivalent of US$3.07.[60] Such an amount is nowhere to be found. Government budget data leave the Syrian Lira equivalent of US$5.47 billion ($2.4 +$3.07) unaccounted for.

It is an open secret in Syria that the oil account (revenues and spending) was under the exclusive personal authority of Hafiz Assad and his son ever since the Assads came to power. It is also an open secret that anyone questioning any aspect of the oil account risks arrest or even charges of treason.

Characteristics of Assad Rule—Police State: Syria's president enjoys absolute powers, enshrined in the constitution of 1973 during Hafiz Assad's tenure and in the 2012 constitution of his son's regime. He appoints his deputies (Article 91.1), the prime minister, the government ministers and their deputies (Article 97), civilian and military employees. He also has the authority to end their services (Article 106). He promulgates laws that the parliament has passed, but he has the right to veto any law. Parliament can, theoretically, overrule his veto by a two-thirds majority (Article 100). The president, however, may then dissolve the assembly (Article 111). When parliament is not in session, or in cases of extreme need or when national interest so demands, the president can exercise legislative powers by himself. Amending the constitution requires a three-fourths majority in parliament and the approval of the president (Article 150.4).

Although Syria's constitution contains all of the clauses and appearances of a modern democratic document, it is simply a yellow sheet of paper of little value. Emergency Law, imposed since 1963, nullifies every

---

[57]180,000 bbl./day x 365 days x $50/bbl. = $3.28 billion per year.

[58]*$3.28 billion x S£50* (at the exchange rate of S£50 to $1—the rate was S£47 in 2009, S£47 in 2008, S£50 in 2007) = S£164 billion.

[59]S£120 billion /S£50 = $2.4 billion.

[60]240,000 bbl./day x 365 days x $50 x 70% = $3.07 billion.

constitutional protection, whether it is Article 33.1, which guarantees personal freedoms, dignity, and security of citizens, or Article 42.2, which establishes the right of every citizen to freely and openly express their views in writing or orally or by all other means of expression, or Article 43, in which the state guarantees freedom of the press, printing and publishing, or Article 53.2, which stipulates that no one may be tortured or treated in a humiliating manner.

There is no separation of governmental powers. The parliament and the judiciary are rubber stamp entities. Parliamentary committees cannot question government policy on security, defense, military budget, oil accounting, foreign affairs, corruption, or sectarianism in officialdom. The prospect of the regime's security dungeons terrifies the most hardened of parliamentarians and the most fearless of judges. Anyone under the slightest suspicion may end his life at the hands of sadistic torturers. A steady diet of exaggerated and invented victories provides psychic rewards to regime's operatives.

How Did the Assads Justify Fifty Years of Emergency Law? In a word, Israel. Like exploitation of Sunni Islam, the Assad regime has turned the conflict with Israel into an instrument to control the country.[61] The confrontation with Israel culminated in the disastrous defeats of 1967 and 1973 wars. Israel's occupation of the Golan Heights since 1967 turned the Arab-Israeli conflict into a core issue in Syria's domestic and foreign politics. To stay in power, the regime promotes the confrontation as Syria's and the Arab world's supreme challenge. The two Assads claim that they are the leading defender of Palestinian rights, Arab honor, and Syria's sovereignty. The conflict with Israel is constructed to be their benchmark against which patriotism is measured. To the regime, the Arab-Israeli conflict is a magic wand that vanquishes all domestic opposition.

The conflict with Israel is the regime's excuse to eliminate its enemies. Opponents are thrown in prison on charges like, "treason in the middle of the battle" or "weakening the national spirit." A daily diet of nationalistic rhetoric helps rally the masses behind the regime's agenda of the moment. The long list of restrictions in the name of the confrontation with Israel is

---

[61]Elie Elhadj, "Why Syria's Regime is Likely to Survive," *Middle East Review of International Affairs (MERIA) Journal*, (August 21, 2011). http://www.rubincenter.org/2011/08/why-syria's-regime-is-likely-to-survive/

in reality a means to secure the regime and maintain the privileged status and wealth of the ruling group and their relatives. Free press is banned. Advocates of reform are imprisoned without trial.

The conflict justifies allocating a substantial proportion of the country's scarce resources to a huge standing army to protect the regime, at the expense of desperately needed investment in infrastructure, health, and education. As for military spending, not even the parliament can ask questions. The "impending" confrontation with Israel justifies lack of transparency or accountability in state finances. It also means prison and torture for whoever questions, let alone criticizes, any of the regime's sanctioned national discourse propaganda.

Emergency Law turned life in Syria into a living hell the likes of which has rarely existed in history. Finally, on Tuesday March 18, 2011, the pressure cooker exploded. The barrier of fear was broken. Fifty years of police state cruelty and injustices exploded into a revolution. The revolution was not sparked by Israel, the CIA, global imperialism, global warming, the drought, or migration from rural communities to urban centers (see below: *Was the March 2011 Revolution Triggered by Drought and Migration?*). To deal with the demonstrations, unarmed protestors were met with live ammunition and barrel bombs.

Torture Dungeons: Multiple security services operate independently of one another: General Intelligence, Political Intelligence, Military Intelligence, Air Force Intelligence, and the National Security Bureau of the Ba'th Party. They all report directly to the president. They overlap without coordination, and operate outside the law. They watch every move and encourage people to spy on everyone, even their own families. Stories abound of political opponents being arrested, never to be heard from again. Innocent family members of dissidents are routinely taken away as hostages. Female relatives are tortured, often raped on camera to force the dissident into submission. Such practices in Syria's conservative society are absolutely terrifying.

The cruelty of the Assad regime is legendary. Amnesty International documented 38 types of torture used against detainees; including, electrical shocks, pulling out fingernails, burning genitalia, forcing objects into the rectum, beatings while the victim is suspended from the ceiling and on the soles of the feet, alternately dousing victims with freezing water and beating them in extremely cold rooms, hyperextending the spine, bending the body into the frame of a wheel and whipping exposed body parts, using a backward-bending chair to asphyxiate the victim or fracture the spine, and stripping prisoners naked for public view.[62]

Massacres in the Palmyra Prison and the City of Hama: On June 26, 1980, Hafiz Assad escaped an assassination attempt in Damascus. The next day, two units of Hafiz's brother Rif'at's Defense Companies committed a massacre in the Palmyra Prison. They destroyed 500 helpless inmates with machine gun fire and hand grenades. Patrick Seale described the massacre: "In Palmyra, deep in the desert, where Muslim Brothers were being held ... about sixty men were driven to the desert prison, split up into six or seven squads and let loose on the prison dormitories with orders to kill anyone inside. Some five hundred inmates died in cells echoing to the fearful din of automatic weapons, exploding grenades, and dying shrieks of 'God is great.'"[63]

The brutality with which the regime dealt with its enemies in the defenseless city of Hama in western Syria in February 1982 was beastly. A three-week orgy of bombardment and destruction from the air and the ground demolished this city of around 200,000 residents. Patrick Seale wrote of the Hama carnage: "The battle for Hama raged for three grim weeks ... Hama was besieged by some 12,000 men ... Many civilians were slaughtered in the prolonged mopping up, whole districts razed ... Scores of mosques, churches and other ancient monuments were damaged and looted ... Just how many lives were lost in Hama must remain a matter of conjecture, with government sympathizers estimating a mere 3,000 and critics as many as 20,000 and more."[64] Rif'at Defense Companies destroyed three-quarters of the city and an estimated 20,000 were killed, but Rif'at boasted that the death toll was actually 36,000.[65]

Machiavellianism is Alive and Well in Damascus: The Assads' regime is built on three pillars: exploitation of Sunni Islam, brutal sectarian security forces, and rhetorical theatrics against Israel. The regime destroyed Syria's democratic institutions. In 1963, Syria had a robust political life conducted by ten political parties of different philosophies, ethnic and religious

---

[62]GlobalSecurity.org, "Syria Intelligence & Security Agencies." https://www.globalsecurity.org/intell/world/syria/index.html

[63]Patrick Seale, *Assad, the Struggle for the Middle East*, P. 329.

[64]Ibid, PP. 333–334.

[65]Adrian Bloomfield, "Maher Assad: Profile of the Syrian President's Feared Brother," *The Telegraph*, (June 9, 2011). http://www.telegraph.co.uk/news/worldnews/middleeast/syria/8565025/Maher-Assad-profile-of-the-Syrian-presidents-feared-brother.html

compositions, agendas and platforms.[66] The parties promoted their programs freely. They shared power democratically in a coalition government. Immediately following the 1963 coup, the political parties were dissolved, their leaders scattered in and outside the country, and democracy died.

The pre-1963 democratic structures were replaced by the Ba'th Party. The Ba'th Party, is a huge mass of hangers-on. The president is the secretary-general of the Party. As if to convey the image of a multi-party system, five incarnations of the Ba'th Party were created. Together, the six parties were cobbled together under an umbrella called the National Progressive Front. In the May 2012 parliament, the Front was composed of the Ba'th Party, the Socialist Unionists, Communist Party of Syria (2 factions), National Vow Movement, and Arab Socialist Union. The security services watch every move of every parliamentarian for the slightest deviation from the regime's official line.

The Assad regime decapitated Syria's democratic political organizations. The heavy hand of the intelligence services eliminated regime opponents. Most anti-regime activists were killed or became refugees in foreign countries. Stories of torture by the captives who were lucky enough to be released put the fear of God in would be dissenters. Fifty years of a police state bred a culture of fear and distrust.

Parents became fearful of their own school-aged children who might inadvertently divulge anti-Assad conversations heard at home. Friends would not trust each other for fear that a cynical ear might be listening. Thus, when the March 18, 2011 revolution erupted, there was no organized opposition, no political parties or non-regime community leaders in place to lead the uprising. According to Royal United Services Institute for Defense and Security Studies (RUSI), approximately 1,500 different rebel groups appeared on the scene, showing there was no centralized movement.[67]

Assad's troops fired live ammunition at unarmed demonstrators.[68] Fearing that killing unarmed civilians might raise the ire of Western public opinion, Assad Islamicized the confrontation by claiming that his troops were killing the likes of al-Qaeda, al-Nusra, and the so-called Islamic State

---

[66]Peoples Party, National Party, Arab Socialist Ba'th Party, Muslim Brotherhood, Arab Liberation Movement, Socialist Cooperation Party, Syrian Social Nationalist Party, Syrian Communist Party, Kurdistan Democratic Party, Assyrian Democratic Organization.

[67]Royal United Services Institute for Defence and Security Studies (RUSI), *Understanding Iran's Role in the Syrian Conflict*, (August 2016), P. 33.

[68]Richard Spencer, "Four Jihadists, One Prison: All Released by Assad and All Now Dead," *The Telegraph*, (May 11, 2016). http://s.telegraph.co.uk/graphics/projects/isis-jihad-syria-assad-islamic/

jihadists in a cynical move to elicit cheers and aid from both the East and the West. In a grand act of blackmail legitimacy, Assad released more than 2,000 hardened jihadists from jail during the second half of 2011. He deliberately spread Islamist warlords throughout Syria.

The Power Pyramid—Armed Forces: Since independence from the French mandate in 1946, Syria's armed forces have taken the country from disaster to catastrophe. Nonetheless, the military is exalted in the government sanctioned national discourse as the defender against the Zionist threat. However, the armed forces have never won a battle against Israel. For decades, Israel could bomb Syria at will without a whimper from the regime, save for empty rhetoric.

The French mandate started in 1920, following the defeat of the Ottoman Empire in the First World War. Between 1946 and 1954, Syria experienced four military coups, three of which were in 1949. In February 1958, Syria and Egypt were united. They formed the United Arab Republic under the presidency of Gamal Abdul Nasser. A Damascus military coup on September 28, 1961 separated the two countries. Another military coup in March 1963 brought the Ba'th Party to power. By 1970, at the end of a vicious internal power struggle, Hafiz Assad succeeded in eliminating his compatriots from the 1963 coup. In all, between 1946 and 1970, the Syrian army carried out seven coups d'états, eight if the union with Egypt is included. It was the military generals who forced the country's civilian politicians into the union with Egypt. The eight successful coups were in addition to many failed coup attempts.

During the first twenty-four years after independence (1946–1970), the Syrian army was an instrument of turmoil. During those years, the armed forces were composed of officers from disparate ethnic and religious backgrounds and more than half a dozen rival political parties. Since 1970, however, all commanding and sensitive positions in the security apparatus and the armed brigades around Damascus were composed entirely of Alawite officers.

The army has kept the Assads in power for the past fifty years. It protected them from rival Alawite officers and Sunni popular opposition. In ordering the massacre of 500 helpless inmates in the Palmyra Prison in 1980, and in demolishing most of the City of Hama in 1982, Hafiz Assad proved himself to be a tyrant prepared to destroy Syria in order to stay in power. In the event, the task of burning and demolishing most of the country was left to his son. Since the start of the March 2011 revolution, a dilapidated air force using primitive barrel bombs pulverized most of Syria, killing and injuring two million people, possibly more, and displacing 60% of the population internally and into refugee camps in neighboring countries.

Yet, the confrontations of the father and the son with Israel were humiliatingly different. Despite extreme rhetoric and bravado, both men suffered one crushing defeat after another. When Hafiz was defense minister, he lost the Golan Heights in the 1967 Six-Day-War. When he was president, his performance in the 1973 war over the Golan Heights was no better. Subsequent armed confrontations with Israel were disastrous. On June 9, 1982, twenty-nine Syrian MIGs were shot down over Lebanon.[69] The next day, another thirty-five planes were lost.[70] In addition to the loss of the pilots, the cost of this confrontation may be estimated at more than one billion dollars, a fortune for a country like Syria that had a gross national product of $10 billion that year.

During the son's reign, Israel attacked the suspected al-Kibar nuclear facility in the eastern Deir Ezzor region on September 5–6, 2007, destroying the site totally.[71] The son's reaction was silence save for the usual empty posturing. Since the start of the revolution in March 2011 and February 10, 2018, Israel launched at least 100 strikes in Syria.[72] During the February 10, 2018 raid, one of the eight attacking planes was shot down, the first such loss for Israel in decades.[73]

The Cost of Syria's Armed Forces: Syria's armed forces increased from 2,500 men in 1948,[74] to 61,000 in 1967,[75] to 100,000 in 1970,[76] and to 408,000 in 1990.[77] In 1997, however, the number dropped to 320,000

[69]Ibid, Patrick Seale, *Assad, the Struggle for the Middle East* P. 381.

[70]Ibid, P. 382.

[71]Eleven years after the attack, on March 21, 2018, Israel admitted that eight of its jets destroyed the close-to-be-completed nuclear site. The admission came after Israeli military censors lifted an order banning officials from discussing the operation: "Israel admits striking suspected Syrian nuclear reactor in 2007," *BBC*, (March 21, 2018). http://www.bbc.co.uk/news/world-middle-east-43481803

[72]"Syria war: Israel 'strikes Damascus military complex'," *BBC*, (February 7, 2018). http://www.bbc.co.uk/news/world-middle-east-42973662

[73]Maayan Lubell and Lisa Barrington, "Israeli Jet Shot Down after Bombing Iranian Site in Syria," *Reuters*, (February 10, 2018). https://www.reuters.com/article/us-israel-iran/israeli-jet-shot-down-after-bombing-iranian-site-in-syria-idUSKBN1FU07L

[74]Philip Khoury, *Syria and the French Mandate*, P. 80.

[75]US Statistical Abstract of the Census Bureau (1968), *Comparative International Statistics, Personnel in the Armed Forces*, Table No. 1256, P. 844, https://www2.census.gov/library/publications/1968/compendia/statab/89ed/1968-13.pdf

[76]Volker Perthes, *The Political Economy of Syria under Assad* (I. B. Tauris, London, 1997), P. 141.

[77]US Statistical Abstract of the Census Bureau (2000), *Comparative International Statistics, Military Expenditures and Armed Forces Personnel by Country: 1990 and 1997*, Table No. 1412, P. 856. https://www2.census.gov/library/publications/2001/compendia/statab/120ed/tables/sec30.pdf

men.[78] In 2005, the number was 296,000.[79] It is reasonable to think that when the revolution erupted in March 2011, the armed forces were around 300,000. Seven years later, the strength of the military is probably a fraction of its pre-revolution level in numbers and effectiveness.

Syria's military impoverished the country. For decades, a large proportion of Syria's modest resources has been wasted on the army. Military finances are conducted independently from the rest of government ministries. Not even the central audit office, ministry of finance, nor parliament may question, let alone examine, army appropriations or spending. Between 2001 and 2011, Syria might have spent $25 billion:

Military Spending in Syria[80]

Year	2001	2002	2003	2004	2005	2006	2007	2008	2009	2010	2011
$ Billion	1.951	2.025	2.322	2.326	2.339	2.104	2.236	2.027	2.301	2.366	2.495
% GDP	5.5	5.4	6.2	5.5	5.0	4.4	4.1	3.6	4.0	4.1	N/A

Government statistics are notoriously unreliable. These figures represent, most probably, the military's operating budget only. Spending on arms purchases is anyone's guess. Between 1970 and 1990, an estimate put the amount at $28.5 billion.[81] After 1990, spending on arms is open to speculation. As discussed above, under *Dubious Oil Accounting*, government budgets left billions of dollars unaccounted for—more than five billion dollars in each of the three years under examination (2007, 2008, and 2009). Government budget figures in prior years must have followed the same pattern. There is little doubt that a part of the unreported billions must have been spent on the acquisition of weapons. The suspected al-Kibar nuclear project must have been funded from the unreported oil billions.

The Power Pyramid—Arab Baath Socialist Party: The Ba'th Party (meaning renaissance) was founded in 1947 by French-educated Syrian intellectuals Michel Aflaq, a Greek Orthodox, and Salah al-Din al-Bitar, a Sunni Muslim. In 1953, the Ba'th Party merged with the Arab Socialist

---

[78] Ibid.

[79] Anthony Cordesman, "The Middle East Military Balance: Definition, Regional Development, and Trends," *Center for Strategic and International Studies*, Washington D.C., (March 23, 2005), P. 12. https://csis-prod.s3.amazonaws.com/s3fs-public/legacy_files/files/media/csis/pubs/050323_memil-baldefine[1].pdf

[80] MilitaryBudget.org, http://militarybudget.org/syria/

[81] Volker Perthes, *The Political Economy of Syria under Assad*, P. 32.

Party of Akram al-Hourani to become the Arab Ba'th Socialist Party. Article 8 of Hafiz Assad's 1973 constitution enshrined the Ba'th Party at the heart of life in Syria, "The leading party in the society and the state is the Socialist Arab Baath Party. It leads a patriotic and progressive front seeking to unify the resources of the people's masses and place them at the service of the Arab nation's goals."

Under the two Assads, the Ba'th Party has become a supplemental tool of the security services to control Syrian society, just as Wahhabism is a cult to control Saudi society. A Quasi-military hierarchical structure under the direct authority of Hafiz Assad replaced the old collective leadership of the party in 1971. A decision by the first party conference after Hafiz monopolized power in 1970 declared that, "The leadership had realized … that the people … emphasize the necessity for a leader, rally around a leader, and consider comrade Hafiz al-Assad the leader they seek."[82] In his new role as secretary general of the Baath Party, Hafiz Assad was empowered to appoint members of the Ba'th Party's central committee.

In 1963, the Ba'th Party had a few hundred members. By 1981, 375,000 members had joined. By 2010, the number had reportedly risen to 1.2 million.[83] To put this figure in perspective, it represents around 20% of Syria's population between the ages of 25 and 54.[84] It also represents the majority of government civilian and military and security employees. The swift growth in membership is not surprising. Ba'thification of civil servants and military and security personnel was in high gear during those years. New job applicants had to join the Party if they were to stand a chance of securing employment. In a job market with limited opportunities, a government job is a coveted prize.

The Ba'th Party penetrates all walks of life. It serves as an extensive network of eyes and ears that supplements a brutal security machine. It organizes high school and university students, teachers, workers, peasants, government employees, and military personnel. Party membership includes all religious and ethnic affiliations. The party's propaganda machine turns the personality of the president into a cult. It praises his every move and word. It praises the regime's rhetoric and orchestrates the

---

[82]Volker Perthes, *The Political Economy of Syria under Assad*, P. 155.

[83]"Profile: Syria's ruling Baath Party," *BBC*, (July 9, 2012). http://www.bbc.co.uk/news/world-middle-east-18582755

[84]Central Intelligence Agency, "The World Fact Book, Syria." https://www.cia.gov/library/publications/the-world-factbook/geos/sy.html

national discourse. To the Assad regime, the Ba'th Party functionaries is what the Wahhabi ulama class is to the al-Saud regime.

The Assad regime relies on peoples' organizations for societal control. It mobilizes the citizenry under all kinds of organizations. There are unions for peasants, non-farm workers, women, teachers, artisans, and writers. For students, there are the Pioneers of the Ba'th (for primary schools), the Revolutionary Youth Organization (for preparatory and high schools), and the National Union of Students (for universities). There are professional organizations for lawyers, engineers, physicians, journalists, and others. These entities are hierarchical, with leaders appointed by the regime.

The Power Pyramid—Peasants and Farmers: For millennia, agriculture in Syria has supported large population centers and produced thriving civilizations along rivers and coastal areas. Of Syria's 185,000 sq. km, 25% is arable. Peasants and farmers are a major constituency. Until the start of the revolution in 2011, approximately one-half of the population lived in rural communities. In 2007, agriculture accounted for one-quarter of GDP. One-quarter of the labor force is engaged in farming, with another one-half of the manufacturing workforce dependent on agriculture for employment. Seven years after the revolution had started, with over five million refugees outside Syria, plus 6.3 million internally displaced, it is impossible to estimate who lives where anymore.[85]

Political Motives Behind Syria's Hydraulic Mission: Three political motives are behind the Assads' emphasis on agricultural development. The first was self-preservation. To destroy the power base of the age-old establishments of feudalists, capitalists, and urban notables, their agricultural land had to be redistributed, and industrial assets nationalized/confiscated. The second motive was pragmatism. The new leaders had to legitimate their seizure of power. The predominance of agriculture provided the opportunity to appeal to a major proportion of the population. The third motive was self-enrichment. As sons of farmers in the villages of the Alawite mountains, the officers who seized power quickly transformed the poverty-stricken towns and villages to modernity.[86]

---

[85]UNHCR, Syria Emergency, (accessed, November 6, 2017, http://www.unhcr.org/uk/syria-emergency.html

[86]Patrick Seale wrote, "In 1970, only 10% of households in the Latakia governorate had piped drinking water; fifteen years later, the figure was over 70% and roads had been built to every hamlet. Hundreds of upland villages were so expanded in an orgy of breeze-block building that scarcely a trace remained of the old rough-stone hamlets of al-Assad's youth." Patrick Seale, Assad, the Struggle for the Middle East, P. 454.

Water politics in Syria go back to the 1958 Land Reform Act, promulgated by President Nasser during the three-and-a-half-year union between Egypt and Syria (February 1, 1958–September 28, 1961). The Act changed the political and societal power structures. The Land Reform Act removed 3,000 wealthy families from the country's farmland. These were feudalists experienced in farming businesses. The Act replaced the old professional farm-owners with new peasant-owners who had little or no financial strength, management expertise, or marketing networks. The exhilaration of owning a piece of land quickly faded, and land ownership became a burden for most peasants. The government had to rush in with assistance ranging from subsidies on fuel and short-term loans for seeds, fertilizers, and machinery, to the construction of dams and reclamation of lands, especially around the new Tabqa Dam on the Euphrates river.

While it would seem sensible to insulate water issues from politics in an environment of water stress and high population growth, Damascus chose a political water strategy to chase the mirage of food self-sufficiency. It ushered the government into an expensive hydraulic mission.

The Hydraulic Mission: The Assad regime's irrigation agriculture cost billions of dollars. Over-extraction of groundwater has led to negative balances in five out of the country's seven basin, deteriorated water quality, and contributed to water shortages in most major urban centers.[87] A more sensible strategy would have left agriculture to rain-fed lands and focused instead on investing in low-water-using manufacturing industries for export to generate the needed foreign currency with which to import high-water using foodstuffs.

Beginning in 1960, the eight 5-year plans spent $20 billion on the agricultural sector (at the official foreign exchange rates of that period). Three-quarters of the investment was made between 1988 and 2000. However, the results were not brilliant: Of the half million hectares added during this period, the private sector developed 75% and the government contributed 25%, of which 90% was in the salt-affected and drainage-poor Euphrates Basin.

The Tabqa Dam on the Euphrates river failed to achieve even a fifth of its planned land reclamation targets twenty-seven years after its construction.

---

[87]This section is an abridgement of Chapter Six: *Syria's Government Investment in Water for Agriculture: A Cost/Benefit Analysis*, in: Elie Elhadj, *Experiments in Achieving Water and Food Self-Sufficiency in the Middle East*, PP. 123–145.

Gypsum in the soil caused irrigation networks to collapse. The World Bank had identified 43% of the land in the Euphrates Basin as having drainage problems or the potential to develop problems in the future.

Placing Syria at the Mercy of Turkish Water Politics: The Euphrates river originates in eastern Turkey and flows through Syria and Iraq. Over 700 km of its 3,000 km flow within Syria. The Tabqa Dam, hailed as the Assad regime's proudest accomplishments, wastes a huge volume of water to evaporation, estimated at 1.6 billion m3 annually. To put the figure in perspective, Syria's 20 million inhabitants use around one billion cubic meters for drinking and household needs per year. This loss of water is all the more significant in light of the 50% reduction in the flow of the Euphrates river into Syria (to 15 billion m3 per annum), as a result of Turkey's construction of the huge GAP project in Eastern Turkey.

Planning for the GAP project started in 1938. Progress was interrupted during the Second World War. Work on the project started in the early 1950s. Construction of the Keban Dam started in 1966, two years before work on Tabqa had started. When the Tabqa Dam was on the drawing board, Syrian officials were aware of the looming drop in the water volume flow from Turkey. Damascus' assertion that Tabqa was necessary to avoid seasonal flooding is disingenuous. The series of dams of the GAP project control flooding in Turkey and, by extension, in Syria.

Hafiz Assad ignored, or failed to realize, the water impact of the GAP project on Syria's part of the Euphrates river. In his failure, he plunged Syria into a long-term conflict with Turkey and Iraq over trans-boundary water rights. He placed Syria (and Iraq) at the mercy of Turkish water politics.

A Flawed Decision Making Process: Under the regime's non-representative, non-participatory system of governance, national decisions are made by the small circle of the Assad family to serve its own interests. As a result, the Assads' irrigation strategy, like most spheres of public policy, has been a failure. It reflects haphazard planning and a failed, politically-determined economic and ecological policy created by a poorly informed ruling group. There are no voices from civil society speaking out to protect the country's water basins from depletion and the environment from degradation.

Failure to address critical issues openly and truthfully, like water scarcity, is not surprising. The regime's ban on free press, egalitarian non-governmental organizations, and environmental groups have made it impossible to have any kind of effective dissent about the folly of pursuing food independence in a water-stressed country, or the risks of depleting the nation's water supply. Under such conditions, it is difficult to introduce a balancing economic, political, or environmental perspective into water policy. There has been no effective voice to point out that irrigation projects, especially those on the Euphrates river, would have serious negative economic and environmental consequences.

Food self-sufficiency in Syria is a romantic notion, not a reasoned strategy. Inefficient and environmentally unsound schemes to pursue food self-sufficiency are packaged with national security slogans designed to evoke patriotism. Slogans and politics aside, food self-sufficiency in Syria is impossible to attain. A rapidly growing population and insufficient water resources make food self-sufficiency strategy a mirage.[88] The regime's propagandists have succeeded in incorporating into the national discourse the false notion that food security is critical for national security. There is no mention that medical equipment and pharmaceuticals, among a long list of other imports, are as essential to national security as foodstuffs, if not more.

Was the March 2011 Revolution Triggered by Drought and Migration? Propagandists and apologists of the Assad regime contend that the drought that struck Syria's northeast region between 2006 and 2010, and the ensuing migration of a million people to cities all around the country, were among the main factors that triggered the March 2011 revolution.[89] Indeed, the entire Eastern Mediterranean was subjected to drought during the same period, but only Syria sank into civil war. The following shows that the government's contentions are false, on both accounts.

Drought: Between 2006 and 2010, only one year, 2008, had a serious drop in wheat production (from 4 million tons in 2007 to 2.1 million tons in 2008). However, the next year, 2009, wheat production jumped to 3.6 million tons. In 2010, the volume was maintained at 3.6 million

---

[88]The World Bank concluded that the government, "will need to recognize that achieving food security with respect to wheat and other cereals in the short-term, as well as the encouragement of water-intensive cotton appear to be undermining Syria's security over the long-term by depleting available groundwater resources." The World Bank, "Syrian Arab Republic Irrigation Sector Report," Report No. 22602-SYR. P. xi.

[89]Mark Fiscetti, "Climate Change Hastened Syria's Civil War," *Scientific American*, (March 2, 2015). https://www.scientificamerican.com/article/climate-change-hastened-the-syrian-war/

tons, then increased to 3.9 million tons in 2011. The following table shows wheat production from 2001 to 2011:

Wheat Production in Syria (2001–2011)[90]

Market Year	Production	Unit of Measure	Growth Rate
2001	4745	(1000 MT)	52.82 %
2002	4775	(1000 MT)	0.63 %
2003	4913	(1000 MT)	2.89 %
2004	4537	(1000 MT)	−7.65 %
2005	4669	(1000 MT)	2.91 %
2006	4200	(1000 MT)	−10.04 %
2007	4041	(1000 MT)	−3.79 %
2008	2139	(1000 MT)	−47.07 %
2009	3600	(1000 MT)	68.30 %
2010	3600	(1000 MT)	0.00 %
2011	3850	(1000 MT)	6.94 %

Migration: Migration from rural areas to urban centers in Syria has been taking place since 1960. Data from the World Bank show that the ratio of rural to total population has been declining gradually and steadily over the past 50 years. Between 1960 and 2008 the ratio of rural to total population actually dropped by 18% (63% to 45%). The drop from 2008 to 2011 was a mere 1% (45% to 44%). The largest movement from rural communities to urban centers took place during the 1960s, dropping by a huge 6% (from 63% in 1960 to 57% in 1970). That period belonged to the 1963 military coup, which relocated Alawite villagers to cities, especially Damascus, to fill army and civilian government positions.

Syria's Rural Population (% of total population)[91]

Year	1960	1970	1980	1990	2000	2005	2006	2007	2008	2009	2010	2011
%	63	57	53	51	48	46	46	46	45	45	44	44

[90]Index Mundi, "Syrian Arab Republic Wheat Production by Year, as sourced from United States Department of Agriculture." https://www.indexmundi.com/agriculture/?country=sy&commodity=wheat&graph=production

[91]The World Bank, "Rural Population (% of total population), Syria." http://data.worldbank.org/indicator/SP.RUR.TOTL.ZS?locations=SY

A study titled *Climate change and the Syrian civil war revisited* found that "There is no clear and reliable evidence that anthropogenic climate change was a factor in Syria's pre-civil war drought; this drought did not cause anywhere near the scale of migration that is often alleged, and there exists no solid evidence that drought migration pressures in Syria contributed to civil war onset."[92]

The Arab Spring[93]

Encouraged by the successes of the Arab Spring revolutions in Tunisia against the 23-year dictatorship of President Zine al-Abidine bin Ali, and in Egypt against the 30-year dictatorship of President Hosni Mubarak, Syrians rose to end the 50-year dictatorships of the illegitimate regime of Hafiz al-Assad and his son Bashar. While Tunisia and Egypt replaced their tormentors within one month, Bashar al-Assad has been fighting for seven years, thus far.

As of March 15, 2016, five years after the revolution started, The *Telegraph* newspaper reported that Assad's forces had killed an estimated 470,000 people.[94] Up to 1.9 million Syrians have been injured, which means that more than a tenth of the population has either been killed or wounded.[95] An estimated 200,000 prisoners, many of whom died under torture should be added to this number. Additionally, 7.6 million people are internally displaced and nearly four million became refugees in other countries, including 2.4 million children, according to The UN Children's Fund, UNICEF.[96] Further, attacks on medical facilities have partially or completely destroyed more than 50% of the country's hospitals, with UNICEF estimating that doctor to people ratio increased from around 600 people to 4,000 as noted by the World Bank in January 2016.[97]

Four years after the revolution started, satellite photographs taken over Syria show the country as 83% darker at night than when the war started,

[92]"Climate Change and the Syrian Civil War Revisited", *Elsevier*, Volume 60, (September 2017), PP. 232–244. https://www.sciencedirect.com/science/article/pii/S0962629816301822

[93]Parts of this section are sourced from my article titled "Why Syria's Regime is Likely to Survive", in *Middle East Review of International Affairs (MERIA) Journal*, (August 21, 2011). http://www.rubin-center.org/2011/08/why-syria's-regime-is-likely-to-survive/

[94]Raziye Akkoc, "What has been the real cost of Syria's civil war?," *The Telegraph*, (March 15, 2016). http://www.telegraph.co.uk/news/worldnews/middleeast/syria/12146082/What-has-been-the-real-cost-of-Syrias-civil-war.html

[95]Ibid.

[96]Ibid.

[97]Ibid.

with Aleppo, Syria's largest city, 91% darker at night, and Damascus 35% darker at night.[98]

In opening Syria's doors to Russia, Iran, Hezbollah and other mercenaries, Assad failed his oath of office. "I swear by the Almighty God to respect the country's constitution, laws and Republican system, to look after the interests and freedoms of the people, to safeguard the homeland's sovereignty, independence, freedom and to defend its territorial integrity and to act in order to achieve social justice and the unity of the Arab Nation."

Popular Uprisings in Tunisia and Egypt: When Muhammad Bouazizi, the 26-year-old vegetable street vendor from the town of Sidi Bouzid, Tunisia, set himself on fire on December 17, 2010, he sparked widespread protests against President Zine al-Abidine bin Ali. Less than a month later, after 23 years of rule, bin Ali fled to Jeddah, Saudi Arabia. The Tunisian army, being drawn from a homogeneous non-sectarian society, refused to shoot at protesters and thereby struck a mortal blow to the bin Ali regime. In its refusal, the army effectively transformed Tunisia's popular uprising into a coup d'état. In an interview with *Le Parisien* newspaper, quoted by Reuters, Admiral Jacques Lanxade, a former French chief of staff and later ambassador to Tunisia said, "The chief of staff of the land army, General Rachid Ammar, resigned, refusing to get the army to open fire, and it is probably he who advised Ben Ali to go, telling him 'You're finished.'"[99] The Tunisian uprising was swift, effective, and inspirational to the Arab masses everywhere.

In Egypt, on January 18, 2011, one man died and another was injured after they set themselves on fire.[100] On January 25, 2011, a few days after bin Ali's flight, thousands of anti-government protesters clashed with riot police in Tahrir Square in the center of Cairo, demanding the end of President Hosni Mubarak's 30-year rule. The protests spread to other cities. During the first week of the demonstrations, the violence resulted in some 300 deaths, according to UN estimates.[101] On January 31, 2011,

[98]Diana al Rifai and Mohammed Haddad, "What's left of Syria?," *Al Jazeera*, (March 17, 2015). https://www.aljazeera.com/indepth/interactive/2015/03/left-syria-150317133753354.html

[99]William Maclean, "Tunisia Army Pivotal to Ben Ali Ousting: Reports," *Reuters*, (January 17, 2011). http://www.reuters.com/article/idUSTRE70G52B20110117

[100]"2 in Egypt torch themselves; 1 dead," *CNN*, (January 18, 2011). http://edition.cnn.com/2011/WORLD/africa/01/18/egypt.self.immolation/index.html

[101]John Simpson, "Egypt Unrest: Protesters Hold Huge Cairo Demonstration," *BBC*, (February 1, 2011). http://www.bbc.co.uk/news/world-middle-east-12331520

the Egyptian army had declared its respect for the legitimate rights of the people, stating that it would not use force against protesters. By February 5, 2011, Mubarak announced a series of concessions; he replaced the cabinet, appointed a vice-president for the first time, and declared that he would not run for re-election for a sixth term in September 2011. He also replaced the politburo of the ruling party, including his son Gamal, and pledged dialogue with opposition parties.[102]

Egypt's new vice-president, Umar Sulaiman, invited all protest groups and opposition parties to immediate negotiations on constitutional reform.[103] Six groups, including the banned Muslim Brothers organization, met with the vice president on February 6, 2011. The participants agreed to form a joint committee of judicial and political figures tasked with proposing constitutional amendments.[104] On February 8, 2011, it was reported that public sector workers received a 15% pay increase.[105] Finally, on February 11, 2011, Hosni Mubarak resigned, handing over Egypt's affairs to the high command of the armed forces, headed by the defense minister.[106]

It should be noted that, as in the case of Tunisia, the Egyptian army, being drawn from a homogeneous non-sectarian society, had publicly declared that it respected the legitimate rights of the people and would not use force against its protesting citizens.[107]

Shared Characteristics Among the Regimes of Syria, Tunisia, and Egypt: Assad's regime in Syria, on one hand, and Tunisia's bin Ali and Egypt's Mubarak on the other, share some common characteristics and differ on others, which offer clues as to why the regimes in Tunisia and Egypt collapsed within a few weeks, while in Syria, Assad has been battling the people for seven years with unprecedented savagery.

In the three countries, a politicized military is the kingmaker, the supreme power. The countries also had in common an illegitimate,

[102]Frank Wisner, "Egypt Unrest: US Disowns Envoy Comment on Hosni Mubarak," *BBC*, (February 5, 2011). http://www.bbc.co.uk/news/world-us-canada-12374753

[103]Lyse Doucet, "Egypt Protests: Army Rules Out the Use of Force," *BBC*, (January 31, 2011). http://www.bbc.co.uk/news/world-middle-east-12330169

[104]"Egyptian VP Vows Changes to Appease Protesters," *CNN*, (February 7, 2011). http://edition.cnn.com/2011/WORLD/africa/02/06/egypt.protests/index.html

[105]John Leyne, "Egypt Unrest: Protesters Frustrate Normalisation Effort," *BBC*, (February 7, 2011). http://www.bbc.co.uk/news/world-middle-east-12378828

[106]Yolande Knell, "Egypt Crisis: President Hosni Mubarak Resigns as Leader," *BBC*, (February 12, 2011). http://www.bbc.co.uk/news/world-middle-east-12433045

[107]Lyse Doucet, "Egypt Protests: Army Rules Out the Use of Force," *BBC*.

non-representative, non-participatory governance: a single political party dictatorship, a rubber-stamp parliament, a politicized judiciary, the absence of press freedom, brigades of brutal security forces infamous for appalling human-rights abuses, and a presidential cult of personality. They are also alike in mismanagement, rampant corruption, the absence of transparency or accountability in government finances, high unemployment, and huge disparities of income—poverty for the great majority of the population, and great wealth for the tiny minority of the ruling groups and their business associates. Breaking the law with impunity is a common denominator for the elites among the three regimes. Furthermore, in each of the three countries, the dictators contrived comical, uncontested referendums intended to justify decades of tyranny.

Differences Among the Regimes of Syria, Tunisia, and Egypt: The regime of the two Assads differs from the regimes of bin Ali and Mubarak in three respects. These differences stopped the Tunisian and Egyptian armies from massacring their fellow citizens. It is these differences that made for a successful popular uprising leading to regime change in Cairo and Tunis, which is still unlikely in Damascus.

Unlike the homogeneous Sunni majority population and government in bin Ali's Tunisia, Syria is ruled by a 10% Alawite minority led by the Assad clan. Tunisia's population of 11 million is 98% Arab, 99% Sunni Muslims.[108] By contrast, Syria is home to a colorful tapestry of religions, religious sects, and ethnicities (see above: *The Alawites*). Secondly, Tunisia's secularism is genuine. It differs from Assad's exploitation of Sunni Islam. For more than fifty years, there has been a meaningful separation between religion and the Tunisian state. Tunisia's first president, Habib Bourguiba (1957–1987), was the Arab world's most serious secularist. He implemented a genuine program of secularization and modernization. He abolished Shari'a courts and polygamy. He reformed education and banned the headscarf for women. In this respect, bin Ali followed in Bourguiba's footsteps. By contrast, Assad's "secularism" is adulterated. Thirdly, the geopolitical environment dictates different domestic and foreign agendas in Damascus and Tunis, especially regarding the Arab-Israeli conflict.

---

[108]Central Intelligence Agency, "The World Factbook, Tunisia." https://www.cia.gov/library/publications/resources/the-world-factbook/geos/ts.html

The regime of the two Assads differ from Mubarak's in three respects as well. First, Syria's Alawite-minority rule differs from the homogeneous Sunni majority-led government of former President Mubarak. Egypt's population is around 95 million, 99% are Egyptian Arab, about 90% Sunni Muslims, and about 9% Coptic.[109] Secondly, the Muslim Brotherhood organization in Syria has been greatly weakened and gone underground since the massacres in Palmyra (1980) and the city of Hama (1982) and the ban on its existence under penalty of death. By comparison, the Muslim Brotherhood organization in Egypt has had a long history of being well-organized and powerful. Although the Mubarak administration precluded the Brotherhood from openly fielding candidates in the November-December 2005 parliamentary elections, they ran as independents and won 88 seats to become the major parliamentary opposition bloc, with 20% of the seats in parliament.[110] Thirdly, Syria is in a technical state of war with Israel, though impotent to confront Israel, whereas peaceful relations have existed between Egypt and Israel since March 26, 1979.

Damascus attributes the Tunisian uprising to bin Ali's reliance on "fair-weather foreign allies."[111] Damascus' rhetoric on Tunisia applies to Egypt as well. Assad claims that Syria is insulated from popular uprisings because he understands the needs of the Syrian people and his policies fulfill their aspirations. In an interview with the *Wall Street Journal* on January 31, 2011, Assad claimed that he was very closely linked to the beliefs of his people.[112] Yet, the regime of the two Assads has never been closely linked to the beliefs of Syrians: The gun has kept the two Assads in power. Most of the 75% Sunni population regarded them as belonging to a heterodox sect. It is the Assads' sectarian security forces that destroyed much of Syria. In Egypt and Tunisia, it is the absence of sectarianism and the homogeneity of Sunnis that saved the two countries from the abyss.

---

[109]Central Intelligence Agency, "The World Factbook, Egypt." https://www.cia.gov/library/publications/the-world-factbook/geos/eg.html

[110]"Egypt Islamists Make Record Gains," *BBC*, (December 8, 2005). http://news.bbc.co.uk/1/hi/world/middle_east/4509682.stm

[111]Martin Chulov, Giles Tremlett, and Ian Black, "Tunisian Uprising Fires a Warning to Region's Hardliners," *The Guardian*, (January 17, 2011). http://www.guardian.co.uk/world/2011/jan/17/tunisia-uprising-regional-reaction

[112]"Interview with Syrian President Bashar al-Assad," *The Wall Street Journal*, "January 31, 2011). http://online.wsj.com/article/SB10001424052748703833204576114712441122894.html

The Syrian Revolution

In February 2011, in the southern city of Dar'a, school children wrote anti-Assad slogans on the school wall. Some 15 children were arrested. Dar'a was outraged at the mistreatment of the children. Peaceful stirrings on March 18, 2011 resulted in the killing of at least three demonstrators by the regime. By March 26, 2011, peaceful demonstrations had spread to other Syrian cities. On April 25, 2011, the army entered the city of Dar'a with tanks.

Braving bullets, tanks, arrest, and torture, demonstrations had grown in size and become features of the noon prayer on Fridays and during the burial rituals in dozens of cities, towns, and villages. Tanks rolled into Banyas, Dara'a, Hama, Jableh, Jisr al-Shughour, and Homs, among others. By August 1, 2011, the number of protestors killed exceeded 1,600, plus thousands injured, thousands more arrested and thrown into the regime's torture dungeons, (many to meet a horrible death), while tens of thousands fled to neighboring Turkey. After fifty years of tyranny, the barrier of fear was finally broken. The demonstrators demanded the removal of the Assad family.

In his public address to parliament on March 30, 2011, Assad was defiant. He repeated the well-known cliché that the protests against him were a disguise for a foreign conspiracy to "fragment Syria   an Israeli agenda." Assad insisted that Syria's protesters had been "duped." While acknowledging popular demands for reform, he declared that it would be either him or the gun.[113] This speech was reiterated by his notorious cousin, Rami Makhlouf, a billionaire, infamous for his illicit enterprise. Makhlouf has been under US sanctions since 2008 for "manipulating the judicial system and using Syrian intelligence to intimidate rivals."[114]

In an interview with the *New York Times* reported on May 10, 2011, Makhlouf revealed the workings and thinking of the Assad family's inner circle. He warned, "Syria's ruling elite, a tight-knit circle at the nexus of absolute power ... will fight to the end ... The ruling elite ... had grown even closer during the crisis," he continued, and "the decision of the government now is that they [have] decided to fight." Makhlouf, who holds

---

[113]Liam Stack, "Syria Offers Changes Before Renewed Protests," The *New York Times*, (March 31, 2011). http://www.nytimes.com/2011/04/01/world/middleeast/01syria.html?_r=1&ref=global-home
[114]"Bashar al-Assad's inner circle," *BBC*, (July 30, 2012). http://www.bbc.co.uk/news/world-middle-east-13216195

no official position, postured further, "If there is no stability here, there's no way there will be stability in Israel."[115]

The Geopolitical Environment

Syria has become the battle field for competing interests for local, regional, and international powers: The United States, Israel, Russia, Iran, Lebanon's Hezbollah, Shi'ite mercenaries from Pakistan and Afghanistan, GCC member states, Turkey, and Syrian anti-Assad groups. Troops from Iran, Russia, Turkey, and the United States have occupied parts of Syria.

The Unites States

US politics in Iraq and Iran are intertwined with its politics in Syria. G.W. Bush, exploiting 9/11, reshaped the Muslim Middle East. By destroying much of Iraq, he handed Iraq to Iran, whether he intended to do so or not. Mr. Obama empowered Iran further as a result of:

– Tolerating Prime Minister Maliki's abuse of Iraq's Sunni population.
– Withdrawing US forces from Iraq Prematurely.
– Facilitating the P5+1 nuclear agreement, which lifted UN sanctions against Iran.
– Handing Syria to Iran.

To help explain Obama's politics in the Muslim Middle East, his interview with the *Atlantic* magazine in April 2016, after seven and a half years in the Oval Office, was revealing. It sheds light on the thinking that could have shaped his politics in Iran, Iraq, Saudi Arabia, and Syria. President Obama revealed the following in the interview:[116]

1. "Derision" toward the "Washington Playbook," which "compels him to treat Saudi Arabia as an ally."
2. Fulmination at the Arabization of Indonesia's Islam.
3. Denunciation of Saudi Arabia's "state-sanctioned misogyny."

---

[115]Antoine Shadid, "Syria Elite to Fight Protests Till 'the End'," The *New York Times*, (May 10, 2011). http://www.nytimes.com/2011/05/11/world/middleeast/11makhlouf.html?_r=1&ref=global-home
[116]Jeffrey Goldberg, "The Obama Doctrine."

4. White House's National Security Council consciousness that "the large majority of 9/11 hijackers were not Iranian, but Saudi."
5. Belief that the Saudis need to 'share' the Middle East with their Iranian foes.

Obama's statements suggest that the empowerment of Iran could have been a calculated strategy to punish Saudi Arabia for its culpability of 9/11, for manipulating the Washington Playbook, for radicalizing Indonesia's Islam, and for state-sponsored misogyny.

- **Tolerating Prime Minister Maliki's Abuse of Iraq's Sunni Population:** For the six years between 2008 (when Obama became president) and 2014 (when Maliki was removed from the office of prime minister), Obama looked the other way at Iran's growing influence over Iraq and Maliki's abuse of Iraq's Sunnis. US diplomats and senators warned Obama about the dangers to US interests his policies were creating, to no avail.[117]
- **Withdrawing US Forces from Iraq Prematurely:** The decision to withdraw the last US soldier from Iraq on December 18, 2011 left a vacuum, filled promptly by Tehran. Emptying Iraq of US forces allowed Maliki to increase his abuse of Iraq's Sunnis. Three years later, the so-called Islamic State was born.
- **Facilitating the P5+1 Nuclear Agreement, which Lifted UN Sanctions Against Iran:** In 1992, the US Congress passed the *Iran-Iraq Arms Nonproliferation Act of 1992*.[118] For seventeen years, the US refused to negotiate with Iran. It required Iran to meet UN demands to suspend all nuclear activities first. On April 8, 2009, however, soon after Obama took office, the White House announced that the US would participate fully in the P5+1 talks with Iran.[119] On November 24, 2013 the interim Joint Plan of Action (JPOA) was signed.[120] On July 14, 2015, the P5+1 reached the Joint Comprehensive Plan of Action (JCPOA).[121] In

---

[117]Peter Beinart, "Obama's Disastrous Iraq Policy: An Autopsy," *The Atlantic*, (July 23, 2014).

[118]Congress.gov, "Iran-Iraq Arms Non-Proliferation Act of 1992," *H.R.5434 102nd Congress (1991–1992)*, https://www.congress.gov/bill/102nd-congress/house-bill/5434

[119]Arms Control Association, "Timeline of Nuclear Diplomacy with Iran." https://www.armscontrol.org/factsheet/Timeline-of-Nuclear-Diplomacy-With-Iran

[120]Ibid.

[121]US Department of State," Joint Comprehensive Plan of Action." https://www.state.gov/e/eb/tfs/spi/iran/jcpoa/

return for a delay in its nuclear program for 15 years, Iran gained access to some $100 billion in frozen assets and became able to export oil.[122]

– **Handing Syria to Iran:** The Syrian revolution erupted in mid-March 2011. For six years, until he left the White House, Obama not only refused to supply defensive anti-aircraft guns to Syria's anti-Assad forces, but also prevented other countries from supplying such weapons. In effect, he handcuffed the Syrian revolution. He refused to punish the Assad regime for its use of chemical weapons on August 21, 2013 in Eastern Ghouta near Damascus, in which 1,400 people were killed,[123] repudiating his own infamous "red line," which he had established a year earlier. Getting away with this presumably first use of chemical weapons, Assad was emboldened to carry more such atrocious attacks. US Ambassador to the United Nations revealed in the Security Council on April 13, 2018 that Washington estimates that Assad have used chemical weapons at least 50 times during the seven-year-long conflict.[124]

That Obama allowed Syria to be destroyed by Iran's surrogate regime in Damascus because he feared entangling America a new war in the Middle East is a weak excuse. The US could have trained and armed the Free Syrian Army in a serious manner, particularly with anti aircraft guns to neutralize Assad's dilapidated helicopters and primitive barrel bombs. The FSA could have done the fighting alone, with help from a limited number of US military advisers. Syria has a sufficiently large Sunni population to supply the needed soldiers.

However, Syria was not going to be allowed to derail Obama's drive toward a successful conclusion of the Iran nuclear deal.[125] Nor was Iran going to allow Obama to attack Assad, even if that meant walking away from the nuclear deal. The Assad regime is Iran's highway to the Mediterranean, the source of power for Iran's other surrogate, Lebanon's Hezbollah, and the cornerstone of the Shi'ite Crescent sphere of influence from Tehran and Baghdad to Beirut, via Damascus. Reportedly, Obama declined to enforce the red-line after Iran threatened to back out of the

---

[122]"Iran Nuclear Deal: Key Details," *BBC*, (January 16, 2016).

[123]"Syria Chemical Attack: What we know," *BBC*.

[124]"U.S. envoy to UN says Syria used chemical weapons 50 times," *Reuters*, (April 13, 2018). https://www.reuters.com/article/us-mideast-crisis-syria-un-usa/u-s-envoy-to-u-n-says-syria-used-chemical-weapons-50-times-idUSKBN1HK243

[125]Obama's keen interest in a successful conclusion of the nuclear deal could have been driven by his eagerness to produce some success somewhere, given his lack of legislative achievements on the US domestic front and the international scene.

nuclear deal if Assad's forces were bombed.[126] According to *The Wall Street Journal* reporter Jay Solomon, "When the president announced his plans to attack [the Assad regime] and then pulled back, it was exactly the period in time when American negotiators were meeting with Iranian negotiators secretly in Oman to get the nuclear agreement."[127]

American Experts' Call on Obama to Strike Assad: On February 3, 2013, Reuters reported that a plan developed in the summer of 2012 by then-Secretary of State Hillary Clinton and then-CIA Director David Petraeus to arm and train vetted Syrian rebels was rebuffed by the White House over concerns that it could draw the United States into the Syrian conflict and that the American arms could fall into the wrong hands.[128] In June 2016, more than 50 State Department diplomats involved with advising on Syria policy signed an internal memo sharply critical of US policy in Syria, and calling for military strikes against Assad forces.[129]

Obama shares with Assad and the ayatollahs and Putin the responsibility of condemning millions of Syrians to death, injury, and destitution. His inaction in Syria was cruel and short sighted, a blight on US and Western morality, not different from US and Western silence during the Rwanda genocide in 1994.[130]

How Might Mr. Obama Justify the Empowerment of Iran? Obama set the stage for the restoration of US relations with Iran after 38 years of estrangement, ever since Ayatollah Khomeini deposed the Shah of Iran in 1979 and held 52 US diplomats and citizens as hostages for 444 days. His and G.W. Bush actions triggered Shi'ite/Sunni proxy wars, caused Riyadh to buy tons of new weapons and seek Israeli friendship, and opened Iran's markets to US companies.

Trump Administration's Likely Syria Policy: Defense Secretary Mattis stated on November 14, 2017: "We're not just going to walk away right now before the Geneva process has traction."[131] On January 17, 2018,

---

[126]Pamela Engel, "Obama Reportedly Declined to Enforce Red line in Syria After Iran Threatened to Back Out of Nuclear Deal," *Business Insider UK*.

[127]Ibid.

[128]"White House Rebuffed Clinton-Petraeus Plan to Arm Syrian Rebels: report," *Reuters*.

[129]"US Diplomats Rebuke Obama On Syria and Call for Strikes On Assad," *Huffpost*, (June 20, 2016). http://www.huffingtonpost.com/entry/diplomats-obama-syria-assad_us_5763668ce4b0fbbc8be9e7ed

[130]Speaking to *CNBC Meets'* Tania Bryer, former President Bill Clinton "admitted that if the U.S. had gone into Rwanda sooner following the start of the 1994 genocide, at least a third or roughly 300,000 lives could have been saved." "Bill Clinton: We could have Saved 300,000 lives in Rwanda" *CNBC*, (updated July 29, 2013). https://www.cnbc.com/id/100546207

[131]Phil Stewart, "US to Fight Islamic State in Syria 'as Long as They Want to Fight': Mattis," *Reuters*, (November 14, 2017). https://ca.reuters.com/article/topNews/idCAKBN1DE037-OCATP

former Secretary of State Tillerson, outlined five US goals in Syria: "The defeat of ISIS and al-Qaida, a UN-brokered resolution for Syria that involves Bashar al-Assad's departure, a curb on Iran, conditions for the safe return of refugees, and the complete elimination of remaining chemical weapons."[132] On March 29, 2018, however, Mr. Trump changed all that. He announced unexpectedly, in a speech in Ohio, that the US "will withdraw from Syria 'very soon'."[133] Assad, Iran, Turkey, and Russia must be pleased.

On April 14, 2018, the US, UK, and France fired more than 100 missiles in what US Defense Secretary called a "one time shot," against Syrian government chemical weapons sites in response to Assad's use of poison gas in the town of Duma, a suburb of Damascus, on April 7, 2018 that killed dozens of civilians.[134] UK Prime Minister Theresa May said the strikes were not about "regime change".[135] The Mattis and May statements must have delighted Assad and his Russian and Iranian protectors. A year earlier, on April 7, 2017, the US fired 59 missiles at the Shayrat air base after Assad dropped nerve gas bombs on the town of Khan Sheikhoun, near Idlib, killing more than 80 people.[136] That strike failed to change Assad and his Russian and Iranian protectors' behavior. It was a tactical strike, devoid of strategic aims. The new strike is expected to be as ineffective as the one in 2017.

Israel

Seven years of destruction have eliminated all Syrian military risk toward Israel. Before the recent mega destruction, whether on the Golan Heights in 1967 and 1973, in the skies over Lebanon in 1982, or at al-Kibar's suspected nuclear facility in 2007, the two Assads suffered crushingly humiliating defeats at the hands of Israel. Realizing his impotence in a fight with Israel, and to justify the suspension of the constitution and imposition of

---

[132]Julian Borger, Patrick Wintour, and Kareem Shaheen, "US military to maintain open-ended presence in Syria, Tillerson says," *The Guardian*, (January 17, 2018). https://www.theguardian.com/us-news/2018/jan/17/us-military-syria-isis-iran-assad-tillerson

[133]Ryan Browne and Barbara Starr, "Trump says US will withdraw from Syria 'very soon'," *CNN*.

[134]Steve Holland and Tom Perry, "U.S., Britain, France launch air strikes in Syria," *Reuters*, (April 13, 2018). https://uk.reuters.com/article/uk-mideast-crisis-syria/u-s-britain-france-launch-air-strikes-in-syria-idUKKBN1HK16M

[135]"Syria air strikes: US and allies attack chemical weapons sites," *BBC*, (April 14, 2018). http://www.bbc.co.uk/news/world-middle-east-43762251

[136]"Syria war: Why was Shayrat airbase bombed?" *BBC*, (April 7, 2017). http://www.bbc.co.uk/news/world-us-canada-39531045

state of emergency, Hafiz formed a strategic alliance with Iran. Together, Damascus and Tehran built Hezbollah into a credible fighting force.

Syria's revolution presented Israeli leaders with a choice between tolerating the devil they knew in the form of the Shi'ite Crescent (Iran/Iraq/Assad/Hezbollah), or accepting the risk of a new regime in Syria that might, in a worst case scenario, bring the likes of al-Qaeda/Nusra jihadists to Damascus. In May 2015, the Israeli Defense Minister said that Israel's policy regarding Syria is, "on the one hand not to intervene, and on the other hand to keep our interests. We have three red lines: One is not to allow the delivery of advanced weapons to any terror organization, whether by Iran or by Syria. Second, not to allow delivery of chemical agents or weapons to any terror faction. The third is not to allow any violation of our sovereignty, especially in the Golan Heights. When it happens, we act."[137]

Consistent with this strategy, Israel launched at least 100 clandestine strikes in Syria since 2011.[138] During the February 10, 2018 raid, one of the eight attacking planes was shot down, the first such loss for Israel in decades.[139]

A Strategy Cooked in Washington: Given Israeli dependency on the US and the close co-operation between the two countries on regional defense and security, the Israeli Defense Minister's policy must have been formulated in Washington. The aim of the policy was to prevent Israel from attempting the removal of Assad and antagonizing Mr. Obama and Iran in the middle of the nuclear agreement negotiations. Notwithstanding the fact that Israel's interest would be well served if Assad were removed, Israel could not defy the Obama administration.

Why is the removal of Assad in Israel's best interest? Without Assad, the Shi'ite Crescent would be broken, weakening Iran, and dealing a severe blow to Hezbollah. Also, the cost of removing Assad would be far less than the cost of other options, such as waging war against Iran and Hezbollah.[140] As long as Assad is in power, the Shi'ite Crescent will remain alive and well, with Iran more powerful than ever, and Hezbollah more menacing than ever.

[137]Ehud Elam, "Israel and the Civil War in Syria," *ISRAELDEFENSE*, (February 1, 2017). http://www.israeldefense.co.il/en/node/28095

[138]"Syria war: Israel 'strikes Damascus military complex'," *BBC*, (February 7, 2018). http://www.bbc.co.uk/news/world-middle-east-42973662

[139]Maayan Lubell and Lisa Barrington, "Israeli Jet Shot Down after Bombing Iranian Site in Syria," *Reuters*, (February 10, 2018). https://www.reuters.com/article/us-israel-iran/israeli-jet-shot-down-after-bombing-iranian-site-in-syria-idUSKBN1FU07L

[140]The least expensive action to remove the ayatollahs would be a regime change in Tehran through a popular uprising or a military coup.

There are two possible scenarios after Assad. One possibility is a secular parliamentary democracy which would side with other Arab Sunni countries against Iran, especially the GCC member states, and shut down Iran's weapons pipeline to Hezbollah. The second possibility is a Sunni Islamist regime, which would wage a furious sectarian war against the Shi'ite Hezbollah. An Islamist regime does not necessarily mean it would be anti-West or anti-Israel. The Saudi Wahhabi regime is the world's most extreme Islamist regime; yet, Riyadh has been America's most obsequious servant since the Saudi state was formed in 1932 with London's help. Moreover, Syria's Sunnis follow the moderate Hanafi rite. Either possibility would be bad for the Shi'ite Crescent.

Why Is Israel Anti-Iran? Now that Israel has become immune from Arab military threats as a result of the destruction of much of Iraq and Syria, and Israel's peace treaties with Egypt and Jordan, Israel needs a new enemy to keep its domestic front united. Just like Iran's invention of Israel as a mortal enemy in order to rally the Iranian masses behind the ayatollahs (see below: *Why Is Iran Anti-Israel?*), threats and provocations from Iran and the Shi'ite Crescent keep Israel's home front united.

And, as an added benefit, Iran's regional threat brings Saudi Arabia and its GCC allies close to Israel.

Russian Federation

Syria's geographic location is important for Moscow due to its coastline on the Mediterranean, its borders with Turkey, Iraq, Jordan, Lebanon, and Israel, and its close proximity to the oil-rich Arabian Peninsula, with Iran to the east and Europe to the northwest. The Soviet Union had been Syria's main supplier of arms since the mid-1950s. Egypt was the Soviet Union's gateway to Syria. In October 1955, the late President Gamal Abdul Nasser signed a major deal with Czechoslovakia to supply Egypt with Soviet arms.[141] Around that same time, Syria received its own Soviet arms shipments from Czechoslovakia. During the three and a half years when Egypt and Syria were united, (February 1, 1958–September 28, 1961), Moscow's access to Syria expanded.[142]

---

[141]"Suez Crisis: Key players," *BBC*, (July 21, 2006). http://news.bbc.co.uk/1/hi/5195582.stm

[142]After Egypt and Syria were united under the United Arab Republic on February 28, 1958, Soviet naval units became frequent visitors to the port of Latakia.

In 1971, Hafiz Assad signed an agreement giving the USSR control of a naval facility in Tartous on the Mediterranean Coast.[143] In May 2005, Russia wrote off 73% of the $13.4 billion Syria owed the former USSR in return for continuing with the 1971 naval facility agreement.[144] Arms contracts in January 2012 were estimated to be worth $1.5 billion.[145]

On September 30, 2015, Russia came to Assad's rescue after the serious losses Syria and Hezbollah and Iran had suffered in areas considered key to the government's survival.[146] A spokesperson for the Russian Defense Ministry said Russia's Air Force sent to Syria over 50 warplanes and helicopters.[147] In addition to weapons and troops, Russia vetoed twelve United Nations Security Council resolutions between October 4, 2011 and April 10, 2018 for Assad.[148]

What Are Russia's Aims in Syria? Russia's protection of the Assad regime is driven by the following factors:

1. Building naval and air force bases.
2. Testing Russia's new weapons.
3. Projecting Russia's power on the world stage.
4. Fighting jihadism.
5. Using Syria as a bargaining chip to remove Western sanctions following Russia's annexation of the Crimean Peninsula.

Building Naval and Air Force Bases: Reuters reported on January 20, 2017, that Russia and Syria have signed an agreement to expand and modernize the Tartus facility to enable 11 Russian warships to be located there simultaneously.[149] The agreement is valid for 49 years and will accommodate cruisers and possibly aircraft carriers, including nuclear-powered warships.[150]

---

[143]The Soviet Navy had similar support facilities in Egypt, until closed by the late President Sadat in 1972. Ron Synovitz, "Why Is Access To Syria's Port at Tartus So Important To Moscow?," *RadioFreeEurope RadioLiberty*, (June 19, 2012). https://www.rferl.org/a/explainer-why-is-access-/24619441.html

[144]Ibid.

[145]Richard Galpin, "Russian Arms Shipments Bolster Syria's Embattled Assad," *BBC*, (January 30, 2012). http://www.bbc.co.uk/news/world-middle-east-16797818

[146]Zeina Karam, "Russia's Pro-Assad Airstrikes Restore Syria Stalemate," *The Times of Israel*, (December 17, 2015). https://www.timesofisrael.com/russias-pro-assad-airstrikes-restore-syria-stalemate/

[147]"Russian Air Force in Syria Deploying over 50 Planes & Chopper-Defense Ministry," *RT*, (October 1, 2015), https://www.rt.com/news/317179-russian-airforce-syria-aircraft/

[148]"Russia's 12 UN Vetoes on Syria," *Arab News*, (April 10, 2018). http://www.arabnews.com/node/1282481/middle-east

[149]"Russia, Syria Sign Agreement on Expanding Tartus Naval Base," *Reuters*, (January 20, 2017). http://www.reuters.com/article/us-mideast-crisis-russia-syria-tartus-idUSKBN1541U8

[150]"Russia to Start Upgrading Tartous Facility in Syria for Hosting Aircraft Carriers," *Sputnik International*, (March 3, 2017). https://sputniknews.com/military/201703101051435468-tartus-russia-base/

Tartous is strategically important to Russia. It is the only naval facility Moscow has outside the former Soviet Union. It allows the stationing of naval assets in the Mediterranean instead of sailing them from the Black Sea through Turkey's NATO controlled Bosporus. Russia has been seeking uninterrupted access to the warm waters of the Mediterranean for centuries. The Ottoman Empire, and its successor, Turkey with its NATO allies, have stood in its way for the past seven centuries.

What does Russia pay for the Tartous privilege? That is a secret. However, in the 2005 debt re-negotiation agreement, Russia forgave Syria almost $10 billion. How many years does this sum cover? To Assad, the answer is irrelevant. He will pay whatever invoice Russia demands, in order to stay in power. In addition to the Tartus naval facility, Russia and Syria signed an agreement in January 2017 for the Russian air force to use the Hmeymim air base near Latakia for 49 years.[151]

Testing Russia's New Weapons: Russia's Deputy Defense Minister revealed that Russia has tested over 600 new weapons and military equipment items on the battlefields of Syria, "Practically all new items have passed through the Syrian theater of war in order for us to have an opportunity to see what their real characteristics are and how these weapons are behaving."[152] Using Syria as a testing field for new Russian weapons serves as a marketing demonstration of the destructiveness of those weapons to potential buyers. In 2014, Russia exported weapons worth $15.5 billion. The *Moscow Times* wrote that a 1% increase in sales ($150 million) would be equivalent to only a month of spending on bombs in Syria, estimated at $4 million per day ($120 million per month).[153] Further, in Syria, Russian soldiers have been gaining real battlefield operational experience.

Projecting Russia's Power on the World Stage: Tartus and Hmeymim strengthen Russia's great-power image. Russia's protection of Assad is a part of an assertive Russian campaign to act on the world stage, following the collapse of the Soviet Union and attempts by Washington, NATO and the European Union to encroach on what Russia sees as its sphere of influence in Eastern Europe. President Putin, in his annual State of the Nation

[151]Samuel Osborne, "Russia to Stay in Syria for Another Half a Century as Putin Signs Air Base Deal with Assad Regime," *The Independent*, (July 27, 2017). http://www.independent.co.uk/news/world/middle-east/russia-syria-50-years-half-century-air-base-deal-putin-assad-regime-president-rebels-isis-a7863031.html

[152]Damien Sharkov, "Russia Is Using Syria to Test Its Next Generation of Weapons," *Newsweek*, (August 24, 2017). http://www.newsweek.com/russia-using-syria-test-next-generation-its-weapons-654689

[153]Peter Hobson, "Calculating the Cost of Russia's War in Syria," *The Moscow Times*, (October 20, 2015). https://themoscowtimes.com/articles/calculating-the-cost-of-russias-war-in-syria-50382

address on April 24, 2005, stated, "The collapse of the Soviet Union was the greatest geo-political catastrophe of the century."[154]

Putin's military interventions in Georgia's South Ossetia in August 2008, in Crimea in March 2014, and in Syria since September 30, 2015 are chapters in Mr. Putin's book on how to restore Russia to its former super-power status, lost on December 26, 1991, with the collapse of the Soviet Union.

Fighting Jihadism: The so-called Islamic State in Syria has become a magnet to jihadists from Chechnya and the Caucasus. Assad's survival might be seen in Moscow as a useful trap to kill Russia's own Islamist citizens who might otherwise return to terrorize Russian cities.

Using Syria as a Bargaining Chip to Remove Western Sanctions: In mid-March 2014, Putin annexed Crimea. In an immediate response, the US and the EU imposed sanctions on Russia. Eighteen months later, Putin entered Syria to possibly use it as a bargaining chip to lift the sanctions.

Moscow is anxious to get the sanctions removed. They have had a heavy toll on Russia's economy. A Congressional Research Service report dated February 17, 2017 stated:

> Russia faced a number of economic challenges in 2014 and 2015, including capital flight, rapid depreciation of the ruble, exclusion from international capital markets, inflation, and domestic budgetary pressures. Growth slowed to 0.7% in 2014 before contracting sharply by 3.7% in 2015. The extent to which US and EU sanctions drove the downturn is difficult to disentangle from the impact of a dramatic drop in the price of oil, a major source of export revenue for the Russian government, or economic policy decisions by the Russian government.
>
> The International Monetary Fund (IMF) estimated in 2015 that US and EU sanctions in response to the conflict in Ukraine and Russia's countervailing ban on agricultural imports reduced Russian output over the short term by as much as 1.5%.[155]

---

[154]Andrew Osborne, "Putin: Collapse of the Soviet Union Was 'Catastrophe of the Century'," *The Independent*, (April 25, 2005). http://www.independent.co.uk/news/world/europe/putin-collapse-of-the-soviet-union-was-catastrophe-of-the-century-521064.html

[155]Rebecca M. Nelson, "US Sanctions and Russia's Economy," *Congressional Research Service*, (February 17, 2017). https://fas.org/sgp/crs/row/R43895.pdf

The likelihood of an imminent removal of sanctions on Russia disappeared, when on August 2, 2017, President Trump had to sign legislation that imposes new sanctions on Russia and limits his own authority to reverse or relax them.[156] The bill, passed almost unanimously by the House of Representatives (419-3) and the Senate (98-2), prohibits the White House from lifting sanctions on Russia or even easing their impact without first reporting to Congress on what the US will get in return from Moscow.[157] In reaction, Russia's prime minister said the sanctions were tantamount to a "full-scale trade war."[158]

With the United States Congress determined to punish Russia for meddling in the 2016 US presidential elections, annexing Crimea, destabilizing Eastern Ukraine, and protecting the Assad regime, Putin must realize that his gamble in Syria has thus far been a failure. In order to have the sanctions removed, Putin needs to accommodate US interests in Crimea and/or Syria, and/or Ukraine.

Russia's Vulnerability in Syria: Syrians never developed an affinity towards Russia, its language, culture, or way of life. Despite six decades of government loyalty to Moscow, very few Syrians speak Russian. Instead, Syrians who study a second language speak English, French, or German. Those who wish to migrate from Syria dream of living in New York, London, or Paris, not in Moscow. After sixty years of government alliance with Russia, it would be difficult to find Syrian students who wish to study in Russian universities, save for those who are on government scholarships. Instead, the great majority of young Syrians desire to study at Harvard, Princeton, Stanford, or Oxford. Syrian graduates dream of working and building their lives in Western cities, not in Russia. Standing in the way of Russia's popularity in Syrian society is Russian protection of the hated Assad regime, Russia's police-state, the USSR's history of atheism, the limited reach of the Russian language, and Russia's poverty compared to US/EU affluence. Since the revolution, the Syrian people's coldness towards Russia has grown into enmity.

---

[156]Kaitlan Collins, Jeremy Herb, and Daniella Diaz, "Trump Signs Bill Approving New Sanctions against Russia," *CNN*, (August 3, 2017). http://edition.cnn.com/2017/08/02/politics/donald-trump-russia-sanctions-bill/index.html

[157]Ibid.

[158]Julian Borger, "Russia Sanctions: Trump Signs Bill Imposing New Measures," *The Guardian*, (August 2, 2017). https://www.theguardian.com/us-news/2017/aug/02/donald-trump-sanctions-russia-signs-bill

The US could take advantage of this situation. By weaponizing a new Syrian army, the US could turn the war in Syria into a defeat for Putin, reminiscent of the Soviet Union's defeat in the war in Afghanistan (December 1979–February 1989). This new army would be recruited from amongst the 12 million Syrians who lost family and friends and were displaced inside Syria and in neighboring refugee camps.[159] These people whose lives have been destroyed represent a ticking bomb primed against Russia and Assad. With the aid of Western advisors, they could provide the necessary soldiers for a war against Assad and Russia, without the need for American forces on the ground in Syria, save for advisers.

Tactically, Mr. Putin extended the life of the Assad regime. Strategically, however, Russia's intervention is unsustainable. Moscow is unable to walk away from Syria because, if it does, Assad will fall. Staying in Syria puts Russia at the mercy of the US, should Washington choose to pressure Russia.

The war in Syria benefited Russia indirectly. It strained relations between two NATO allies, Turkey and the US, over Syria's Kurds. Three developments may serve as a harbinger of potentially even greater disagreements between Ankara and Washington. The first two events are resented by Turkey. First was the US welcome in 2013, to the unilaterally declared self-governing Kurdish region in Northern Syria (see below: *Areas Controlled by the Democratic Federal System of Northern Syria*). The second area of contention was the Pentagon's alliance with Syria's Kurds and Syrian Democratic Forces, which removed the so-called Islamic State from Northern Syria. The third event is resented by the US: Turkey's capture of the Kurdish-majority city of Afrin in defiance of the US.[160]

Iran, Shi'ite Mercenaries, and Hezbollah

In 2016, the Commander of Iran's Revolutionary Guard Corps, Major General Mohammad Ali Jafari, was reported as saying that Iran has

---

[159]UNHCR, Syria Emergency, (accessed, November 6, 2017). http://www.unhcr.org/uk/syria-emergency.html

[160]"Turkey's Erdogan Says Afrin City Centre Under 'Total' Control in Syria," *The Telegraph*, (March 18, 2018).https://www.telegraph.co.uk/news/2018/03/18/turkeys-erdogan-says-afrin-city-centre-total-control-syria/

equipped nearly 200,000 young men with arms in Afghanistan, Iraq, Pakistan, Syria, and Yemen "in order to face terrorism."[161]

The deputy commander of the Iranian Revolutionary Guard Gen. Hossein Salami told the official Iranian news agency, Islamic Republic News Agency, that: "The victory in Aleppo will pave the way for liberating Bahrain," and further that "the people of Bahrain will achieve their wishes, the Yemeni people will be delighted, and the residents of Mosul will taste victory … these are all divine promises."[162]

The March of Shi'ism: Emboldened by gains in Iraq and Syria, the Qom theocrats in Iran have been exploiting the Shi'ite sectarian card to enhance Iran's regional reach. Being the largest Shi'ite country, the ayatollahs have appointed themselves protectors of Shi'ites everywhere.

Former US Ambassador to Iraq, Zalmay Khalilzad, one of the architects of the Iraq misadventure claimed, "The 2003 toppling of Saddam Hussein's regime had opened a Pandora's box of volatile ethnic and sectarian tensions."[163] Khalilzad described a "worst-case scenario in which religious extremists could take over sections of Iraq and begin to expand outward."[164] Khalilzad's prophesy came true in 2014 when the so-called Islamic State was born (see Chapter Seven). With Iraq and Syria under control, an overconfident Ayatollah Khamenei launched an aggressive march of Shi'ism crusade against his Sunni neighbors.

Iran in Syria: As conditions on the ground for the Assad regime deteriorated between 2011 and early 2013, Iran's Revolutionary Guard's Quds Force helped create Syria's National Defense Forces (NDF), a paramilitary organization composed of 100,000 fighters.[165] NDF is funded by Iran, according to Mohammad Reza Naghdi, the commander-in-chief of Iran's own paramilitary force, the Basij.[166] As it became clear that there were insufficient Syrian forces to fight rebel groups, Iran facilitated the

---

[161]"Iran's Revolutionary Guards: We Have Armed 200,000 Fighters in the Region," *Middle East Monitor*.

[162]"Iran: After Aleppo, We Will Intervene in Bahrain, Yemen," *Al Arabiya*, December 16, 2016, https://english.alarabiya.net/en/features/2016/12/16/Iran-s-Revolutionary-Guard-After-Aleppo-we-will-intervene-in-Bahrain-and-Yemen.html

[163]Borzou Daragahi, "Envoy to Iraq Sees Threat of Wider War," *Los Angeles Times*, (March 7, 2006). http://articles.latimes.com/2006/mar/07/world/fg-envoy7

[164]Ibid.

[165]Royal United Services Institute for Defence and Security Studies (RUSI), *Understanding Iran's Role in the Syrian Conflict*, P. 4.

[166]Hossein Bastani, "Iran Quietly Deepens Involvement in Syria's War," *BBC*, (October 20, 2015), http://www.bbc.co.uk/news/world-middle-east-34572756

deployment of foreign Shia militias,[167] starting with Iraqi Shia groups and Lebanon's Hezbollah (see below: *The Roots of the Iran/ Hezbollah Axis*).

Iran recruited Afghan Shi'ite fighters to form the Zaynabiyoun Brigade.[168] The word Zaynabiyoun holds a special significance to Shi'ites. It refers to Zaynab, sister of Imam Hussein bin Ali, daughter of the fourth caliph Ali bin abi Talib and his wife Fatima (daughter of the Prophet). Zaynab was with Hussein's party when the Imam was killed by the forces of the Damascus Umayyad Caliph Yazid bin Mu'awiyah (680–683) in the cataclysmic battle of Karbala on the 10th of the Arabic month of Muharram in 680. Zaynab's tomb is allegedly located just outside Damascus in the Sayyida Zaynab district. However, Zaynab's tomb is also allegedly located in Cairo's Sayyida Zaynab Mosque. For obvious political reasons, the Qom ayatollahs promote Damascus as the real site of Zaynab's tomb. Under the guise of guarding Zaynab's mausoleum, Iranians and other Shi'ites protect the Assad regime from collapse (see below: *Why Is Iran Wedded to the Assad Regime?*).

Another brigade, Fatemiyoun, named after the Shi'ite Fatimid caliphate in Cairo (973–1171), is an Afghan Shi'ite militia formed by Iran to protect the Assad regime. According to Colonel Hussain Kenani Moghdam of Iran's Revolutionary Guards, the brigade "numbers in the tens of thousands."[169] Iran pays recruits between $500 and $1,000 a month.[170]

Until April 2016, the number of Iranian paramilitary personnel operating in Syria was estimated at between 6,500 and 9,200. In April 2016, Iran dispatched its special forces to Syria.[171] To Syria's Sunnis, the presence of Iranian soldiers is particularly provocative, not only because of their Shi'ite sectarianism but also their non-Arab ethnicity.

Financially, Iran is heavily invested in Syria. Staffan de Mistura, UN special envoy for Syria, is quoted as saying that Iran spends $6 billion annually on Assad's government, while some researchers estimate that "Iran spent between $14 and $15 billion in military and economic aid to

---

[167]Ibid.

[168]Philip Smyth, "Iran's Afghan Shiite Fighters in Syria," *The Washington Institute*, (June 3, 2014), http://www.washingtoninstitute.org/policy-analysis/view/irans-afghan-shiite-fighters-in-syria

[169]Hashmatallah Moslih, "Iran 'Foreign Legion' Leans on Afghan Shia in Syria War," *Al Jazeera*, (January 22, 2016). https://www.aljazeera.com/news/2016/01/iran-foreign-legion-leans-afghan-shia-syria-war-160122130355206.html

[170]Royal United Services Institute for Defence and Security Studies (RUSI), *Understanding Iran's Role in the Syrian Conflict*, P. 4.

[171]Ibid, P. 5.

the Damascus regime in 2012 and 2013."[172] Additionally, Iranian credit lines and oil sales to Syria have softened and limited the drop in the value of the Syrian Lira in terms of the US dollar.

Why Is Iran Wedded to the Assad Regime? Syria provides Iran with the overland route to supply Hezbollah in Southern Lebanon with weapons. Without Syria, delivering Iranian weapons to Hezbollah would become exceedingly difficult. Without Syria, Hezbollah would be strangled. Hezbollah is of critical strategic importance to Iran. It brings Iran's borders 1,500 kilo meters closer to Israel. A military confrontation between Israel and Iran will automatically bring Hezbollah into the battle.

In capturing Damascus, the Umayyad Caliphate's capital city, the Shi'ite masses feel jubilant, not only for avenging Imam Hussein's killing by the Damascus Caliph Yazid but also for redressing the first Muslim civil war in 657 between Yazid's father, Mu'awiyah (661–680), and Hussein's father, Ali (656–661). Even today, Shi'ites curse Mu'awihah and Yazid publically.

Why Is Iran Anti-Israel? For the Tehran regime to survive, it must rally Iran's masses behind a confrontation with a powerful external enemy. If such an enemy does not exist, it must be invented. Conveniently, Israel is the perfect enemy for the Qom ayatollahs from a religious and political point of view. The confrontation with Israel gives the ayatollahs a license to crush the slightest opposition at home for "weakening the morale of the populace in the middle of the confrontation with the Israeli enemy."

As an added benefit, the anti-Israel game ingratiates the ayatollahs with the Palestinian people and Arab masses. Qom's ayatollahs use anti-Israel rhetoric as a proselytization tool to convert Sunnis to Shi'ism.

The fact that Israel has not threatened Iran's security does not matter. The ayatollahs have constructed an image of Israel in the Iranian national discourse as if it were Iran's most dangerous threat, an existential risk. Until the Shah of Iran was deposed by Ayatollah Khomeini, on February 11, 1979, Iran and Israel had cordial relations.

Historically, Persia and the Jewish people were not enemies. Prime Minister Benjamin Netanyahu, in a speech at the United Nations General Assembly in 2013 noted, "Some 2,500 years ago, the great Persian king Cyrus ended the Babylonian exile of the Jewish people. He issued a famous edict in which he proclaimed the right of the Jews to return to the land of

---

[172]Shahir ShahidSaless, "Iran's Plan to Confront a Post-Assad Era," *Huffington Post*. http://www.huffingtonpost.com/shahir-shahidsaless/irans-plan-to-confront-a_b_8510186.html

Israel and rebuild the Jewish temple in Jerusalem. That's a Persian decree. And thus began an historic friendship between the Jews and the Persians that lasted until modern times."[173]

To prove their anti-Israel credentials, the ayatollahs built Hezbollah on Israel's borders in order to unleash it whenever it becomes politically convenient. This happened on July 12, 2006. "Hezbollah guerillas crossed into Israel, killed three Israeli soldiers, and kidnapped two others, precipitating a war with Israel."[174] The war ended on August 14, 2006.[175] Israel's losses were surprisingly high.[176]

There could have been a connection between the 2006 war and the P5+1 nuclear deal negotiations with Iran. The discussions were tough. On April 11, 2006, Iran announced that it has enriched uranium for the first time to about 3.5% at the Natanz pilot enrichment plant.[177] The 2006 war was a demonstration to Western powers and Israel of the shape of things to come if they were tempted to bomb Iran's nuclear facilities.

The Roots of the Iran/Hezbollah Axis: A close religious connection has existed between Iran and the Shi'ites of Lebanon for the past five centuries. To add religious fervor into Persia's wars against the Sunni Ottoman Empire, Shah Ismail (1501–1524) made Shi'ism the state religion of the Safavid dynasty (1502–1737) instead of Sunnism. Lacking the necessary clerics to effect the conversion, Shi'ite scholars from southern Lebanon's Mount Amel were imported to establish schools and train Persian clerics in Shi'ite laws, rituals, and way of life. Ever since that time, a bridge between Iran and Lebanon has flourished.

For centuries, Lebanon's Shi'ite population was discriminated against. Their fortunes began to improve in 1959 with the arrival of Musa al-Sadr to the coastal city of Tyre. Al-Sadr was an Iranian-born Lebanese Shiite cleric, son of a long line of distinguished Shi'ite scholars. At the turn of the

---

[173]"Full Text of Netanyahu's 2013 Speech to the UN General Assembly," *The Times of Israel*, (November 21, 2013). https://www.timesofisrael.com/full-text-netanyahus-2013-speech-to-the-un-general-assembly/

[174]From the US Department of State statement on Dec. 1, 2011, "What Was the 2006 Israel-Lebanon War?," *ProCon.org.* (February 22, 2012). https://israelipalestinian.procon.org/view.answers.php?questionID=000981

[175]Ibid.

[176]Alistair Crooke and Mark Perry, "How Hezbollah Defeated Israel," *Counterpunch*, (October 13, 2006). https://www.counterpunch.org/2006/10/13/how-hezbollah-defeated-israel-2/

[177]"Timeline of Nuclear Diplomacy with Iran," *Arms Control Association*. https://www.armscontrol.org/factsheet/Timeline-of-Nuclear-Diplomacy-With-Iran

nineteenth century, Sadr's ancestors escaped Ottoman mistreatment from Tyre and moved to Iraq's holy city of Najaf, and then to Iran.

For the Shiites of Lebanon, Musa al-Sadr awakened a sense of dignity and self-worth previously unknown. He replaced their innate self-pity, sorrow, and submission with a fiery spirit of hope, defiance, and revolution. In 1974, he formed the Movement of the Disinherited, a political movement aimed at social justice. In 1975, the Amal movement was formed as the militia wing of the Movement of the Disinherited.

In 1982, after Sadr's suspicious disappearance in 1978, while on a visit to Colonel Qaddafi in Libya, the momentum of his work gave rise to Hezbollah, a trained, organized militia, funded by Ayatollah Khomeini's Revolutionary Guards. In 2016, Hezbollah had about 21,000 active duty fighters and 24,000 reservists, with a stockpile of around 130,000 rockets of different types and ranges (up to 400 kilometers), hundreds of drones, and thousands of anti-tank missiles.[178]

Hezbollah is the only body of Shi'ites outside Iran that pledges allegiance to the Iranian faqih. Hezbollah's deputy secretary general Sheikh Naim Qassem's was quoted as saying in August 2011 that, "Wilayat al-faqih is the reason for Hezbollah's establishment."[179] On October 8, 1997, the United States designated Hezbollah as a Foreign Terrorist Organization.

Hezbollah in Syria: According to the US Department of State's Foreign Terrorist Organizations Report (2016), there are about 7,000 Hezbollah fighters in Syria.[180] According to *Newsweek* magazine, Hezbollah's involvement in Syria between 2011 and 2016 cost the terrorist organization some 2,000 to 2,500 killed, and some 7,000 injured.[181]

Hezbollah's fighters proved to be more capable than the Syrian army, and their involvement in Syria provided them with serious battlefield experience. Hezbollah's intervention has taken four principal forms: training for regular Syrian forces and irregular Syrian and foreign militia forces, combat advisory roles, combat participation, and a separate and more

---

[178]"Hezbollah, "From Terror Group to Army," *Haaretz*, (December 7, 2016).

[179]"Hezbollah MP Credits Wilayat al Fakih for Saving Lebanon," *YALIBNAN*, (November 2, 2014). http://yalibnan.com/2014/11/02/hezbollah-mp-credits-wilayat-al-fakih-saving-lebanon/

[180]US Department of State, Bureau of Counterterrorism and Countering Violent Extremism, "Foreign Terrorist Organizations," (2016). https://www.state.gov/j/ct/rls/crt/2016/272238.htm

[181]Mona Alami, "Will Hezbollah Remain in Syria Forever?," *Newsweek*, (March 28, 2017). http://www.newsweek.com/will-hezbollah-remain-syria-forever-573818

focused effort to build up capability to strike Israel from southern Syria.[182] Hezbollah may be described today as Iran's weapon of mass destruction on Israel's border with Lebanon.

Turkey

Turkey is caught between US/NATO strategies and Russia's national interest. Ankara's balancing act between the two powers is further complicated by its extreme hostility towards the aspirations for self-rule of Turkey's estimated 20-million Kurds. Turkey's (the Ottoman's) defeat in the First World War and dismemberment in 1918 weighs heavily on the collective memory of Turks. They reject further loss of territory to ethnic groups.

The Turkish government has invested tens of billions of dollars in the Kurdish-majority region of Southeastern Turkey over the past four decades. The GAP project is an integrated regional economic and social development in the Euphrates-Tigris basins comprising infrastructure investment in irrigated agriculture, electricity generation, manufacturing, transportation, education, and health. The GAP involves the construction of 22 dams, 19 hydroelectric power plants, and irrigation networks for approximately 1.8 million hectares in nine provinces in Southeastern Turkey.[183]

In large measure, the Kurdish challenge shapes Ankara's agenda towards the Syrian revolution. In November 2013, Syria's Kurds unilaterally declared a self-governing autonomous region bordering Turkey in three cities (cantons): Afrin, Kobani (Ain al-Arab in Arabic), and Jazira (see below: *Areas Controlled by the Democratic Federal System of Northern Syria*). Turkey fears self-rule fever next-door might spread among its own Kurdish population along the 820 kilometer border it shares with Syria. Turkish President Erdogan vowed on June 26, 2015 that he would "never allow the establishment of a Kurdish state in northern Syria."[184]

---

[182]Royal United Services Institute for Defence and Security Studies (RUSI), *Understanding Iran's Role in the Syrian Conflict.*

[183]Republic of Turkey, Southeastern Anatolia Project (GAP). http://www.gap.gov.tr/en/index.php

[184]"Drawing in the Neighbours," *The Economist*, (July 4, 2015). https://web.archive.org/web/20150705014343/http://www.economist.com/news/middle-east-and-africa/21656692-turkey-and-jordan-are-considering-setting-up-buffer-zones-war-scorched

In its zeal to frustrate Kurdish autonomy, the Turkish government stands ready to support any group, including Islamists, who would help thwart Kurdish aspirations for self-rule. Ankara would even exploit the so-called Islamic State in an engagement of political convenience. The territorial ambitions of the so-called Islamic State in the Kurdish space makes the terror group of use to Turkey—it is like the cat that can be used to kill the Kurdish mouse.

Francis Ricciardone, former US ambassador to Ankara until June 2014, told journalists that Turkish authorities might have thought that they could work with the extremist groups and "at the same time push them to become more moderate."[185] He also stated that Turkey has directly supported al-Qaeda's wing in Syria in defiance of the United States.[186]

Turkey's Confrontations with the So-Called Islamic State: Notwithstanding their rendezvous of convenience, the so-called Islamic State and Turkey have had some bloody confrontations. According to a report by Turkey's Interior Ministry in July 2017, the Islamic State killed 304 people in 14 attacks in Turkey, including 10 police officers and one soldier. Of the attacks, ten were suicide attacks, one was a bomb attack and three were armed attacks. Additionally, 1,338 people, including 62 police officers and seven soldiers were wounded. According to the report, three of the attacks were carried out in Istanbul and five of the others were in the southeastern provinces of Diyarbakır, Şanlıurfa and Gaziantep and the capital Ankara.[187]

Turkey's Confrontations with Syria's Kurds: Alarmed by the unilaterally declared self-governing towns (cantons), and by the large Kurdish component in the US-supported Syrian Democratic Forces (see below: *SDF*), Turkey imposed an economic blockade and military action against the Kurds.[188] On January 20, 2018, Turkey launched air strikes on Afrin.[189] The following day, Turkish troops, along with 25,000 fighters from the

---

[185]Richard Spencer and Raf Sanchez, "Turkish Government Co-operated with al-Qaeda in Syria, Says Former US Ambassador," *The Telegraph*, (September 12, 2014). https://archive.is/38XNV# selection-717.0-717.80

[186]Ibid.

[187]"ISIL Killed 304 in 14 Major Attacks in Turkey," *Hurriyet Daily News*, (September 22, 2017). http://www.hurriyetdailynews.com/isil-killed-304-in-14-major-attacks-in-turkey-.aspx?pageID=238 &nID=115378&NewsCatID=341

[188]"Turkey v Syria's Kurds v Islamic State," *BBC*, (August 23, 2016). http://www.bbc.co.uk/news/ world-middle-east-33690060

[189]"Syria: Turkey war planes launch strikes on Afrin," *BBC*, (January 20, 2018). http://www.bbc. co.uk/news/world-middle-east-42759944

anti-Assad Free Syrian Army, crossed into the Afrin region.[190] Under pressure, the Kurds sought help from their enemy, the Assad regime. Assad, eager to harm his nemesis, Turkey's Erdogan, declared that he would help the Kurds resist the Turkish attacks in Afrin.[191] He failed. On March 18, 2018, President Erdogan declared that Turkish-backed units of the Free Syrian Army had taken control of the center of Afrin.[192]

In view of the war between Turkey and Syria's Kurds, how might the US balance its alliance with these two antagonists? Washington is most likely to abandon the Kurds. An alliance with Syria's Kurds is no longer of much value to the US. The defeat of the so-called Islamic State has largely been achieved. Between February 2015 and October 2017, the Kurds, with US help, defeated the so-called Islamic State in Ain al-Arab (Kobane), Tal Abyad, Hasaka, and Raqqa (see below: *Syrian Democratic Forces*). Now, Turkey, a NATO member bordering Russia, is more valuable to Washington than the Kurds. Already, Mr. Trump signaled on March 29, 2018, the looming US abandonment of SDF. He said the US "will withdraw from Syria 'very soon'."[193]

Syria's refugees in Turkey: Turkey is host to the largest number of registered Syrian refugees—3.2 million, according UNHCR. The majority of the refugees live in urban areas, with around 260,000 accommodated in 21 government refugee camps.[194] Turkey's welcome will always be remembered with gratitude. The refugees nurture the already rich religious and cultural fabric, knitted by Syrians and Turks over four centuries of Ottoman rule (1517–1918). Pulling the two peoples closer together are Hanafi Islam, social customs and habits, food, music, arts, and now the Turkish language.

Gulf Cooperation Council

The Gulf Cooperation Council member states may be described as being US protectorates. 35,000 US soldiers are stationed in Bahrain, Kuwait,

---

[190]"Syria: Turkish ground troops enter Afrin enclave," *BBC*, (January 22, 2018). http://www.bbc.co.uk/news/world-middle-east-42765697

[191]Mark Lowen, "Afrin offensive: Turkey warns Syria against helping Kurds," *BBC*, (February 19, 2018). http://www.bbc.co.uk/news/world-middle-east-43107013

[192]"Turkey's Erdogan Says Afrin City Centre Under 'Total' Control in Syria," *The Telegraph*, (March 18, 2018). https://www.telegraph.co.uk/news/2018/03/18/turkeys-erdogan-says-afrin-city-centre-total-control-syria/

[193]Ryan Browne and Barbara Starr, "Trump says US will withdraw from Syria 'very soon'," *CNN*.

[194]UNHCR, Syria Emergency, (accessed, November 6, 2017). http://www.unhcr.org/uk/syria-emergency.html

Qatar, and the UAE to ensure the uninterrupted delivery of 35% of world's oil exports to world markets and to protect GCC kings, emirs, and sultans from external threats, internal strife, and one another.

As protectorates, GCC policies on regional security are shaped by US interests. While Turkey could play the Russian card against the US/NATO card, GCC rulers have only one card, the American card, to play. And, while Turkish politics in Syria are primarily defined by the Kurdish issue, Saudi politics in Syria are shaped by the Shi'ite/Wahhabi sectarian divide and age-old tribal rivalries and jealousies.

From the start of the Syrian revolution, Saudi Arabia and Qatar demanded a Syria without Assad. As Assad weaponized the revolution, GCC supporters of Syria's armed groups proved to be long on money, posturing, rhetoric, and promises, but short on effectiveness. The revolution needed anti-aircraft guns, but Obama and the GCC under America's instructions, did not respond. The war dragged on and the destruction reached unspeakable horror.

In addition, the GCC member states prevented Syrians from taking refuge in their cities. There are more than five million refugees registered with UNHCR, in Turkey (3.2 million), Lebanon (more than one million), Jordan (650,000), Iraq (244,000), Egypt (122,000),[195] plus the refugees who are not registered with UNHCR. While Germany welcomed several hundred thousand refugees, their Saudi and GCC brethren shut their doors. Their coarse excuse was that large numbers of Syrians already live and work in Saudi and GCC cities. Those who already live there are expatriate workers with work permits: accountants, architects, bankers, dentists, doctors, engineers, nurses, physicians, teachers, etc. They have been living there for years, many for decade.

Anti-Assad Syrian Groups

No sooner than the March 18, 2011 revolution erupted, Assad pursued a two-pronged strategy. First, he weaponized the protests by ordering live ammunition to be fired at unarmed demonstrators. Fear that killing civilian demonstrators could provoke Western public opinion prompted Assad to pursue his second strategy: He islamicized the revolution by releasing

---

[195]Ibid.

imprisoned jihadists. During the second half of 2011, some 2,000 terrorists were released from prisons. Thus, he turned a revolution against tyranny into a war against terrorism. Killing al-Qaeda, al-Nusra and Islamic State jihadists would bring the East and the West to his aid. Blackmail legitimacy has for fifty years been a tool in the regime's playbook.

Political Groups

When the revolution erupted, there was no organized opposition or political parties or non-regime community leaders to lead. A number of political organizations gradually emerged. The following are among the better known.

The **Syrian National Council (SNC):** Formed in Istanbul on October 2, 2011,[196] it was a coalition of representatives of Local Coordination Committees, the Muslim Brotherhood, and various Kurdish factions. SNC's internal schisms and failure to unite the rest of the opposition behind a clear program and strategy resulted in US Secretary of State Hillary Clinton announcing on October 31, 2012 that the United States no longer considered the SNC to be "the visible leader of the opposition" and called for a new opposition leadership.[197] SNC joined other opposition bodies to form the National Coalition for Syrian Revolution and Opposition Forces.[198]

The **National Coalition for Syrian Revolution and Opposition Forces:** The Syrian National Coalition was founded in Doha, Qatar, on November 11, 2012.[199] It includes the Local Co-ordination Committees, a network of grassroots opposition activists. It also has the support of the Free Syrian Army (FSA).[200] The six Gulf Co-operation Council member

---

[196]"Syrian Council Wants Recognition as Voice of Opposition," *Reuters*, (October 10, 2011). https://www.reuters.com/article/us-syria-opposition/syrian-council-wants-recognition-as-voice-of-opposition-idUSTRE7993NF20111010

[197]"Syrian National Council," *Carnegie Middle East Center*, (September 25, 2013). http://carnegie-mec.org/diwan/48334?lang=en

[198]Rania El Gamal, "Syrian Opposition Agrees Deal, Chooses Preacher as Leader," *Reuters*, (November 11, 2012). https://www.reuters.com/article/us-syria-crisis-doha/syrian-opposition-agrees-deal-chooses-preacher-as-leader-idUSBRE8AA0H320121111

[199]"Syria's Opposition Chooses President, Formally Signs Coalition Deal," *Al-Arabiya News*, (November 12, 2012). https://english.alarabiya.net/articles/2012/11/12/249032.html

[200]"Guide to the Syrian Opposition," *BBC*, (October 17, 2013). http://www.bbc.co.uk/news/world-middle-east-15798218

states were the first to recognize it as the legitimate representative of the Syrian people, followed by France, the UK, EU and US.[201] In December 2012, a hundred countries at the Friends of the Syrian People conference in Marrakesh also recognized the Coalition. Absent were Russia, China and Iran, which have backed the Assad regime.[202] The National Coalition has been unable to assert full command over Syria's jihadist groups.[203] On January 20, 2014, the Syrian National Council withdrew from the Coalition in protest against the Coalition's attendance of the Geneva talks.[204]

National Coordination Committee for Democratic Change: Formed in June 2011, the National Co-ordination Committee (NCC) for Democratic Change is an alliance of 16 left-leaning political parties, three Kurdish political parties, and independent political and youth activists.[205]

The Kurdish Supreme Committee: It was formed in July 2012 by the Democratic Union Party (PYD) and the Kurdish National Council (KNC), an alliance of 13 Kurdish parties, all under the initiative of Massoud Barzani, the former President of Iraq's semi-autonomous Kurdistan region.[206]

Armed Groups

In addition to political organizations, hundreds of anti-Assad groups of ordinary citizens were formed in Sunni areas, armed with rudimentary means to defend themselves against the security forces. According to Royal United Services Institute for Defense and Security Studies (RUSI), approximately 1,500 different rebel groups appeared on the scene during the years of the revolution.[207]

In terms of control on the ground, anti-regime fighting groups control three main geographic areas outside the regime's control. The borders and dimensions of these areas are fluid, as fighting against the regime and against each other changes their borders constantly.

---

[201]Ibid.

[202]Ibid.

[203]Ibid.

[204]"Main Bloc Quits Syrian National Coalition over Geneva," *The Times of Israel*, (January 21, 2014). http://www.timesofisrael.com/main-bloc-quits-syrian-national-coalition-over-geneva/

[205]Ibid.

[206]Ibid.

[207]Royal United Services Institute for Defence and Security Studies (RUSI), *Understanding Iran's Role in the Syrian Conflict*. P. 33.

1. Areas Controlled by the Democratic Federal System of Northern Syria: Taking advantage of the revolution, the Kurdish dominated region in the North of Syria along Turkey's borders unilaterally declared in November 2013 a self-governing autonomous region encompassing three towns (cantons) of Afrin, Kobane (Ain al-Arab in Arabic), and Jazira and adjacent areas. The Kurdish move was made possible as a result of the withdrawal of the regime's army from Kurdish areas in order to defend Aleppo and other cities. The region was called the Northern Syria Democratic Federal System, commonly known as Rojava (meaning "West" in Kurdish, a reference to the location of Rojava in Western Kurdistan).[208] On December 28, 2016, the three regions announced dropping the word 'Rojava' from the name of the proposed federal system, making the name of the autonomous region with its three cantons the Democratic Federal System of Northern Syria.[209]

According to the Kurdistan National Congress (KNK), each canton has its own constitution, government, parliament, courts, and municipalities.[210] The cantons enjoy administrative autonomy and freedom of decision-making. They have control over their educational systems, social services, police, People's Defense Forces and Women's Defense Forces.[211] Decision-making is said to federate upwards from communes, to neighborhood/district councils, to city councils, and then to the cantons. In Jazira canton for instance, Qamishli city has six neighborhoods or districts, each has 18 communes, and each commune is made up of 300 households.[212]

The Syrian Kurdish Democratic Union Party declared that the intention for Rojava is to become a model for a future democratic federal Syria along the lines of the Swiss self-governing cantonal system, not independence.[213]

---

[208]Tamya Goudsouzizn, "Why Syria's Kurds Want Federalism, and Who Opposes it," *Al Jazeera*. https://www.aljazeera.com/news/2016/03/syria-kurds-federalism-opposes-160317080412664.html

[209]Hisham Arafat, "'Rojava' no longer exists, 'Northern Syria' adopted instead," *Kurdistan 24*, (December 28, 2016). http://www.kurdistan24.net/en/news/51940fb9-3aff-4e51-bcf8-b1629af00 299/-Rojava--no-longer-exists---Northern-Syria--adopted-instead-

[210]Kurdistan National Congress (KNK), "Canton Based Democratic Autonomy of Rojava (Western Kurdistan—Northern Syria), A Transformations Process from Dictatorship to Democracy," (May 2014), P. 13. https://peaceinkurdistancampaign.files.wordpress.com/2011/11/rojava-info-may-2014.pdf

[211]Ibid.

[212]Rana Khalaf, "Governing Rojava—Layers of Legitimacy in Syria," *Chatham House*, (December 2016), P. 11. https://www.chathamhouse.org/sites/files/chathamhouse/publications/research/2016-12-08-governing-rojava-khalaf.pdf

[213]"Why Syria's Kurds want federalism, and who opposes it," *Al Jazeera*, (March 17, 2016).

For fifty years, the Assad/Ba'ath Party's Arab nationalism ideology discriminated against Syria's Kurdish population. The regime's Arabization policies reduced the Kurds to second-class citizens. Deportation, prohibition of the Kurdish language, denial of Syrian citizenship, among other restrictions, turned their lives upside down.[214] Arab nationalism also meant "Arab Cordon" (al-Hizam al-Arabi), resulting in the Kurds' fertile lands being taken over by the Assad regime and later given to Arab tribes.[215] The "Arab Belt" is 350 kilometers long and 15 kilometers wide, according to the Kurdistan National Congress.[216] The insertion of the word "Arab" in the old name of the Syrian Republic, the making of the country's name since the 1963 military coup as Syrian Arab Republic, ignores the existence of Kurds (around 10% of the population) and the other ethnic minorities; namely, Assyrians, Turkmen, Armenians, Chechens, Circassians. In the mid-1960s, under the banner of Arab nationalism, thousands of soldiers from the Syrian army were dispatched to Iraq to help the Iraqi army in its war against Iraqi Kurds.

On June 27–28, 2016, a Constituent Assembly approved the draft of an 85-article constitution, called "The Social Contract," notable for its explicit declaration of minority rights and gender equality. The preamble emphasizes the importance of federalism. It states, "We, the people of Rojava: Northern Syria, Kurds, Arabs, Assyrians, Turkmen, Armenians, Chechens, Circassians, Muslims, Christians, Yazidis and various others, are aware that the nation-state has brought our people problems, acute crises and tragedies."[217] The document recognizes Syria's territorial integrity. Article 12 states, "The Autonomous Regions form an integral part of Syria. It is a model for a future decentralized system of federal governance in Syria."[218]

Rojava is not recognized by the Assad regime nor the Syrian opposition nor by any international state or organization. Iran and Turkey fear that a self-ruled Kurdish region in Syria alongside a Kurdistan Regional Government in Iraq could encourage the Kurdish populations in Iran and Turkey to demand similar rights. Their nightmare is that a Kurdish

---

[214]Ibid.

[215]Rana Khalaf, "Governing Rojava–Layers of Legitimacy in Syria," P. 7.

[216]Kurdistan National Congress (KNK), Canton Based Democratic Autonomy of Rojava, P. 4.

[217]Peace in Kurdistan, "Charter of the Social Contract," (January 29, 2014). https://peaceinkurdistancampaign.com/charter-of-the-social-contract/

[218]Ibid.

region might eventually lead to the creation of a Kurdish state spanning Iran, Iraq, Syria and Turkey. Curiously, the US Secretary of State suggested on February 23, 2016 that partition could form part of an eventual solution in Syria,[219] and the Russian Deputy Foreign Minister told a news briefing on February 29, 2016 that Syria could become a federal state.[220]

Population and Resources: At the start of the Syrian revolution in March 2011, the region was home to around 3.5 million people. Six years later, nearly a million people have fled.[221] Hasaka (Jazira Canton), cradled between the Tigris and Euphrates rivers, is rich in agriculture. Of Syria's 13 billion m3 of water available annually for irrigation, 7 billion m3 are in the Euphrates Basin, a good proportion of which is in Hasaka.[222] Of Syria's 1.2 million hectares of irrigated areas, 760,000 hectares are in the Euphrates Basin, a good proportion of which is in Hasaka.[223] Rimelan (Jazira Canton) is rich in oil and gas.[224]

Syrian Democratic Forces (SDF): The Kurds crushed the so-called Islamic State in Kobane (Ain al-Arab) in February 2015, Tal Abyad in June 2015, and Hasaka City in July 2015.[225] In October 2015, the Syria Democratic Forces (SDF) was formed. Its mission is to fight terrorism and to create a secular, democratic and federal Syria. The Syrian Democratic Forces is a coalition of Kurdish, Sunni Arab and Syriac Christian[226] and Yazidi[227] fighters. According to a Carnegie Middle East Center report, it is a political umbrella designed to provide legal and political cover for US military support to the Kurdistan Workers'

---

[219]Patrick Wintour, "John Kerry Says Partition of Syria Could Be Part of 'Plan B' if Peace Talks Fail," *The Guardian*, (February 23, 2016). https://www.theguardian.com/world/2016/feb/23/john-kerry-partition-syria-peace-talks

[220]"Russia Says Federal Model Is Possible for Syria in Future," *Reuters*, (February 29, 2016). http://in.reuters.com/article/mideast-crisis-russia-syria/russia-says-federal-model-is-possible-for-syria-in-future-idINKCN0W21TP

[221]Libcom.org, "A Mountain River Has Many Bends: An Introduction to the Rojava Revolution." https://libcom.org/library/mountain-river-has-many-bends

[222]The World Bank, "Syrian Arab Republic Irrigation Sector Report," Report no. 22602, P. viii,

[223]Ibid.

[224]Kurdistan National Congress (KNK), "Canton Based Democratic Autonomy of Rojava," P. 5.

[225]Aron Lund, "Syria's Kurds at the Center of America's Anti-Jihadi Strategy", *Carnegie Middle East Center*.

[226]Ibid.

[227]"From the Front Line in Raqqa: Isis to Lose Syrian 'Capital' in Days after 'Surprise Attack' by US-Backed Forces," *The Independent*, (September 20, 2017). http://www.independent.co.uk/news/world/middle-east/isis-raqqa-front-line-in-syria-sdf-assad-islamic-state-iraq-forces-battle-a7957931.html

Party, better known as PKK, in the fight against the so-called Islamic State.[228] Turkey views Syria's Kurdish progress with consternation and hostility.

On the composition of Arabs and Kurds, the US Department of Defense revealed in a press briefing dated March 1, 2017 that, "We have watched and operated alongside the Syrian Democratic Forces, of which about 40% are composed of YPG Kurds, the People's Protection units—YPG, and about 60% now are composed of the Syrian Arab Coalition."[229]

According to the London *Independent* newspaper on September 20, 2017, the Pentagon said, "The SDF numbers 40,000 troops, but they are for the most part a quickly trained and inexperienced army, and the bonds holding its various Kurdish, Arab and other component units together are not strong."[230]

The liberation of Raqqa and Deir Ezzor from the So-Called Islamic State: On October 17, 2017, after about four years of being the capital city of the so-called Islamic State, the destroyed city of Raqqa, on the eastern side of the Euphrates river, was liberated by Syrian Democratic Forces, with American help.[231] A few days later on October 22, 2017, the SDF captured Syria's largest oilfield, al-Omar, also on the eastern side of the Euphrates river near Deir Ezzor.[232]

On November 3, 2017, government forces backed by Russia recaptured the city of Deir Ezzor from the so-called Islamic State.[233]

With Raqqa and the al-Omar oilfield in the hands of American supported Syrian Democratic Forces and the adjacent Deir Ezzor city in the hands of Russian supported Assad and allied forces, a potentially serious

---

[228]Aron Lund, "Syria's Kurds at the Center of America's Anti-Jihadi Strategy," *Carnegie Middle East Center.*

[229]US Department of Defense Press Briefing by Gen. Townsend via Teleconference from Baghdad, Iraq, (March 1, 2017). https://www.defense.gov/News/Transcripts/Transcript-View/Article/1099469/department-of-defense-press-briefing-by-gen-townsend-via-teleconference-from-ba/

[230]"From the Front Line in Raqqa: Isis to Lose Syrian 'Capital' in Days after 'Surprise Attack' by US-backed forces", *The Independent.*

[231]"Trump Praises Syrian Democratic Forces for Fall of Raqqa," *Voice of America (VOA)*, (October 21, 2017). https://www.voanews.com/a/after-raqqa-new-phase-in-syria/4080699.html

[232]"SDF Says it Captured al-Omar Oilfield from ISIL," *Al Jazeera*, (October 22, 2017). https://www.aljazeera.com/news/2017/10/sdf-captured-al-omar-oil-field-isil-171022194321039.html

[233]Chris Pleasance, "The End of the 'Caliphate': Syrian Army Takes Control of Deir Ezzor from ISIS as Government Forces Enter Al-Qaim, the Terror Group's Final Bastion in Iraq," *MailOnline*, (November 3, 2017). http://www.dailymail.co.uk/news/article-5045843/End-ISIS-caliphate-bastions-Syria-Iraq-fall.html

confrontation could be in the making, especially since Assad has vowed to retake the whole of Syria.[234]

US Commitment to SDF: According to the US Secretary of Defense and former Secretary of State the US is set for a long-term presence in Syria (see above: *Trump Administration's Likely Syria Policy*). The US has set up around 20 military bases in Syria on territory controlled by the Kurds, according to Russia's Security Council.[235] However, Mr. Trump signaled on March 29, 2018, the looming US abandonment of SDF. He said the US "will withdraw from Syria 'very soon'."[236] So, whether the President or his Defense Secretary and Secretary of State are right, remains to be seen.

2. Areas Controlled by Al-Qaeda's Two Incarnations: Two incarnations were delivered from al-Qaeda: the al-Nusra Front in Syria and the so-called Islamic State in Syria and Iraq. The Metamorphosis evolved as follows:

On October 18, 2004, Abu Mus'ab al-Zarqawi (killed on June 7, 2006 by the US) declared the allegiance of his five-year old terror organization, Tawheed and Jihad, to Osama bin Laden.[237] The organization became known as al-Qaeda in Iraq (AQI).

On October 15, 2006, AQI joined several smaller Sunni groups and tribes to form the Islamic State in Iraq (ISI) covering Iraq's six mostly Sunni Arab governorates with Abu Omar al-Baghdadi as emir.[238]

In 2007 and 2008, the US "surge" drove ISI out of its safe Sunni areas after suffering huge losses in fights against US troops and Iraqi Sunni Awakening fighters.[239]

On May 16, 2010, following the killing by US forces of Abu Omar al-Baghdadi (April 18, 2010), Abu Bakr al-Baghdadi (no relation to Abu

---

[234]"Assad Adviser says Turkish, US Forces 'Illegal Invaders' in Syria," *Reuters*, (November 7, 2017). http://uk.reuters.com/article/uk-mideast-crisis-syria-adviser/assad-adviser-says-turkish-u-s-forces-illegal-invaders-in-syria-idUKKBN1D72V9

[235]"Russia Says U.S. Has Set Up About 20 Military Bases in Syria: RIA," *Reuters*, (March 1, 2018). https://www.reuters.com/article/us-mideast-crisis-syria-usa-russia/russia-says-u-s-has-set-up-about-20-military-bases-in-syria-ria-idUSKCN1GD3ZY

[236]Ryan Browne and Barbara Starr, "Trump says US will withdraw from Syria 'very soon'," *CNN*.

[237]"Al-Zarqawi Group Claims Allegiance to bin Laden," *CNN*, (October 18, 2004). http://edition.cnn.com/2004/WORLD/meast/10/17/al.zarqawi.statement/

[238]"What is 'Islamic State'?," *BBC*, (December 2, 2015). http://www.bbc.co.uk/news/world-middle-east-29052144

[239]Lenox Samuels, "AL QAEDA IN IRAQ RAMPS UP ITS RACKETEERING," *Newsweek*, (May 20, 2008). http://www.newsweek.com/al-qaeda-iraq-ramps-its-racketeering-89733

Omar al-Baghdadi) was appointed ISI's new leader.[240] He appointed former Saddam Hussein military officers to key positions in ISI.[241]

The Syrian revolution exploded on March 18, 2011. In the following few months, shooting live ammunition to kill unarmed demonstrators led to a gradual militarization of the conflict and Islamization of the revolution.[242]

Jabhat al-Nusra (Syria): In August 2011, Baghdadi started dispatching Syrian and Iraqi ISI jihadists to Syria to establish a foothold under the banner of Jabhat al-Nusra Li Ahl al-Sham (meaning, the Support Front for the people of the Levant). The leader was a Syrian, Abu Muhammad al-Joulani, a veteran of the war against the US in Iraq.[243] On December 11, 2012, the US State Department announced that the al-Nusra Front was simply "a new alias for AQI" and that the group "has sought to portray itself as part of the legitimate Syrian opposition while it is, in fact, an attempt by AQI to hijack the struggles of the Syrian people for its own malign purposes."[244]

On April 9, 2013, Baghdadi announced in an audio message, translated by the SITE Intelligence Group that the al-Nusra Front "is but an extension of the Islamic State of Iraq and part of it."[245] It also mentioned that the two groups were merging under the name Islamic State of Iraq and al-Sham (ISIS).[246] The next day, April 10, 2013, Joulani said in an audio message: "The sons of al-Nusra Front pledge allegiance to Sheikh Ayman al-Zawahri," distancing the group from claims that it had merged with al-Qaida in Iraq.[247] On June 9, 2013, Al Jazeera reported that it had obtained

---

[240]"Iraqi Insurgent Group Names New Leaders," The *New York Times*, (May 16, 2010). https://atwar.blogs.nytimes.com/2010/05/16/iraqi-insurgent-group-names-new-leaders/?_php=true&_type=blogs&_r=0

[241]Liz Sly, "How Saddam Hussein's Former Military Officers and Spies Are Controlling Isis," *The Independent*, (April 5, 2015). https://www.independent.co.uk/news/world/middle-east/how-saddam-husseins-former-military-officers-and-spies-are-controlling-isis-10156610.html

[242]"Syria: The story of the Conflict," *BBC*, (March 11, 2016). http://www.bbc.co.uk/news/world-middle-east-26116868

[243]Rania Abouzeid, "The Jihad Next Door-The Syrian Roots of Iraq's Newest Civil War," *Politico*, (June 23, 2014). http://www.politico.com/magazine/story/2014/06/al-qaeda-iraq-syria-108214_full.html#.WbL8Ba2ZP6k

[244]Thomas Joscelyn, "Al-Qaeda in Iraq, Al-Nusra Front Emerge as Rebranded Single Entity," *FDD's Long War*, (April 9, 2013). http://www.longwarjournal.org/archives/2013/04/the_emir_of_al_qaeda.php

[245]Ibid.

[246]Ibid.

[247]"Al-Nusra Commits to al-Qaida, Deny Iraq Branch 'Merger'," *Naharnet*, (April 10, 2013). http://www.naharnet.com/stories/en/78961-al-nusra-commits-to-al-qaida-deny-iraq-branch-merger/

a letter written by Zawahiri, addressed to both men, in which he ruled against the merger.[248] A week later, on June 15, 2013, Baghdadi released an audio message rejecting Zawahri's ruling and declaring that the merger was going ahead.[249]

On November 8, 2013, Zawahri ordered the disbanding of ISIS, putting al-Nusra Front in charge al-Qaeda's jihad in Syria.[250] Some jihadists stayed with Joulani after the split-up, while others, especially the foreign fighters, followed Baghdadi's edict and joined ISIS with their weapons. ISIS started to set up its state in Raqqa in the northeast of Syria bordering Iraq.[251] On January 14, 2014, Raqqa was reported to be under the full control of ISIS.[252]

Two and a half years later, on July 29, 2016, Jabhat al-Nusra's leader Joulani, announced in a recorded message that it had split from al-Qaeda. Its new name would be Jabhat Fateh al-Sham [Front for the Conquest of Syria/the Levant].[253] The US responded by saying it saw no reason to change its view of the group as a terrorist organization.[254]

Fall of Mosul to the So-Called Islamic State: Meanwhile, on June 10, 2014, the Islamic State in Iraq and al-Sham (ISIS) seized Mosul, Iraq's second largest city of two million inhabitants.[255] Two and a half years after US troops left Iraq, about 1,000 lightly armed men, riding in Toyota pick-ups forced 30,000 soldiers with tanks, helicopters, and heavy guns to flee.[256]

---

[248]"Qaeda Chief Annuls Syrian-Iraqi jihad Merger," *Al Jazeera*, (June 9, 2013). https://www.aljazeera.com/news/middleeast/2013/06/2013699425657882.html

[249]"Iraqi al-Qaeda Chief Rejects Zawahiri Orders," *Al Jazeera*, (June 15, 2013). https://www.aljazeera.com/news/middleeast/2013/06/20136151722178827810.html

[250]"Zawahiri Disbands Main Qaeda Faction in Syria," *The Daily Star*, (November 8, 2013). http://www.dailystar.com.lb/News/Middle-East/2013/Nov-08/237219-zawahiri-disbands-main-qaeda-faction-in-syria-jazeera.ashx

[251]Rania Abouzeid, "The Jihad Next Door-The Syrian Roots of Iraq's Newest Civil War," *Politico*.

[252]"ISIL Recaptures Raqqa from Syria's Rebels," *Al Jazeera*, (January 14, 2014). https://www.aljazeera.com/news/middleeast/2014/01/isil-recaptures-raqqa-from-syrias-rebels-2014114201917453586.html

[253]"Syrian Nusra Front Announces Split from al-Qaeda," *BBC*, (July 29, 2016). http://www.bbc.co.uk/news/world-middle-east-36916606

[254]Ibid.

[255]Martin Chulov, "Isis Insurgents Seize Control of Iraqi City of Mosul," *The Guardian*, (June 10, 2014). https://www.theguardian.com/world/2014/jun/10/iraq-sunni-insurgents-islamic-militants-seize-control-mosul

[256]"Mosul: Iraq's Beleaguered Second City," *BBC*, (October 18, 2016). http://www.bbc.co.uk/news/world-middle-east-37676731

The So-Called Islamic State: On June 29, 2014, ISIS proclaimed itself a caliphate. Its name became Islamic State, with Raqqa as its capital city,[257] and Abu Bakr al-Baghdadi as caliph.[258] Rebranding itself as a caliphate, with a caliph, not a kingdom, with a king, was clever. The Qur'an takes a jaundiced view of kingships and kings:

> Qur'an 27:34: *Surely when kings enter a city, they destroy it and despoil the honor of its nobility.*

Liberation of Mosul from the So-Called Islamic State: Three years of savagery came to an end on July 10, 2017 when Iraq's prime minister declared victory over the so-called Islamic State in Mosul. "A 100,000-strong alliance of Iraqi government units, Kurdish Peshmerga fighters and Shi'ite militias launched the offensive to recapture the northern city from the militants in October, with key air and ground support from a US-led coalition."[259] However, nine months of fighting had left Mosul in total ruins.

The So-Called Islamic State Beyond Iraq and Syria: In an audio message purportedly from an Islamic State spokesman, reported on March 16, 2013, the group announced that a pledge of allegiance from Nigerian-based Boko Haram had been accepted by Abu Bakr al-Baghdadi. The message said that the caliphate had expanded to western Africa.[260] In April 2016, it was reported that co-operation between the so-called Islamic State and Boko Haram was increasing.[261]

---

[257]Muslims' first civil war took place in 657 along the banks of the Euphrates river in Siffin, near Raqqa, Syria. It was over the succession to the Prophet between the fourth caliph Ali bin Abi Talib (656–661), the Prophet's cousin and son in law, and Mu'awiyah bin Abi Sufyan, Governor of Syria (639–661) and fifth caliph of Islam (661–680), first caliph of the Umayyad caliphate in Damascus (661–750). 1360 years later, the Assad regime lost Raqqa to the Wahhabi so-called Islamic State.

[258]"ISIS Fast Facts," *CNN*, (August 24, 2017). http://edition.cnn.com/2014/08/08/world/isis-fast-facts/index.html

[259]Isabel Coles and Stephen Kalin, "Iraqi PM Declares Victory Over Islamic State in Mosul," *Reuters*, "July 10, 2017". https://www.reuters.com/article/us-mideast-crisis-iraq-mosul/iraqi-pm-declares-victory-over-islamic-state-in-mosul-idUSKBN19V105

[260]Hamdi Alkhshali and Steve Almasy, "ISIS Leader Purportedly Accepts Boko Haram's Pledge of Allegiance," *CNN*, (March 16, 2013). http://edition.cnn.com/2015/03/12/middleeast/isis-boko-haram/index.html

[261]Lizzie Dearden, "Isis Increasing Co-operation with Boko Haram—the 'World's Most Horrific Terrorist Group'," *The Independent*, (April 21, 2016). http://www.independent.co.uk/news/world/africa/isis-increasing-co-operation-with-boko-haram-the-worlds-most-horrific-terrorist-group-a6994881.html

Wahhabi Proselytization in the Age of the Internet: What is most dangerous in the age of the internet and social media, is the ease with which Wahhabi activists can proselytize and radicalize the gullible individual. In the past, Saudi trained clerics in mosques and religious schools (madrassas) preached to local audiences. Today, these face to face lessons have been replaced by a computer. Wahhabi inspiration, through the internet, has recently been turning otherwise peaceful young Muslims in Western cities into killers, using cars to mow down pedestrians or machete to terrify shoppers.

Whether radicalization is done in person or through the internet, two elements must be present to make a jihadist explode: the first, which is the dynamite, is a belief in predestination, jihad, and the delights of paradise. The second is the spark to explode the dynamite: Personal frustration, exasperation, and anger.

Hay'at Tahrir Al-Sham (HTS): On January 28, 2017, five Islamist groups in Syria announced their merger to form Hay'at Tahrir al-Sham (HTS), or the Assembly for Liberation of the Levant.[262] The head of the new grouping is a jihadist known as Abu Jaber (also known as Hashem al-Sheikh).[263] The Assad regime knows Abu Jaber well. In 2005, he was imprisoned in the notorious Sednaya Prison. Assad released Abu Jaber from prison on September 25, 2011, six months after the revolution had started, as part of his manipulation strategy.[264]

The new grouping is dominated by al-Qaeda's affiliate, al-Nusra Front (renamed on July 29, 2016 as Jabhat Fatah al-Sham). Hay'at Tahrir al-Sham, boasts some 31,000 fighters.[265] The merger expanded the group's presence from one front to multiple cities: Idlib, Hama, Aleppo in the North and Dar'a in the South.[266] HTS had a presence in Eastern Ghouta, just outside Damascus.[267]

---

[262]The five are: Jabhat Fath al Sham, Harakat (Movement) Nur al-Din al-Zanki, Liwa Al Haqq, Ansar Al Din, and Jaysh Al Sunnah.

[263]Thomas Joscelyn, "Al Qaeda and Allies Announce 'New Entity' in Syria," *FDD's Long War Journal*, (January 28, 2017). http://www.longwarjournal.org/archives/2017/01/al-qaeda-and-allies-announce-new-entity-in-syria.php

[264]Thomas Joscelyn, "Hay'at Tahrir al Sham Leader Calls for 'Unity' in Syrian Insurgency," *FDD's Long War Journal*, (February 10, 2017). http://www.longwarjournal.org/archives/2017/02/hayat-tahrir-al-sham-leader-calls-for-unity-in-syrian-insurgency.php

[265]Nazeer Rida, "Syria: Surfacing of 'Hai'at Tahrir al-Sham' Threatens Truce," *Asharq al-Awsat*, (January 30, 2017). https://english.aawsat.com/nazeer-rida/news-middle-east/syria-surfacing-haiat-tahrir-al-sham-threatens-truce

[266]Mattisan Rowan, "Al Qaeda's Latest Rebranding: Hay'at Tahrir al Sham," *Wilson Center*, (April 24, 2017). https://www.wilsoncenter.org/article/al-qaedas-latest-rebranding-hayat-tahrir-al-sham

[267]BBC Monitoring, "Explainer: Who's Fighting Whom in Syria's Ghouta?," *BBC*, (February 22, 2018). https://monitoring.bbc.co.uk/product/c1douzrw

HTS wants to establish in Syria what may be described as an "IS-light" Wahhabi type of governance. Nonetheless, Syrians, steeped in the moderate Hanafi culture for the five centuries during Ottoman rule are unwelcoming to Wahhabism in all its shades, colors, and incarnations.

Discord among the parties started to undermine HTS. On July 20, 2017, Harakat (Movement) Nour al-Din al-Zanki, one of the original five main battalions in HTS, announced its defection from HTS.[268] Following internal strife, defections, and resignations, HTS announced on October 2, 2017, the resignation of Abu Jaber and the appointment of Joulani as interim leader.[269] On November 7, 2017, Harakat Nour al-Din al-Zanki, announced that its fighters repelled an attack of HTS.[270] On February 18, 2018, Ahrar al-Sham and Harakat Nour al-Din al-Zenki announced in a joint statement that they are merging their forces to form a new armed group in Idlib called The Syria Liberation Front (SLF).[271]

Al-Qaeda's Metamorphosis Summary:
October 2004: al-Qaeda in Iraq (AQI)
October 2006: Islamic State in Iraq (ISI)
August 2011: Jabhat al-Nusra (Syria). Re-named on July 29, 2016 as Jabhat Fatah al-Sham.
April 2013: Islamic State of Iraq and al-Sham [Iraq and Syria (ISIS)].
June 29, 2014, ISIS made itself a caliphate, so-called Islamic State. Raqqa, Syria was capital.
July 29, 2016, Jabhat al-Nusra announced divorce from al-Qaeda.
January 28, 2017, Jabhat Fatah al-Sham became the main part in Hay'at Tahrir al-Sham (HTS).

---

[268]The Carter Center, "Relations Between Hai'yat Tahrir al-Sham and Nour al-Din al-Zinki in 2017," (November 7, 2017), P. 4, https://www.cartercenter.org/resources/pdfs/peace/conflict_resolution/syria-conflict/2017.11.03-hts-ndz-report.pdf

[269]"Joulani Interim Leader of HTS," *HUFFPOST (Arabic)*, (October 2, 2017). http://www.huffpostarabi.com/2017/10/02/story_n_18159996.html

[270]"Nour Al-Din Al-Zenki Foils Hay'at Tahrir Al-Sham Attack on Toqad Town in West Aleppo," *The Revolutionary Forces of Syria*, (November 12, 2017). https://rfsmediaoffice.com/en/2017/11/12/nour-al-din-al-zenki-foils-hayat-tahrir-al-sham-attack-toqad-town-west-aleppo/ Also: "Calm returns to Aleppo as Syrian inter-rebel clashes subdue," *The New Arab*, (November 15, 2017). https://www.alaraby.co.uk/english/blog/2017/11/15/calm-returns-to-aleppo-as-syrian-inter-rebel-clashes-subdue

[271]"Syrian Rebels Form Merger against Jihadists," *The New Arab*, (February 19, 2018). https://www.alaraby.co.uk/english/news/2018/2/19/syrian-rebels-form-merger-against-jihadists

Are Assad and Al-Qaeda/Al-Nusra/IS Enemies or Friends? There is ample evidence to conclude that a mutuality of interest has existed between the Assad regime and terrorist groups. The London *Daily Telegraph* reported on January 20, 2014, that Western intelligence agencies, rebels, and al-Qaeda defectors assert that the Assad regime has co-operated with Jabhat al-Nusra and the so-called Islamic State in a complex double game of selling oil and gas from wells under their control to and through the regime.[272]

According to US Secretary of State John Kerry, in a testimony before Congress in September 2014, the Syrian government has been flirting with al-Qaeda and its incarnations:

> If Assad's forces indeed do decide to focus on ISIL significantly, which they haven't been doing throughout this period, one of our judgments is, there is evidence that Assad has played footsie with them, and he has used them as a tool of weakening the opposition. He never took on their headquarters, which were there and obvious, and other assets that they have. So we have no confidence that Assad is either capable of or willing to take on ISIL.[273]

According to NBC News, quoting IHS Jane's Terrorism and Insurgency Center database, just 13% of the militants' attacks during 2014 targeted Syrian security forces. As for the Assad regime's targeting of the Islamist enemy, it was even more halfhearted: only 6% of the 982 operations against the enemy had targeted ISIS during the same time period.[274]

On June 1, 2015, the US Embassy in Syria stated that the Syrian government was "making air-strikes in support" of an ISIS advance on Syrian opposition areas north of Aleppo.[275] The president of the Syrian National Coalition, Khaled Khoja, accused Assad of acting "as an air force

---

[272]Ruth Sherlock, "Syria's Assad Accused of Boosting al-Qaeda with Secret Oil Deals," *The Telegraph*, (January 20, 2014). http://www.telegraph.co.uk/news/worldnews/middleeast/syria/10585391/Syrias-Assad-accused-of-boosting-al-Qaeda-with-secret-oil-deals.html

[273]Ian Schwartz, "Kerry: There Is Evidence That Assad Has Played "Footsie" With ISIl," *Real Clear Politics*, (September 18, 2014). https://www.realclearpolitics.com/video/2014/09/18/kerry_there_is_evidence_that_assad_has_played_footsie_with_isil.html

[274]Ammar Cheikh and Cassandra Vinograd, "Syria, ISIS Have Been 'Ignoring' Each Other on Battlefield, Data Suggests," *NBC News*, (December 11, 2014). https://www.nbcnews.com/storyline/isis-terror/syria-isis-have-been-ignoring-each-other-battlefield-data-suggests-n264551

[275]US Embassy Syria Verified Account: Reports indicate that the regime is making air-strikes in support of #ISIL's advance on #Aleppo, aiding extremists against Syrian population 1:28 PM—1 Jun 2015

for ISIS."[276] Haaretz reported in June 2015 that regime forces abandoned the city of Palmyra and allowed ISIS to take it over unopposed.[277] The Defense Minister in the Revolutionary Provisional Government, Salim Idris, stated that approximately 180 Syrian government officers were serving in ISIS and coordinating the group's attacks with the Syrian Army.[278]

Sources of Funding of Terror Groups: It is difficult to estimate the relative contribution of each of the categories below to al-Nusra or the so-called Islamic State. To gain an idea of magnitude, if the annual financial requirement to maintain a jihadi in a state of readiness is around $10,000 (~$300 in monthly salary + ~$500 in monthly ammunition, and other expenses), the cost of, say, 10,000 jihadists would be some $100 million:

- Confiscation of cash from banks.
- Oil revenues.
- Taxing business owners.
- Selling stolen artefacts.
- Transit fees.
- Kidnapping for ransom.
- Donations from Islamists.
- Munitions seized from Syrian army units.
- Targeting other groups to capture their weapons.[279]

According to a Brookings Institution study in July 2016, while ISIS maintains almost all sources of income originating within their territory, Jabhat al-Nusra is heavily reliant on external sources of financial donations to sustain its operations.[280] This formula must change as cities in Iraq and Syria get liberated from the Islamic State. As it changes its modus operandi, its funding sources will come from stealing, kidnapping for ransom, and

[276]"Assad's Forces May Be Aiding New ISIS Surge," The *New York Times*, (June 2, 2015). https://www.nytimes.com/2015/06/03/world/middleeast/new-battles-aleppo-syria-insurgents-isis.html

[277]Zvi Bar'el, "Assad's Cooperation with ISIS Could Push US into Syria Conflict," *Haaretz*, (June 3, 2015). http://www.haaretz.com/middle-east-news/1.659340

[278]Ibid.

[279]In 2014, Jabhat al-Nusra, Allegedly Captured 10 Tanks and 80 TOW Missiles from the US Backed Syrian Revolutionaries Front. "Hay'at Tahrir al-Sham (Formerly Jabhat al-Nusra)", *Stanford University, Mapping Militants project*, (updated August 14, 2017), http://web.stanford.edu/group/mappingmilitants/cgi-bin/groups/view/493?highlight=Hayyat+Tahrir+al-Sham

[280]Charles Lister, "Profiling Jabhat al-Nusra," *The Brookings Project on US Relations with the Islamic World*, (July 2016), PP. 31–32. https://www.brookings.edu/wp-content/uploads/2016/07/iwr_20160728_profiling_nusra.pdf

donation from Islamists. On individuals accused of alleged involvement in financially supporting Jabhat al-Nusra from outside Syria, the Brookings study, quoting US Department of Treasury, continues, "The majority, seven of ten, are Kuwaitis based in Kuwait, with the remaining three being a Jordanian currently in prison in Lebanon, a Turk in Turkey, and a Qatari in Qatar."[281] Additionally, "Jabhat al-Nusra is widely alleged to acquire more substantial sums from the ransoming of foreign hostages ... Well placed media reports have cited figures of between $4 million and $25 million for hostage releases, almost all mediated and secured by Qatar." The study adds, "Should allegations over ransom payments be accurate, it would suggest that kidnapping for ransom represented a highly significant source of income for Jabhat al-Nusra, likely of existential importance."[282]

The War Between al-Qaeda and the So-Called Islamic State—An Observation: It is curious that recommendations made in the RAND Corporation's report in 2008, *Unfolding the Future of the Long War*, identified a number of strategy options to weaken Islamist terror organizations. One of the strategies became a reality with the birth of the so-called Islamic State in 2014 and the war that ensued between it and al-Qaeda. RAND recommended a 'divide and rule' strategy that seeks to turn jihadist groups against each other using covert action and support to indigenous security forces.

3. Areas Controlled by the Free Syrian Army: The Free Syrian Army (FSA) was founded in July 2011 by officers who deserted from the Syrian army. Initially, it was headquartered close to the Syrian border with Turkey. In September 2012, it moved to the city of Idlib in Northern Syria, near the Turkish border.[283] FSA leader Colonel Riad al-Assad expressed in November 2011 the aim for the FSA to be the "military wing of the Syrian people's opposition to the regime."[284] The Free Syrian Army functions more as an umbrella organization of hundreds of small loosely connected local units, mostly secular, some religious, than

---

[281]Ibid.

[282]Ibid.

[283]Ruth Sherlock, "Syria Rebel Army Shifts from Turkey," *The Telegraph*, (September 23, 2012). www.telegraph.co.uk/news/worldnews/midSyria rebel army shifts from Turkeydleast/syria/9560925/Syria-rebel-army-shifts-from-Turkey.html

[284]Ruth Sherlock, "'15,000 Strong' Army Gathers to Take on Syria," *The Telegraph*, (November 3, 2011). http://www.telegraph.co.uk/news/worldnews/middleeast/syria/8868027/15000-strong-army-gathers-to-take-on-Syria.html

a traditional military chain of command.[285] *Time* magazine described the FSA in October 2012 as being "never more than an umbrella term that provided political cover for the loose franchise of defectors and armed civilians fighting Assad's regime."[286] Gen. Salim Idriss, who leads the FSA Supreme Military Command, admitted in May 2013 that his movement is badly fragmented and that he faces difficulty in creating a chain of command in the highly localized rebellion, a shortcoming he blamed on the presence within the rebel movement of large numbers of civilians without military experience.[287]

Suffering from a lack of discipline and a shortage of ammunition and weapons, the FSA struggled to assert itself on the battlefield. It stagnated while Islamist groups prospered, despite valiant attempts to unify the anti-Assad democratic forces.[288] One such attempt was the signing of an agreement in Turkey on September 25, 2014 by more than 20 Syrian opposition commanders, including members of Christian opposition groups to unite in the fight against ISIS and Assad's forces. The agreement came out of a meeting facilitated by staff from the US House Foreign Affairs Committee and the Syrian Emergency Task Force, based in Washington.

At the top of the anti-FSA list was Jabhat al-Nusra. It became the best-equipped, financed and motivated fighting force battling the Assad regime.[289] The FSA has lost a quarter of all its fighters to al-Nusra, according to one estimate revealed in the *Guardian* in May 2013—its own Ahrar al-Shimal brigade, joined al-Nusra en-masse.[290]

[285]Joseph Holliday, "Syria's Armed Opposition," *Middle East Security Report*, (March 2012). http://www.understandingwar.org/sites/default/files/Syrias_Armed_Opposition.pdf

[286]Rana Abouzeid, "Syria's Up-and-Coming Rebels: Who Are the Farouq Brigades?," *Time magazine*, (October 5, 2012). http://world.time.com/2012/10/05/syrias-up-and-coming-rebels-who-are-the-farouq-brigades-2/

[287]David Enders, "Syrian Rebel Leader Salim Idriss Admits Difficulty of Unifying Fighters," *McClatchy*, (May 7, 2013). http://www.mcclatchydc.com/news/nation-world/world/article24748906.html

[288]Scott Bronsten, "Syrian Rebel Groups Unite to Fight ISIS," *CNN*, (September 26, 2014). http://edition.cnn.com/2014/09/25/world/meast/us-syria-rebel-agreement/

[289]Martin Chulov, "Free Syrian Army Threatens Blood Feud After Senior Officer Killed by jihadists," *The Guardian*, (July 12, 2013). https://www.theguardian.com/world/2013/jul/12/free-syrian-army-officer-killed

[290]Mona Mahmood and Ian Black, "Free Syrian Army Rebels Defect to Islamist Group Jabhat al-Nusra," *The Guardian*, (May 8, 2013). https://www.theguardian.com/world/2013/may/08/free-syrian-army-rebels-defect-islamist-group

Many FSA soldiers moved to al-Nusra and the so-called Islamic State for better weapons, possibly better salaries and the prospect of more booty. Others must have fantasized that by joining either group, a jihadist would get closer to God and enjoys bigger victories. The belief in predestination and the imagined, tantalizing pleasures of paradise must have made the prospect of dying for al-Nusra and the so-called Islamic State more attractive than dying for the cause of democracy.

It was only a matter of time before Nusra and IS would go to war against the generally secularist FSA. Within two years, al-Qaeda's Nusra and IS started shooting at FSA. Also, rivalry and personal animosity among al-Qaeda leaders (Ayman al-Zawahiri) and his al-Nusra lieutenant (Abu Muhammad al-Joulani), on one hand, and the so-called Islamic State's self-appointed caliph (Abu Bakr al-Baghdadi) on the other led to wars within the Islamist brigades.

The leader of the Salafist-jihadist movement in southern Jordan, Mohammed Shalabi, found that war between Nusra and IS against FSA was inevitable and justified. He told Lebanese al-Hayat newspaper in a phone conversation on July 14, 2013 that "the recent armed clashes between us and the secular fighters of the Free Syrian Army are a necessary evil, due to differing methods and programs."[291]

Turkey, however, continues to support the Free Syrian Army along Syria's northwest border. On January 21, 2018, Turkish ground troops were joined by 25,000 FSA fighters in crossing into Afrin to push out Kurdish militia.[292] On March 18, 2018, President Erdogan declared that Turkish-backed units of the Free Syrian Army have taken "total" control of the center of Afrin.[293]

In his release of Islamist terrorists from Syrian prisons, Assad practiced his standard blackmail legitimacy ploy. He let loose Islamist terrorist forces that sidelined the FSA and turned a revolution against tyranny into a war against jihadism. The birth and growth of al-Nusra and the so-called Islamic State dealt a severe blow to the Syrian revolution. Incoherence among the anti-Assad political groups and the absence of a central

---

[291]Tamer al-Samadi (translator), "Jordanian Salafist Leader Foresees Conflict with Secular Syrian Opposition," *Ammon News*, (July 16, 2013). http://en.ammonnews.net/article.aspx?articleno=22322#. Wc6r7kyZP6l

[292]"Syria: Turkish Ground Troops Enter Afrin Enclave," *BBC*, (January 22, 2018). http://www.bbc.co.uk/news/world-middle-east-42765697

[293]"Turkey's Erdogan Says Afrin City Centre Under 'Total' Control in Syria," *The Telegraph*.

military authority over the Free Syrian Army resulted in the hijacking of the revolution by Islamist terror groups.

The Refugees

The UN Refugee Agency (UNHCR) Website[294] (accessed on November 6, 2017), states that over five million Syrians have become refugees, registered in Turkey, Lebanon, Jordan, Iraq, and Egypt. The figures do not include those who escaped from Syria but are not registered with UNCHR. Internally displaced persons are estimated at 6.3 million. Filippo Grandi, UNHCR High Commissioner stated that, "Syria is the biggest humanitarian and refugee crisis of our time, a continuing cause of suffering for millions which should be garnering a groundswell of support around the world."

UNHCR's Website put the suffering of the refugees aptly:

> Millions of Syrians have escaped across borders, fleeing the bombs and bullets that have devastated homes.
>
> Turkey hosts over 3.2 million registered Syrians. The majority of them live in urban areas, with around 260,000 accommodated in the 21 government-run refugee camps.
>
> In Lebanon, life is a daily struggle for many Syrian refugees who have little or no financial resources. Around 70 percent live below the poverty line. There are no formal refugee camps and, as a result, more than a million registered Syrians are scattered throughout more than 2,100 urban and rural communities and locations, often sharing small basic lodgings with other refugee families in overcrowded conditions.
>
> In Jordan, over 650,000 men, women and children are currently trapped in exile. Approximately 80 percent of them live outside camps, while more than 140,000 have found sanctuary at the camps of Za'atari and Azraq. Many have arrived with limited means to cover even basic needs, and those who could at first rely on

---

[294]UNHCR, Syria Emergency, (accessed, November 6, 2017). http://www.unhcr.org/uk/syria-emergency.html

savings or support from host families are now increasingly in need of help. 93 percent of refugees in Jordan live below the poverty line.

Iraq has also seen a growing number of Syrians arriving, hosting more than 244,000, while in Egypt, UNHCR provides protection and assistance to more than 122,000.

But although life in exile can be difficult, for Syrians still at home, it is even harder.

As for the several hundred thousand Syrians who climbed the mountains, sailed the seas, and walked hundreds of miles to reach Europe, they represent the epitome of determination, endurance, tenacity, and fortitude. Amongst them are Artists, doctors, engineers, lawyers, nurses, teachers, and writers. They are able, educated, and creative; valuable human capital in any society.

Germany acquired impressive human capital resources through its Syrian refugees. The cost of raising and educating a 25-year old doctor may be estimated at $500,000; an engineer, $400,000; a lawyer, $300,000; a nurse or a teacher, $200,000; a high school graduate, $100,000. Assuming that on average the human capital per refugee was $50,000, the value of the human capital embedded in 1,000 refugees would be $50 million. Although accurate numbers are difficult to obtain, assuming that the number of Syrian refugees Germany hosted is 500,000 persons, Germany acquired from Syria around $25 billion in the form of human capital. Syrians who are settled in Germany will forever be indebted and grateful to their "Mama Merkel."

A Crystal Ball View

The Assad regime decapitated Syria's democratic political structures. When the revolution erupted on March 18, 2011, there was no organized opposition to lead. Quickly, Assad weaponized the protests and Islamicized the revolution in a Machiavellian act of blackmail legitimacy. Mr. Obama then handcuffed the Syrian revolution. He refused to supply anti-Assad forces with anti-aircraft guns and prevented others from supplying the weapons. His intentions to empower Iran were confirmed when he refused to honor his own red-line warning against the use of chemical weapons in Syria, which Assad used on August 21, 2013, killing 1,400 citizens outside Damascus.

The revolution's civilian leadership lacked unity and a firm hand at the top. The Free Syrian Army lacked a central authority, a chain of command, and the necessary weapons. The combination resulted in the hijacking of the revolution by Islamist Jabhat al-Nusra and the so-called Islamic State. These terror groups dealt a severe blow to the objectives and effectiveness of the revolution.

Turkey's support for the revolution has been constrained by the tightrope Mr. Erdogan must tread between Washington and Moscow, and by Turkey's abhorrence of Kurdish aspirations for self-rule.

The revolution suffered from relying on hapless GCC supporters, like Saudi Arabia and Qatar. The two states are rivals with conflicting agendas. Their two ruling families are erratic and hate each other. Aside from money, both are short on stature in Washington, and Obama did not take them seriously.

In retrospect, as soon as Obama showed his pro-Iran colors, the revolution was doomed. Obama's inaction was explained in April 2016 in the interview he gave to *The Atlantic* magazine. He expressed loathing toward Saudi Arabia for its culpability for 9/11, manipulating the Washington Playbook, radicalizing Indonesia's Islam, state-sponsored misogyny, suppressing dissent, and tolerating corruption and inequality. He was clear that *Saudis need to 'share' the Middle East with their Iranian foes*.

The Syrian crisis has become exceedingly complicated. Only Moscow and Washington can resolve it, not Damascus, Ankara, Beirut, Riyadh, or Tehran. The settlement might involve a barter exchange between Russia and the US. However, should a barter exchange prove unattainable, the US possesses a lethal option it can use against Russia.

Syrians' traditional coldness toward Russia has turned to enmity since the revolution. The 12 million Syrians who lost family and friends and are displaced internally and in refugee camps are like a bomb, primed against Russia. Washington can, at any time, weaponize a new anti-Assad army, or enlarge the Syrian Democratic Forces, for a repeat of the USSR's experience in Afghanistan. Whether Washington will decide to exploit this option is unclear, given Trump's mysterious affinity toward Putin and Russia. Regarding the Shi'ite Crescent, if the US, Israel, and Saudi Arabia are truly serious about containing Tehran and weakening Hezbollah, the least expensive option would be the removal of Assad.

It is difficult to imagine how harmony among Syria's many ethnic and religious groups could be restored. Nonetheless, a possible way forward, should Messrs. Putin and Trump agree, might involve:

- A United Nations and/or an Arab peace keeping force to implement a cease fire agreement throughout the country.
- Removal of Assad and his senior operatives in the military and security forces.
- Free and democratic elections for a parliament of national unity representing all religious and ethnic groups.
- A truth and reconciliation commission.

For Syria to remain a single country and attain a semblance of harmonious living, a federal system with self-ruled regions ought to be taken seriously. The self-governing autonomous region in Northern Syria, declared unilaterally in November 2013 and modelled on the Swiss federal system can be a good model to build upon. Otherwise, Syria might be divided into enclaves dominated by foreign powers. Russia's Deputy Foreign Minister said on April 20, 2018: "We don't know how the situation is going to develop on the question of whether it is possible to keep Syria as a single country."[295]

The two Assads demolished most of Syria. In addition, they saddled the Alawite community and Christian and other minorities with a terrible legacy. The Assads regimes have proven that in a religious country like Syria, a non-representative, totalitarian, minority regime of 10% of the population, from a sect seen as heretical by most of the 75% Sunni majority, is unsustainable. Unless genuine representative democracy replaces the Assad regime, a second revolution, a third, and a fourth will inevitably erupt.

A Diagnosis of Bashar Assad's Personality: To destroy most of one's homeland, to kill, injure, and displace two thirds of its population, Bashar Assad must suffer from a severe mental disorder, compounded by his wicked upbringing.

He grew-up in a home of intrigues, conspiracies, and violence. He learned lessons in duplicity, deceit, and treachery throughout his childhood. In 1980 (when he was 15 years of age) and in 1982 (when he was 17 years old), he witnessed his father and uncle Rif'at commit unspeakable atrocities in Palmyra and Hama. In 1984, he watched his uncle Rif'at come close to overthrowing his father from office, only for the father to

---

[295]"Russia says hard to know if Syria's borders will remain as they are: Ifax," *Reuters*, (April 20, 2018). https://www.reuters.com/article/us-mideast-crisis-syria-borders/russia-says-hard-to-know-if-syrias-borders-will-remain-as-they-are-ifax-idUSKBN1HR10Q

throw the uncle into exile, never to live at home again. In 1993, he witnessed his older brother Basil imprisoning his future brother-in-law, Asef Shawkat, to prevent him from marrying his sister, Bushra, and in 1999, his brother Maher shooting and wounding Asef.

Bashar Assad exhibits psychopathic behavior.[296] Not until he leaves office, will the Syrian people begin to heal.

---

[296]Signs and Symptoms of Psychopathy: Superficial charm and glibness, inflated sense of self-worth, lying pathologically, conning others, being manipulative, lack of remorse, shallow emotions, lack of empathy, using others, poor control over behavior, lack of realistic long-term goals, being impulsive, being irresponsible, blaming others and refusing to accept responsibility, criminal acts in several realms (criminal versatility). Natasha Tracy, "Psychopathy: Definition, Symptoms, Signs and Causes," *HealthyPlace*. https://www.healthyplace.com/personality-disorders/psychopath/psychopathy-definition-symptoms-signs-and-causes/

EPILOGUE

Neglecting the importance of Islam in the study of Middle Eastern politics is like sailing a ship without a compass. Islam's influence in the home and city hall is as relevant today as it was a thousand years ago. Chapters Two and Three introduced the important role Islam plays in the lives of Muslims, particularly in the Arab world.

Religious extremism surfaced in the Middle East after the defeat of the Ottoman Empire at the end of the First World War in 1918. On the ashes of the Ottoman Empire, Britain and France created new states with different religious agendas in the Middle East.

The firm hand of the Sunni Hanafi Sultans kept religious extremism in the Ottoman Empire under control for six centuries (1280–1918). The Sultans ruled over most of the Arab world for four centuries (1517–1918). They were tolerant. They did not force their Christian subjects in the Balkans in the sixteenth century, for example, to convert to Islam. Had they done so, the cruel Christian/Muslim battles and Catholic/Orthodox fights (1991–1999) in the former Yugoslavia four centuries later would probably not have happened. The tolerance of the Turkish Sultans was also demonstrated in 1492, when Sultan Bayezid-II (1481–1512) allowed Jews, driven out from Spain and Portugal, to settle in Ottoman territories and rebuild their lives.

Within a hundred years after the fragmentation of the Ottoman Empire, the Middle East sank into nasty religious wars. Millions were killed and injured and millions more were displaced. Aside from mayhem and tragedy in the Middle East, Muslim refugees set off alarm bells in Christian Europe. Acts of terror by followers of the so-called Islamic State rocked Western cities. Fear of more acts of terror put security forces on a constant state of alert. Far right anti-immigrant politicians in Europe and America were elected. They widened the religious, cultural, and ethnic divide between the East and the West. President Trump's anti Muslim statements and travel ban on citizens of certain Muslim majority countries helped to fan the fires of Islamophobia. He encourages far right politicians in other countries to follow suit.

This transformation during the past century demonstrates the validity of Samuel P. Huntington's hypothesis on the "Clash of Civilizations. Recognizing the stresses cultural differences may create, Samuel P. Huntington wrote in Foreign Affairs in 1993:

> It is my hypothesis that the fundamental source of conflict in this new world will not be primarily ideological or primarily economic. The great divisions among humankind and the dominating source of conflict will be cultural. Nation states will remain the most powerful actors in world affairs, but the principal conflicts of global politics will occur between nations and groups of different civilizations. The clash of civilizations will dominate global politics. The fault lines between civilizations will be the battle lines of the future.[1]

The validity of Huntington's hypothesis extends beyond conflicts between one religion and another. It also explains fights among sects within the same religion, such as Shi'ites and Sunnis, or Catholics, Protestants, and Orthodox.

Significant Events That Loom Large Behind the Huntington Hypothesis

Chronologically, five events loom large: The formation of the Wahhabi state of Saudi Arabia (1932), the creation of the State of Israel (1948), the Khomeini Shi'ite Revolution in Iran (1979), the September 11, 2001 terror attacks against the US, and the birth of the Shi'ite Crescent (2003).

---

[1]Samuel Huntington, "The Clash of Civilizations?" Foreign Affairs, (Summer 1993).

The first is Wahhabism. Kemal Ataturk's secularization of the Turkish Republic in the 1920s blamed the decline and defeat of the Ottoman Empire on a rigid Islam in a European world of the Enlightenment, Reformation, and the Industrial Revolution. On the other hand, Abdulaziz al-Saud and his Abdulwahhab compatriots blamed the decline on the Sultans for corrupting the "true" tenets of Islam. They saw the road to greatness through the imposition of the most extreme among the four of Sunni rites. They rebelled against Istanbul. With British help, the rebellion succeeded in creating the Wahhabi state of Saudi Arabia in 1932. With US protection, the Wahhabi enterprise has flourished to this day thanks to Saudi Arabia's vast oil resources. Not even the atrocities of 9/11 were serious enough for G.W. Bush to retaliate against Riyadh. Instead, he demolished Iraq.

Wahhabism radicalized Islam and polarized Muslims. Propagated in schools, mosques, and the media, Wahhabi palace clerics made hatred of non-Wahhabis a part of Wahhabi culture, especially Christians, Jews, and Shi'ites. They attack democracy as a Western conspiracy to destroy Islam. Billions of dollars have been spent to convert Arab and non-Arab Muslims to the Wahhabi creed, especially Sunni clerics in neighboring countries. Expatriate workers who lived in Saudi Arabia and became indoctrinated in the Wahhabi ways act as foot soldiers in the Saudi campaign. During the past twenty years, Wahhabism metastasized. What was al-Qaeda has become Boko Haram, the so-called Islamic State, Shabab, and Taliban. Also, a new breed of terrorist emerged—the lone-wolf. Using a knife or a car, he has terrorized Berlin, London, New York, Nice, Paris, and Stockholm.

The second event was the creation of Israel. When the Jews politicized the Old Testament of the Bible, the Arabs responded by politicizing the Quran. This ignited a conflict that will burn for generations if not resolved. Israeli and US denial of a connection between Israel's occupation, oppression, and humiliation of Arabs and Palestinians and the growth of jihadism is as obtuse as Saudi Arabia's denial of a connection between the Wahhabi way of life and the atrocities of 9/11. To compound matters, on December 6, 2017, President Trump recognized Jerusalem as Israel's capital. To coerce Palestinians to accept the decision, he cut by 50% US contribution to United Nations Relief and Works Agency for Palestinian Refugees (UNRWA) and threatened the Palestinian Authority with cutting American aid funds. He added salt on the wounds of Palestinians and Arabs and Muslims. He escalated the religious nature of the conflict.

The third event was the Khomeini revolution of 1979. It may be said that the Iranian revolution was in part, at least, a reaction to Wahhabi hatred and abuse of Shi'ites. Shi'ism incorporates the ethnic and cultural differences between Persians and Arabs. It is a repository of the memories of their wars and rivalries over the long sweep of history. Shi'ism may be described as a Persianized version of Arabian Islam. The Iranian revolution exacerbated the Shi'ite/Sunni divide. It led to the eight-year war between Iran and Iraq (September 1980-August 1988), which deepened the already deep sectarian enmity between Riyadh and Tehran.

The fourth event happened on September 11, 2001, when nineteen Wahhabi terrorists flew passenger air planes into buildings in New York and Washington D.C. The heinous attacks may be seen as a conscious strategy by Osama bin Laden to provoke a devastating and long-term American retaliation against Muslims in order to deepen Muslim/Christian hatred of one another.

The fifth event was the birth of the Shi'ite Crescent as a result of the American occupation of Iraq in retaliation for 9/11, among other ostensible reasons. The attack on Iraq opened the gates of sectarian hell in the Muslim Middle East. G.W. Bush's misadventure in Iraq handed Baghdad to Tehran, and Obama's inaction in Syria empowered Iran further. Proxy wars between Saudi Arabia and Iran devastated Iraq, Syria, and Yemen. Tension escalated between the Sunni and Shi'ite populations in Bahrain, Kuwait and Saudi Arabia.

As life becomes harsher in the Middle East due to constant warfare, occupation, oppression, and humiliation, the downtrodden faithful turn to God. The belief in predestination, jihad, and the delights of paradise make martyrdom more attractive than their current lives.

Oil and God contends that once oil is replaced by sustainable sources of energy, Saudi oil will cease to be of interest to Washington. The day will be brought closer if US rivals like China, continental Europe, India, and Japan develop sufficient green energy capacity to stop the importation of oil. Without America's protection and oil wealth the power of Saudi Arabia will fade, religious and democratic reforms in the Arab Middle East will stand a chance, and Wahhabi terror will diminish. When that happens, Huntington's "great divisions among humankind" will start to narrow.

BIBLIOGRAPHY

Abedin, Mahan. "The Supreme Council for the Islamic Revolution in Iraq (SCIRI)." *Middle East Intelligence Bulletin* 5, no. 10. https://www.meforum.org/meib/articles/0310_iraqd.htm

Allan, Tony. *International Water & Irrigation, Virtual Water-Economically Invisible and Politically Silent-A Way to Solve Strategic Water Problems*, Vol. 21, No. 4, 2001.

Ali, Suad T. *A Religion, Not a State. Ali Abd al-Raziq's Islamic Justification of Political Secularism.* Utah: The University of Utah Press, 2009.

Allan, Tony. *The Middle East Water Question Hydropolitics and the Global Economy.* London: I.B. Tauris, 2000.

Al-Nowaihi Mohamed. *Problems of Modernization in Islam, Arab Society: Social Science Perspectives.* Edited by N. S. Hopkins and Saad Eddin Ibrahim. Cairo: The American University in Cairo Press, 1992.

Al-Rasheed, Madawi. *Muted Modernists—The Struggle Over Divine Politics in Saudi Arabia.* Cambridge: Oxford University Press, 2015.

———. *A History of Saudi Arabia.* Cambridge: Cambridge University Press, 2003.

Arafat, W. N. *Early Critics of the Poetry of the Sira.* In Bulletin of the School of Oriental and African Studies, Vol. XXI, part 3. London: University of London, 1956.

———. "New Light on the Story of Banu Qurayza and the Jews of Medina." *Journal of the Royal Asiatic Society of Great Britain and Ireland*, (1976).

Arms Control Association. "Timeline of Nuclear Diplomacy with Iran." https://www.armscontrol.org/factsheet/Timeline-of-Nuclear-Diplomacy-With-Iran

Azami, Muhammad Mustafa. *Studies in Hadith Methodology and Literature.* Indianapolis, Indiana: American Trust Publications, 1977.

Bard, Mitchell. *The Palestinian Refugees.* The American-Israeli Cooperative Enterprise, Jewish Virtual Library. http://www.jewishvirtuallibrary.org/jsource/History/refugees.html

Bilmes, Linda J. "The Financial Legacy of Iraq and Afghanistan: How Wartime Spending Decisions Will Constrain Future National Security Budgets." *Harvard University, Faculty Research Working Paper Series,* (March 2013). https://research.hks.harvard.edu/publications/workingpapers/citation.aspx?PubId=8956&type=WPN

Burton, John. *An Introduction to the Hadith.* Edinburgh: Edinburgh University Press, 1994.

Burg, Avraham. "The End of Zionism." The *Guardian,* (September 15, 2003). Reprinted with permission of *The Forward,* which translated and adapted the essay from an article that originally appeared in *Yediot Aharonot.* http://www.guardian.co.uk/israel/comment/0,10551,1042071,00.html

Carnegie Middle East Center. "The Syrian Constitution—1973–2012." http://carnegie-mec.org/diwan/50255?lang=en

Congress.gov. "Iran-Iraq Arms Non-Proliferation Act of 1992, H.R.5434 102nd Congress." (1991–1992) https://www.congress.gov/bill/102nd-congress/house-bill/5434

Cordesman, Anthony. "The Middle East Military Balance: Definition, Regional Development, and Trends." *Center for Strategic and International Studies,* (March 23, 2005). https://csis-prod.s3.amazonaws.com/s3fs-public/legacy_files/files/media/csis/pubs/050323_memilbaldefine[1].pdf

Coulson, Noel J. *A History of Islamic Law.* Edinburgh: Edinburgh University Press, 1999.

Council on Foreign Relations. "Iraq: Grand Ayatollah Ali al-Sistani." (September 1, 2004). http://www.cfr.org/iraq/iraq-grand-ayatollah-ali-al-sistani/p7636

Crone, Patricia. *Roman, Provincial and Islamic Law: The Origins of Islamic Patronate.* Cambridge: Cambridge University Press, 1987.

Department of Defense, Report to Congress. "Measuring Stability and Security in Iraq." (September 26, 2008). http://archive.defense.gov/news/d20080930iraq.pdf

Disraeli, Benjamin. *Coningsby, or The New Generation.* Whitehish, MT: Kessinger Publishing, 2004. http://www.amazon.com/Coningsby-Generation-Benjamin-Beaconsfield-Disraeli/dp/1419113887/ref=reader_auth_dp/102-7296008-3005735

Doha Institute for Graduate Studies, Arab Center for Research & Policy Studies. "The 2015 Arab Opinion Index: Results in Brief." (December 21, 2015). http://english.dohainstitute.org/content/cb12264b-1eca-402b-926a-5d068ac60011

Donner, Fred M. *Narratives of Islamic Origin: The Beginnings of Islamic Historical Writing*. Princeton, New Jersey: The Darwin Press, Inc., 1998.

Drory, Rina. "The Abbasid Construction of the Jahiliyya: Cultural Authority in the Making." *Studia Islamica 1*, no. 83. (1966).

Elhadj, Elie. *Experiments in Achieving Water and Food Self-Sufficiency in the Middle East: The Consequences of Contrasting Endowments, Ideologies, and Investment Policies in Saudi Arabia and Syria*. London University, School of Oriental and African Studies. Boca Raton, Florida: Dissertation.com, 2006.

———. "Dry Aquifers in Arab Countries and the Looming Food Crisis." *Middle East Review of International Affairs Journal (MERIA)*, (December 7, 2008). http://www.rubincenter.org/2008/12/elhadj-asp-2008-12-07/#_ednref7

———. "The Arab Spring and the Prospects for Genuine Religious and Political Reforms." *Middle East Review of International Affairs (MERIA) Journal* 16, no. 03, (Nov. 14, 2012). http://www.rubincenter.org/2012/11/the-arab-spring-and-the-prospects-for-genuine-religious-and-political-reforms/

———. "The Shi'i Crescent's Push for Regional Hegemony and the Sunni Reaction." *Middle East Review of International Affairs Journal (MERIA)*, (April 8, 2014). http://www.rubincenter.org/2014/04/the-shii-crescents-push-for-regional-hegemony-and-the-sunni-reaction/

———. "Why Syria's Regime is Likely to Survive." *Middle East Review of International Affairs (MERIA) Journal* 15, no. 01 (August 21, 2011). http://www.rubincenter.org/2011/08/why-syria's-regime-is-likely-to-survive/

Felter, Joseph and Fishman, Brian. "Iranian Strategy in Iraq Politics." *Combating Terrorism Center at West Point*, (October 13, 2008). https://ctc.usma.edu/iranian-strategy-in-iraq-politics-and-other-means/

Garraty, John A. and Peter Gay, eds. *The Columbia History of the World*. Harper & Row, 1981.

Goldberg, Jeffery. "The Obama Doctrine." *The Atlantic, (April 2016 Issue)*. https://www.theatlantic.com/magazine/archive/2016/04/the-obama-doctrine/471525/

Goldziher, Ignaz. *Muslim Studies*. Edited by S. M. Stern, Translated by C. R. Barber and S. M. Stern, Vol. II. Chicago and New York: Aldine Atherton, 1967. (First published 1890).

———. *The Life of Muhammad: A Translation of Ibn Ishaq's Sirat Rasul Allah* (Nineteenth Impression, Oxford University Press, 2006).

GlobalSecurity.org. "Saudi Arabian National Guard." http://www.globalsecurity. org/military/world/gulf/sang.htm

———. "Syria Intelligence & Security Agencies." http://www.globalsecurity.org/ intell/world/syria/intro.ht

Guillaume, Alfred. *Islam*. London: Penguin Books, 1954. Reprinted 1990.

Hadawi, Sami. *Palestinian Rights & Losses in 1948: A Comprehensive Study*. London: Saqi Books, 1988.

Hitti, Philip. *History of the Arabs*. London: MacMillan Press Ltd, 10th edition, 1970.

Hodgson, Marshall G. S. *The Venture of Islam: Conscience and History in a World Civilization: the Classical Age of Islam, Vol. 1*. Chicago, IL: University of Chicago Press, 1977.

Hourani, Albert. *Arabic Thought in the Liberal Age 1789–1939*. Cambridge: Cambridge University Press, 1997.

———. *History of the Arab Peoples*. London: Faber and Faber, 1991.

Huntington, Samuel. "The Clash of Civilizations?" *Foreign Affairs*, (Summer 1993). https://www.foreignaffairs.com/articles/united-states/1993-06-01/clash-civilizations

International Rescue Committee. "Syria Crisis Briefing." Accessed September 29, 2017, https://www.rescue-uk.org/country/syria?gclid=EAIaIQobChMIvLCr 7dvJ1gIVA-EbCh2KJwcXEAAYAiAAEgJz3fD_BwE

Institute for the Analysis of Global Security. "How Much Did the September 11 Terrorist Attack Cost America? (2003–2004)." http://www.iags.org/costof911. html

International Constitutional Law. "Syria—Constitution, Adopted on March 13, 1973." http://www.icla.up.ac.za/images/un/use-of-force/asia-pacific/Syrian ArabRepublic/Constitution%20Syrian%20Arab%20Republic%201973.pdf

Iran Chamber Society. "History of Iran: Historic Personalities: Ayatullah Khumayni." http://www.iranchamber.com/history/rkhomeini/ayatollah_khomeini.php

Jewish Virtual Library. "Fact Sheet: Jewish Refugees from Arab Countries." (Updated December 2015). http://www.jewishvirtuallibrary.org/jewish-refugees-from-arab-countries

Jewish Policy Centre. "The Attack on Syria's al-Kibar Nuclear Facility." (Spring 2009). https://www.jewishpolicycenter.org/2009/02/28/the-attack-on-syrias-al-kibar-nuclear-facility/

Juynboll, G. H. A. *Muslim Tradition: Studies in Chronology, Provenance and Author-ship of Early Hadith*. Cambridge: Cambridge University Press, 1983.

Katzman, K. "Report for Congress—Iraq: US Regime Change Efforts and Post-Saddam Governance." *Library of Congress*, (October 2003). i.cfr.org/content/publications/attachments/RL31339_2006Jan13.pdf

———. "CRS Report for Congress—Iraq's Opposition Movements, Order Code 98–179 F." *Congressional Research Services*, (Updated June 27, 2000): CRC-5. http://www.au.af.mil/au/awc/awcgate/crs/98–179.pdf

Kennedy, Hugh. *The Prophet and the Age of the Caliphates, the Islamic Near East from the Sixth to the Eleventh Century*. London and New York: Longman, 1996.

Kepel, Giles. *The War for Muslim Minds. Islam and the West. Belknap/Harvard*. 2004.

Khoury, Philip. *Syria and the French Mandate: The Politics of Arab Nationalism, 1920–1945*. Princeton NJ: Princeton University Press, 1987.

Khlaf, Rana. "Governing Rojava—Layers of Legitimacy in Syria." Chatham House, (December 2016). https://www.chathamhouse.org/sites/files/chathamhouse/publications/research/2016-12-08-governing-rojava-khalaf.pdf

Kramer, Martin, ed. *Shi'ism, Resistance, and Revolution*. Boulder CO: Westview Press, 1987.

Kurdistan National Congress (KNK). "Canton Based Democratic Autonomy of Rojava (Western Kurdistan—Northern Syria), A Transformations Process from Dictatorship to Democracy." Information File, (May 2014). https://peaceinkurdistancampaign.files.wordpress.com/2011/11/rojava-info-may-2014.pdf

Lehrs, Lior. "A Comparative Analysis of the "Saudi Initiative" (Thomas Friedman Document, February 2002), the "Arab Peace Initiative" (Arab League Document, March 2002), and the "Israeli Peace Initiative" Document (April 2011)." *Jerusalem Institute for Israel Studies*, (August 2011). http://en.jerusaleminstitute.org.il/.upload/Peace%20Initiatives-English-%20last%20version.pdf

Lewis, Bernard. *The Emergence of Modern Turkey*. Oxford: Oxford University Press, 1961.

———. *The Jews of Islam*. Princeton NJ: Princeton University Press, 1987.

Momen, Moojan. *An Introduction to Shi'i Islam*. New Haven CT: Yale University Press, 1985.

Moosa, Matti. *The Nusairi mass, Extremist Shi'ites*. Syracuse NY: Syracuse University Press, 1987.

Muslim Brotherhood Official English Website. http://www.ikhwanweb.com/index.php

Nader, Alireza. "Iran's Role in Iraq," *Rand Corporation*, (2015): 4. http://www.rand.org/content/dam/rand/pubs/perspectives/PE100/PE151/RAND_PE151.pdf

Nelson, Rebecca M. "US Sanctions and Russia's Economy." *Congressional Research Service*, (February 17, 2017). https://fas.org/sgp/crs/row/R43895.pdf

Office of the Under Secretary of Defense for Acquisition, Technology, and Logistics. "Report of the Defense Science Board Task Force on Strategic Communication (DSB)." (September 2004): 17. https://fas.org/irp/agency/dod/dsb/commun.pdf

Organization of the Petroleum Exporting Countries. "Saudi Arabia Facts and Figures, 2015." http://www.opec.org/opec_web/en/about_us/169.htm

Palestine Land Society. http://www.plands.org/en/books-reports/books/right-of-return-sacred-legal-and-possilble/from-refugees-to-citizens-at-home

Pernin, Christopher G. Brian Nichiporuk, Dale Stahl, Justin Beck and Ricky Radaelli-Sanchez. "Unfolding the Future of the Long War—Motivations, Prospects, and Implications for the US Army." *RAND Corporation*, (2008): 171–172. https://www.rand.org/content/dam/rand/pubs/monographs/2008/RAND_MG738.pdf

Perthes, Volker. *The Political Economy of Syria under Assad*. London: I. B. Tauris, 1997.

Pew Research Center. "The World's Muslims: Unity and Diversity." (August 9, 2012). http://www.pewforum.org/2012/08/09/the-worlds-muslims-unity-and-diversity-executive-summary/

———. "The World's Muslims: Religion, Politics and Society." (April 30, 2013). http://www.pewforum.org/2013/04/30/the-worlds-muslims-religion-politics-society-overview/

———. "Iranians' Views Mixed on Political Role for Religious Figures." (June 11, 2013). http://www.pewforum.org/2013/06/11/iranians-views-mixed-on-political-role-for-religious-figures/

Rangwala, Glen. "British Intelligence Iraq Dossier Relies on Recycled Academic Articles." *Center for Research on Globalisation*, (February 5, 2003). http://globalresearch.ca/articles/RAN302A.html

Republic of Turkey. Southeastern Anatolia Project (GAP), Regional Development Administration. http://www.gap.gov.tr/en/index.php

Richards, Alan and Waterbury, John. *A Political Economy of the Middle East*. Boulder CO: Westview Press, 1998.

Rubin, Uri. *The Eye of the Beholder—The Life of Muhammad as Viewed by the Early Muslims: A Textual Analysis*. Princeton, New Jersey: The Darwin Press, Inc., 1995.

Sadek, George. "The Role of Islamic Law in Tunisia's Constitution and Legislation Post-Arab Spring." *Library of Congress*, (May 2013). https://www.loc.gov/law/help/tunisia.php

Seale, Patrick. *Assad, the Struggle for the Middle East*. Berkeley, California: University of California Press, 1995.

———. *The Struggle for Syria. A study in Post-War Arab Politics 1945–1958*. London: I. B. Taurus, 1986.

"Saudi Minister Yamani: 'Kissinger Was Behind 1974 Oil Shock.'" *Executive Intelligence Review* 28, no 4, (January 26, 2001). http://www.larouchepub.com/eiw/public/2001/eirv28n04-20010126/eirv28n04-20010126_008-saudi_minister_yamani_kissinger.pdf

Schacht, Joseph. *An Introduction to Islamic Law*. Oxford. England: Oxford University Press, 1982.

Sharabi, Hisham. *Neopatriarchy: A Theory of Distorted Change in Arab Society*. Oxford, England: Oxford University Press, 1998.

Stanford University. "Mapping Militant Organizations Project: Mahdi Army." (April 2003). https://web.stanford.edu/group/mappingmilitants/cgi-bin/groups/view/57

———. "Mapping Militants Organizations Project: Hay'at Tahrir al-Sham (Formerly Jabhat al-Nusra)." (December 2011). http://web.stanford.edu/group/mappingmilitants/cgi-bin/groups/view/493?highlight=Hayyat+Tahrir+al-Sham

State of Palestine: Palestinian Central Bureau of Statistics. "Estimated Population of Palestinians in the World by Country of Residence." http://www.pcbs.gov.ps/Downloads/book2261.pdf

Stiglitz, Joseph and Bilmes, Linda. *The Three Trillion Dollar War, The True Cost of the Iraqi Conflict*. Allen Lane, an imprint of Penguin Books, (2008).

Tabrizi, Aniseh Bassiri and Rafaello Pantucci, eds. "Understanding Iran's Role in the Syrian Conflict." *Royal United Services Institute for Defence and Security Studies*. (August 2016). https://rusi.org/sites/default/files/201608_op_understanding_irans_role_in_the_syrian_conflict_0.pdf

The Ba'th Party. "The Constitution of the Ba'th Arab Socialist Party." http://www.baathparty.org/index.php?option=com_content&view=category&id=307&Itemid=327&lang=en

The Commission on the Intelligence Capabilities of the United States Regarding Weapons of Mass Destruction. (Online). http://govinfo.library.unt.edu/wmd/about.html

The Heritage Foundation. "Index of US Military Strength, Assessing the Global Operating Environment, Middle East." (2015). http://index.heritage.org/military/2015/chapter/op-environment/middle-east/

The Institute for Advanced Strategic and Political Studies, Study Group on a New Israeli Strategy toward 2000. "A Clean Break: A New Strategy for Securing the Realm." https://www.sourcewatch.org/index.php/Study_Group_on_a_New_Israeli_Strategy_Toward_2000

The National Security Archive, *National Security Archive Electronic Briefing Book No. 214.* http://nsarchive.gwu.edu/NSAEBB/NSAEBB214/index.htm

The Project for the New American Century. "Rebuilding America's Defenses—Strategy, Forces and Resources for a New Century." (September 2000). http://www.informationclearinghouse.info/pdf/RebuildingAmericasDefenses.pdf

The Royal Aal Al-bayt Institute for Islamic Thought. "The Amman Message." https://docs.google.com/viewer?a=v&pid=forums&srcid=MDE5NTA5N-DY4NTM4NDk1OTU5MjkBMDI5OTAxNzQwNDQxNDUwNzg1MzI-Bc1ZMZEdQSEVGMklKATAuMQEBdjI

"The Six Books—Sahih al-Bukhari, Sahih Muslim, Sunan Abi Dawood, Sunan Ibn Maja, Sunan al-Nasai, Jame' al-Tirmithi." In The Hadith Encyclopaedia. Riyadh, Saudi Arabia: Darussalam Publishing and distribution, 2000.

The United States Senate. "Report of the Select Committee on Intelligence on Post War Findings about Iraq's WMD Programs and Links to Terrorism and How They Compare with Prewar Assessments with Additional Views (RSCI)." (September 8, 2006). https://fas.org/irp/congress/2006_rpt/srpt109–331.pdf

The White House. "President Bush Outlines Iraqi Threat." (October 7, 2002). https://georgewbush-whitehouse.archives.gov/news/releases/2002/10/print/20021007-8.html

————. "The Vice President Appears on NBC's Meet the Press." (December 9, 2001). https://georgewbush-whitehouse.archives.gov/vicepresident/news-speeches/speeches/print/vp20011209.html

The World Bank. "Worldwide Government Indicators." http://info.worldbank.org/governance/wgi/index.aspx#home

————. Rural Development, Water, and Environment Group: Middle East and North Africa Region. "Syrian Arab Republic Irrigation Sector Report," Report No. 22602-SYR, (August 6, 2001).

————. "Rural population (% of total population), Syria." http://data.worldbank.org/indicator/SP.RUR.TOTL.ZS?locations=SY

United Nations General Assembly, 194 (III). "Palestine—Progress Report of the United Nations Mediator." (December 11, 1948). https://unispal.un.org/DPA/DPR/unispal.nsf/0/C758572B78D1CD0085256BCF0077E51A

———. "Relief and Works Agency for Palestine Refugees in the Near East (UNRWA): Palestine Refugees." https://www.unrwa.org/palestine-refugees

———. "Weapons Inspectors Report to Security Council on Progress in Disarmament of Iraq." (March 7, 2003). http://www.un.org/press/en/2003/sc7682.doc.htm

UNHCR. "Syrian Arab Republic: Constitution." (2012). http://www.refworld.org/docid/5100f02a2.html

———. "Syria Emergency." (October 1, 2017). http://www.unhcr.org/uk/syria-emergency.html

UNICEF. "Nowhere to Go: Children in Iraq Trapped in Cycles of Violence and Poverty." (June 27, 2017). https://www.unicef.org/media/media_96529.html

US Congress. "Iraq Liberation Act of 1998." https://www.congress.gov/bill/105th-congress/house-bill/4655

US Department of Defense Press Briefing by Gen. Townsend via teleconference from Baghdad, Iraq. (March 1, 2017). https://www.defense.gov/News/Transcripts/Transcript-View/Article/1099469/department-of-defense-press-briefing-by-gen-townsend-via-teleconference-from-ba/

US Department of State, Bureau of Counterterrorism and Countering Violent Extremism. "Foreign Terrorist Organizations." (2016). https://www.state.gov/j/ct/rls/crt/2016/272238.htm

———. Bureau of Democracy, Human Rights and Labor. "International Religious Freedom Report for 2012, Saudi Arabia." https://www.state.gov/j/drl/rls/irf/2012religiousfreedom/index.htm?year=2012&dlid=208398#wrapper

———. "International Religious Freedom Report for 2015, Saudi Arabia." http://www.state.gov/j/drl/rls/irf/religiousfreedom/index.htm?year=2015&dlid=256287

———. "International Religious Freedom Report for 2016, Bahrain." https://www.state.gov/j/drl/rls/irf/religiousfreedom/index.htm#wrapper

———. "Country Reports on Human Rights Practices for 2016, Saudi Arabia." https://www.state.gov/j/drl/rls/hrrpt/humanrightsreport/index.htm#wrapper

———. "International Religious Freedom Report for 2016, Kuwait." https://www.state.gov/j/drl/rls/irf/religiousfreedom/index.htm#wrapper

US Library of Congress, Federal Research Division. "Country Studies—Saudi Arabia." http://countrystudies.us/saudi-arabia/55.htm

————. "Iran Country Report." http://lcweb2.loc.gov/frd/cs/irtoc.html.

US Statistical Abstract of the Census Bureau. "Comparative International Statistics, Personnel in the Armed Forces, Table No. 1256." 1968. https://www2.census.gov/library/publications/1968/compendia/statab/89ed/1968-13.pdf

Van Dam, Nikolas. *The Struggle for Power in Syria. Politics and Society under Assad and the Ba'th Party.* London: I. B. Taurus, London, 1997.

Wansbrough, John. *Qur'anic Studies. Sources and Methods of Scriptural Interpretation—Forward, Translations, and Expanded Notes by Andrew Rippon.* Amherst, New York: Prometheus Books, 2004.

Watt, Montgomery W. *Islamic Political Thought.* Edinburgh, Scotland: Edinburgh University Press, 1999.

———— and Richard Bell. *Introduction to the Qur'an.* Edinburgh, Scotland: Edinburgh University Press, 1997.

Zogby Research Services, LLC. "Muslim Millennial Attitudes on Religion and Religious Leadership," *Tabah Foundation,* (2015). https://d3n8a8pro7vhmx.cloudfront.net/aai/pages/11165/attachments/original/1452881049/Millenials_2015_FINAL.pdf?1452881049

INDEX